REFLECTIVE HISTORY SERIES

Barbara Finkelstein and William J. Reese, Series Editors

Power and the Promise of School Reform:
Grassroots Movements During the Progressive Era
Reissued with a New Introduction by Jeffrey E. Mirel
WILLIAM J. REESE

Access to Success in the Urban High School:
The Middle College Movement
HAROLD S. WECHSLER

The Irony of School Reform:
Educational Innovation in Mid-Nineteenth
Century Massachusetts
MICHAEL B. KATZ

Curriculum & Consequence:
Herbert M. Kliebard and the Promise of Schooling
BARRY FRANKLIN, EDITOR

Schooled to Work:
Vocationalism and the American Curriculum,
1876–1946
HERBERT M. KLIEBARD

Moral Education in America:
Schools and the Shaping of Character
from Colonial Times to the Present
B. EDWARD McCLELLAN

The Failed Promise of the
American High School, 1890–1995
DAVID L. ANGUS & JEFFREY E. MIREL

D0908040

Power and the Promise of School Reform

GRASSROOTS MOVEMENTS DURING THE PROGRESSIVE ERA

WILLIAM J. REESE

Reissued with a New Introduction by Jeffrey E. Mirel

Teachers College, Columbia University
New York and London

Sections of this work have appeared in previous publications by the author:

"After Bread, Education: Nutrition and the Urban School Children, 1890–1920" in *Teachers College Record, 81* (Summer 1980): 496–525.

"Between Home and School: Organized Parents, Club Women and Urban Education in the Progressive Era." (1978). *School Review.* Chicago: University of Chicago Press. © 1978 by The University of Chicago. All rights reserved.

"Partisans of the Proletariat: The Socialist Working Class and the Milwaukee Schools, 1980–1920" in *History of Education Quarterly, 21* (Spring 1981): 3–50.

"The Control of Urban School Boards in the Progressive Era" in *Pacific Northwest Quarterly, 68* (October 1977): 164–174.

"Progressive School Reform in Toledo, 1890–1920" in *Northwest Ohio Quarterly, 47* (Spring 1975): 44–59.

Published by Teachers College Press, 1234 Amsterdam Avenue, New York, NY 10027

Library of Congress Cataloging-in-Publication Data

Reese, William J., 1951–
    Power and the promise of school reform : grassroots movements during the Progressive era / William J. Reese ; reissued with a new introduction by Jeffrey E. Mirel.
        p. cm. — (Reflective history series)
    Originally published: Boston : Routledge & Kegan Paul, 1986. With new introd.
    Includes bibliographical references (p.   ) and index.
    ISBN 0-8077-4227-9 (pbk.) — ISBN 0-8077-4228-7 (cloth)
        1. Education, Urban—Social aspects—United States—History.   2. Progressive education—United States—Philosophy—History.   3. Social reformers—United States—History.   I. Title.   II. Series.
    LC5131 .R44 2002
    370'.9173'2–dc21   2001060370

ISBN 0-8077-4227-9 (paper)
ISBN 0-8077-4228-7 (cloth)

Printed on acid-free paper
Manufactured in the United States of America

09 08 07 06 05 04 03 02   8 7 6 5 4 3 2 1

To the memory of Sterling Fishman

Contents

Introduction

JEFFREY E. MIREL

University of Michigan, Ann Arbor

Bill Reese's *Power and the Promise of School Reform* first appeared at a particularly auspicious time in the development of American educational history as a distinct field in the broader area of American social history. During the decade and a half that had preceded the publication of Reese's book, historians of American education, particularly historians of urban education, had been embroiled in a ferocious debate about how to interpret the history of public education in this country. But by 1986, that debate seemed to have arrived at an intellectual impasse. The importance of *Power and the Promise of School Reform* and the source of its continuing influence is that it showed a way out.

The great debate of the 1970s and early 1980s turned on one essential question: What has been the nature and function of public education throughout American history? During the first half of the twentieth century, virtually all of the major studies in the history of American education such as Ellwood Cubberley's *Public Education in the United States*, never doubted the answer to that question—the development of public schools and the advancement of American democracy were inseparable (Cubberley, 1919). As far as these early educational historians were concerned, Horace Mann accurately had summed up the essence of public schools in 1848 when he declared that education "beyond all other devices of human origin, is the great equalizer of the conditions of men, the balance wheel of the social machinery" (Cremin, 1957, p. 87).

Early in the 1960s, however, a number of prominent historians began to question and intensely scrutinize key assumptions in these earlier works. Bernard Bailyn, for example, accused Cubberly and his colleagues of three "sins against Clio": parochialism (looking narrowly at schooling rather than other forms of education), anachronism (reading the present back into the past), and evangelism (using history as a way to inspire future educators) (Bailyn, 1960, pp. 8–10; Cremin, 1965, p. 43). In attempting to avoid the last of these sins, these historians increasingly identified and examined the failings of the public schools. Nevertheless, they accepted, as surely as did Cubberley, the belief that the basic nature and function of public education was positive.

No one articulated this belief more clearly than Lawrence Cremin who wrote:

> I happen to believe that on balance the American education system has contributed significantly to the advancement of liberty, equality, and fraternity, in that complementarity and tension that mark the relations among them in a free society. . . . The institutions of American education are human institutions: they have been guilty of their full share of evil, venality, and failure, and my phrase "on balance" is intended to take account of that fact. But it is also intended to convey my sense that the aspirations of American education have been more noble than base, and that its performance over the last two centuries has been more liberating of a greater diversity of human energies and potentialities than has been the case in most other eras and most other places (Cremin, 1976, p. 127).

Yet even as Cremin was declaring his faith in the positive nature of public schools, a new generation of scholars was coming of age and calling almost every aspect of that faith into question. Writing in the 1970s and 1980s, these historians largely rejected the assumption that public education had been "on balance" a positive force in American life. Inspired, in part, by Marxist or anarchist theories, many of these revisionist historians, as they came to be called, argued that public education was defined more by its contribution to the oppression of minorities, women, and the working class than by any supposed success in advancing American democracy (Bowles & Gintis, 1976; Katz, 1971; Spring, 1972; Violas, 1978). Rejecting Horace Mann's vision of the schools as "the great equalizer", Samuel Bowles and Herbert Gintis, two of the most widely cited revisionist scholars, argued that one of the main historical functions of public schools has been to "reproduce inequality" (Bowles & Gintis, 1976, pp. 4–5).

Michael B. Katz, another leading voice in this new generation of historians, provided a succinct summary of this interpretation when he stated:

> The basic structure of American education had been fixed by about 1880 and that it has not altered fundamentally since that time. . . . Acceptance of that proposition that the basic structure of American education has remained unchanged rests, quite obviously, on the definition of "basic." I mean by the term that certain characteristics of American education today were also characteristic nearly a century ago: it is, and was, universal, tax-support, free, compulsory, bureaucratic, racist, and class-biased (Katz, 1971, p. xviii).

Not surprisingly these views, diametrically opposed to the traditional notions about the nature and function of public education, provoked considerable debate and controversy. These debates also seemed to have profound implications for educational policy. If, for example, as Cremin maintained, the basic elements of public education were sound, then improving the institution was primarily a matter of identifying imperfections and crafting appropriate policies to correct them. If, on the other hand, Katz was right, then such tinkering would be, in large part, futile. From a revisionist perspective such basic features of public education as racism and class-bias were bound to undermine whatever policies and programs that were introduced to improve public schools. American education, they maintained, needed greater change than modest, liberal reforms.

These debates intensified in 1978, when Diane Ravitch published *The Revisionist Revised*, a comprehensive critique of many of the major studies produced by this new generation of scholars. Ravitch staunchly defended public education against the revisionist attack by questioning these scholars' evidence and methods (Ravitch, 1978). Two years later, some of the historians that Ravitch had criticized published *Revisionists Respond to Ravitch* to answer her charges and reassert their vision of the history of American public education (Feinberg et al., 1980). These exchanges seemed to push the controversy to a new and more fractious level. By the early 1980s, this debate seemed to dominate the field.

Those of us who were graduate students in those years heard stories about one infamous conference of the History of Education Society where a "discussion" of these interpretations deteriorated into a melee in which enraged senior scholars supposedly threw chairs at one another. These stories later proved to be false, but given the passions raised by this debate, at the time, many of us were quite ready to believe them.

Some people look back on this period as a Golden Era in the field, an exciting and heady time when educational historians seemed to be disputing issues of profound importance with outcomes that could substantially influence policy. As exciting as this period certainly was, that perspective is colored as much by nostalgia and longing for lost youth, as it is a reflection of the time. Moreover, it misses two significant, negative consequences of the great debate between the pro-and anti-revisionist historians. First, the controversy left a long, angry scar down the center of the field and created animosities and bitter feelings that still have not completely healed.

Second, by the mid-1980s, once people had lined up on either side of the historiographic divide, there was almost nowhere else for them to go. The debate had assumed religious proportions. People either accepted or rejected certain basic premises and, almost as a matter of faith, no amount of evidence or argument could sway them to amend, or change, their views. At its worst, the debate began to seem like a then-popular sketch on "Saturday Night Live," in which Dan Ackroyd and Jane Curtin appeared as political pundits whose supposedly reasoned discussions on important issues increasingly escalated into volleys of nasty ad hominum insults.

The importance of Bill Reese's *Power and Promise of School Reform* was that it transcended the angry exchanges that were threatening the very fabric of the field and gave educational historians a way out of this intellectual impasse. Specifically, it offered a conceptually rich approach to the problems raised by the great debate that did not demand unquestioning loyalty to either side. Three aspects of Reese's book captured the fresh approach that he took. First, he shifted the focus of research from the history of large urban school systems to new, previously unexplored urban sites. Second, based on this research he introduced new historical actors into the literature on Progressive school reform, individuals and groups that heretofore had rarely stepped onto the historiographic stage. Third and, most importantly, he challenged the growing influence of theories that seemed to be shaping rather than responding to research. Consequently, he produced a study thoroughly informed by the ongoing historiographic debate, but that was nevertheless neither celebratory nor damning in its depiction of the history of urban education.

Reese's concentration on the Progressive Era also added to the significance of *Power and the Promise of School Reform*. Much of the debate between revisionists and their critics centered on this key period in the history of urban public education. Historians such as Cremin viewed the era as the time in which the schools became increasingly democratic in terms of the population they served and in the broad array of services they provided (Cremin, 1961, 1988). Conversely, revisionists argued that during this era public schools grew increasingly undemocratic and instead became firmly wedded to the demands and interests of corporate capitalism (Bowles & Gintis, 1976). These arguments rested, in large part, on interpretations of several important Progressive Era initiatives and policies, including the shift from ward-based to at-large school board elections, the centralization and professionalization of school organization and operation, and the increasing use of schools to address social problems. These are precisely the areas that Reese explores in his study.

By examining these initiatives and policies in four moderate-sized cities—Kansas City, Milwaukee, Toledo, and Rochester—Reese took a distinctive approach to understanding education in the Progressive Era. Writing in the 1960s and 1970s, scholars such as Stephan Thernstrom and Alan Dawley had led the way in exploring nineteenth-century social history in small cities such as Newburyport and Lynn, Massachusetts rather than in the emerging great metropolises of the era (Thernstrom, 1964; Dawley, 1976). A number of important works in educational history had followed this lead. For example, a key section of Michael Katz's seminal work, *The Irony of Early School Reform*, investigated events in the town of Beverly, Massachusetts and Carl Kaestle and Maris Vinovskis's *Education and Social Change in Nineteenth-Century Massachusetts* examined several small cities in Essex County (Katz, 1968; Kaestle & Vinovskis, 1979).

Reese drew on these earlier works, but he parted company from them in two ways. First, he shifted the research focus about small cities out of the antebellum period and into the late nineteenth and early twentieth centuries. Second, he explicitly concentrated on the politics of education. Some of these earlier works *had* addressed political issues; the section of Katz's book on Beverly, for example, explored the outcome of an election about the town's high school, but none of them contained the kind of rich case studies of municipal and educational politics that Reese provided.

Some detailed case studies on progressive school reform did exist, but they mainly focused on large urban school systems such as Boston, Chicago, and New York (e.g., Hogan, 1985; Wrigley, 1982). These are unquestionably important systems, yet for a number of reasons each has drawbacks in regards to school politics in the Progressive Era. For example, municipal and educational politics in Chicago and New York were strongly shaped by political machines, a situation that was not as common in many smaller American cities. Moreover, progressive reformers in Chicago and New York never completely realized their goal of "taking the schools out of politics." While the reformers did abolish ward-based school boards, in both cities they failed to replace them with at-large elections. Instead they settled for a system in which the mayor appointed school board members, hardly what the reformers had hoped for in terms of removing the schools from politics (Hogan, 1985; Wrigley, 1982).

By examining progressive politics in a range of small cities, several of which had more open political cultures than Chicago and New York, Reese was able to present a picture of progressive school reform untainted by organizations like Tammany Hall. In the cities that Reese examined, the shift from ward-based to at-large elections essentially followed the progressive blueprint for changing school governance. These cities were then more representative of certain types of progressive reform than places that hitherto had received the most scholarly attention.

The most important aspect of the generally open political cultures of Kansas City, Milwaukee, Toledo, and Rochester was that these cities were the home to a host of disparate individuals and grassroots organizations that played important roles in educational politics and the development of progressive school reform. In highlighting these individuals and groups, Reese made another major contribution to the literature by introducing a more diverse cast of historical actors than had appeared in any earlier studies.

Most previous research into the politics of progressive school reform, whether conducted by revisionists or by other historians, had concentrated largely on the actions of a relatively small number of socially elite or professionally prominent individuals or groups.[1] Reese did not ignore these individuals and groups, but he demonstrated that in addition to them a large number of less socially prominent people and organizations were equally deserving of the title of progressive reformers. Reese introduced educational historians to such individuals as Meta and Victor Berger, leaders of Milwaukee's socialist movement who played key roles in school reform in that city (Meta serving on the Milwaukee school board for 30 years!); Sam "Golden Rule" Jones, the progressive mayor of Toledo, one of the most colorful political and educational leaders in American history whose vision of social justice was inspired by the Sermon on the Mount; and Rochester's Edward Ward who sought to use schools as social centers and encouraged adults who used those centers to form civic clubs that would promote democratic ideals. He also demonstrated in all these cities how trade unions and a host of middle-class women's organizations contributed to progressive educational politics and policy making. Joining these individuals and organizations were leaders of the growing Italian, German, and Polish communities, many of whom were active participants in campaigns for educational change.

What emerged from the detailed studies of so varied an array of political actors and organizations was a portrait of progressive reform that transcended all the prevailing historiographic discussions of the era. His investigation of grassroots movements in these small cities led Reese to question a number of widely held assumptions about educational reform in the Progressive Era. For example, Reese's discussion of the role of middle-class women's organizations in these reform efforts challenged traditional narratives in which men dominated progressive educational politics and women played, at best, a secondary role. Contrary to that view, Reese argues that these women's organizations were "central" to the success of some of the best features of progressive school reform and that they battled to thwart some its most benighted efforts. As he put it, "The history of school innovation in these years is integrally bound with the history of activist women, whose hopes and dreams, successes and failures are hidden in diverse kinds of local materials on school and society" (p. 29, this volume).

Perhaps the most significant insight that this research into grassroots educational politics provides is that disparate individuals and groups were not merely involved in these struggles, they also had a profound influence on their outcome. In the conclusion to *Power and the Promise of Reform*, Reese declares, "To argue that schools were divorced from the masses of people and controlled exclusively by the forces of privilege captures only one aspect of Progressive era reform movements and misses the dialectical nature of social innovation" (p. 233). This emphasis on the dialectical nature of educational reform provided a path out of the revisionist/anti-revisionist morass.

The fruits of this approach to understanding Progressive era educational politics were substantial. In addition to his insights into the role of women in educational politics, Reese demonstrated that the shift from ward-based to at-large school board elections was not the great triumph of enlightened democracy over corruption and self-interest that progressive leaders and some later historians had claimed. Nor was this change the unalloyed victory of elite, business-oriented reformers over representatives of "the poor and the dispossessed" as some revisionists had described it (p. 82). Rather, Reese argues, that despite the political advantages that business-oriented progressives had in at-large elections, school politics under the new regime remained as fiercely contested as they had been and the results of these conflicts were not assured.

Similarly, Reese found that bitter enemies such as business leaders and socialists could occasionally find common ground when seeking to implement such programs as penny lunches for poor children, even though the former may have sought the meals as a means for producing healthier workers while the latter advocated them as step toward greater social justice. Reese also noted that frequently more radical groups on both sides of the political spectrum denounced such efforts because, for example, they undermined the traditional responsibilities of families, on the one hand, or they failed to undermine the foundations of capitalism, on the other.

What these examples highlight is that rather than accepting the either–or straitjacket that had come to define the revisionist/anti-revisionist debate, Reese offered a new perspective on the Progressive Era, one perhaps best described as "both/and." *Power and the Promise of School Reform* depicts a broad array of people and organizations that shaped and reshaped the character of school reform through conflict, compromise, and shifting political coalitions. The crux of his argument is that during these years "America's urban schools were largely 'contested terrain'" (p. xx).

That new perspective on progressive reform was shared by an increasing number of scholars in the field, many of who were students of people deeply involved in the revisionist/anti-revisionist debate. Like Reese, this new generation of educational historians produced studies guided by, but not overwhelmed by, that debate. *Power and the Promise of School Reform*, with its thoughtful, vibrant, and highly nuanced account of a crucial period in the development of American public education, was one of the first of these new works. It is still one of the very best.

NOTE

1. An important exception to that generalization is Wrigley's study of Chicago that specifically examined the role of organized labor in educational politics from 1900 to 1950 (Wrigley, 1982).

REFERENCES

Bailyn, Bernard. (1960). *Education and the Forming of American Society*. New York: W.W. Norton.

Bowles, Samuel; & Gintis, Herbert. (1976). *Schooling in Capitalist America: Educational Reform and the Contradictions of Economic Life*. New York: Basic Books.

Cremin, Lawrence A. (1957). *The Republic and the School: Horace Mann on the Education of Free Men*. New York: Teachers College Press.

Cremin, Lawrence A. (1961). *The Transformation of the School*. New York: Knopf.

Cremin, Lawrence A. (1965). *The Wonderful World of Ellwood P. Cubberley*. New York: Teachers College Press.

Cremin, Lawrence A. (1976). *Traditions in American Education*. New York: Basic Books.

Cremin, Lawrence A. (1988). *American Education: The Metropolitan Experience, 1876–1980*. New York: Harper and Row.

Cubberley, Ellwood P. (1919). *Public Education in the United States*. Boston: Houghton Mifflin.

Dawley, Alan. (1976). *Class and Community: The Industrial Revolution in Lynn*. Cambridge, MA: Harvard University Press.

Feinberg, Walter; Kantor, Harvey; Katz, Michael; & Violas, Paul. (1980). *Revisionists Respond to Ravitch*. Washington, DC: National Academy of Education.

Hogan, David John. (1985). *Class and Reform: School and Society in Chicago, 1880–1930*. Philadelphia: University of Pennsylvania Press.

Kaestle, Carl; & Vinovskis, Maris. (1979). *Education and Social Change in Nineteenth-Century Massachusetts*. New York: Cambridge University Press.

Katz, Michael B. (1968). *The Irony of Early School Reform: Educational Reform in Mid-Nineteenth Century Massachusetts*. Boston: Beacon Press.

Katz, Michael B. (1971). *Class, Bureaucracy, and Schools: The Illusion of Educational Change in America*. New York: Praeger.

Ravitch, Diane. (1978). *The Revisionists Revised: A Critique of the Radical Attack on the Schools*. New York: Basic Books.

Spring, Joel. (1972). *Education and the Rise of the Corporate State*. Boston: Beacon Press.

Thernstrom, Stephan. (1964). *Poverty and Progress: Social Mobility in a Nineteenth Century City*. Cambridge, MA: Harvard University Press.

Violas, Paul. (1978). *The Training of the Urban Working Class*. Chicago: Rand McNally.

Wrigely, Julia. (1982). *Class Politics and Public Schools: Chicago, 1900–1950*. New Brunswick, NJ: Rutgers University Press.

Acknowledgments

Power and the Promise of School Reform was first published in 1986 by Routledge and Kegan Paul in the Critical Social Thought series, edited by Michael W. Apple. I remain grateful to Mike for his early faith in my scholarship and would also like to thank Routledge for reversion of the publishing rights. While the original book acknowledged a long list of friends, teachers, and colleagues in whose debt I remain, I would especially like to affirm the kindness and generosity of a few: Carl F. Kaestle, who shepherded me and this study through graduate school; the late David Roller, who directed my master's thesis; and B. Edward McClellan, steadfast friend and constructive critic.

Brian Ellerbeck of Teachers College Press invited me to prepare a second edition of this book for publication, for which I am extremely grateful. Anita Lightfoot of the University of Wisconsin-Madison typed a new version of the book, which was first written in the age of the typewriter, and Mary Jo Gessler and Lisa Loutzenheiser skillfully brought the final version to its present form. (Except for occasional editing, the prose remains identical to the first edition; the Notes have been altered from the original Routledge format to save space.) I would also like to thank the editors of the *History of Education Quarterly*, the *Pacific Northwest Quarterly*, *School Review* (now the *American Journal of Education*), and the *Teachers College Record* for permission to draw upon materials previously published in different form in their respective journals. I am especially grateful, too, to Karen Benjamin, a doctoral student at the University of Wisconsin-Madison, for her exceptional talents in securing the illustrations for this new edition.

Finally, this edition of *Power and the Promise of School Reform* is dedicated to the memory of Sterling Fishman. Our friendship was regrettably brief but a high point of my adult life. Through the ages authors have tried to define friendship. Among its characteristics, Francis Bacon noted centuries ago, was its "two contrary effects, for it redoubleth joys, and cutteth griefs in half." I'll always remember Sterling's wise counsel, love of learning, and courage. And our conversations over dark beer at The Laurel.

Preface

I

Long the symbol of an indigenous American democracy, public schools were the center of intense controversy and debate in the early twentieth century. Victor Berger, the famous Socialist, wrote in the *Milwaukee Leader* in 1915 that "two ideas are fighting for mastery in the educational world." Indeed, two contradictory movements struggled for dominance. One movement, Berger warned, was engineered by capitalists and "would make the schools into 'efficient,' card catalogued, time clocked, well bossed factories for the manufacture of standardized wage slaves." An opposite effort, led by political radicals and progressive citizens, reflected a fundamentally different conception of schools in a changing social order. Instead of shaping education to serve privilege, this movement "would have the schools a part of our social life, specialized to hasten the development of children into free human beings." From "the kindergarten to the university," these contradictory forces clashed and competed in the world of education. From this struggle, Berger asserted, America's modern public school system would emerge replete with the contradictions of the larger capitalist society.[1]

Efficiency versus democracy, freedom versus control, respect for labor versus power for the capitalist: these were the many conflicts that citizens confronted on the shop floor as well as in the local neighborhood school. Unlike the ubiquitous school administrators of the period who viewed educational decision making as "above politics," most citizens realized that schools were a decidedly political enterprise. Socialists and non-Socialists, trade unionists and manufacturers, and educational experts and ordinary citizens recognized that schools had become key institutions in children's lives. The power to influence the curriculum, to select textbooks, to appoint teachers, or to inaugurate innovative programs depended upon political strength, no matter what school superintendents with their advanced academic degrees proclaimed.[2]

How to reshape state-sponsored mass education in response to massive immigration, increased urbanization, and the emergence of monopoly capital was the central issue among school reformers during the Progressive era. Comrade Berger and countless contemporaries understood that some of the most important debates of their age focused on school policy. Consensus on the significance of education in the lives of youth never produced agreement on school policy. Rather, the public schools symbolized many different things to various citizens during the period. There was tremendous enthusiasm for the elusive concept called "reform" but vigorous dissent over specific school innovations. To a banker on the Milwaukee Board of Education in 1910, school organization represented business ethics, and teachers were hired to instill proper values into incipient workers. To the members of middle-class women's organizations, however, schools were humanitarian institutions that sponsored free breakfasts for the hungry and safe playgrounds for guttersnipes. Political radicals and progressive trade unionists, by contrast, often saw schools as evolving democratic forms that nevertheless required vigilance and continual protection from the serpentine arms of manufacturers and capitalists.[3]

Given the eclectic nature of reform ideology in the early 1900s, any attempt to capture the essence of school reform must, therefore, abandon analytical theories such as imposition and social control, despite their popularity with some historians. Reformers of all political persuasions wanted to impose their values on the schools, and everyone realized that children would be controlled by the ruling ideas of specific adults. Schools existed to socialize youth, to train them in basic subjects, and to impose adult authority. Debates centered on whose values would predominate in the neighborhood school, not on whether imposition and control would occur. This guaranteed that from the depression of the 1890s to the Palmer Raids of World War I, America's urban schools were largely "contested terrain."[4]

Few people in 1890 could have sketched the exact contours of urban education thirty years hence, but the central characteristics of twentieth-century schooling slowly emerged amid the conflicts and controversies of the Progressive era. In less than three decades America's urban schools had adopted numerous educational experiments that promised to transform the very character of public education. Slowly and unpredictably, a wide range of voluntary associations of men and women in dozens of cities coalesced into local movements for reform, pressing the schools to assume novel responsibilities. The distinction between public and private duty, so carefully articulated in previous years, soon lost its clarity. Whether or not contemporaries agreed with Victor Berger's claim that the schools were enmeshed in a struggle between capitalists and democratic reformers, educator and layperson alike sensed that education had reached an important historical juncture.

Education reform in its multiple, often contradictory guises constituted a major municipal concern in the late nineteenth and early twentieth centuries. There was striking interest in educational innovation after Americans faced a major economic depression beginning in 1893. The depression ended within four years, but social consciousness continued to flourish. Berger and numerous activists realized, of course, that capitalist consolidation and economic specialization in the business world had their counterpart in changes in school organization. School boards were centralized, eliminating ward-level representation, and superintendents were empowered, eroding lay influence. At the same time, large numbers of citizens struggled to make public schools more responsive to the children of ordinary people, especially the poor. Shaped largely in reaction to business- and elite-inspired reforms that centralized power, these grassroots Progressives did not equate schools with capital investments and did not confuse children with human capital. These local reformers, whose own histories and place in shaping history have rarely been told, form the basis of this study.[5]

Most histories of urban school reform at the turn of the century examine the perspectives and actions of school board members, superintendents, and other educational elites. One cannot underestimate the importance of these individuals, but school innovation was a dynamic, interactive process involving diverse community groups. Women's organizations, parent associations, labor unions, Social Gospelers, and the Populist and Socialist Parties—hardly the featured actors in analyses of Progressive school reform—nevertheless played a seminal role in school innovation. They often arose in dialectical fashion in opposition to the centralizing and bureaucratic reforms embraced by business and professional elites. The lives and activities of these grassroots, community-oriented Progressives remain hidden in articles in trade union and Socialist newspapers as well as in the regular party press, in petitions to local school boards, and in various obscure archival collections. These reformers resisted efforts to remove lay influence from educational policy making and make the classroom the anteroom to the factory.

In city after city these Progressives labored to democratize schools and to make them more responsive to local neighborhoods. At a time when businessmen and professionals dominated on school boards and when superintendents consolidated their power, local community groups emerged as vital elements in the history of social reform. They fought to convert schools into social centers to bring institutions closer to the people.

They petitioned for free breakfasts and lunches for the poor, for vacation schools, for rudimentary medical and dental care, and for safe places for children's play. Besides trying to expand the social services available in local schools, they organized political rallies to ensure that women, Socialists, workers, and constituents of other minority interests—ignored by Democratic and Republican machines that often controlled "nonpartisan" school systems—were elected to office to secure essential reforms. These community-oriented Progressives understood that schools were undergoing rapid change in response to the rise of a corporate economy, and they warned against the dangers of elite rule in institutions that educated the majority of children and were steeped in an ideology of democracy and equal rights.

Voluntary organizations were hardly novel phenomena by the turn of the twentieth century, yet they were integral to the history of school reform during the Progressive era. Some voluntary associations had a diverse membership and eclectic interests; others had a narrower social base and a more parochial outlook. Since social change in education was often championed by women's organizations, parent groups, labor unions, and radical political parties, their histories are central and not incidental aspects of educational transformation. Whether or not organizations were composed of liberals or radicals, grassroots reformers—like the corporate capitalists who often opposed them—viewed schooling as a leading instrument for social improvement. Since visions of how to improve society through educational innovation often differed enormously during this period, conflict in many forms characterized urban school policy early in this century.

Men and women from diverse social, ethnic, and occupational backgrounds joined competing organizations after 1890 to lobby for educational change. However much these groups differed on specific means and ends, they all promoted the expansion of the social functions of education and the extension of public responsibilities into areas once considered private. Responding to the imperatives of an emerging political economy based on specialization and centralization, in which the state usually protected the rights of capital by defending trusts, pools, and monopolies, grassroots reformers—for all of their internal differences— accepted the increasing power of government in social and family life. Whether Socialist or non-Socialist, clubwoman or union representative, these reformers asked how, rather than whether, the state should intervene in children's lives. And as the schools acquired new roles in social improvements, they increasingly grew in political significance and nurtured rising expectations among taxpayers and community leaders.

By the 1920s, America's urban school system had expanded not only in size but also in the complexity of services offered to local citizens.

Innovation represented by the rise of curricular innovations, social service programs, and changing practices in school governance altered the lives of millions of children and set important precedents for subsequent decades. But exactly how and why did schools assume additional social functions during the Progressive era? Why was there such an upsurge of interest in school reform at the turn of the century? Which social groups and community organizations lobbied for which changes and with what kinds of success? In particular, how widespread were the various services that expanded the social role of schools, how willingly and readily did parents and children utilize these innovations, and what difference did they make in their lives?

Searching for the origins of social welfare programs in urban education in the early twentieth century requires discovering the intricate processes of social change and how they ultimately influenced institutions and their clientele. After studying various cities, one encounters a fascinating problem. Turn-of-the-century reformers who had diametrically opposed political and ideological perspectives, such as Socialists and capitalist efficiency experts, often endorsed the same innovation. Their reasons for doing so, of course, differed enormously, proving Berger's contention that competing visions of social life sought mastery in the schools. Even the acceptance of the need for the same reform produced noticeable conflict, as a single example at this point demonstrates.

Like their counterparts in Europe, American Socialists were often the first reformers to campaign for free meals for schoolchildren. Even a simple breakfast or lunch might help compensate the poor for the unequal distribution of wealth and income produced by capitalism; the reform was a matter of social justice. Efficiency reformers, however, viewed the same programs as a form of capital investment, a way to build healthier and stronger children to defend and support the existing free enterprise system. Which perspective predominated in the creation of the innovation? Did new programs such as social centers or health services or playgrounds fulfill the needs of one ideological interest group but not another? To what degree did innovations actually function as competing reform groups desired? Did new social services and programs place the power of the state on the side of capital or labor?

One strategy to assess the origins, implementation, and significance of social welfare reforms in Progressive-era schools is to use detailed case studies of various cities. Case studies enable historians to locate social change in its immediate, local context and to examine particular reforms from their genesis as ideas to their actual implementation. Studies of famous cities such as New York and Boston have been models of historical analysis and enormously influential in the historiography of American schooling. By exploring several cities and venturing beyond the urban East, I hope to provide a more solid ground on which to construct a thesis on the importance of grassroots, community-oriented reformers in the history of schooling during the Progressive era. The cities selected provide insights into changes that were occurring in differing degrees across the urban landscape, but they are hardly "representative." More modestly, they may serve as illustrations of the multifaceted nature of school reform and welfare innovation in the early twentieth century. If all the world is not Boston, neither is it Comrade Berger's Milwaukee.[6]

II

America's urban schools generated an enormous quantity of relevant historical documents during the Progressive era, and my own graduate training in history and education at universities in Ohio, Missouri, and especially Wisconsin gave me access to major archival collections on local school systems. The cities basic to this study are Rochester, New York; Toledo, Ohio; Milwaukee, Wisconsin; and Kansas City, Missouri. For each of these cities I read the available school board minutes and proceedings, annual school reports, competing newspapers, various manuscript collections, and other extant materials. The official version of how and why school innovations were inaugurated at certain times and in certain places was, therefore, corrected through reconstruction of the lives of various grassroots reformers, from middle-class women's club members to Socialist trade unionists. Showing that history never changes, school officials were never above taking credit for innovations that were conceived outside their institutions.

All four cities had their own distinctive political, economic, and social characteristics. Yet they all to different degrees produced contradictory movements for school reform: one that aimed to consolidate and centralize power, and one that resisted this effort by making schools more serviceable to local neighborhoods. Despite the real differences that varying ethnic mixes, political traditions, and local patterns of leadership had on school innovation in different cities, what remains striking is how grassroots reformers continually surfaced to demand more responsive schools that offered many new programs. The pace and timing of innovation were often shaped by local circumstance, yet urban schools everywhere were gripped by polar extremes: by forces that pushed schools away from popular control and by forces that tried to counteract that trend. The schools of Rochester, Toledo, Milwaukee, and Kansas City— like scores of other cities—all faced the problem of how to prepare youth for a society whose economic and political institutions were increasingly specialized, centralized, and controlled by a narrow, elite class.

Rochester, New York, has a prominent place in the history of Progressive-era school reform, particularly in the area of social services. Rochester was the leading American city in the promotion of social centers, a popular innovation that many civic groups championed across the United States. Rochester's reputation flourished because of the activities and influence of Edward J. Ward, the so-called father of the social center movement. Ward became a national leader in social service expansion. Through his well-publicized conflicts with local ward bosses, who vigorously opposed the centers, Ward turned the national social center spotlight on his adopted city. In many regards, Rochester is uniquely suited to the study of welfare reform in the schools. Its reform leadership formed close bonds with civic activists in many cities. When the Socialists assumed power in Milwaukee in 1910, for example, party leaders hired Ward as an advisor in social center development, and one of Ward's associates later operated Milwaukee's Socialist Sunday schools.

The significance of Toledo, Ohio, during the Progressive era rested on fundamentally different grounds. Throughout the period, Toledo attracted national attention because of its famous mayors: the charismatic Samuel M. "Golden Rule" Jones (in office from 1897–1904) and his close friend and successor, Brand Whitlock (1905–13). To contemporaries and later historians, both men symbolized a grassroots expression of "social justice" in the early twentieth century. Indeed, Golden Rule Clubs formed across the country after Jones popularized his views on brotherly love and the social gospel in politics. Jones and Whitlock pressed for many new social reforms in the Toledo schools, following and often furthering movements initiated by labor groups, women's clubs, and parent-teacher associations in child welfare innovations such as social centers, playgrounds, and penny lunches. After Jones's death in 1904, Whitlock became the acknowledged leader of the local Independent Movement, a third-party effort that was central to Toledo politics until 1913. While the Republican Party dominated in Rochester (except for occasional challenges from upstart Socialists and liberal Good Government reformers), a vigorous variety of third-party activism prospered in Toledo throughout the Progressive era.

Milwaukee provides another attractive city for studying social change in the schools. Just as the attempts of Jones and Whitlock to establish a new municipality based on the Golden Rule and Independent politics brought Toledo its share of attention, so too did the activities of organized labor and the Socialist Party make Milwaukee distinctive throughout the Progressive era. Like Toledo, Milwaukee had a large immigrant population. More than that, the Social Democratic Party, whose strength primarily rested in the local trade unions, captured the city administration in 1910, marking the first time that Socialists succeeded politically in a large American city. Compared with Toledo and Rochester, Milwaukee had a highly politicized and militant trade union movement. Formally aligned with the Socialists, the trade unions agitated for many education innovations and social service reforms and fought the influence of economic elites. By electing their own members to the school board and cooperating with other civic groups, they became a remarkable and consistent force for grassroots reform.

Offering a comparison with the political traditions and reform impulses in Rochester, Toledo, and Milwaukee, Kansas City provides still another useful setting for examining the history of Progressive school reform. Unlike Milwaukee and Toledo, the city was ruled by an entrenched two-party system that was never effectively challenged by any coalition of third-party dissidents. Even more so than in Rochester, the major political parties reigned and ruled. Largely composed of native-born citizens, Kansas City lacked the ethnic cast of most midwestern and eastern cities. It therefore offers a unique opportunity on many levels to determine how a different urban area with unusual characteristics influenced the history of schooling. Kansas City's educational history also directly contrasts with these other three cities because its school board was already small and centralized by the 1870s. It underwent administrative centralization much earlier than most cities, producing a network of educational control unlike the systems found in nineteenth-century Rochester, Toledo, and Milwaukee.

In all these cities, as in much of the urban nation, educational innovation became an integral facet of reform movements during the Progressive era. A wide range of individuals who often assembled into competing camps turned to the schools as a source of human betterment. In many respects educational innovation reflected the power of the major economic forces at work in the late nineteenth century, forces that included centralization, consolidation, and specialization. While efficiency reformers might try to use vocational education programs and other innovations to fit children into the existing market system, many other reformers contested such policies and agreed with Victor Berger that schools should become "a part of our social life" and "hasten the development of children into free human beings."

Whether they favored state capitalism or state socialism, reform-minded men and women joined innumerable voluntary organizations in the 1890s dedicated to the improvement of the public schools. A spirit of reform, variously interpreted but always present, infused the political environments of cities such as Rochester, Toledo, Milwaukee, and Kansas City. The history of educational reform in these locales exemplified a much larger process by which urban schools across America adjusted to the demands of a changing society. Reformers agitated for change and believed that schools should be a seminal force in the education and socialization of young people in the twentieth century. As one famous Milwaukee socialist had argued, throughout America contradictory forces competed for mastery in the schools.

Chapter 1

The Origins of Mass Education and the Dawn of Progressivism

I

In the spring of 1854, a ship chugged across Lake Erie with precious cargo for the citizens of Toledo. Although the town founders predicted that the city would be an international crossroads for trade, industry, and culture, the *Propellor Toledo* did not convey jasmine or lace or even glittering metals. Instead, the Whig *Blade* announced the arrival of something far more useful to this bustling community: a forty-three-hundred-pound schoolhouse bell. Raised to the tower of Toledo's expensive new high school, the bell soon rested beside a brass town clock, "which will strike the hours upon this ponderous bell, and announce the time to the inhabitants of the city and for miles around it." With dials that spanned a diameter of seven feet, the clock was an imposing centerpiece of the local school system, now less than a decade old. As the secretary of the board of education later recorded in his minute book, school officials even appointed a "Keeper of the Town Clock" who was paid "for keeping . . . all School Clocks in order." The school system was young, but it would run on time.[1]

During the nineteenth century, clocks, whistles, and bells told the children of Toledo and most cities when to begin and conclude their school day. If their parents were factory workers, they too labored in a world of morning and evening whistles. Clocks ticked incessantly in neighborhood schools across urban America, demonstrating that the private virtues especially valued by the elite classes could be stamped upon the face of public institutions. During the formative years of state-sponsored, mass education between the 1840s and the 1890s, public schools became a battleground between various contending interests. Schools became linked in the minds of elite reformers with progress and reform, and gradually over time the schools were wedded to an emerging free-market economy. And so, decades before the rise of grassroots community reformers in the 1890s, mass education had already been the site of extensive controversy and conflict in local cities.

School reformers of the late nineteenth and early twentieth centuries cannot be understood apart from an understanding of how mass education evolved in local settings and how state-controlled schooling became embedded in social life. The depression of the 1890s and the emergence of industrial monopoly capitalism set the main immediate background for the rise of Progressive reform, but urban schools had already been undergoing formation and change for nearly half a century. Progressives of all stripes faced institutions that had existed for decades and had acquired characteristics that would impede the efforts of various reformers. To understand Progressive-era school innovation in cities such as Rochester, Toledo, Milwaukee, and Kansas City, one must step back from the social conflicts of the 1890s and examine school and society before the onset of a new era of reform.

What were the major historical forces that shaped the rise of mass education in urban America? Who had been the major protagonists in early school reform? Why did the state intervene in educational decision making, despite the protests of certain opponents? What social and political roles did schools play in mid- to late-nineteenth-century America? What particular social and cultural characteristics existed in Toledo and these other cities as the Progressive era dawned? By the early twentieth century, reformers with diametrically opposed ideological viewpoints agreed upon the need for state-dominated education. Was this consensus on state power and conflict over the precise nature of state power in education already a powerful tradition in local communities by the 1890s?

II

Nineteenth-century working people in Toledo and other urban areas believed in the utility of schooling for their children, but there is no evidence that they urged the purchase of two-ton bells or supported other schemes to make schools more efficient. In fact, the most striking phenomenon concerning the origins of mass institutions is how, in city after city, white males with similar ideological and class perspectives helped found public school systems. These men were comfortable in both the countinghouse and the schoolhouse. As men of affairs they were involved in an inordinate variety of commercial and philanthropic projects. They helped direct, for example, the construction of canals, plank roads, railroads, newspapers, small and large businesses, libraries, lyceums, asylums, private charities, and, when time allowed, public schools.

Antebellum and postbellum school reformers moved from the private sector to public arenas with considerable skill and zeal. Prime forces in

economic life, they viewed themselves as natural leaders in social and
political life as well. Between the 1840s and 1860s, aggressive elite community leaders in Rochester, Toledo, Milwaukee, and Kansas City more actively involved their municipalities in educational development. Thanks to
their efforts, systems of schools emerged on the urban frontier. This was
not accomplished without effort or conflict. Besides assailing the district
system of schooling, which gave parents considerable power over their
children's education, early school reformers wrote editorials, attended
meetings, and drafted memorials for the state legislature to impose centralization and order upon education. The ringing of school bells across
the city must have engendered in them a feeling of triumph.

Antebellum reformers had, therefore, set new educational ideas into
motion, propelling the state forward as a more powerful element in the
education and socialization of youth. Despite the claims of many local
historians, however, the Rochester, Toledo, Milwaukee, and Kansas City
school systems did not arise from some movement for American "democracy." Put simply, school reformers were intensive, energetic, and acquisi-
tive individuals who had broad visions of commercial and industrial
empire. Their biographers, usually close friends, approvingly called them
"capitalists." Endorsing the principle of state intervention in the political
economy and in schooling, local school reformers were usually Whigs
and town boosters as they fought for tax-supported, centralized, and uniform systems of mass education. They continually cajoled contented parents and suspicious taxpayers, urging support for their righteous cause.
Despite these efforts, the plain people or local mechanics never rose up
to demand new systems of state-supported education for their children.
Instead, elite members of the professional, economic, and social classes
controlled the timing and pace of educational innovation.[2]

Public school systems evolved at a time when many parents and
citizens loyally supported district schooling and questioned the benefits
of a centralized school board and graded, uniform instruction. The *Toledo
Blade* complained in 1849 that parents seemed either indifferent or antago-
nistic toward the Akron Law (1846), which mandated an elected board
of education and graded schools for cities such as Toledo. Rochester's
early school reports similarly reveal many home and school antagonisms,
and parents often grumbled about centralization long after elites disman-
tled the district system in the 1840s. Whig editors in Milwaukee and
Kansas City frequently complained that elite reformers were forced to
overcome apathy or hostility to direct the course of social progress. In
1845, for example, the *Milwaukee Sentinel* called for the creation of many
more schools and lambasted the public for its "*criminal* apathy" concerning
public education. Kansas City's leading Whig reformer similarly com-

plained a few years later that "not one-twentieth [of the citizenry] have an intelligent idea of the condition of things, and not one-fiftieth can be induced to attend any meeting."[3]

Newspaper journalists in city after city boosted the cause of school centralization and related reforms to guide the process of social transformation. They welded programs of state intervention in schooling to dynamic schemes of internal economic improvement, shaping as well as reflecting the desires of an emerging civic elite. Personalities differed somewhat from place to place and Democrats often aided the effort, but everyone held buoyant visions of the future of school and society. Henry O'Reilly, an Irish immigrant who edited Rochester's first newspaper in 1826, exemplified the spirit of urban boosterism. Most notably, he pressed for numerous economic and civic improvements, from the expansion of the Erie Canal to the replacement of district schooling with a comprehensive and centralized system of education. This editor, banker, and later inventor agitated for many of the citizens' meetings that considered the establishment of a school board in the early 1840s, when Rochester's population already surpassed twenty thousand. Like many contemporaries, O'Reilly feared that vice, crime, and sedition would proliferate without a system of schools.[4]

In Toledo, the Whig and later Republican *Blade*, founded as a tri-weekly in 1847, similarly agitated for a full system of public improvements. One favorite idea was the linkage of the Wabash Canal in the hinterland with the Erie Canal through to the shipping lanes of the Great Lakes. Hosmer Graham, the *Blade*'s editor, characteristically wrote that "in this age of improvements, this great, and all important subject of *educating the whole people*, the masses, should not be lost sight of nor neglected." For although his city still possessed fewer than four thousand inhabitants, he realized that canals and the iron bands of the railroads would soon integrate enterprising communities into national markets. And certainly the nation's expansive plans of "Internal Improvement" seemed incomplete without a corresponding network of education.[5]

The rise of urban school systems was largely promoted by these advocates of internal economic and social development. Already by the 1820s, Rochester was heralded not as the next Syracuse or Utica but as a leading metropolis. Lofty expansionist dreams, based primarily on economic development, prevailed in every aspiring captain of commerce. The Democratic press of different cities gloried in the coming of the American imperium, but Whigs in particular propelled the ideology of economic and educational expansion forward at a dizzying speed. The *Milwaukee Sentinel*, for example, predicted in 1845 that the area was "destined to be the chief commercial and manufacturing city of this WESTERN

EMPIRE." Like Henry O'Reilly, his Rochester counterpart, Rufus King of the *Sentinel* was a pioneer school board member and civic booster. King was also Milwaukee's first school superintendent, and his political prowess made him a member of the Wisconsin Constitutional Convention in 1847.[6]

Decades after urban school systems began in New York, Ohio, and Wisconsin, Robert T. Van Horn's inspirational editorials for Kansas City's Whig and later Republican newspapers made all these men seem like amateurs. That the "city" had approximately four thousand residents in 1860 mattered little. Soon Van Horn and the community business leaders who lured him to the bend of the Missouri River were trumpeting the virtues of their promised land. An itinerant printer with an undistinguished past, as editor Van Horn was well suited to become one of the West's leading civic promoters and champions of schooling. As a young man, he worked on the Erie Canal, where he learned of internal improvement firsthand. Soon after, he rightly predicted that the nation was on the brink of vast commercial expansion.

With other local notables, Van Horn rejected the common characterization of the West as a great American desert. Instead, he perceived an American version of the Garden of Eden in which national and international markets supported by a vast system of railroads crisscrossed his fair city. But the American paradise required more than trains and banks, buyers and sellers. "Here will soon be the commercial center of a vast and energetic population," Van Horn acknowledged in the *Kansas City Journal of Commerce* in 1869, "and it is proper that the means of education, scientific and literary, should keep pace with the progress of material wealth and advancement." Education was the handmaiden of economic development, and Van Horn's clear and bountiful vision has encouraged many historians of Kansas City to emphasize his remarkable influence upon early school reform.[7]

Boosters frequently misrepresented the state of education in local communities. When it came to mass instruction, they condemned district schooling and most forms of private initiative in education. In their eyes, district schools were as ineffective in educating the people as were pay schools, select schools, and itinerant schoolmasters. The whole method of educating children was too irregular, too informal, and too often subject to parental discretion: parents determined how, when, and whether their offspring would be educated and schooled. Too much seemed left to chance to those who equated parental choice with social chaos and disorder. Like every editor who prayed for metropolitan status, Van Horn complained in 1867 that Kansas City lagged behind other urban areas, ignoring the existence of some district schools and a variety of private institutions. Van Horn nevertheless warned that children languished in an atmosphere of vice and ignorance: "We can furnish them billiards and whiskey, but we have no public school."[8]

In Toledo, the superintendent of schools further claimed that before centralization the "schools were 'without form and void,' and the private schools were *so* private as scarcely to be known even by the man who took the census, or to be found in the memory of 'the oldest inhabitant.'" Toledo's census worker must have been remarkably inept and local memories exceedingly dim, but editors and other school allies feared that internal improvement plans would be undermined unless parents abandoned the existing educational arrangements. But parents seemed lethargic and resistant to change; they looked to the past, not to the future. And so newspaper writers in city after city called "citizens' meetings" to rally people behind a more centralized and uniform system of education, in line with the march of commercial and economic progress. These meetings testify to the elite origins of mass education.[9]

Historians of these four cities have described the men who lobbied for centralized schooling in many ways: as "civic minded" elites, "public minded" citizens, and "urban statesmen." Perhaps they were all of these. Contemporaries, however, more accurately described them as "men of affairs," a term that indicated their membership in a select economic and social group that shaped general urban development. Citizens' meetings that promoted the establishment of school systems were not attended by a cross section of leaders. These men were dominant civic leaders active in all spheres of urban politics, and they certainly were unrepresentative of the lower classes. Henry O'Reilly and other enterprising commercial and professional elites led the crusade against the district system in Rochester. I. F. Mack, a prominent Whig and custom miller in a city with an economic stake in flour production and trade, lobbied for centralization and became Rochester's first school superintendent in the early 1840s, illustrating the intimate bonds between commercial development and educational change. The local *Workingman's Advocate* encouraged the working classes to pay more attention to their children's formal education, but they were hardly the prime movers in early school reform.[10]

Those Toledoans most responsible for school reform in the 1840s were also powerful individuals. Prominent among them was Charles W. Hill, a Whig politician, plank road promoter, attorney, and city clerk in the 1830s who subsequently served as the president of the school board for decades. Another Whig and advocate of state intervention in education, Daniel Swift, was locally renowned as the contractor for area canal construction. Edward Bissell, who joined them in Toledo's citizens' meetings, built the first mill in the city (still called the Corn City, for its corn processing; Rochester, by contrast, was the Flour City); otherwise he was active in harbor improvements, railroad development, and land speculation. Dennison Steele, a Democrat until he became a Republican in 1854, was an attorney, a commission merchant, and a council member in the 1840s, besides having investments in lumbering and shipbuilding. Along with representatives of other mercantile interests, these prominent men founded Toledo's new public school system.[11]

Similarly, civic elites concerned with comprehensive internal improvement laid the foundation of Milwaukee's schools. When Rufus King and the *Sentinel* staff organized school-related meetings in 1845, Dr. Lemuel W. Weeks took command of a movement that included the major professional and economic interests in the new city. Like King a Yankee by birth, Weeks was a promoter of improved harbors and of railroad development, a pioneer merchant in the grain trade, and a real estate speculator. An admiring friend and biographer recalled that he was "fond of making money, and as fond of spending it" and was "one of the most industrious men that ever lived in Milwaukee." The inner circle also included another Yankee, Increase Lapham, a nationally renowned scientist who doubled as an urban booster. Lapham's father was a contractor for the Erie Canal, and the younger Weeks became prominent in the construction of Ohio's network of inland waterways in the 1830s. Arriving in Milwaukee in 1836, he accumulated considerable property and prestige. The men who built the local schools were not all native born, however; this famous city of immigrants also produced influential ethnic leaders. Moritz Schoeffler, the Democratic owner and editor of the first German newspaper in the city, the *Wiskonsin-Demokrat*, and Richard Murphy, a leading Irish politician, helped frame the early school laws after participating in many citizens' meetings. Whether foreign born or native, elite leaders overcame public indifference and opposition and inaugurated a new educational order.[12]

Despite Milwaukee's later reputation for its Socialist trade unions, local mechanics and laborers were not visible elements in the establishment of a unified system of schools in 1846. The age of regular trade union involvement in school reform in these cities still lay in the future. Similarly, the architects of Kansas City's schools in the 1860s included the famous Van Horn, William Sheffield (a leading attorney and civic promoter), and some of the most influential bankers and merchants in this boom town. For that reason, John Phillips, Kansas City's first school superintendent, especially thanked "our leading citizens" in 1869 for advancing the cause of reform. These men guided the pace of change and the nature of educational innovation in their new city.[13]

Nineteenth-century school superintendents, school board members, and other educators adopted the booster spirit as their own. They hailed economic development and welcomed population growth and additional school buildings as enthusiastically as boards of commerce applauded an increase in trade. They publicized the positive connections between economic prosperity and educational growth, and never as an afterthought. In 1849 President S. L. Rood of the Milwaukee Board of Education commonly noted that a sound system of education attracted the "better class" of immigrants who would stimulate commercial enterprise. Urging the construction of more schoolhouses, he wrote: "To the question so often asked by persons upon their first visit to our city, 'What is the state of education among you?' a much more satisfactory answer must be given than can now be done, if we wish our city to continue to prosper and flourish."[14]

President Charles W. Hill of the Toledo school board echoed these sentiments in 1855, affirming the connections school promoters perceived between education and commercial prosperity. When his administration was attacked for mismanagement and for squandering tax dollars on palatial school buildings, he simply responded that the school board "should be held responsible for a large per cent of the increased population bro't to your town and the enhanced value of your town property." A booster sheet for Kansas City—the "Queen and imperial mistress of the West"—argued in 1879 that families with school-age children would love the area for its schools and commercial prospects: "Here you will find good schools, and, at the same time, not be shut off from business opportunities." J. V. C. Karnes, one of Kansas City's leading attorneys and a powerful school board member, routinely asserted in his presidential address in 1880 that "[e]very year is an improvement on the previous one. Our educational growth is keeping pace with our commercial."[15]

School representatives, therefore, commonly equated rising school enrollments with regional economic development. During the early years of these school systems, roughly between the 1840s and the 1880s, commerce and trade formed the linchpins of the local economies. Early school reform was not the product of factory development but the result of agitation by mostly preindustrial commercial, professional, and civic elites whose successes formed the basis for later industrial expansion. The commercialization of agriculture, along with the construction of canals and then railroads to transport goods and finished products to various markets, enabled local cities to exploit their unique geographical position. This fostered the growth of an interdependent, national economy. Large-scale industrial capitalist development did not develop very rapidly until long after these four school systems were already established. By 1880, however, manufacturing became increasingly integral to these local economies. By then Kansas City already had $2.1 million invested in manufacturing establishments, compared with $5.5 million for Toledo, $13.1 million for Rochester, and $18.7 million for Milwaukee.[16]

The men of affairs who promoted these school systems were the most progressive elements of a local ruling elite. Commercial advancement and economic growth, they argued, required the expenditure of public monies to guarantee the spread of a new economic and social order. The schools became a valuable way to inculcate social beliefs that supported political stability and an evolving capitalist system. A handmaiden of economic growth, schools promised to eliminate the immorality of the street and to resolve the problems of parents and children who needed discipline and lessons in thrift. Kansas City's Democratic *Times* simply restated a common ruling belief in 1879 by asserting that "the idea is kept prominently in view that the object of the school is to prepare the children for duties of citizenship, and to make them law-abiding and wealth-producing citizens."[17]

The establishment of a system of urban schools was one tangible accomplishment of mid-nineteenth-century boosterism. The irregular, unsystematic quality of education that had been offered earlier was discredited; new governing structures were erected; and the idea of a single, tax-supported network of schooling gained political legitimacy. Even before the 1890s, however, school officials and their political allies would have to face the contradictions nurtured by educational instructions that were created for the people, but not by them.

III

"In this country, to a more just sense and for a higher purpose than in any other, the youth are the property of the State." Charles W. Hill, the perennial president of the Toledo Board of Education, was rarely equivocal, and local newspaper reporters in 1855 eagerly reprinted such a quotable statement. Whig politicians and elite school reformers such as Hill clearly favored state intervention in children's lives, and they rarely minced words on the power of government in internal improvement and moral reform. The state did not by and large force children to attend school in the nineteenth century, and school attendance was usually voluntary and applauded by various social classes and ethnic and racial groups. A consensus on the value of education, however, did not translate into universal agreement on the role of parents in children's lives, on the particular values taught in school, on the nature of school governance, or on the propriety of state-sponsored schools controlled by a centralized board of education. Whigs and town boosters owned many things, but not everyone concurred with their belief that children could be regarded as property.[18]

School officials struggled mightily, with impressive results, to build a single system of tax-supported public education by the end of the Victorian era. Social conflict was central to the history of early school reform; indeed, it was almost guaranteed by the elite origins of mass education. While citizens did not engage in daily combat with reformers, superintendents, or teachers, certain school policies nevertheless ensured that dissent was ever present in local cities. A single system of schools tried to serve a plurality of competing interests, and educational institutions designed by a narrow segment of the population faced outside critics at many turns.

In dozens of school reports generated in these cities, superintendents, principals, and leading school commissioners repeatedly publicized the tremendous moral and intellectual achievements of public education and exposed the failings of parents and their children. Paragraph upon paragraph condemned the children of "poverty and crime," the "dangerous classes," and on the streets, the "embryo mob" and "hoodlum element." The ignorance and immorality of the poor, whether native born or immigrant, could only be overcome through the redemptive powers of the school. The poor would otherwise become drunkards, public charges, "thieves, pickpockets, incendiaries, or the leaders of mobs, and finally die in the gutter, the almshouse, or the prison."[19]

After describing the poor in such hostile terms, educators and elite reformers then asked for greater cooperation between teachers and the entire community. Even though the schools were not built by the people, parents were asked "to cheer and encourage" the teachers in their arduous labors and to show "an appreciative spirit" without "unkind criticism." Like April showers, parents were supposed to freshen and invigorate the atmosphere. Dark clouds, however, frequently intruded, since parental apathy or conflict was common. I. F. Mack, the Whig superintendent of the Rochester schools in the 1840s, complained, as did reformers in other cities, that parents failed to show much interest in the schools and rarely visited them. The Rochester school board president in 1862 angrily denounced the "criminal neglect and indifference of parents and guardians in respect to the education of their children." In city after city, parents were urged to visit the schools, but as the Toledo school superintendent complained in 1888, "[f]ew of them do so. Many of them have no personal acquaintance with the teacher who instructs their children."[20]

Always accorded a dependent status, parents often listened to their children rather than to teachers or school officials when conflict occurred.

Parents, it was widely believed, uncritically accepted the "garbled statements of their children, and condemn[ed] the teacher unheard. . . . Children are often roguish and lawyer-like in their stories; and parents, without investigation, decide upon ex parte testimony. In this way the child *lights* the flame, the parent *fans* it, and often great mischief is done." The ringing of two-ton bells, part of a larger process of linking schools to capitalist time discipline, emphasized the educational need for punctuality, but time orientation in particular was a sore point that existed between home and school. School reports overflowed with decimal points on tardiness and accusations of parental insubordination. Principals in Toledo, Rochester, Milwaukee, and Kansas City continually lambasted parents for offering harebrained excuses for their children's behavior. Most children came to school on time, but in 1867 principal E. V. DeGraff of Grammar School No. 5 in Rochester published some delightful examples of excuses parents sent him regarding children's tardiness: the child "Had to run an errand," "Went to the drug store," "Was minding the baby," "Had to watch for a thief"; and to cite the most questionable of all reasons, the "Clock stopped."[21]

To nineteenth-century school reformers, punctuality, business success, and moral behavior were all intertwined. James M. Greenwood, whose superintendency in Kansas City ranged from 1874 to his death in 1914, appeared at his office promptly each morning at seven o'clock, whereupon he parsed Latin verbs, read Greek, and within two hours began a full day of administration. He did this until the day he died—an event that occurred appropriately enough at his office—with a book clutched firmly in hand. Could not pupils be ready for their McGuffey Readers at the appointed time? Did they not realize that "promptness and regularity in matters of business" were essential to success as adults, and that the "vacillating, slip-shod, go-easy soul . . . is a nobody, and should be sent back to nature's mint and be recoined?"[22]

Growing up was serious business, much too serious to be left to parents who forgot to wind clocks or internalize time discipline completely. And yet, as Superintendent John Dowd of Toledo argued in 1882, adherence to time was essential for personal advancement in the free-market system:

> The boy who is found promptly in his place at school for five days in the week, for forty weeks in the year, through a period of from four to seven years, will always be found, when he is through with his school life, at the appointed place, at the appointed time, for the appointed business. He has formed the habit of being on time.[23]

Discipline, self-control, adherence to rules and regulations: these things mattered greatly in schools that stressed deference to authority, sanctioned corporal punishment, and tried to integrate apathetic or hostile elements of the community into a single educational system.

The creation of a uniform, standardized curriculum was an essential part of early school reform, and it, too, was the source of continual controversy and debate in the Victorian period. Parents, particularly poor parents, were often criticized for sending their children to school dirty and without the rudiments of scholarship: pencils, paper, and maps. More significant, some parents fought for freedom of choice in the curriculum at a time when elite reformers sought uniformity in learning. More than a dozen years after the formation of the Milwaukee school system, the board of education regrettably revealed that parents still opposed a graded and uniform plan of instruction. "Questions of the kind here indicated have come up frequently during the past year," wrote the board in 1861. "One parent declares that his child should not study Grammar, and refuses her a book even—another says, let Mental Arithmetic alone; I want my son to learn to calculate interest." Examples of parental meddling and muddleheadedness were legion, but the board remained firm: "Economy, success, and duty to all, demand that we hold on to our system of graded schools." Citizens in Rochester as in other cities complained about the collapse of the district system, the dangers of turning schools into Procrustean institutions, and the preoccupation with time discipline that would not serve laborer and employer equally well when one's school days ended.[24]

The familiar educational configurations that many parents in the midnineteenth century had known in their youth—an assortment of district schools, pay schools, and itinerant schoolmasters, mixed with home instruction—were under assault by town boosters and proponents of elite interests in local communities. Systems of tax-supported schools replaced the unsystematic, unpredictable methods of education in the past, while the attitudes of many parents remained fastened to past educational practices. Although by the Victorian era everyone agreed upon the value of education and schooling, opinions differed on the wisdom of uniformity, time orientation, the nature of school authority, and most important, moral instruction in the schools. It was here in particular that elites furthered the extensiveness of educational dissent.

Town boosters and school leaders of the nineteenth century offered numerous justifications for the establishment of public school systems, including training for citizenship in a republic, character formation, the mastery of basic literacy, and the assimilation of the foreign born. Moral reform was essential to their efforts, since beneath many of their eclectic arguments lay an open hostility to immigrants and the poor, particularly those who were Catholic. Immigrants were "pests" and "vicious," and as one Rochester Whig argued, America had become "a depository of filth for the old world." All was not lost, however, since elite reformers believed deeply in the power of schools to solve social problems. Poverty led to criminality, and schools could cure both maladies. As the *Toledo Blade* editorialized in 1849, children would become "discontented, useless, and bad citizens" without systematic schooling. Ignorant, poor people committed most of the crimes that "destroy the peace, prosperity, and happiness of society," it warned. Moreover, poorly educated persons would neither govern nor be easily governed, and they "cannot be good statesmen, or divines, or lawyers, or doctors, or artizans, or mechanics, or tradesmen, or manufacturers, or farmers—and they make very poor laborers, and worse citizens."[25]

The moral aims of schooling, which triggered major social reactions in local cities, were demonstrated in many ways: the use of Bibles in the classroom, the early morning recitations of prayer, the singing of religious hymns, and the overall dissemination of Protestant-oriented values through textbooks. The schools taught more than the three R's and basic subjects. Reflecting the beliefs of boosters and elite interests, they also emphasized social respectability, political stability, and an acceptance of free enterprise. Schools taught "character building" above all, claimed Superintendent Greenwood of Kansas City, who added that the "central thought in the public school system is not how much grammar, arithmetic, and geography, but how to train the children—educate them—into orderly, quiet, methodical citizens." Greenwood's close friend and political ally Robert T. Van Horn put it more bluntly in 1869: "No schools, and a check is given to our prosperity, and a fearful blow to our moral and pecuniary interests."[26]

From their inception through the Victorian period, the schools of Rochester, Toledo, Milwaukee, and Kansas City emphasized the importance of producing sober, punctual, trustworthy, reliable, and God-fearing citizens. These values would contribute to the nation's "moral and pecuniary interests" and reduce the "licentiousness" and criminal potential of the poor. Indeed, schoolchildren often discovered that teachers were more interested in their morals than in their minds. Schools promised to eliminate both ignorance and immorality. "Let mothers remember that there is no sickness like that of the mind, cramped with ignorance; and no death so dreadful as the extinction of all that is Godlike in the soul," claimed one Rochesterian. A fellow citizen remarked that "good manners in children and youth are worth far more than good mathematics—gentility than geography." Anson Smyth, Toledo's first school superintendent, was a graduate of the Yale Divinity School and the former pastor of the wealthy First Congregational Church. His early school reports indicated that schools taught "useful knowledge" but also "what is of the highest possible importance, moral principles, order, decorum, truthfulness, purity and virtue."[27]

By suggesting that morality could be expressed in absolutes and that many parents were immoral and incompetent, early school reformers provoked numerous conflicts in local cities. Catholics in Rochester, Toledo, Milwaukee, and Kansas City—as in many cities across the nation—objected to the pan-Protestantism of the public schools, called for the division of the school fund for the support of parochial schools, and otherwise challenged the hegemony of Protestant Whigs, Republicans, and school officials. In each of these cities, town boosters and school leaders locked horns with thousands of Catholics who questioned the legitimacy of the evolving public system. In Toledo, for example, the bishop of the local diocese ordered priests to deny the sacraments to any adult Catholic whose children attended the public schools, which used the Protestant Bible in the classroom. Unable to eliminate the power of Protestantism in the schools, Toledo's Catholics, as those elsewhere, began the slow process of building their own system of private schools. School officials viewed Catholics as detrimental to the consensus desired in educational reform, as indeed they were, and usually dismissed them as aliens, unpatriotic citizens, and dupes of the Vatican.[28]

Bishop Bernard J. McQuaid's famous assault on the Rochester public schools illustrates the religious conflicts that occurred in so many cities in the nineteenth century. As the first bishop of the Rochester area, McQuaid received national attention in the 1870s when he lectured and published tracts against the public schools. He argued that public schools were communistic, Protestant, promoters of vice, more expensive than prisons, and a burden on the immigrant poor, who, he claimed, preferred sectarian instruction in "Christian Free Schools," supported by their own taxes. "Parents have the right to educate their children," he insisted, "and it was wrong for the State to interfere with the exercise of this right." By using everyone's tax dollars for a single state system of education, Protestant town boosters and public school officials unjustly denied other parents the right to select and finance their own forms of moral instruction for their young.[29]

McQuaid's conflicts with the schools continued in the 1880s, when he assailed "Godless" public education and urged the division of the tax fund. The bishop emphasized that morality for Catholics meant church-controlled education and that calling schools "public" did not make them less Protestant. Superintendent S. A. Ellis of Rochester tried to respond to McQuaid's attacks on his system, but he only agreed with McQuaid that "moral training" and "true character building" were central to "correct living and good citizenship." Like so many Victorian educators, Ellis was unwilling to seriously entertain the notion that public schools taught selected moral values that some citizens could legitimately oppose. And in the anti-Catholic atmosphere that infused American culture, the schools became an extension of free-market, Protestant values.[30]

With the continuing availability of some private schooling and the rise of competing parochial education systems in each of these four cities, school leaders searched for additional ways to gather more support for public education. They feared that too many parents might be attracted to parochial schools and other institutions if the public sector failed to respond to some of the criticisms leveled against it. Local boosters and school leaders made unexpected concessions in some areas of educational policy. One especially crucial reform was the addition of foreign-language instruction, particularly German. With a large number of German immigrants inhabiting Rochester, Toledo, and Milwaukee, German instruction was a politically contentious issue, one final example of the various kinds of conflicts central to nineteenth-century school innovation.

German parents who were proud of their culture and language pressured school boards for the adoption of German in dozens of American cities. Parents often triumphed in direct proportion to their numbers and political power. In Kansas City, where German foreign-born residents were only 6 percent of the total population in 1870, their petitions were rejected. In Rochester, where they accounted for 12 percent of the population, German was adopted as an elective in the 1870s, but this was overturned shortly thereafter. In Toledo and Milwaukee, where German immigrants constituted 17 percent and 32 percent of the total population respectively, German instruction fared much better.[31]

The adoption of German was a politically astute decision by school boards in Milwaukee and Toledo. School leaders in the 1850s in both cities realized that Germans were an important voting bloc and that German academies undermined the popularity of the fledgling public system. A knowledgeable Milwaukeean pointed to the political importance of adopting German when he noted in 1899 that it had been championed by "shrewd politicians who cared neither for the educational value of German nor for the beauty of its literature, but who recognized the . . . strength of the so-called German vote." In Toledo, a local German teacher recalled in the 1870s that foreign-language instruction helped to sweep many private schools and German academies "out of existence," and the school superintendent bluntly wrote that the teaching of German helped enlist the support of "a large body of citizens . . . who, while supporting private schools, could feel little interest in the Public Schools."[32]

Once again, school leaders undermined outside criticism and strengthened the state system. As in every area of educational policy, German instruction emerged in an atmosphere of conflict and debate. Contradictory pressures—parental desires for foreign-language training, and school promoter designs to undermine the private sector—forced the adoption of a new program in the public schools. At the dawn of the Progressive era in the early 1890s, public schools had done an impressive job of consolidating their power and emerged as virtual state-financed monopolies in the world of education. Elite reformers had not shaped schools just as they pleased, but in a few decades they had nevertheless constructed a single system of publicly financed schools in cities across America. Whigs and elite educators had withstood challenges and insults from vicious homes, contrary parents, tardy children, angry Germans, and even Bishop McQuaid. In the 1890s, when a severe depression led a new generation of critics to question the policies of local schools, conflicts would intensify in public education. Reformers who ranged from class-conscious workers to middle-class clubwomen ensured that conflict remained central to social change and educational innovation. The conditions of economic life, rife with contradictions in the early 1890s, produced a new age of reform.

IV

By the early 1890s, most children and their parents in urban America lived in the shadow of state-sponsored public school systems. Private schools on the primary and secondary level continued to serve the needs of diverse citizens who dissented from the public school monopoly, but a single system of education received the bulk of government favor. Shaped in an atmosphere of economic boosterism and capitalist growth, public schools could not help but reflect the contradictory dimensions of life beyond the classroom door. Conflicts over value systems regarding time discipline and cultural beliefs about religious choice were common in the larger society and in local schools. Throughout the Victorian period, schools also promised to serve equally well the needs of native born and foreign born, rich and poor, capitalist and worker, Protestant and Catholic. But schools were especially responsive to economic elites, the professional classes, and school officials, whose shared values strengthened the public system and whose political power gave their ideas added weight. Even when they responded to outside criticisms, the schools absorbed conflict and solidified their place in social life.

By the dawn of the Progressive era, therefore, schools were multifaceted institutions that reflected the economic, political, and cultural tensions of local communities. By the 1890s, school systems had already existed for many decades, and public schools had become the predominant site for mass education in America. This meant that competing reform groups of the 1890s faced institutions that were firmly linked to the political economy and had already demonstrated their resilience. For many, the central political question was how to capture the control of the state and its supporting institutions. But exactly why did a new era of school reform commence in the early 1890s? Although schools had long been regarded as an agency of reform, what prompted this revived interest in educational innovation? What immediate historical forces gave rise to a new spirit of reform?

Reconstructing the social and industrial characteristics of places such as Rochester, Toledo, Milwaukee, and Kansas City in the late nineteenth century enables the historian to situate schools and educational innovation in their immediate historical context. The emergence of a more intensively urban, industrial capitalist society, which composed the backdrop for the origins of Progressive era school reform, occurred so rapidly by the late nineteenth century that even local boosters viewed it with a mixture of awe and delight. A German businessman in Milwaukee in 1886 sounded the common refrain that in a few short years his own town "had become a genuinely important industrial city." Gross statistics on manufacturing highlight these tremendous social transformations, the onset of a new way of life across urban America. With a larger industrial base than Rochester, Toledo, and Kansas City, Milwaukee experienced a spectacular growth in the number of manufacturing establishments by the turn of the century.[33]

Milwaukee already had eight hundred manufacturing facilities of varying sizes by 1880. Within two decades the number had quadrupled. Besides its famous breweries, the city regained its world leadership in leather processing and also became a competitive force in the steel and iron industry. In 1900 almost one out of every five workers in Milwaukee industry was an iron- or steelworker or employed in closely related machine shops. Heavy industry was centered in the city's South Side, where Polish immigrants competed for unskilled jobs in the rolling mills and established ethnic communities in this otherwise heavily German city. In a relatively short period of time, Milwaukee had a sizeable industrial working class, workers who exchanged their labor for a wage and who did not own the means of production. The number of "wage earners" engaged in manufacturing and mechanical jobs increased from twenty thousand to approximately fifty thousand in less than twenty years. More than $110 million was invested in manufacturing in Milwaukee in 1900, well over five times the amount of investment twenty years earlier.[34]

Rochester's growth during this period was also very impressive. Long noted for its beautiful nurseries and horticulture, the Flower City increasingly became the Factory City. It had less than half the capital investment in manufacturing of Milwaukee in 1900 because of its smaller population base, but it had nevertheless tripled the number of manufacturing establishments in two decades. One-half of Rochester's gainfully employed citizens in 1900 worked in manufacturing and mechanical endeavors, a figure that was slightly higher than the percentage in Milwaukee. Unlike Milwaukee or Toledo, however, Rochester was never a major center for heavy industry, a fact that had important effects on the nature of its labor movement. Travelers in this city did not see puffs of smoke from steel mills or blast furnaces, but heard the humming of sewing machines and conversations on the price of shoes.[35]

Like many New England cities, Rochester became a regional center for clothing and shoe production. Census figures reveal that one out of every four men and women with occupations in 1900 worked in the textile industry. With the rise of industrial capitalism, as Socialist Eugene Debs eloquently argued, these men and women were often reduced to "hands" in the productive process, part of the larger degradation of modern work:

> In the capitalist system the soul has no business. It cannot produce profit by any process of capitalist calculation.
> The working hand is what is needed for the capitalist's tool and so the human must be reduced to a hand. . . .
> A thousand hands to one brain—the hands of workingman, the brain of a capitalist.
> A thousand dumb animals, in human form—a thousand slaves in fetters of ignorance, their heads having to run to hands—all these owned and worked and fleeced by one stock-dealing, profit-mongering capitalist.
> This is capitalism![36]

Debs's insights accurately captured the perspectives of Rochester's business leaders, heirs of the booster tradition. Business elites embellished local publications with their own names, pictures, and biographies, saving a line or two for their "hands," while remaining silent on their own anti-union sentiments. The changing character of the local economy, however, decidedly shaped Rochester's labor movement. While Socialists had infiltrated Milwaukee's strong trade union movement by the turn of the century, Eastman Kodak and related industries diversified Rochester's economy in the same period, and it became increasingly known as a white-collar, nonunion city.[37]

Sparked by the natural-gas boom in Northwestern Ohio in the late nineteenth century, Toledo also engaged in an aggressive drive for industrial supremacy. Its 440 manufacturing establishments in 1880 mushroomed to more than 1,000 in 1900 as Toledo's business community made an important bid for regional economic dominance. With less than half of the population of Milwaukee in 1900 (and smaller than Rochester), Toledo had only one-third of the manufacturing establishments of Wisconsin's largest city. Like Milwaukee, however, it developed considerable heavy industry; it had almost the same percentage of workers engaged in the steel and iron industry (16 percent).[38]

Just as heavy industry was concentrated in Milwaukee's immigrant South Side, Toledo built its steel and iron plants in one corner of town on the East Side. This area was separated from the rest of the city geographically by the Maumee River and culturally by its unskilled Hungarian residents. Part of the East Side was called Birmingham, since its drab skies and working-class appearance resembled England's famous industrial center. The Hungarians largely operated the steel plants and made Birmingham their home. Toledo also became widely known for its glass production, particularly through the work of Edward D. Libbey, and its proximity to Detroit furthered its economic expansion. The city annually supplied millions of dollars worth of parts and accessories to the auto industry after the turn of the century. Less white collar than Rochester, its labor unions were certainly more aggressive than those of Rochester, but timid compared with their Socialist counterparts in Milwaukee.[39]

Robert T. Van Horn's boasts during the Civil War that Kansas City would soon become the crossroads for western trade and manufacturing have been publicized by many historians as archetypal elements of frontier journalism and nineteenth-century boosterism. A tiny trading post in 1850, Kansas City witnessed dizzying rates of economic and social expansion in less than forty years. Commerce and trade rather than manufacturing per se remained the key prop of Kansas City's economy. The percentage of workers engaged in manufacturing and mechanical pursuits in 1900 provides a rough though useful index to Kansas City's economic development. Approximately 25 percent of its total male and female laborers worked in industries, compared with 35 percent in Toledo, 45 percent in Milwaukee, and 50 percent in Rochester. That does not mean that Kansas City's industrial growth was insignificant. The rate of increase of capital investment in the city's manufacturing development between 1880 and 1900 was higher than in the other three cities: an amazing 1,260 percent. Such notable efforts at industrialization should not disguise the fact that

Kansas City was still primarily a center of commerce, rather than a manufacturing town. For example, in 1900 Kansas City and Rochester both had slightly more than 160,000 people. Rochester nevertheless had several hundred more factories with double the capital investment; it also had twice as many wage earners in manufacturing jobs. Kansas City was simply less industrial.[40]

While Rochester was famous for its textiles, Toledo for its glass and mills, and Milwaukee for its beer, tanning, and heavy industry, Kansas City was a vital entrepot for western trade. It was a gateway to the West and its many alluring markets. For this reason, by 1900 the largest group of city workers (38 percent) was employed in occupations related to trade and transportation, much higher than either Toledo (32 percent), Milwaukee (27 percent), or Rochester (26 percent.) In addition, Kansas City's extensive stockyards by the 1870s reflected its importance in the meatpacking industry. Railroads transported thousands of cattle to the city annually, and hog slaughtering and meat processing assumed considerable prominence. By the early 1890s, roughly half of the factory workers were associated in some way with industries owned by Armour, Swift, and their competitors. The flavor of the Wild West, with tales of cattle drives and roundups, remained vital to local folklore and civic identity well into the new century.[41]

Population grew at a frenzied pace in these cities in the late nineteenth century. With a population of more than 115,000 in 1880, Milwaukee was the largest of the four cities, followed by Rochester (nearly 90,000), Kansas City (more than 55,000), and Toledo (more than 50,000). This ranked order remained essentially stable in 1900, except that Kansas City narrowly surpassed Rochester to earn second place. The percentage increase in population between 1880 and 1900 for Rochester (182 percent), Toledo (263 percent), Milwaukee (247 percent), and Kansas City (294 percent) typified the movement to the cities that contemporaries witnessed as immigration from Europe intensified and millions of rural citizens sought new homes and opportunities. These cities grew in size, in industrial complexity, and in the kinds of residents who brought life and profits to local communities.[42]

There were notable differences in the varieties of people who inhabited these four cities just as there were variations in the kinds of industries and commercial developments that sustained their economies. A closer look at the character of these people in 1890, just prior to the onset of various reform movements ushering in the Progressive era, reveals some of the human flavor and social dynamics of these communities. Cities were made of more than iron and steel, or machine shops, foundries, and garment factories. There was more to life than the driving rhythms of the machinery and the ubiquitous morning and evening whistle. Clashing against the sights and sounds of the factories were older cultural practices of the thousands of foreign-born residents and displaced rural folk who now called these cities home.

By 1890, Milwaukee's ethnic heritage was quite distinctive. Fully 39 percent of the total population of 204,000 was foreign born. Known as the Deutsch-Athens in the midnineteenth century, Milwaukee retained a strong Teutonic cast; nearly one-third of the total population was born in Germany. A distinct ethnic culture flourished in the northwestern and western parts of town, though Germans lived throughout the city. One historian has appreciatively written that "there were public buildings that might have stood in Strassburg or Nuremburg, ornate residences that were influenced by the German Renaissance, and German faces, German signs, Teutonic speech." German foods, music, shooting clubs, and singing societies as well as the ever-present beer gardens provided camaraderie and recreation. Astonishing as it may seem, Milwaukee's beer gardens in 1890 had a seating capacity exceeding 105,000, room enough for more than half the entire city! In the world of business and politics, in the schools and the press, Germans had made an unmistakable mark on city life.[43]

Dozens of different immigrant groups inhabited Milwaukee, but it was still primarily a German city. The "new" immigration of southern and central Europeans had not yet altered the character of the population, though their visibility would increase dramatically in the next decade. Once politically influential and a challenge to German hegemony, the Irish became a small part of the total population, and they generally resided in the poorest, least desirable section of town: the Bloody Third. By the end of the 1890s, the Italians, who accounted for less than 1 percent of the population in all these cities in 1890, would move into the Bloody Third and make it their new home. Visitors to the industrial South Side encountered additional signs of the growing importance of the new immigration. Over the years the South Side became a haven for the Poles. They were already 5 percent of the population, but few realized that they would surpass the Germans as the leading ethnic group within three decades. Intensely Roman Catholic, these largely unskilled newcomers quickly established segments of their own culture and built a large parochial school system as a bulwark of their faith. There were fraternal orders, singing groups, and athletic clubs for the men and rosary societies for the women. Travelers to the South Side could find only names "that end with a sneeze," as Ignatz rivaled Fritz as a leading name in Milwaukee.[44]

After Milwaukee, Rochester was the next city with a significant percentage of foreign-born residents, totaling 30 percent of the 113,000 inhabitants in 1890. Here, too, the Germans represented the largest foreign-born group in the total population (13 percent). As in Milwaukee, the Irish began to lose their once visible role in municipal politics, and the Poles and Italians still accounted for less than 1 percent of the people. Second-generation Germans continued to exhibit considerable influence in Rochester after the 1890s, as old and new immigrant groups struggled for cultural dominance. Walter Rauschenbusch, whose father had been a prominent German newcomer, became internationally known for his writings on the Social Gospel. And men such as Isaac Adler, also a second-generation German, were leading lights in Good Government and education reforms at the turn of the century.[45]

As in Rochester and Milwaukee, Germans constituted the largest foreign-born group in Toledo in 1890, constituting 15 percent of the total population. The Poles, however, later surpassed the Germans as the major ethnic group in the Progressive era, just as they did in Milwaukee. While the Germans scattered across much of Toledo, the Poles primarily settled in two separate communities in the northern and southwestern parts of town. Polish foods, dialects, and traditions added variety to civic life. The Hungarians, another important new group, worked in the grueling heat of the steel mills on the East Side, where they lived in an enclave separated from the rest of Toledo by the Maumee River and by their own indigenous culture. The new immigration increasingly altered the composition and flavor of urban life, as Italians, Hungarians, Poles, Czechs, and other groups arrived by the thousands in these cities.[46]

Whereas many first- and second-generation immigrants inhabited Milwaukee, Rochester, and Toledo in the 1890s, Kansas City was a bastion of the native born. In 1890, only 16 percent of its population of 132,000 was foreign born, compared with the higher rates in Toledo (27 percent), Rochester (30 percent), and Milwaukee (39 percent). Kansas City was less industrial and less foreign than these cities. Its demographic structure was very distinctive, since it had a higher percentage of African Americans than the other cities and only a small percentage of Germans (5 percent) and Irish (4 percent) residents. The great majority of its population was native born; southerners in particular swelled its population after the Civil War. And only after the turn of the century did a new immigrant group, the Italians, finally surpass the Germans as Kansas City's largest ethnic population.[47]

Even though the Poles and the Italians constituted only a small portion of the residents of these cities in the early 1890s, their increased visibility brought them scorn and ridicule in the native press. Called the "dusky sons of the Orient" by those who slept through geography class, the Italians and other new residents were stereotyped as murderers, thieves, and drunkards. Rochester's *Democrat and Chronicle* and Kansas City's *Star* endorsed immigrant restriction as early as 1894, especially for the newcomers. Illiterate, poor, and ignorant of American ways, these new arrivals reportedly formed the pool of recruits for "labor riots" and were an "embarrassment" to the entire country. "The Russians, Poles, Portuguese, Hungarians, and Italians who come to America . . . as a class are not desirable citizens," wrote an editor in Rochester. "They do not easily assimilate with the American people, but form classes and communities among themselves, greatly increasing the difficulty of administering law and order."[48]

Growth in commerce, industry, and population was, therefore, everywhere evident in these cities in the late nineteenth century, and these industrial and human characteristics set the main background for the rise of Progressive reform movements in education. "The age is going ahead at a two-forty pace," wrote one Kansas City resident in 1875, and town boosters gloated over urban growth and industrial expansion. But by the early 1890s, the contradictions within an evolving industrial capitalist economy again grew apparent. Once again, as in previous decades, the schools found themselves gripped by competing forces for improvement and change.[49]

"This age is peculiarly prolific of the 'genus, crank,'" wrote a Kansas City newspaper in 1893. "Wild-eyed, howling, vicious, and preposterous cranks abound. You see them every day. They pop up on our rostrums, in our pulpits, and as frequently as our legislative halls." Cranks exist in the eyes of the beholder, but the depression certainly nurtured many competing visions of economic, social, and educational reconstruction. Critics exposed the contradictions of poverty and progress. Against the bravado of the Van Horns and the city boosters, a wide variety of men and women—Socialists, Populists, workers, and assorted parents—organized into reform groups that challenged the views of those on the top of the social system. Reformers asked why poverty haunted a land of plenty, why corruption festered on school boards, why some children went to school with tattered clothes and empty bellies. At a time of economic despair, various reformers dreamed about a new social and educational order.[50]

When the first national business failures occurred in the spring of 1893, newspaper editors in Rochester, Toledo, Milwaukee, and Kansas City either ignored them or dismissed them as aberrations. Throughout the early summer of 1893, for example, the *Kansas City Star* warned against pessimism and predicted glorious economic revivals. The reality was very different. After seeing numerous articles portraying growth in local trade and industry, Kansas City readers were informed of the obvious: the onset of depression. The influential National Bank of Kansas City collapsed in early July; several smaller banks soon followed its fate. By the end of the month layoffs in local industries were expected and public confidence in the economy declined. Even the *Star* now recognized that it was "a time of financial disturbance and popular apprehension."[51]

The depression affected other local economies by September. Noting reports of hunger among workers in Cincinnati, the *Toledo Evening Bee* feared that millions of hardworking producers were becoming "an army of tramps and paupers." "With such scenes in a land where crops have been abundant, where nature has passed forth her richest treasures, where there is every indication of outward prosperity, there is evidently something deplorably wrong." In city after city, the prevailing hard times forced many urban citizens to account for the widespread poverty that coexisted with obvious national wealth. Too many people were unemployed and actively searching for work to blame the situation on intemperance, laziness, or sinfulness, the traditional explanations for personal failure. There were claims and counterclaims on the extensiveness of the depression, but most social observers agreed that suffering was widespread and too great to be explained by personal deficiencies. The economic system seemed on the verge of total collapse, as conditions reached a crisis stage.[52]

By the autumn of 1893 half of Rochester's tailors and shoemakers were unemployed. Equally gloomy figures characterized the building trades. Since clothing production was central to Rochester's economy, the decline in sales caused by tight money and unemployment elsewhere greatly affected the shape of the local labor market. "The poor we have always with us," wrote the Reverend William C. Gannett, a liberal Unitarian minister, "but this winter we have with us more poor than usual." When a handful of jobs on municipal public works projects opened in early 1894, an "army of unemployed" stood in line hoping for the chance to earn their daily bread. Within a few months an estimated ten thousand workers were unemployed—one-third of the entire labor market. Charity groups such as the Rochester Humane Society, which cared for abused animals and people, early reported that "we find ourselves overwhelmed with work without the machinery, or the funds to successfully carry on."[53]

Conditions in Toledo, Milwaukee, and Kansas City were very similar. In 1894, approximately one-third of Toledo's workers were unemployed, an unprecedented percentage in the city's history. The *Toledo Blade* would have preferred hiding the darker side of progress but finally ran front page stories on poverty by November 1893. Already nearly 2,500 people received charitable relief; and 360 individuals on the average applied daily for food and medical assistance at the city infirmary, ten times the number of requests for the preceding year. Milwaukee suffered the same forms of economic dislocation as many workers faced layoffs, pay cuts, and overall despair. An estimated 35 to 40 percent of the local working population was unemployed during the depths of the depression. The Milwaukee County Poor List had varied from year to year but had never exceeded several hundred families before the depression; it reached an unprecedented 3,420 families in the winter of 1894. As late as the 1930s, Emil Seidel, a wood-carver who was Milwaukee's first Socialist mayor in 1910 and a product of his times, recalled the untold suffering of the period, even though he was lucky enough to hold his job. It was a familiar tale, for numerous radicals and moderate reformers alike acknowledged the effects of hard times on their social conscience.[54]

"Hard times is the cry of everyone nowadays," wrote the *Kansas City Mail* in the summer of 1893. The *Star* agreed, saying that there was already "a tendency to speak of 'the unemployed' as of a permanent, recognized, and even organized class." "The air is vocal with the dismal voices of demagogues who talk as if this were Poland or Siberia." While failing to identify these "demagogues," the editor accurately noted the rise of various forms of social discontent as the depression worsened. The visible gap between rich and poor and the specter of class conflict and mob violence remained constant subjects of public discussion in American cities. Thoughtful men and women reconsidered their opinions on who benefited from existing arrangements in school and society.[55]

In Kansas City, people without visible means of support slept every evening on the floor in the basement of the police station; as one group left another took its place. A job notice for fifty laborers attracted almost four thousand applicants. "Idle men, willing to work, stood in a long line for three blocks, waiting for a chance to secure employment." The foreman in charge of the hiring claimed it was "the biggest demonstration I ever saw." In this context, the local Socialist Labor Party announced in 1895 that "never before in the history of mankind has there been so much suffering from hunger and privations of all kinds alongside of luxury and abundance of nature's gifts and the products of labor." Poverty and progress marched arm in arm, though much of the suffering and pain were hidden in so many obscure news reports and in the proceedings of different civic meetings. Not all workers or citizens were miserable, impoverished, or converted to radicalism by these events, but for many the realities of urban existence were grim and uncertain.[56]

The depression finally ended in 1897. Local newspapers such as Rochester's *Democrat and Chronicle* hoped that the "calamity howlers" who had stirred up discontent would be silenced. They were not. Many men and women who had never actively participated in social and educational reforms made their initial commitments to activism during these difficult years, and the local cities were never quite the same. Women's clubs and suffrage leaders were especially potent sources of innovation in every city. A Socialist trade union movement emerged in Milwaukee that gave it a radical heritage surpassing those of most municipalities. Kansas City's parents' and mothers' organizations tried to take power away from Superintendent Greenwood and an entrenched elite on the school board. Samuel M. Jones, a Toledo businessman and teetotaler turned Social Gospeler, hoped to reshape social and industrial relations along the lines of the Golden Rule. Little wonder, then, that some frustrated citizens threw up their arms in disgust and proclaimed: "This is the age of cranks."[57]

Chapter 2

Municipal Housekeepers

I

"Once upon a time, in a beautiful city situated on Lake Michigan, there lived a little girl who was a perfect nuisance," recalled Lizzie Black Kander in a paper before the Wednesday Afternoon Club in Milwaukee in 1902:

> Time rolled on and on, this little girl grew and grew
> And then she married and still she grew—
> And the selfsame "spirits" that did simmer and brew
> And caused her teachers to fret and to stew
> Now bubbled and boiled and then overflew!!
> She crocheted wonderful tidies for sofa and chairs
> She made paper flowers for birthdays and fairs.
> She made noodles and strudel and knit sox by the pair
> And e'en sewed rag carpet for bedroom and stair.
> But, alas, things have changed, she sews carpets no more
> For her "spirits" have taken an upward soar.
> She's a *Joiner of Clubs*, Women's clubs by the score
> Oh, husband, fond husband, your fate we deplore!
> She settles grave matters—she tried to save souls
> And would you believe, she now votes at the polls![1]

Thus, in characteristic form, Lizzie Kander chronicled her emergence as a "new" woman in the late nineteenth century. She personified the activism of many women who helped usher in an age of Progressive reform during the depression of the 1890s. Like so many of her generation, she found herself in a whirligig of municipal politics and social welfare reform, as Milwaukee's leading settlement house worker, a school board member for two decades, and an outspoken pacifist and champion of reform during the difficult days of World War I.

Living in a troubled but rapidly expanding urban and industrial society, activists such as Kander occupied a crucial position in the evolution and implementation of early Progressive school reforms. Unquestionably, women's organizations in the late nineteenth and early twentieth century gave urban reform in general much of its strength, stamina, and moral fervor. Separate female organizations had been central to the women's movement in the early 1800s, and various women's clubs and associations at the turn of the twentieth century continued this tradition. Separatism enabled activist women to extend their rights beyond the private home to the public, largely male-dominated world. And as female-dominated voluntary organizations expanded in size and power after the 1890s, these groups "turned more frequently to the state" as a key element in social policy.[2]

While foreign commentators, including Alexis de Tocqueville, had long recognized that Americans were joiners, something new was clearly under way in the Progressive era. The consolidation of capitalist enterprise in the form of pools, trusts, and monopolies protected by the state meant that reformers of all varieties functioned in a new political economy. Like other social institutions, schools were caught in the tensions between older traditions of political democracy and individual rights and modern forms of economic concentration and social inequality. Disenfranchised in the political arena, many women at the grassroots fought for the right to vote, but they did not limit their goals to securing suffrage. Progressive women wanted to shape public policy and expand women's opportunities more broadly, and they demonstrated this most forcefully in multifaceted campaigns to improve neighborhood schools.

Even though women were influential sponsors of child welfare reforms, they faced numerous competing groups that also sought increased state intervention in the lives of youth. How did women's conception of the role of the state compare with that of labor unions, Socialist leaders, or businessmen or professionals on local school boards? What types of consensus and conflict existed between dominant women's organizations and other elements of the grassroots? Why did these disparate groups find themselves traveling on various roads to reform, all of which led to the expansion of the social functions of the modern school?

II

During the Progressive era, women played a more pronounced role in school reform than ever before. Samuel T. Dutton and David Snedden, two nationally respected educators, noted in 1908 that "perhaps no one factor has done more to give popular education a place in the thought of the community than the activity of women's clubs. These organizations, so numerous and so earnest, have both in their meetings at home and in their great federated gatherings always made education in its various forms their chiefest topic." Women helped initiate many of the social welfare reforms that became commonplace in urban education; various women's club members were the central figures in early discussions of the "new" education popularized nationally by John Dewey, Francis Parker, and Joseph Mayer Rice; and they were continually forces to reckon with in local communities.[3]

Between 1890 and 1920, as Lizzie Kander had indicated in rhyme, women's role in society changed dramatically, and the appearance of the "new" woman was a crucial element in the origins of municipal reform. Along with the numerous reform organizations they often cooperated with, women's organizations championed a wide range of innovations then considered advanced and "Progressive": vacation schools, playgrounds, social centers, school breakfasts and lunches, manual training and domestic science programs, parent-teacher associations, and other new programs. With the passage of school suffrage laws that affected cities such as Rochester, Toledo, and Milwaukee (but not Kansas City), women served on school boards in these cities for the first time and finally shared power with men who had customarily viewed school governance as their exclusive domain. Women taught in the schools in overwhelming numbers, particularly in the lower grades, but male ward leaders mostly controlled the schools of the nineteenth century. By the 1890s, however, organized women emerged as ever present factors in the shaping of certain aspects of educational policy.[4]

Historians of Progressive educational reform often emphasize the importance of the "new middle class" school superintendents who augmented their power in educational policy through school board centralization reforms in the 1890s. Considerably less has been written about the centrality of women and voluntary organizations in administrative and curricular reform. This is partially explained by the wide use of school reports and mainstream educational journals that often emphasized the importance of male administrators in initiating innovations. These materials served as the official record of the process of innovation; they often slighted the role of the private sector in educational experimentation and ignored much of the local context for reform. The history of school innovation during these years is integrally bound with the history of activist women, whose hopes and dreams, successes and failures, are hidden in diverse kinds of local materials on school and society.[5]

The ascent of the "new" woman to an influential though not dominant position in educational change was totally unexpected in places such as Rochester, Toledo, Milwaukee, and Kansas City. It was as unpredictable as the depression that accelerated the formation of competing voluntary associations and hence competing views on educational policy and the state. As a result of the depression, as well as the changing character of the middle- and upper-class household, new organizations developed that soon overshadowed the smaller and older literary women's clubs that already existed in these cities. The "society" women who dominated in these earlier groups promoted general intellectual improvement by studying poetry, history, philosophy, music, and art. They showed little interest in the larger concerns of the working world, favoring personal development over social reform. Their behavior mirrored perfectly the prevalent notion that politics—the rough and tumble by which public policy evolves—was exclusively for men, for one looks in vain in school proceedings before the 1870s for petitions by them or other indications of their interest in urban education. Milwaukee's superintendent reported in the 1870s that some women planned to investigate their schools, but then they were never heard from again.[6]

The *Toledo Blade* wrote in 1890 that the existing literary clubs were snobbish little affairs wholly divorced from the active life of the city. Even the many church-related women's organizations, tied as they were to local neighborhoods, displayed more interest in social issues. The *Milwaukee Sentinel* likewise claimed in 1891 that locally "there are several 'sets' which carry on separate lines of social activity, and the members of each are quite satisfied with their own position and associates, and make no effort to get out of their own 'set' and into any other." Society women on the East Side, like competing church groups, remained apart. The *Kansas City Star* likewise contended that women seemed unsuited for the strenuous life of politics. "Women, as a rule, have little taste for politics," claimed one of its editors. "The peace and quietude of the home present to them much stronger attractions than the excitement and turmoil of the public arena. They are not fitted by nature for contact with the world and participation in its strife and rivalry."[7]

During the hard times emanating from the panic of 1893, women emerged as potent sources of social change and reform. Three years after the *Blade* attacked clubs for their elitism and pretentiousness, it asserted that "Toledo is becoming noted for the number and variety of its club organizations. Everyone must have observed the rapid growth of the 'club spirit' within the past few years," which happily denoted the rise of "a broad, liberal metropolitan spirit." In Rochester, more than forty clubs, most of them formed during the depression, organized into a Local Council of Women, causing one citizen to boast without evidence that "there is probably no other city of its size which supports more women's clubs."[8]

Like thriving newspapers in many cities, the *Milwaukee Sentinel* and its rival *Daily News* welcomed the arrival of the new women. Regular women's columns soon appeared in local papers, providing news for the curious and footnotes for future historians on the social and educational ideas of organized women. Women editors, who themselves often belonged to activist clubs, frequently reprinted speeches and addresses, information on membership dues, and the date, time, and location of the next meeting. Starting in October and running through June, the club season was the source of considerable controversy and news coverage throughout the Progressive era. Kansas City's newspapers, which previously dismissed the organizations and women's activism as whimsical, now warned the school board to beware of women with fire in their eyes. "The school board need not invest in chest protectors or lay in a stock of revolvers," asserted the working-class *Mail*, "but it may live in hourly expectation of a visitation nevertheless."[9]

The most important women's association that agitated for school reform in the Progressive years assembled in the early 1890s. The Women's Educational and Industrial Union of Rochester, modeled directly after organizations in Buffalo and other cities, early revolved around the dynamism of Susan B. Anthony, the national matriarch of the suffrage movement and one of the city's senior citizens. Formed in 1893, the Union was a direct descendant of the Ignorance Club, a self-effacing though elite literary group that had become Rochester's first modern woman's organization in 1880. The Union was to Rochester what the Woman's Educational Club was to Toledo: the leading feminine organization for school reform. This Ohio club formed near the end of the depression, when local women tried to elect a woman to the school board. Unity meant strength, wrote the Toledoan who defined the club as "the first weapon of primitive man" but "the last of the Twentieth Century Woman."[10]

Milwaukee and Kansas City also had notable female organizations. The Woman's School Alliance was especially distinctive, since it was the only club in all of Wisconsin that was exclusively interested in school affairs. First organized in 1891, the Alliance reassembled two years later, when the depression impoverished thousands of Milwaukeeans; from an uncertain existence the group evolved into the most powerful woman's organization in the local schools. At the same time there emerged the Social Economics Club and numerous social reform groups that were active throughout the next three decades in this growing metropolis. Similarly, Kansas City witnessed in 1894 the birth of the Athenaeum, whose name belied the nonliterary interests that guided the group over the years. Moreover, every one of these cities had their first organized and permanent parent-teacher organizations in the 1890s; they were heavily dominated by women. By 1920 Kansas City was the world leader in parent-teacher organizations, with more than ten thousand members.[11]

Except for the Woman's School Alliance of Milwaukee and neighbor-hood parent groups, women's organizations were never exclusively con-cerned with school reform, though most of them made education their dominant interest. Like all organizations, clubs had their own division of labor. Most of them had departments on education, literature, industrial change, domestic science, city beautification, and legislation. Many of the prominent activists in these cities aggressively sought women's suffrage. Susan B. Anthony, for example, formed early suffrage organizations in Rochester as well as in Toledo, Milwaukee, and Kansas City. Anthony was an exceptional figure but typified the zeal of lesser-known individuals such as Mary E. Law and Emily Bouton of Toledo.[12]

Many club activists found suffrage less attractive, yet these organiza-tions provided every member with useful outlets from the restraints of the home. The club was a place of refuge from children and husbands and a means to discover one's hidden talents. The women's clubs and mothers' organizations became female community meeting places: friend-ships were strengthened, solitary individuals found fellowship, and every-one escaped from the narrowness of domestic life for a few hours. There were social teas and lectures, papers and informal discussions. Here one could gossip about trivial matters as well as unite for a new school activity. Here women who were unaccustomed to public speaking overcame some of their shyness. And here, too, many first confronted the contradiction of progress and poverty, an experience that often proved exhilarating. For these reasons a club such as the Kansas City Athenaeum quickly mush-roomed from a few dozen members in 1894 to several hundred women and was called the local "women's university."[13]

The personal motivations behind these joiners of clubs were im-mensely complex and varied, though not inscrutable. For example, Lizzie Black Kander was a member of the Woman's School Alliance and Milwau-kee's leading settlement worker. She was driven by a mixture of intense idealism, love for the poor, and fear for her middle-class standing. The child of Jewish immigrants who secured a comfortable livelihood in Mil-waukee, Kander was moved by the spectacle of immense human suffering and the gap between rich and poor that accompanied nineteenth-century progress. Speaking to her classmates at her high school graduation exer-cises in 1878, she called for public control over the industrial giants to secure social welfare. "The wealth of the nation is in the hands of a few individuals who are accumulating more every day, while the poor are becoming more and more miserable," she bluntly argued. "Our men are forgetting that truth, honesty, virtue, and love are far more valuable to the happiness of mankind than extravagant modes of living."[14]

With such a strong conviction in support of social justice evident so early in her life, it is not surprising that Kander's speeches, correspondence, and settlement house reports over the following several decades revealed an intense concern with the victims of industrial progress. At the same time she acknowledged that helping others was simultaneously a form of self-advancement. She feared that the many poor Russian Jews who inhabited late-nineteenth-century Milwaukee would hurt the reputations of assimilated Jews like herself; she was also frightened by the prospects of new outbreaks of anti-Semitism of the sort her parents had once faced. In the 1880s she thereupon joined a Jewish Ladies' Sewing Society to mend tattered clothes for recent immigrants. Together with the School Alliance in the 1890s, she gathered shoes and clothes for underprivileged schoolchildren and also began a "Keep Clean Mission" in the densest Jewish immigrant neighborhood to teach cleanliness and morality. This mission soon evolved into her locally renowned Settlement House.[15]

Kander was popularly known as the "Jane Addams of Milwaukee." Even critics who thought her liberalism and pacifism were tainted by some of her Socialist friends said she had "a heart big enough to mother every child in town." It was a compliment she could appreciate. She spent decades as a school board member agitating for new social service programs in the public schools such as penny lunches and supervised playgrounds. She demonstrated the efficacy of these programs for children of the poor at the settlement and increasingly viewed them as desirable objects of public policy for all children. Remarkably honest about her own fears of a threatened loss of social status, she tried to reeducate others about the social rather than the personal origins of immigrant poverty. "The people are really not to blame, they are the result of tyranny and oppression, of the persecutions that have been heaped upon them from generation to generation," Kander always noted.[16]

A confirmed teetotaler, Kander respected the social role of the saloon in working-class life and attacked prohibitionists and advocates of immigrant restriction. In defending immigrant lifestyles from bigots and extreme Americanizers, she partially transcended some of her own middle-class prejudices. Her preoccupation with the immigrant poor also made her marriage, to a realtor, a very difficult one, especially in the early years of the 1890s, since her husband wanted his wife at home. Lacking any moral support, Kander confided in her diary in 1895 that "my husband hates to have me speak or think much about . . . the poor little children and their mothers at the mission."[17]

Personal information on the lives of other women similarly reveals why they participated in service groups. While younger women such as Kander represented the newer generation of female activists, Progressive women's organizations also contained many older suffrage leaders who used the clubs in part as possible vehicles for full citizenship. Susan B. Anthony was already in her seventies when she helped form Rochester's Women's Educational and Industrial Union. She agitated for the group along with younger suffrage leaders such as Helen B. Montgomery, an irrepressible reformer who became the first woman school board member in Rochester in 1900.[18]

Anthony had joined temperance groups, lobbied with labor organizations, and even gone on trial in the 1870s when she cast her ballot in a local election. When found guilty of voting, this highly principled woman refused to pay the fine; she was given a suspended sentence. For Anthony as well as for thousands of less famous women, suffrage and broadened roles for women in higher education and society generally were, in their words, matters of "simple justice." Service clubs were a means to that end. Rosa Segur, a pioneer suffrage worker, German immigrant, and prominent clubwoman in Toledo in the 1890s, typically interpreted school suffrage as a "crumb" but agreed with many that such legislation and club work generally aided in the struggle for full citizenship.[19]

Whatever their diverse motivations, women for the first time were able to escape from the restrictiveness of the home, particularly the middle- and upper-class homes from which many club members came. The availability of labor-saving devices that they could afford and the declining birth rate over the nineteenth century freed many comfortable women from the fireside, physically if not emotionally. Middle- and upper-middle-class women benefited enormously from the release from mundane domestic responsibilities, especially if they had servants or other domestic help. The availability of prepackaged and prepared foods, improved water supplies, electric lighting, and rudimentary washing machines revolutionized their homes, as a consumer phase of capitalism emerged in the late nineteenth century. Housework remained largely women's work, but the clubs they formed became bridges to the larger society, and it often took an act of bravery to cross them.[20]

Helen B. Montgomery of Rochester epitomized the outspoken nature of the new woman. The perennial president of the Women's Educational and Industrial Union, she was a social gadfly by the 1890s. A popular public speaker, she spoke to labor organizations, Socialist groups, and other voluntary associations on an assortment of topics. On more than one occasion, Montgomery was attacked as a Socialist, since she endorsed the national ownership of utilities and condemned the conspicuous consumption and antisocial behavior of the Vanderbilts. "Real" Socialists, of course, quickly pointed out that she was not a member of their party. Yet one of Rochester's leading Socialist radicals in 1897 attacked her critics and praised her for her spunk and "keen insight into economic injustice."[21]

Montgomery boldly attacked the local curmudgeons who commonly complained that club work ruined the value of many housewives. "We are tired of the flabby philosophy that there was something unwomanly in any matters outside their own doorsteps," she retorted. "The time is past when women are content to play with dolls, or devote themselves to their little calling list, and the association of a few social friends." Montgomery's allies in the Women's Educational and Industrial Union, like women across the country, similarly defended the existence of the clubs and their role in educating their minds and broadening their social views. Mrs. William C. Gannett, who was the wife of a liberal Protestant minister, typically asserted that "the club not only widens the horizon, but tends to open-minded and good-tempered discussion of widely divergent opinions."[22]

Women in various cities emphasized the value of the clubs in furthering self-awareness and understanding a changing social life. One of Toledo's prominent clubwomen, Mary E. Law, ran a local kindergarten training school and narrowly lost in her bid for election to the school board in the 1890s. For her and many others, the clubs were invaluable, despite recurrent disappointments at the polls. "The club woman," she claimed, "has found that breadth of culture comes from the association of women of different classes and pursuits and that selfishness and exclusiveness tend to narrowness and provincialism."[23]

Everywhere Progressive women agreed. In their clubs women debated the merits of the tariff, free trade, Socialism, child-labor laws, working conditions for their poorer sisters, suffrage, and other timely subjects. Many shy women grew in self-confidence as they engaged in debate and discussion with friends old and new. Invited speakers, both men and women, introduced novel ideas into the lives of the club members, challenging old perspectives and offering fresh perspectives on contemporary problems. Because of the social and personal benefits, millions of housewives ultimately joined turn-of-the-century women's clubs.

It was, of course, an age of organization, from the business monopolies above to the trade unions below that fought for control over the work process and fruits of production. Now women formed an additional force that could possibly shape local politics and the direction of social institutions. In 1890 organized women were an insignificant factor in urban educational policy. For the following three decades, however, they influenced every important administrative change, curricular reform, and social service established in local cities. The history of urban school reform in the Progressive era became inextricably related to the history of this multifarious women's movement.

III

Through various means women were locked out of the political process of school decision making in the early 1890s. In Kansas City they lacked the right of school suffrage. Wisconsin permitted school suffrage for women, but Milwaukee's school board was appointed by male aldermen. In Toledo and Rochester, where the boards of education were elected, the male-dominated Republican and Democratic caucuses controlled ward nominations, thereby weakening school suffrage as an instrument of positive change. Women's clubs, therefore, became the collective arm of thousands of reform-minded citizens whose political dependence on men otherwise sapped their strength. If women could not vote, wrote one Kansas City resident, the mothers "will demand to be heard from in a different way, and the school board may discover to its horror what that way is. Mothers will arrive probably with blood in their eyes."[24]

What remained uncertain in the 1890s was not whether women would organize, for the prominence of their associations was a matter of public record. There was common agreement that "this is an era of organizations—of clubs, societies, and associations, devoted to purposes the number and scope of which are bewildering." To many observers, the main issue was how women—even middle- and upper-class women—could justify greater participation in a male-dominated world, retain what contemporaries called their feminine and domestic traits, and use the powers of the state for public good. This required a convincing and acceptable platform of reform, one that enabled women to venture beyond the seclusion of the home and to question the validity of the existing educational order. By the end of the 1890s the die had finally been cast.[25]

To fully comprehend the zeal with which women promoted social service reforms such as vacation schools, playgrounds, breakfasts and lunches, social centers, medical inspection, and other forms of state intervention in the Progressive era requires an understanding of the ideology of this women's movement. Clubwomen were not disinterested reformers but espoused a coherent body of ideas that varied greatly from the beliefs of organized workers, trade union leaders, Socialists, Populists, Social Gospelers, and other Progressive reformers. Nearly all grassroots Progressives found themselves on a road to greater state involvement in schooling and welfare, but different groups traveled alternate routes to their common destination. Most organized women did not share the daily experiences of the skilled workers facing monopoly capitalism, or the vision of a heaven on earth that inspired Social Gospelers, or the Socialist faith in the coming of a fundamentally new social order. Some women would indeed be greatly affected by these considerations as reform movements gathered momentum in local cities, yet they had to reconcile their own contradictions: how to resolve the tensions between domesticity and political activism, how to defend the home while espousing more state intervention in family life, how to cater to the perceived needs of the poor even though they were not poor themselves.

The creation of a new form of domesticity was at the heart of the ideological world constructed and inhabited by Progressive women. Women did not ordinarily refer to themselves as "citizens" or "taxpayers" in their petitions to the school board, as their male counterparts so often did; more frequently, they invoked the image of parent or mother to justify what critics saw as meddling in men's affairs. Hence they used a seemingly traditional faith in the power of motherhood as their inroad to social activism. The General Federation of Women's Clubs, the national organization that united thousands of women's associations from every state, was popularly known as that "Great Mothers' Organization." The forerunner of the modern parent-teacher association was the National Congress of Mothers, which assembled in the final days of the depression in 1897. And from national journals of opinion to local publications such as the *Toledo Blade*, one found the common statement that "the hand that rocks the cradle is the hand that rules the world." Or at least *should* rule the world. Motherhood became the war cry of those who met face to face with the male ward bosses who controlled the urban school.[26]

The nineteenth-century consensus that women's place was in the home was gradually reinterpreted in Rochester, Toledo, Milwaukee, and Kansas City. In the past, the belief that women were the defenders of the purity and safety of the home was sufficient argument for denying them a place in city politics. By the turn of the century, however, subtle changes in women's interpretation of domesticity made the prospects of larger involvement in municipal life a reality. Women in the vanguard of urban education reform advanced the age-old argument that they had special talents in child nurture. But they deftly altered the meaning of domesticity to warrant leaving the home to engage in many public activities. What the new woman opposed was not domesticity, but a static interpretation of women's rights and duties. In the rural past, when the processes of production and distribution centered in the home, it was argued, mothers could best protect the home by remaining near the fireside. Because of urban and industrial transformation, parental control over children's food, clothing, and schooling was diminished, necessitating corresponding changes in maternal behavior. Effective motherhood now required the expansion of the home's boundaries to include the entire community.

The new woman often sounded like an old woman in her platitudes on the wonders of motherhood, thereby disguising genuine changes in women's ideology and often the class dimensions of feminine reform. "A partnership with God is motherhood," claimed the elite West Side Mothers' Club in Milwaukee. "What strength, what purity, what self-control." Despite these time-honored assertions, women were nevertheless changing their actual social practice and reaching out in new ways to school and city. By expanding the definition of the home to include more than an individual household, urban women proved that homemaking and social activism were not incompatible, but part of a domestic continuum. "The environment of every woman is the home, wherever she goes she carries this with her," wrote the president of the Wisconsin Federation of Women's Clubs in 1900. "The time has come, however, when it is not enough that woman should alone be a homemaker, she must make the world itself a larger home." Since powerful corporate interests increasingly controlled the basic amenities of life, from food and water to clothing, heat, and light, modern motherhood necessitated extending the four walls of the home out into the street until they reached city hall.[27]

Home-related metaphors dotted the speeches and writings of municipal club women. Helen Montgomery of Rochester characteristically interpreted widened opportunities for reform as a prerequisite for sound motherhood and citizenship. "It is not enough that the house is kept clean, if the street be wrong, and the ward unhealthful," she asserted in an interview in the *Democrat and Chronicle* in 1896. "There should be a broadened housekeeping, to extend out of doors and all over the city. All these things will help women to gain full enfranchisement." "What rights do mothers have in regard to the public school education of their children?" asked some angry representatives of the local Political Equality Club to the ward leaders on the school board. When they learned that they only had the right to vote for school commissioners—who were always men, since the party caucuses were male-dominated—the women quickly retorted that modern mothers could only ensure children's welfare if they stepped beyond their own front door.[28]

The Woman's Suffrage Association of Toledo, whose roots extended back to the 1870s, was revitalized in the 1890s when new legislation gave women the right to vote on school issues and to serve on boards of education. Its members argued that modern motherhood required women to vote to defeat the ward bosses. As the *Blade* revealed in 1894, these activists had started to attract to their meetings women who "had probably never before attended a suffrage meeting, and had never publicly expressed any opinion on public affairs." While moving out of the traditional home sphere, these women were slowly refashioning their domestic identity.[29]

Mrs. John Kumler, for example, demanded at one of these meetings that "she should be allowed to vote because she did not think it right or just that her influence over her children should end at her doorstep. She desires to vote especially on school affairs, that school officers shall be elected, who are qualified to act in the best interests of the youth of the city." In response to those who believed that voting and larger involvement in social and political life were unfeminine, an unmarried suffrage activist responded that "the true woman is no less womanly, no less conscientious, in the performance of her home duties . . . than the woman of a hundred years ago, though the expression of this devotion may wear a different aspect."[30]

Women indeed expressed their devotion in new ways. They often notified men in every city that they refused to stay home and out of public view. Mrs. Charles B. Whitnall, a liberal reformer who later joined the Socialist Party, announced with other members of the Milwaukee's Woman's School Alliance that "ours is a great work in a never-ending cause, a cause which will never die so long as a child lives on this big earth." However much women disagreed on total suffrage and the Socialist movement, clubwomen were inseparable on issues related to school reform and the welfare of urban youth. Historians have emphasized that the Progressive era discovered the adolescent, but reformers were also interested in children of all ages. Certainly the education of the children of the poor and of immigrants of all ages was a preeminent contemporary concern. At any rate, the new domesticity was steeped in images of mothers' role in child nurture, home care, and schooling. "Nine-tenths of the work they have undertaken," wrote the historian of the women's club movement in 1910, "relates to children, the school, and the home."[31]

By continually emphasizing their insights as parents and mothers in child welfare and education, many clubwomen assumed that they were morally superior to men. They perceived themselves as an incorruptible, purifying force that would cleanse urban politics and overturn the rule of immoral men. Dr. Mary Munson, a "new woman" from Toledo, advanced the usual position in 1894 that women had historically borne the burdens of the "philanthropic work of the world." "When she enters the arena of politics she will not be untrue to her woman's nature. Laying aside partisanship, she will rise to the full dignity of her responsibilities as the mother of the race." However much their actions contradicted their claim of nonpartisanship, women persistently argued that they lacked base political motives but always represented the higher interests of the child.[32]

Women were the healers, the guardians of children, and the protectors of hearth and home. Like women's groups elsewhere, the Woman's School

Alliance in its constitution emphasized "the great and good influence that women may exert in a community." And everywhere it was assumed that women could rise above personal prejudices and class background to secure the common good. "Women would vote more directly for what would concern the highest interests of the schools without regard to politics or to party," argued one suffrage leader, who somehow ignored the fact that women's organizations were intensely political and in the vanguard of new and controversial educational ideas. Another female reformer more sensibly asserted that even if women could not purify urban government, an unlikely occurrence, certainly "women cannot make politics any worse than men have done."[33]

The new domesticity, therefore, provided a necessary ideological rationale for women to broaden their housekeeping responsibilities. This never automatically convinced male politicians to share power with them. As a result, women usually found themselves forming alliances not with the men on the school board but with women teachers. Clubwomen assaulted the system on two fronts. With the support of other community groups, they pressured ward leaders to adopt their experimental programs in the schools, and they also struggled to build alliances with neighborhood teachers. Although not uncritical of the prevalence of sing-song teaching methods and the liberal use of corporal punishment in the schools, organized women championed better working conditions for women laboring in the classroom. Women's groups throughout the Progressive era were in the forefront of efforts to increase teachers' salaries, reduce class sizes, and bring parents and teachers into closer association.

Every prominent women's club interested in social service had an active school visitation committee. The educational committees of the Women's Educational and Industrial Union of Rochester, the Women's Educational Club of Toledo, the Woman's School Alliance of Milwaukee, and the Athenaeum of Kansas City had volunteers who visited the schools and tried to establish close ties with neighborhood teachers. These visitors were thorns in the sides of many ward commissioners, but they laid the basis for modern parent-teacher associations. School officials throughout the nineteenth century had urged greater school and home cooperation. Women now took matters into their own hands, with little encouragement from the educational establishment. They investigated everything in the schools from the cleanliness of the floors to the numbers of children per classroom. They ultimately formed a gallery-like assembly at many school board meetings in the 1890s.[34]

One reason why many of the organizations from the 1890s survived for so many decades was that many of their members were former teachers. Fired from their jobs upon marriage, since custom dictated that domestic obligations took precedence over careers, they nevertheless retained a keen interest in schooling. Clubwomen therefore had considerable empathy for the urban schoolteacher, whose plight was once theirs. In that way, middle- and upper-class women could partially transcend their current class position by fighting for better working conditions for their less favored sisters. Without tenure or guaranteed job security, teachers could be removed from office for almost any reason, and marriage precluded the continuation of their teaching careers. Class sizes still hovered above fifty per class in the lower grades with low pay as a reward, so teachers often sorely needed friends on the outside of the schools who could sustain them in their arduous jobs. More systematic attention was now given to the plight of the local teacher than ever before.[35]

The prominence of former teachers and of wives of current male teachers in these women's clubs helped cement stronger bonds between home and school. Since many of these former teachers were now mothers, they took an even greater interest in the welfare of the schools. Of the fifty women on the educational committee of the Women's Educational and Industrial Union in Rochester, most were mothers and former teachers who used their experiences to engage in neighborhood reform. The Union characteristically met on weekends, to accommodate the maximum number of teachers who attended its conferences. Former and current teachers were well represented in the Women's Educational Club of Toledo and the Athenaeum of Kansas City. Mary E. Law of Toledo, for example, was a native Toledoan, a former grade school teacher, and the founder of a local kindergarten training school. When clubwomen and suffrage advocates complained to local school boards, they based their criticisms on personal experiences and recent contact with actual school conditions.[36]

A brief examination of the backgrounds of the members of the Women's School Alliance of Milwaukee, drawn from the earliest membership data available in 1897, reveals some of the social origins of voluntary group membership. Formed in 1891 and reorganized two years later, the Alliance was the outgrowth of a series of "Mothers' Meetings" that some literary club members organized in the 1880s. Throughout the Progressive era the Alliance was in the thick of educational debate and innovation, championing a number of social welfare reforms. Like organizations in other cities, the Alliance applauded the work of women in school reform. The preamble to its constitution stated that the Alliance's chief concern was with "investigating conditions, studying methods of instruction, and promoting the best interests of our Public Schools."[37]

Clubs such as the Alliance often regarded themselves as "representative" organizations. Under closer scrutiny the backgrounds of members assume greater clarity, revealing the basis for the growing connections between home and school. Of the 170 members in 1897, 155 have been uncovered in the city directory. Teachers (17 percent) and wives of male teachers (9 percent) formed 26 percent, or about one-quarter of the entire membership; they constituted the largest segment of the association. The next largest groups included the wives of businessmen and manufacturers (20 percent), of professionals such as physicians, lawyers, and dentists (17 percent), of agents and salesmen (8 percent), and of realtors (7 percent). The wives of skilled workers (hatters, brass finishers, painters, and so on) formed 10 percent of the organization.[38]

Exactly how many of these members were former teachers is unknown, but the Alliance continually pushed for better ties with local schools and physical and educational improvements in the poorer neighborhoods. Alliance members were primarily from the elite East Side, the traditional source of literary club membership, and the working-class South Side. The most prominent teachers who were members worked in some of Milwaukee's poorest areas, inhabited largely by unskilled Polish immigrants. One very active member of the Alliance was Mary F. Flanders, the principal and a former teacher at the Jones Island School. A close friend and supporter of Lizzie Kander, Flanders regularly blasted the school administration for the unsanitary, rickety, understaffed facility in her district.[39]

Jones Island was an impoverished area inhabited by Germans and Poles, many of whom were employed as fishermen. Photographs of the area from the turn of the century depict closely packed, dilapidated houses hugging the Lake Michigan shore. Flanders championed better home and school relations, supported several successful parent associations in the mid-1890s, and continually lobbied for local improvements. Many of the teachers in the Alliance similarly worked in poor neighborhoods, for although the ward system in theory promised to serve each district equally, the schools in the poorest areas, especially near the South Side, were almost always the most understaffed, overcrowded, and least aesthetically pleasing. Many of the Alliance members did not have to worry about economic reprisals when they complained to the school board, yet enough teachers and wives of male teachers were members to ensure that their petitions were based on thorough knowledge of local conditions. School visitors, if not the area children, always did their homework.[40]

Members of the Women's School Alliance and other organizations openly defended parents' and mothers' rights as well as those of the teacher. They were sensitive to the problem of determining how to unite parent and teacher in the best interests of the child. A member of the Women's Ethical Club in 1896 caused a stir in Rochester when she told a principal that "often teachers forget that the first allegiance of the child is to its parents, and while parents may not in all cases keep up with the times . . . their opinion should always be listened to with the greatest deference in the presence of the child."[41]

In this instance the principal retorted that teachers and principals disliked interference and meddling by parents. Despite such disagreements, relations between Rochester women's groups and teachers in the 1890s always seemed cordial; the school board's claim that school visitors would be regarded by teachers as spies was unfounded. When a leading school commissioner attacked the teaching staff in 1898 for trying to control textbook selection, a perennial source of graft from the book companies, the Women's Educational and Industrial Union quickly defended the teachers for asserting their rights against the all-male school board.[42]

Such outspoken behavior was a reflection of the Progressive woman's new ideology of domesticity. Identifying strongly with their parental and maternal traits, women broadened their conceptions of home responsibilities and tried to foment an educational awakening among the citizenry. The quest for what the Kansas City Athenaeum called a "wider educational spirit" in the community continued throughout the 1890s. The Citizens Educational Association of Rochester sounded like so many other organizations when it tried "to encourage every other means of popular education, to bring about needed reforms in the administration of school affairs, and to maintain an active interest among the people in the matter of general education." Women club members were critical of traditional teaching methods, excessive discipline, and other non-progressive elements of schooling. In these and other ways they tried to energize large numbers of people behind the cause of reform.[43]

Women wanted to cooperate with teachers as well as to focus attention on the rights of parents and children. When teachers ignored these rights, they were occasionally chastised, sometimes severely. "One of the strongest criticisms against our public schools is the total ignoring of the rights of children and parents when they come in question with those of teachers," complained one of Toledo's leading suffrage leaders. "The axiom of many Toledo school teachers is: 'The King can do no wrong, I am the King.' When parents have appealed to members of the board of education, their grievances have usually been turned over to the teachers' committee, under whom parents' rights have almost always been nil." This grievance was penned in the heat of battle between local women and the male school board. It was unusually critical in its tone and atypical of female reformers' attitudes toward schoolteachers. But its extreme stance reflected the frustration of those who were through various means barred from public office and who feared that their control over children ended when they passed through the schoolhouse door.[44]

For the most part women's clubs were sympathetic to teachers though eager to transform the schools along the lines of the "new education," a phrase coined in earlier decades but increasingly a broadly defined goal of reform organizations in the 1890s. Their quarrel was less with teachers, who they realized would be essential allies in any progressive campaign, than with the male power brokers who implemented programs and guided school policy. Soon these joiners of clubs boldly confronted ward bosses, superintendents, and the leading men of the city. Women's ability to portray themselves simply as mothers defending the home belied their talents as outspoken political agitators and obscured their role in expanding state responsibility for social welfare.

IV

By the mid-1890s organized women were firmly convinced that modern housekeeping necessitated updated ideas on domesticity. When they entered the male domain of school politics, however, they quickly learned that Progressive school reform would be difficult and would require more than appeals to the new motherhood. In Kansas City, which had a small, elite school board elected at large, women lacked school suffrage, so they had to pressure male leaders to implement their ideas. Although the Milwaukee school board was based on ward lines and Wisconsin women enjoyed school suffrage, the local board was appointed by the all-male city council, which had little interest in the women's movement. The prospects for women in Rochester and Toledo seemed brighter, since their ward-based school boards were elective and women enjoyed suffrage on school matters. The major rub was that the Republican and Democratic machines controlled the nominating process, and the local politicians never nominated women. Women were frustrated at every turn.

Women refused to despair despite these obvious roadblocks. They firmly believed in themselves and mustered the courage to confront unexpected challenges. Organized women and civic-minded mothers were regularly insulted for their innovative educational ideas and told to go home, wash their dishes, and leave the rarified atmosphere of school administration to wiser men. Clubwomen nevertheless refused to withdraw from the public arena; they stood their ground and squarely faced their opponents. They visited the local schools, discussed the latest educational ideas, and even funded some experimental programs at the settlement houses, such as hot lunches, playgrounds, and vacation schools. When permission was granted, they ultimately ran many of these programs in selected neighborhood schools. They formed mothers' clubs with kindergarten teachers who were imbued with Friedrich Froebel's faith in the moral superiority of motherhood. Starting from a weak power base, the new woman helped bring the new education to many cities.[45]

The new education directly contradicted the basic tenets of nineteenth-century pedagogy. In its earliest years in the 1890s, the new education emphasized individuality, mild forms of discipline, and an end to excessive memorization, recitation, and testing; it also endorsed the addition of innovative subjects, including manual training, domestic science, kindergartens, and nature study. Convinced that schools could be more humane and children more active in shaping the classroom experience, organized women and reformers in general thus called for new forms of municipal intervention in the lives of youth. They wanted an enhanced parenting role for the state in social welfare, a natural position for anyone guided by theories of expansive motherhood.[46]

Searching for different ways to expand power beyond their own homes, organized women found countless outlets for their activities during the depression. Despite all the boosterism that continued to inform the public literature of the 1890's, the contradictions of progress and poverty were everywhere apparent as large numbers of able-bodied people were denied work. The old, the weak, and the destitute were in special need during these difficult times, yet women turned again and again to the child, not only to their own children, but especially to the children of the poor. As one Rochesterian contended in 1898, there was now a "growing realization of the value of the maternal element in society—the concern of all for the good of mothers and children." "It is no longer my child, his rights, his comforts—but the rights and comforts of all children," since "what concerns my neighbor's child, concerns me; a wrong or injustice to childhood anywhere in the city touches every mother in the city."[47]

Growing parental criticisms of the educational establishment surfaced in the most unlikely places. Even before the depression struck local cities, or Joseph Mayer Rice and John Dewey had written their early essays and books on the new education, ordinary parents in places such as Kansas City had attacked the worst aspects of local schooling. In late December 1892, an unnamed parent wrote a critical letter to the editor of the conservative and Republican *Journal of Commerce*, the booster paper made famous by Robert T. Van Horn. Soon a raging controversy flared between parents and Superintendent James Greenwood. At first slightly deferential to the school administration, the letters became so strident that the editor refused to publish them after several weeks. Out of the debate came some of the earliest stirrings and examples of Progressive reform.[48]

Parents complained in a series of letters of their dissatisfaction with the school system. They were particularly incensed by the system's emphasis on rigid discipline and rote memorization in the classroom and their effects on children's health. One parent cited an outbreak of the Saint Vitus's dance, a nervous disease that reportedly resulted from the "daily routine" and the constant "worry over school lessons." Others complained about the grading and testing and the ubiquitous forms required when children were tardy or absent. When one child complained that "I got ten demerit marks this forenoon just because I didn't keep my eyes in one certain place," it angered his mother and her neighbors. "Every child in the school seems to be a machine. If one asserts any individuality he gets demerit marks in 'form,' and his promotion is endangered. . . . Is that education, which leaves the child's individuality undeveloped, or crushes it out altogether? Should our schools make automatons, educationally, of our boys and girls?"[49]

Superintendent Greenwood was never afraid to state his opinions locally on any number of subjects. He never hid in the shadows or avoided a confrontation. On the contrary, he strutted through town impeccably dressed with top hat and cane as he made his rounds from school to school. He was a sight not easily forgotten. He was also impatient with outside criticism and privately called Francis Parker, John Dewey, and other innovators fools. The Kansas City school board gave Greenwood almost full reign in administering the schools during his forty years at the helm. He had an interesting way of dealing with parents: he attacked them when they seemed apathetic and attacked them when they disagreed with him. He always deflected criticism of him or the system back upon the parents themselves. Only when one letter appeared that likened the schools to military drill—with "eyes front," "hands erect," and "hands folded"—did Greenwood decide to enter the current fray.[50]

Greenwood blasted parents for not appreciating the value of military form as a central part of "character training." During such emergencies as fires, he argued, parents would certainly applaud "instant obedience and military movement" that would "save lives and prevent the disastrous trampling of a mob." Moreover, discipline, corporal punishment, and toeing the line (that is, aligning toes to the lines formed by wooden floors) prepared children for the rough and tumble of the competitive world. Greenwood then calculated the exact number of hours children spent at home instead of at school, supposedly proving that parents were primarily responsible for such maladies as the Saint Vitus's dance.[51]

Greenwood's blunt rejoinder inflamed local debate. An "anxious

Math Class at the Dawn of the Progressive Era, Benton School, Kansas City, 1892

Courtesy: Special Collections, Kansas City Public Library, Kansas City, Missouri

mother" responded that "the dissatisfaction regarding the surplus amount of red tape used is widespread." Children were forced to learn long lists of words in exact order, recite them accordingly, or get marked down. There were "pencil raps" and lowered deportment grades when children innocently stretched their arms and turned their heads. Some mothers called for school suffrage laws to eliminate the unresponsive male administration. Others pointed out that the teachers, who were the subject of considerable negative publicity, were themselves victims of the system; they were forced to crush "the natural abandon of eager, happy children" as a matter of survival. Teachers preserved "order" to preserve their jobs, and the feminine qualities of love and kindness toward children were transformed into rigid methods of instruction. Anonymous teachers themselves added that through their exposés, parents had "struck the nail on the head." Without tenure provisions, however, even sympathetic teachers were powerless to change the system. Greenwood reportedly platooned critically minded teachers to schools on the outer edges of the city.[52]

Calls for greater freedom for teachers and individual attention for pupils were difficult requests in such overcrowded schools, but Greenwood and the school board never accepted these ideas as legitimate concerns. They controlled the schools and used the major political parties to isolate themselves from outside critics. A bipartisan clique of Republicans and Democrats manipulated nominations to the school board, a plan that Greenwood had personally arranged in 1880. This clique had little respect for the women's movement. Only the working-class *Mail* was friendly toward new educational ideas and "soft" pedagogy. In late 1892 it championed women's rights and parental involvement in schools and questioned elite dominance of the school board. But the paper fell victim to the depression. It went into receivership, changed ownership, and ultimately became an outspoken critic of labor unions, liberalism, and socialism.[53]

The *Kansas City Star* recognized the potential transforming force of the new ideas presented by local parents in the rival *Journal of Commerce*. After considering them, the *Star* concurred with the conservative school administration. One editorial written during the heart of the educational debate spoke volumes:

> What has become of the old fashioned youth who pursued an education with patient search and vigil long, who did not mind poor clothes or bare feet; who was willing to sit on any kind of bench . . . who laid prone on his stomach and read by the light of the fire till far into the night; who would walk miles in snow or rain to borrow a book and as far to return it? Where has he gone? In his place, with all the modern facilities, with fine school houses and patent furniture and furnaces, and cabinets and blackboards, maps and charts, there has come another who complains of "nerves" and "St. Vitus Dance" and for whom fears are entertained lest he learns too much.[54]

With the press, politicians, and the school administration united against them, Kansas City mothers and sympathetic parents turned inward and by 1920 had formed the largest network of parent-teacher associations in the world.

Women had similar problems with the school administration in Milwaukee. The appointed, ward-based school board formed a phalanx against the Woman's School Alliance and the new education. Only a handful of men broke ranks and supported the women. In the 1890s Alliance members regularly attended school board meetings, where they petitioned for better sanitary methods, the adoption of manual training and domestic science, nature study, and the abolishment of corporal punishment. Many of their programs were aimed at freeing children from some of the book-oriented aspects of schooling and to providing more activity-oriented programs for hand-and-eye coordination and muscle development. These innovations were neither class biased nor trade oriented, for when many of them were finally adopted in some form after the turn of the century, they were found in every elementary school. In the 1890s, however, the Alliance specifically championed the needs of the poorest districts of Milwaukee.[55]

Like many urban women's groups, the Alliance focused on many problems related to school sanitation in the 1890s. A few months after the Alliance organized, its school visitors surveyed sanitary conditions in the entire city, like all municipal housekeepers who promoted better health for all school children. Visitors discovered that the poorest districts were also the areas with the highest levels of unsanitary conditions and infant mortality. The worst environment, in their opinion, was at "the Seventeenth District school at Bay View, which is located near the nail mill and puddling mill of the Illinois Steel Company" on the South Side. Obnoxious fumes "and great volumes of black smoke filled the air" of the classrooms "almost constantly" during their visits. Alliance members correspondingly demanded that the men on the school board correct these vile conditions.[56]

The Alliance had even more complaints about the Tenth District School. Located in one of the most densely populated, working-class sections of Milwaukee, the school had a ventilating system with intake ducts located over "privy vaults and manure heaps." The "disgusting odors" were so bad that "even the janitor cannot endure to remain at his post," wrote the Alliance. "The teachers are pale and languid and assert that their rooms are filled with deadly microbes. The rooms of the younger children are directly over vile closets, and it is the greatest wonder that some epidemic does not break out among them." The school was so overcrowded that some classes met in the cloakrooms. For their concerns with children in the poorer districts, the Alliance received many pledges of support, but even more red tape. The women were routinely told to pressure the city council, which funded the school board, or to harass the Board of Public Works, which was technically responsible for school repairs.[57]

The Woman's School Alliance was such a creative, constant source of new ideas that the president of the school board labeled them "impetuous" and fellow committee members who responded to their frequent charges called their reports "misleading and incorrect" and "their suggestions impracticable." Board members never successfully refuted their ideas, though they often dismissed them, and it would have admittedly been difficult for any school board to implement their ideas rapidly in the hard times of the 1890s. The Alliance demanded the abolishment of corporal punishment, a demand that was refused even though it did not involve money but differences between advocates of stern and "gentle" measures of correction. The Alliance also desired more pay for elementary teachers, adjustable desks for all new schools, playgrounds, sewing classes, manual training, and more kindergartens. It was invited to operate some experimental programs and to hold its meetings in various local schools, which provided an inroad for the wider use of the schools as social centers. However modest its early successes, the Alliance actively championed innovations before a body of men who were hostile to Progressive reform.[58]

Largely as a result of the support given to the women's cause by influential dailies such as the *Milwaukee Sentinel*, the city council finally appointed a woman to the school board, in 1896. The Alliance representative received a token position that was popularly regarded by ward leaders as a joke. She was placed on an unimportant committee and sequestered from the board, yet reportedly impressed some opponents with her zeal and attention to detail. In the 1890s this appointment was simply a recognition of the increased visibility of the new woman. The first woman on the Milwaukee school board did little to alter established educational policy, but the appointment marked the beginnings of a long tradition of female representation in the local school administration.[59]

Even this small accomplishment by the Alliance occurred over the objections of many small and large businessmen, manufacturers, and professionals on the school board as well as many German Americans who opposed the suffrage movement and women's rights generally. When the Alliance first pushed for women on the school board, the *Sentinel* announced that "the trouble is that the Germans are against it solid, not only those with the full German traditions, but those born here in America. They think women are only good to perform household duties and you can't make them believe anything else." In their opinion, housekeeping should be restricted to the private home.[60]

One German ward leader argued that "we don't want them around when we are carrying on business. It is a thing for men to do. . . . It is crowding out the men to let the women in." Some men lost their prejudices against women as school officers over the years and came to respect them as equals. But among the many powerful German dailies in the 1890s, only the independent *Freidenker* ignored ethnic opposition and fully supported women for the school board, emphasizing their purifying influence and domestic and child-rearing talents. Throughout these years the Alliance's chief accomplishment was to stir up discontent and to serve as a fountain of new ideas that challenged the legitimacy of the existing educational system. Its ideas were novel and, therefore, somewhat refreshing if not always accepted by the status quo.[61]

If mothers and women in Kansas City and Milwaukee faced walls of opposition in their respective cities, the same was true for reformers in Toledo and Rochester. In both cities the ward-based school boards were popularly chosen and women by mid-decade had the right to vote in school elections. Unfortunately, school superintendents in both cities followed the lead of the board of education and opposed the innovations and soft pedagogical ideas of the female agitators. Toledo's women faced harassment at the polls, the usual ridicule of German ward leaders, and more heat than they could sometimes stand. Rochester's school officials even conducted a smear campaign against Susan B. Anthony and Helen Montgomery and their friends in the Women's Educational and Industrial Union.

In an early display of grassroots community solidarity that would be common in school reform movements during the Progressive era, middle- and upper-class women, the women's branch of the Knights of Labor, the Women's Suffrage Association, and the Women's Christian Temperance Union appeared before the Toledo school board in 1892 and requested its endorsement of a school suffrage bill pending in the state legislature. The board deliberated briefly, then openly refused. At the time, members of the American Protective Association, an aggressive anti-Catholic organization in the Midwest and elsewhere, had considerable influence on the school board. If not members of the secret organization themselves, the leading elite members on the board sympathized with nativism. The president of the school board, for example, was Guy Major, a Republican and an extremely wealthy linseed oil manufacturer who publicly denounced Catholics. Major and his cohorts attacked suffrage legislation, since it would enfranchise thousands of Polish Catholic women, many of whom sought legislation to divide the school fund. Major especially hated Mary Law, a Roman Catholic clubwoman whose peers urged her election to the school board.[62]

The board's refusal to endorse women's suffrage naturally infuriated many local reformers. Along with other state suffrage organizations, women's groups continued to lobby for a suffrage bill until they finally succeeded in 1894. For the following few years Toledo clubwomen then endeavored to force the Republican and Democratic parties to nominate some women to the school board. After considerable haggling they finally did so. Getting women elected was another matter entirely; ward heelers heckled and jeered most women who appeared at the polls. While "visions of the coming Utopia flitted about in the fancies of the women" upon the passage of the new suffrage bill, the realities of political life quickly revealed that they were still in Toledo.[63]

Party lieutenants in several Toledo precincts refused to let women register to vote. Once registered, other women were still not permitted to vote. There were widespread reports of missing ballots and voter fraud on election day. The new woman had appeared at the polls in 1895 for all to see, claimed the *Blade*, but the elections were foregone conclusions. Women were heckled, insulted, and told to leave politics to the men. An increasingly powerful figure in the schools at this point was Thomas Tracy, since Guy Major had left the school board to become Toledo's mayor. Tracy was a wealthy attorney, banker, and Republican. A woman challenged him for his position at one point, but "Tracy's heelers crowded the polling places, spitting tobacco juice, and ridiculing the women as they deposited their ballots." The closest women ever came to serving on the Toledo school board in the 1890s was in 1898, when Mary Law lost in her electoral bid by fifty votes.[64]

Like the women in Kansas City, Milwaukee, and Toledo, those in Rochester similarly agitated for numerous reforms ranging from the abandonment of corporal punishment to higher pay for teachers to manual training and sewing classes. Rochester's women typically ran some new programs at their own expense, received some municipal funding to implement their ideas, and generally labored in a hostile environment. The superintendent and the school board viewed them as troublemakers and Socialists. One ward leader in 1898 said that offering sewing in the schools was as sensible as teaching "blacksmithing" or "potato digging." It would only encourage other cranks to support lunatic ideas such as the construction of swimming pools in the schools for recreational purposes. Dangerous ideas indeed![65]

The Women's Educational and Industrial Union encountered problems with the school board from the beginning. Henry Noyes, the school board president in the early 1890s, was an attorney and longtime member who had publicly opposed all fads and frills in education. "The effort to teach everything, however desirable, in the schools must end in miserable failure," he warned in 1890. It was the great misfortune of the Women's Union that precisely when it pressed for educational change, Noyes was appointed superintendent. Joseph Mayer Rice, who wrote a series of famous muckraking articles on urban education in the *Forum* in 1892 and 1893, spurred the women on through some local lectures on reform. When he argued that the American schools "sacrifice everything to the hammering process and take little account of the nature or sympathies of the student," the women viewed it as a call to action. To the contented school board, it only meant trouble.[66]

Throughout the 1890s, Superintendent Noyes and the school board basically ridiculed the new education and only permitted the establishment of a few manual-training and domestic science programs at public expense. Helen Montgomery and her friends publicized the benefits of the new education in various lectures and community meetings and urged Noyes to expand the kindergartens to all parts of the city. Noyes and his cohorts bent on some issues but never broke into a position of full acceptance. Noyes made the sensible point in 1897 that new was not necessarily better, then refused to accept any criticisms on existing programs or methods of education. The belief that sewing trained "the whole child through brain and eye and hand" was treated by the school board as ludicrous. And when the Women's Union further enjoined the school board to abolish the required state regent's exam, since it was a hazard to the health of teachers and pupils and a "fogy" of the "old system of education," the animosity between the female reformers and the school board only deepened.[67]

"Parents have frequently expected our public schools to extend instruction outside their proper limitations," wrote a special school board committee in Rochester in response to advocates of the new education. The committee then proceeded to attack the Women's Union on every pedagogical point. The silly suggestion to treat children "with sugar coated kindness" by ending corporal punishment was a threat to authority and "a great mistake." Little children, even those of "tender years," should not "do as they please." Similarly, manual-training and domestic science instruction belonged in the home, not in the school.[68]

The committee members then equated the new education with socialism and state paternalism and reaffirmed their allegiance to the old education: "Fortunately, the school authorities have not yielded to the socialistic demand that the schools be made a panacea for all ills. But the point we particularly wish to make is that our public schools can not be used to relieve parents of their responsibilities." Long after the ward system was abolished in many cities, this claim that new programs and progressive ideas robbed parents of their independence and responsibilities to their children would resound in the speeches of those who continued to oppose the new education. Through these early debates in the 1890s, citizens previewed some future social conflicts in the schools. The battle lines between the old education and the new were formally drawn in many cities as the decade drew to a close.[69]

Advocates of social welfare reform in the schools often refused to face the thorny issues raised by the specter of increased state intervention in social welfare. Organized women, like all reformers, assumed that they were motivated by altruism, by the need to correct glaring injustices and to shape public policy in enlightened ways. Everyone searched for that elusive end called the public good. And yet women never adequately answered the charges of those who asked whether the state could expand its power without inevitably reducing the power of the family. Those who were critical of the rise of municipal welfare work in the schools, even if they did not approve of the methods of ward heelers, agreed with them that the state had no moral or legal right to intervene in family relations. Parents, not the state, should provide the food, recreational activities, health and medical care, and other services advocated by grass-roots reformers. Once power began to flow to the state, it was argued, it would be impossible to halt the erosion of parental and individual responsibilities.

Organized women who advocated more intensive state intervention, particularly in the lives of the poor, however, viewed the situation from their own class and ideological vantage points. State intervention was simply the municipalization of motherhood, a way to balance private and public responsibilities for youth, and it helped the middle and upper classes uplift the entire civilization. A speaker to the National Congress of Mothers at the turn of the century put the matter succinctly: "Your children belong to me, to the neighbors, to everybody else, to every one with whom they come in touch." The poor in particular had to learn that "You can not keep them to yourself. . . . They are only lent to you to care for, to help, until they can stand on their own feet and live their lives independently of you." The state would stand between poor parents and their children, and school service programs would provide children with the opportunities to escape from their impoverished environments and live independent lives. The state would not become a new parent, only a temporary provider.[70]

One might have asked such a woman of standing if poor parents had the same jurisdictional rights over her children, but reformers rarely broached that subject publicly. They presumed that the very poor stood in a dependent position to those who had reached at least middle-class standing. Progressive women, for all their obvious compassion and sympathy for the plight of the poor, for the overworked teachers and women workers, always assumed that they knew what was best for all the children in their community. In the end, as will soon become evident, liberal women's clubs never became as radical as ward leaders in Rochester and other cities feared, and their elite maternalism outweighed their Socialism. With some notable exceptions, women accepted the legitimacy of the larger social system that would force some people to become dependent on state welfare, just as they had often been earlier dependent on private charity. And yet organized women, despite their refusal to move beyond liberal prescriptions for educational reform, fought strenuously for lay influence in education and for the adoption of social welfare services for youth, sometimes for all children but especially for the poor. Whether or not social justice could be achieved within the existing capitalist framework of society remained the central dilemma of social service innovation and Progressive politics.

Women, however, were not the sole champions of the new education and social service innovation in cities such as Rochester, Toledo, Milwaukee, and Kansas City during the Progressive era. Socialists, Populists, Social Gospelers, and labor unions that also contributed to grassroots Progressivism helped shape the new era of reform. Throughout the Progressive era, women interacted with many of these groups on a variety of issues affecting the welfare of urban youth, remaining central to the entire reform process. Urban reform received much of its drive, commitment, and interest in children from those who were content with a public title no higher than municipal housekeeper.

Richard Ely of the University of Wisconsin sensed the trends of the day when in 1902 he noted women's growing importance in *The Coming City*. "Whenever you see any peculiarly excellent work going forward in the twentieth-century you may be sure that the women have something to do with it," he assured his readers. "They are cold and unmoved when we talk about municipal government as business, but when we bring forward the household ideal they think of the children, and when they are once aroused you may be sure that something is going to happen!" Something clearly happened in the 1890s. Women learned the art of association; later they learned how to gain even more power in shaping school policy. In spite of all the elements that went into the shaping of Progressive school reform, it was nevertheless very much a women's movement.[71]

Chapter 3

Voices of Discontent

I

The women's club and parent-association movement symbolized important community trends in the 1890s. A new generation of political activists, men and women ranging from liberal to Socialist, gradually attained more visibility and influence in local cities. Some critics simply dismissed all these grassroots reformers as faddists and cranks, but something was clearly stirring on the municipal scene. Indeed, much of the impetus for educational innovation did not occur through the work of "new middle class" superintendents or other officials, but arose outside the schoolhouse door within the dynamic world of voluntary organizations. Into innumerable voluntary group meetings and protest rallies flowed a new social conscience destined to leave its mark on public education.[1]

The centralization and consolidation of the economic system in the hands of relatively few people in the late nineteenth century meant that schools would almost inevitably experience massive social change. The schools were born in class and cultural conflict, and there was considerable community resistance to new centralizing trends. Professional and business elites, with strong allies among an emerging class of professional school administrators, worked to adapt education to new economic realities. But even this powerful alliance faced various forms of opposition, since cities were alive to competing ideas of how to remake the world of mass education in changing times.

Like all broadly based movements for change, urban Progressivism was remarkably diverse, involving more than female municipal housekeepers. Other voices of discontent were continually heard in the late nineteenth century, adding additional dimensions to urban reform movements. Specific laboring groups such as skilled workers, for example, demanded more control over the workplace and various improvements in local school systems. Socialists, eager to tap such discontent, also searched for avenues of influence and emphasized the highly political nature of mass education. Various Social Gospel ministers, in turn, influential beyond their numbers, strained to reconcile basic Christian ethics with a class-ridden state, and they too became an integral aspect of Progressive era school reform.

The multifaceted quality of grassroots Progressivism became one of its defining characteristics throughout the late nineteenth and early twentieth century. As various groups competed in the civic arena to win the favor of the state, newspaper editors even in the mid-1890s wondered aloud whether a cohesive movement for educational and social reconstruction would rise from the ashes of economic depression. The *Toledo Blade*, for example, asked in 1895 whether dissidents and "faddists" would find some common basis for political unity, whether groups such as the "Prohibitionists, the Populists, the free silver at 16 to 1 advocates, and all others [could] join in one conglomeration of 'reform.'" This Republican editor doubted that cooperation would occur. Yet essential questions remained: could social and educational critics motivated by different aims and shaped by different cultural backgrounds and life experiences unite in common cause to improve state education? Could "faddists" and "cranks" discover common strategies to halt the drift of state policy toward consolidation, centralization, and elite control?[2]

In the 1890s there were already a few glimpses of the social cooperation that would soon characterize local movements for educational reform. Cooperation between liberals and radicals on many (though hardly all) school-related issues soon became a distinctive trait of grassroots reform. With civic power dispersed along many lines of activity, a single voluntary group could not successfully implement specific educational reforms without accommodating to the demands of other community interests. The congenial behavior of liberals and more radical reformers was highlighted early, for example, when suffrage leaders such as Susan B. Anthony actively endorsed labor unions, when politicized women in Milwaukee helped agitate for a workingmen's party in 1888, and when the Knights of Labor in Toledo four years later backed the women's organizations lobbying for school suffrage. Only when competing voluntary groups sacrificed parts of their own reform programs and participated in larger efforts at social amelioration could they overcome their civic isolation and forge an alliance against centralized elites.[3]

If the "new education" was partially a testament to the energies of the new woman, it also drew selectively upon the ideals of more highly politicized working-class interests. Nascent Populist, Socialist, and working-class agitators in the 1890s, especially when joined by radical ministers, offered very critical assessments of school and society and even guided individual women along a path from liberalism to socialism. Progressive workers and Socialists often moved beyond an ideology of municipal housekeeping and state welfare capitalism. This further charged an already highly volatile political environment. Radicals openly condemned the contradictions of a society that produced paupers and millionaires, street urchins and children of privilege. More than did liberal reformers of the day, radicals vigorously questioned the hierarchy of wealth and power that now solidified its control over America and its basic supporting institutions, including the press, church, and school. Could the state, they asked, possibly eliminate fundamental inequalities and tip the balance scale in favor of working people and the newly dispossessed?[4]

Across urban America during the Progressive era, specific trade unions and third-party groups became more articulate and visible social critics and more insistent upon increased state intervention in education and social welfare. For these groups as well as for activist women, the 1890s was a decade of hope, planning, and aspiration. What is striking, of course, is how all these different voluntary association representatives, drawing upon so many rich and diverse ideas and experiences, turned to the child as an object of reform. Socialists and progressive trade unions, especially in Milwaukee, became vigorous and outspoken partisans for children's welfare. Religiously oriented radicals, who hated the effects of capitalism just as vocally, if for different reasons, also joined the rising chorus of reform. Mayor Samuel M. "Golden Rule" Jones of Toledo was renowned throughout the country for his activism, and he was only one of the more famous grassroots Progressives who became dedicated to reform during the depression of the 1890s. Trade union activists, Socialists, and advocates of the Golden Rule soon left their imprint on the evolution of grassroots reform.

II

The sheer numerical increase in the wage-earning class that resided in American cities by 1900 guaranteed that it would have some role in municipal politics and school reform. Industrial statistics revealed that there were now more than fifteen thousand wage earners in Kansas City and Toledo, thirty-three thousand in Rochester, and forty-eight thousand in Milwaukee. Just as capitalists consolidated their economic power through pools, mergers, and trusts, unions helped some workingmen contribute to the organizational spirit of the times. While sounding some-what deterministic, one historian has argued that "the organization of labor to resist the depredations of organized capital was the historical imperative of the industrial working class." By organizing themselves for their own protection and advance, the skilled workers who formed trade unions in the nineteenth century—the carpenters, the cigar makers, the beer bottlers, the sheet workers, and other artisans—soon developed social perspectives that invariably shaped their beliefs on the common school.[5]

Unions, of course, represented only a fraction of the entire labor force and constituted a type of labor aristocracy. Still, unions nevertheless enabled one important segment of the wage-earning class to struggle for social improvements and school reform. Throughout the early 1890s, urban residents became more cognizant of their working-class populations. Organized labor especially attracted attention, since its members sometimes espoused unorthodox ideas such as Populism and Socialism. With the growth of a sizable industrial workforce, many citizens wondered whether the class conflicts of European cities would be replicated in this country, threatening political stability and social order. Like so many contemporary newspapers, the *Rochester Democrat and Chronicle* sensed that the depression thoroughly undermined public order. Many workers were "setting class against class" and hence failed to see that the "relations and interests" of labor and capital were "so co-extensive and mutual."[6]

These fears were not unwarranted. Confrontation rather than compromise often informed labor-capital relations, as evidenced by ubiquitous strikes as well as the violence at Haymarket Square and at Pullman. Given these shocking reminders of class division, the relationship of workers to radical political ideologies became a major public issue by the early 1890s. The *Democrat and Chronicle*, for example, remarked in 1894 that even Rochester had a vast "industrial army" and claimed that "in this city Anarchists flourish as they do elsewhere." One Anarchist exchanged heated words with a local minister, and the newspaper reported that "the man was of the regular Anarchist breed, shaggy whiskers, compressed lips, wizened eyes, retreating forehead, and falling chin, and dressed in poor apparel." Although few of them were Anarchists or so uncomely, twenty thousand citizens marched in the Labor Day parade, which dramatized the emerging self-consciousness of the working classes.[7]

The *Toledo Evening Bee* similarly followed the progress of May Day and Labor Day celebrations before concluding in 1899 that Toledo was divided into two groups: "mechanics" and the "so-called middle class." It was a reluctant recognition of the economic divisions that eventually might lead to industrial warfare. Milwaukee, whose Socialist working-class movement will be examined shortly, already experienced considerable social conflict. In the May Day Riots of 1886, skilled and unskilled workers clashed with the Wisconsin National Guard. Less industrial than other cities, Kansas City nevertheless had its share of boycotts, lockouts, and artisan strikes. Surprisingly large and enthusiastic Labor Day parades convinced the *Star* that the town at the bend of the Missouri River was now "a workingman's city."[8]

A major issue in the 1890s was whether the trade unions and the great mass of unorganized workers could build an alternative to the traditional two-party system. Trade union leaders in particular complained that working people lacked political power commensurate with their numbers. Socialist workers and agitators went a step further, arguing that the major parties supported the capitalist system and, therefore, kept workers economically and politically dependent. They pointed out that wage earners did not control their own working environments or vital governing structures such as the school board. Radical trade unionists, however, realized that most labor leaders opposed union involvement in municipal politics and endorsed bread-and-butter reforms within the existing economic system. The Central Labor Union of Rochester and Toledo and the Industrial Council of Kansas City had failed miserably when they entered politics prior to the 1890s, and their official policy was to avoid entanglement with political parties. Only in Milwaukee, where the Union Labor Party almost captured the city in 1888, did workers sufficiently organize politically and seriously challenge two-party dominance.[9]

When local trade unions organized workingmen's parties after the Civil War, they were repeatedly thrashed at the polls. Their "apolitical" character in later decades resulted from their continual rejection by the voters. Rochester's union coalesced against the major parties in 1861 and organized their own "workingmen's ticket," which was crushed on election day. Toledo's unions also refused to endorse the major parties or to build an alternative after the electorate defeated a full slate of candidates of their Workingmen's Party in 1867. Citizens in a free-market society that glorified individualism and property rights treated labor unions and their political parties with open hostility and opposition. Around the time of the Civil War, the Republican *Blade* attacked striking dockworkers as "roughs and loafers," while the Democratic *Commercial* dismissed them as drunkards. In this environment, the Central Labor Union quite logically shunned all political associations after assembling in 1880.[10]

Prior to the 1890s, therefore, trade unionism was never a powerful political force in these cities. Milwaukee was the only major exception. Yet unions were not paralyzed by their past, only chastened by it. In the 1890s organized labor became conspicuous, loquacious, and occasionally daring. It attacked the conditions leading to the depression and the major parties for failing to eliminate the immediate problems of hunger, inadequate housing, overcrowded schools, and unemployment. Increasingly, many trade unions posed the question raised by a Kansas City worker in 1893: "When will the workingmen and producers learn that republican and democratic politicians are both tarred with the same stick? They worship only Mammon and care for labor only on the eve of an election."[11]

Beginning in the early 1890s, Progressive members of organized labor questioned whether the Republicans or Democrats would save workers from corporate rule and developed critical political perspectives that ultimately reevaluated the legitimacy of every public institution. In 1892 the secretary of the United Brotherhood of Carpenters and Joiners accused Rochester's business elite of ignoring Christian ethics and human rights through their callous exploitation of labor. "No country offers the advantages to tricksters to amass fortunes while they oppress the poor that this country does," claimed this popular speaker to various labor groups. "Great capitalists who go to church today, and sit in cushioned pews while they listen" to the teachings of the Golden Rule, "and say amen to it, will tomorrow cut down the wages of their employees 10 per cent." Other Rochester workers simply called local capitalists their "natural oppressors and robbers," and understandably so, since roughly one-third of the workforce was unemployed during the depression.[12]

Even organizations such as Rochester's Central Labor Union that resisted formal alliance with the Socialist Party proudly argued as a result of a growing pro-labor mood that "all wealth is the result of labor. . . . The working class, is, therefore, the only socially necessary class in the world. Wherever a non-producing class exists it must live parasitically upon the fruits of the toil of the producing class." During the early 1890s the Central Labor Union of Toledo also overcame its usual political reticence and condemned the board of education for employing nonunion labor in schoolhouse construction and attacked the major parties for their usual habit of not nominating a workingman for the city council. As one worker and Populist warned, "the giant Labor will not always sleep, and he is already stirring from his lethargy and girding on his armor for a fight at the ballot box."[13]

In Toledo, Rochester, and other cities, labor groups greeted Eugene Debs and other national trade union heroes with open arms when they addressed the citizenry, much to the chagrin of Democratic and Republican newspapers. Debs's vision of a Cooperative Commonwealth was ridiculed by defenders of the status quo but offered hope to millions of workers who knew poverty as their only standard of living. "The citizen of the ten-thousandth century," wrote the working-class *Mail* of Kansas City in 1892, "will probably look back to the present period as a most barbarous one, in which men were guided in their business and social intercourse by the most heartless principles. The theory of the survival of the fittest nowadays covers a multitude of sins." The abysmal poverty suffered by some and the high rates of unemployment directly impinged on the welfare of the various strata of the working class, who were the most vulnerable to economic dislocation. The specter of class war loomed large in every city, and newspaper editors reluctantly documented the angry tone of public speeches at labor rallies, celebrations, and parades.[14]

The labor press in Rochester, Toledo, Milwaukee, and Kansas City appealed for social justice rather than charity as the depression of 1893 took its toll on human comforts and basic human needs. While reform-minded women increasingly tried to solve some important problems in the schools—the dilemma of undernourished and ill-clad children, dogmatic teaching methods, and overcrowded classrooms—Progressive workers were more concerned with eliminating the causes of those and similar social defects; they wanted to root out the sources of poverty and undemo-cratic government. As early as the 1890s, therefore, the various elements of grassroots Progressivism demonstrated their own distinctive attitudes toward social amelioration and public policy. More so than organized women, radical working-class associations, virtually all white and all male, urged citizens to move beyond liberalism.

Rochester Labor, for example, asked during this decade of economic cen-tralization not for reforms per se, but for a basic recognition of the rights of labor, equal educational opportunity, and collective ownership of the means of production. The editor of the *Kansas City Labor* endorsed the Social-ist Labor Party in 1895 and claimed that "liberty is the theme—the lack of it the occasion. The dream of earth's oppressed millions is yet to be realized: Liberty, Equality, Fraternity." The *Midland Mechanic* likewise asserted that if workers searched throughout history, they "will find no age when the robbery of [the] earnings of the masses has been more systematic, more shameless . . . than today. There was never a time when the worship of great riches, however badly acquired, was more open than today." Everywhere a glaring contradiction surfaced: "labor produces all wealth and provides the luxuries of the rich; but it clothes itself in rags, lives in hovels, is denied justice and ridiculed by plutocracy."[15]

As working-class anger deepened, trade union criticism of the two-party system that claimed to represent all citizens but seemed more re-sponsive to "plutocracy" accelerated. This nurtured alternative ideologies that found expression in new third parties. Becoming political activists was a difficult undertaking for workers in many cities. Urban radicals realized that the Republicans and Democrats, while tied to the prevailing economic order, had political legitimacy. Progressive union members nevertheless struggled against the apolitical character of their own organi-zations and tried to convince all workers to abandon the major parties. Socialist workers in Rochester, for example, addressed thousands of labor-ers in open-air meetings, pointing out the similarities of capitalist Republi-cans and capitalist Democrats. Agitators asked if it mattered whether workers were crucified on a cross made of gold or silver, in reference to

William Jennings Bryan's famous speech during the presidential campaign during the depression. William Lippelt, a radical trade unionist, implored other workers in 1899 "to abandon the two old capitalistic parties and ally . . . with the Socialistic-Labor crusade in the interests of justice and humanity."[16]

The Populist Party in Toledo similarly urged laborers to reject the major parties at the ballot box in 1894. The editor of its newspaper, *The People's Call*, was like many labor activists enamored with Marx's writings, and he asserted that "some of us have carried torches for one party and some for the other. In this way the wage slaves have played into the hands of their masters and nullified their voting strength." But the Federated Trades Council of Milwaukee, still not formally Socialist but certainly leaning in that direction, utilized this environment of social protest most effectively. Of all of the laboring groups in these cities, the Trades Council became the most highly politicized and ultimately most powerful third party in municipal affairs. It was the most consistent and organized working-class force against capitalism in all of these cities.[17]

The Milwaukee labor experience was admittedly somewhat atypical for American cities, since, as one historian has written, "the alliance of labor and Socialism is the outstanding fact in the history of unionism in Milwaukee. Though Socialism achieved notable success in other cities, nowhere was its relationship with labor as strong and enduring as in Milwaukee." Tracing how the Milwaukee Socialists organized labor into a third-party force reveals some of the special attributes needed for the successful entry of working people into school politics. Other cities, as we have seen, had the potential for similar trade union and Socialist agitation; the Milwaukee trade unions realized this potential. Workers in other cities had their own dynamic qualities, but Milwaukee's socialist working class appeared on the political stage with a special air of bravado and sense of destiny, full of new ideas for educational and social reconstruction. Their history not only highlights the contributions that specific working people and Socialist publicists made to school reform and social criticism, but also illustrates the dynamic character of grassroots Progressivism in one unusual environment.[18]

III

"Crop failures or industrial disturbances may at any moment launch upon us an army of the unemployed and unfed," warned a frightened contributor to the *Nation* in 1899 who feared that, under these circumstances, "the red flag lurks just around the corner." During the long years of the depression, Populism and Socialism competed for the affection of unemployed wage earners, troubled ministers, and other citizens whose consciences were pricked by the suffering in their midst. Populist and Socialist parties formed during the 1890s in Rochester, Toledo, Milwaukee, and Kansas City, where they struggled against the established press and even policemen who sometimes disrupted radical meetings. But the largest obstacle before third-party dissidents was the heavy weight of historical tradition, which supported the legitimacy and hegemony of the two-party system. Fighting tradition and an emerging corporate economy, left-wing political parties nevertheless organized and offered radical criticisms of school and society. Out of depression conditions emerged even more voices of discontent.[19]

Milwaukee's German beer bottlers, Local No. 213, reflected the spirit of the times when it publicized Marx's charge: "Workingmen of the world unite, all you have to lose are your chains." Fashioning the tools for this job was difficult, even for skilled artisans. How could working people drawn from different ethnocultural and religious backgrounds form a phalanx against their employers? How could artisans and common laborers possibly join hands in a class-based assault on privilege? How, radicals asked, could unions that considered themselves apolitical now coalesce into third parties that would challenge the capitalist system and its supporting institutions?[20]

One vehicle for reform was the Populist Party, an agrarian organization whose roots extended back to the Greenback struggles in the 1870s. Best remembered historically for its rural heroes, such as General Weaver of the People's Party, and colorful figures such as "Sockless" Jerry Simpson, Populism flourished in many urban areas in the early 1890s; it was a short-lived though vital third-party movement that permitted alienated voters to vent their frustrations against the regular parties. With a largely working-class base, urban Populists grappled with the problems of industrialism, contributed ideas and personnel to evolving Socialist movements, and provided citizens with a forum to articulate their views on schooling and the capitalist order.[21]

The problems that Populists faced in Rochester illuminated the difficulties in constructing an opposition party. A typical meeting in 1894 "was made up of the believers in about all the –isms held by people outside of the two great parties. There were Socialists, Anarchists, Prohibitionists, members of the Workingmen's Party, Populists, Alliance men, and everything else there is." In an effort "to conciliate the different factions," as one Populist revealed, the party platform incorporated a wide range of demands: free textbooks and pencils for children, the municipal ownership of utilities, the enfranchisement of women, and the direct election of senators. These were common demands of the urban Populists, who supported these ideas long before the major parties showed any real interest in them. But Populist dissidents were politically astute, yet numerically weak. Far in advance of public opinion, they were certainly no match for the established parties. For example, the Populist Party of Toledo enjoyed few electoral triumphs, and its members were best known for bolting into the meetings of Good Government Clubs, hoping to convert these liberals to radicalism.[22]

Reputable newspapers published many editorials that equated Populism with anarchism, free love, and a leadership of ne'er-do-wells. Because Populist and Socialist parties were so similar in terms of clientele and immediate social demands, editors had difficulty separating one from the other, no matter how much they hated both of them. The *Kansas City Star* waved the civil rights of radicals, since a man "carrying a red flag . . . should be arrested" like a drunkard "or dangerous man who is flourishing a deadly weapon." Drawing upon the workers and small shopkeepers who hated the "trusts" and "special interests," Kansas City's small Populist Party ticket in 1892 received its largest support from the Jackson County Farmer's Alliance in the countryside and a handful of local trade unions. Party membership peaked at several hundred individuals, and the Populist challenge was further weakened through internal bickering and factionalism. The nativist American Protective Association infiltrated into several Populist cells and began harassing Roman Catholics, rather than, as previously, the local plutocrats.[23]

By 1896, the urban Populists of Rochester, Toledo, and Kansas City had been unable to lure significant numbers of voters from the major parties. The party had provided a home for some dissatisfied citizens, and the Republicans and Democrats would later incorporate some of its programs into their own political platforms. Of course, leaders of the major parties never adopted the ideological cast in which programs had earlier been framed. Yet the initiative, the recall, the referendum, universal suffrage for both sexes, the income tax, and other innovative ideas first stirred systematically in the minds of the Populists. While Republicans and Democrats during these years debated the merits of protective tariffs and free trade as cures for an ailing economy, the urban Populists doubted whether these ideas fully addressed the problems of an urban and industrial civilization. When the Populist Party fused with the Democratic Party in 1896 and popularized the issue of free silver, it was a repudiation of the complex set of programs and ideas that had energized grassroots Populism.[24]

Until the creation of Branch One of the Social Democratic Party of America in 1897, the local Populist Party was the main voice for Milwaukee's dissident workers and Socialists in the early 1890s. Compared with those of Rochester, Toledo, and Kansas City, Milwaukee's workforce was more ideologically sophisticated and politically influential due to the unique character of its trade union movement. The Federated Trades Council formed in 1888 and united skilled workers from different ethnic backgrounds, especially Germans who became the driving element in Milwaukee unionism and Socialism. Trade unions in other cities were often unable to link with Socialist political movements, but Milwaukeeans accomplished that task during the economic crisis between 1893 and 1897. As a result, Milwaukee would have considerable Socialist and working-class leadership in the schools during much of the Progressive era.[25]

Socialist working-class successes built upon the political traditions of this heavily German city and particularly upon the labor and capital struggles of the 1880s. As early as 1875, newsboys and working-class dissidents hawked copies of *Der Sozialist* on street corners along with the trade union papers of groups such as the Knights of Labor, an important force in the 1880s. Moreover, during Milwaukee's May Day Riots in 1886 a number of workers engaged in massive strikes. Summoned to preserve public order and capitalist interests, the Wisconsin National Guard only aggravated local problems. The troops soon faced skilled and unskilled workers who marched through the city streets armed with rocks, sticks, and clubs to defend themselves. The militia fired almost without warning upon one group of workers, killing and wounding several citizens, including a man feeding his chickens and a young lad dragging his feet to school. Angered by the imprisonment of strike leaders and the antilabor sentiments of the two major parties in the incident, dissidents formed the Union Labor Party in 1888, narrowly missing in its bid to control the city.[26]

Socialists sealed the fate of the Union Labor party by voting for their own competing ticket, thereby weakening the labor vote sufficiently to enable the Citizens' Ticket, a fusion of Republicans and Democrats, to squeeze into office. Not only did this fusion effort convince many radical workers that the Republicans and Democrats were mutual defenders of capitalism, but it also temporarily alienated the laborers from the Socialists, whose few votes had prevented the workers' party from defeating the dominant parties. Between 1888 and 1897, political leaders such as Victor Berger, a German-born dissident and school teacher-turned-Socialist-propagandist, mended their differences with the trade unions while affirming the need for a third party of workers. When the depression threw nearly 40 percent of Milwaukee's laborers out of work, the conditions were ripe for change and political agitation.[27]

The several thousand members of the Federated Trades Council, a growing hotbed of Socialist ideas, summed up the new feeling of the

trade unions in 1894 with its poem "There Must Be Something Wrong."
It reflected the influence of the depression on its reform spirit and highlighted the contradiction of American progress and poverty.

> When the earth produces free and fair;
>   The golden wavy corn;
> When the fragrant fruits perfume the air;
>   And Fleecy flocks are shorn;
> Whilst thousands move with aching head;
>   And sing the ceaseless song;
> "We starve, we die, oh give us bread!"
>   There must be something wrong.[28]

"No Bread, No Work!" was the common refrain in the streets, claimed
one disillusioned comrade. "The bosses buy or build costly mansions,
while they rob their workingmen and pay them starvation wages," wrote
another champion of the unemployed.[29]

Under the dynamic leadership of Victor Berger, who edited the Socialist *Wisconsin Vorwarts* after 1893, the trade unions and the Socialists resolved their differences, laying the basis for their growing influence in
civic life after the turn of the century. After the separate failures of the
Union Labor Party and the Socialist Party in 1888, Socialist and trade
union groups slowly aligned in third-party efforts. In 1893 the Federated
Trades Council, the Populist Party, and the Socialists endorsed the
"Co-operative Ticket," which was a Populist workingmen's party that
endorsed democratic political devices such as the initiative, the referendum, the recall, free textbooks for children, the municipal ownership of
utilities, the abolition of the contract labor system, and the eight-hour
day. Workers achieved few electoral victories, but Berger and his allies
retained their vision of what they termed a party of proletarians.[30]

As the editor of the German-language *Vorwarts*, Berger applauded
the progress of the Populist Party. An active party member, he continually
urged it to move further to the left, believing that "the People's Party
contains the basic elements of an Anglo-American Socialist Party."
Through their active political support of the Populist Party for several
years, the Socialists demonstrated that they could be trusted and would
not abandon the workers, as they had done in 1888. However, Berger
and his associates simultaneously tried to popularize Socialist ideas in
Milwaukee. They met in the 1890s in a Sozial-Demokratischer Verein, in
various Turner athletic groups, and in the Mannerchor, a popular singing
organization with many working-class members.[31]

By 1896 the *Vorwarts* demanded that the Populists endorse a "more
doctrinaire" program for "progressive political action," namely, a state-

ment on the goal of establishing a Socialist state. When they refused, Berger vigorously attacked the party, which expelled him. Berger's actions were prompted by his realization that the Federated Trades Council was ripe for grassroots Socialism. By 1897 the Socialists had their own party, many former Populist members, and the endorsement of the Trades Council. In a somewhat premature obituary, Berger announced the following year that "the Populist Party is dead, it lives in Socialism."[32]

From the turn of the century to the 1940s, the Social Democratic Party was the political arm of the Federated Trades Council and the embodiment of grassroots Progressivism in Milwaukee. Events later showed that the Socialists could reach out beyond their German, skilled labor base, cooperate with women's organizations in many school service reforms, and still offer fresh and biting commentary on education and society. Largely a third-party force during its lifetime, the Social Democratic Party provided considerable leadership in the schools and in municipal politics generally. Populism did survive in Socialist thinking, as Berger had noted, exemplified when the Social Democratic Party adopted many of its programs. But the Socialists added some of their own and integrated them into a tighter ideological framework.[33]

The Milwaukee Socialists and the Federated Trades Council were unique among Populist and trade union movements in the sense that they participated in immediate working-class demands for new social programs but never lost sight of their more radical ends. Like the Social Democrats, many labor groups helped form the vanguard of educational reform in the Progressive era, endorsing school welfare reforms, including free lunches, social centers, playgrounds, medical and dental inspection, and other innovations. The majority of non-Socialist trade union groups often saw these reforms as ends in themselves. Compared with the Milwaukee Socialists, these associations were less powerful, less aggressive, less successful politically, and less willing to entertain explicitly noncapitalist ideologies. In most cities after the turn of the century, when the majority of Progressive reforms in education were implemented, radicals were on the fringe of organized labor movements. In Milwaukee they occupied its center.[34]

When the Social Democrats and the Milwaukee trade unions formulated their ideas on school and society after the depression, they did so in a self-consciously radical framework. They quoted Marx's political maxims freely, sometimes with reckless abandon, but they continually tried to adapt his ideas to an American environment. They would not have any direct power over school reforms until 1909, when they elected their first official representative to the school board. Like women's organizations, they were still developing their ideas and trying to gain community support throughout the 1890s.

By the turn of the century, however, the Socialists were widely identified with a number of social and political demands. In the area of schooling, for example, they fought for some of the Populists' favorite reforms: the use of the schools as community centers, the distribution of free textbooks to children, and public lectures for adults. The Socialists and the Federated Trades Council in 1900 unanimously adopted the following resolution on education, steeped in the language of class struggle: "Bear in mind that of all things most feared by the expropriating capitalist class is Knowledge when possessed by the wage-slave! Knowledge is power." The local Socialists took a broad perspective on social issues and saw the radical efforts as "the American expression of the international movement of modern wage earners for better food, better houses, sufficient sleep, more leisure, more education, and more culture!" The Socialists continually evolved in terms of the types of programs they endorsed, from the direct election of Milwaukee school board members to plans to abolish the United States Senate![35]

It is important to differentiate the various elements of grassroots Progressivism that existed as different groups organized in the 1890s. Each reform group—from the Populists to the Socialists to the women's clubs—had elements of historical uniqueness that should be appreciated and remembered. Yet no group was an island until itself, unaffected by the actions of others or sequestered socially from the dominant forces of the age. Comparisons between the Milwaukee Socialists and the average women's organization illuminate this point. Although groups such as the Woman's School Alliance and the Social Democratic Party formed during the depression, Alliance leadership and membership never shared the long range perspective of, say, Victor Berger, who in 1895 predicted in the *Vorwarts* that within fifty years Milwaukeeans would live in a Socialist state. Organized women did not usually desire the redistribution of wealth and income or working-class control over the means of production, and they never considered themselves Socialists. Yet Progressive women were genuinely appalled by poverty and the existence of undernourished and ill-clad street waifs, and they had a notable social conscience when many Americans adhered to crude Darwinian theories of social survival.[36]

The differences between organized liberals and organized radicals did not rest so much in the immediate social programs they endorsed as in their long-range views. Women often saw reforms as ends in themselves; Socialists saw them as means to larger political revolution and social transformation. Very few organized women shared the ideological assumptions of the Federated Trades Council. The Council routinely argued in 1900 that "when wealth producers live in poverty and idlers roll in luxury, it is very evident that the industrial system which permits such conditions must be wrong, and requires a change." It also affirmed that "as the power of capital combines and increases, the political freedom of the masses becomes more and more a delusion." For all their genuine sympathies for the poor and for the children of workers, liberal women were decidedly bourgeois, whereas the Social Democrats viewed themselves as "a proletarian organization in opposition to capitalism."[37]

These more comfortable women could not have shared the ideological perspectives of factory workers, for their personal life histories and experiences were enormously different. Yet the differences between groups that often cooperated in municipal reform were genuine. A variety of motivations, perceptions, personalities, and interests converged in the making of grassroots Progressivism. Reformers came to support social invention and state intervention for diverse reasons. To women the schools were often perceived as an outlet for a new domesticity. Even though they would rally behind Socialist workers for particular school innovations, women viewed the schools in their own unique terms. Socialists, by contrast, saw their involvement in the schools as one more battle against capitalism and its supporting structure. Schools could not create a socialist state, but it was argued that children needed protection from capitalism in every social institution. Grassroots Progressivism, therefore, had its middle-class and feminine as well as working-class and Socialist roots, growing together in the 1890s like entangling vines that crossed but did not always join. The Social Gospel and Progressive religion added the final stimulus to the growth of municipal reform.

IV

"Nearly all forms of charity and human betterment began in the souls of men and women who had the substance of religion within them," wrote Rochester's famous Social Gospeler, Walter Rauschenbusch, in 1914. "Their impulses of mercy and anger may have been uninstructed but at least they saw and struck before science or government moved." Throughout the depression, new religious and moral impulses nurtured the growing movement toward grassroots reform. Members of women's clubs, labor unions, and third parties frequently asked whether the ancient maxims of the Golden Rule or the Sermon on the Mount had real meaning in modern America. Could the ethics of Jesus Christ resolve the contradictions of progress and poverty? Could they define proper ethical behavior in the classroom and on the shop floor? More fundamentally, could one create a morally just social order in a land dominated by the principles of corporate business ownership and management?[38]

Community debates in the 1890s over the nature of society and the institutions that sustained it often centered on ethical beliefs derived from American Protestantism. Religious ideals motivated many mothers, artisans, and socialists. Calls for justice, often colored by a millennial tone, echoed throughout the period and exemplified the power of spiritual values in grassroots reform. Throughout the nineteenth century, for example, Protestantism was a key element in the American labor movement. Its influence was contradictory. On the one hand, it taught values that employers would especially applaud such as hard work, application, delayed gratification, sobriety, and respect for private property. On the other hand, Protestantism at times emphasized the solidarity of human beings and the notion of a fair wage for honest labor. Religion tied workers to the capitalist state, but it also enabled them to criticize businessmen who failed to treat workers fairly, never mind as brothers and sisters.[39]

The Social Gospel emerged across urban America during the depression of the 1890s, reaching especially high visibility particularly in Toledo during the mayoralty of Samuel M. "Golden Rule" Jones from 1897 to 1904. Jones became the leading educational reformer in Toledo by the turn of the century, and, like many grassroots activists, his involvement in civic agitation cannot be understood apart from his religious beliefs. Religious sentiments contributed greatly to the origins of Progressivism. Milwaukee became famous for Socialist rule, Toledo for the Golden Rule.

Jones's rise to power and national fame occurred at a time when American Protestantism had reached a turning point. The social classes produced by industrial capitalism fragmented the attitudes of urban citizens toward their religious institutions. Workingmen abandoned the Protestant churches by the thousands in the Victorian era, yet retained a fervent faith in fundamental Christian ethics that they believed were ignored by the modern church. Protestant churches overwhelmingly stood on the side of capital and order in labor disputes, and ministers routinely inveighed against labor unions, socialism, anarchism, and those who called for the redistribution of wealth and power in the market place. By the late nineteenth century, the many Protestant churches had become institutions "where ill-clad worshippers were unwelcome and where the Nazarene himself would have been snubbed." By the 1890s, many workers disgusted with the two-party system as well as the church found solace and solidarity in unions and third-party movements. Progressive workers lambasted the selling of church pews, the alleged capitalist domination of formal religion, and the failure of Protestant ministers to base their institutions on fundamental Christian values such as "brotherhood" and justice for the poor.[40]

At a meeting in Rochester in 1893, several hundred workers hooted "jeers and sneers" against the church when one agitator reported that ministers refused to open their institutions as lodging houses. "It was very evident that the majority of those present had no friendly feeling for churches or ministers," contended one participant. But that did not mean that working people were irreligious. "We believe in the fatherhood of God and the brotherhood of man," asserted Rochester's leading Populist, who went on to attack those "good people who pray for the laboring men one day in the week and prey off them six days." The time must end when one class enjoyed "themselves at the Lord's table and fill[ed] themselves with wine and bread while the other class is compelled to do the fasting."[41]

In city after city, workingmen and others educated ministers and priests on capitalist ethics and the anti-Christian ways of the modern church. Toledo's Central Labor Union in 1893 patiently listened to the Populist gubernatorial candidate. He was given a hearty round of applause when he called for an end to nativism, business monopoly, and religious prejudices that divided Protestant, Catholic, and Jewish workers. This Populist then attacked the churches for their failure to champion the side of labor and the teachings of Jesus. "The gospel of Jesus dealt more with the labor problem than with soul saving," he claimed.

> The Master, himself a carpenter, had formed a labor organization, which acted for the benefit of soul and body. The twelve not only studied economics, but also struck the labor problem, and the Master saw that the only way to deal with the money changing robbers was to drive them out. Then the bosses of the dominated political party set their heelers to work at the beck of the bankers, and three days after they crucified the Savior.[42]

The labor, socialist, and populist press repeatedly emphasized Jesus' working-class roots, his obvious support for labor unions, and his empathy with the common people. His life sharply contrasted with the institutions founded in his name.

The Federated Trades Council in Milwaukee, whose Socialist members were condemned by Catholic priests as atheists, struck the common blow against the established churches. If the churches, like Jesus, believed in brotherhood, why did they attack strikers and print their sermons on nonunion presses? "While urging upon their faithful followers the practice of sympathy and charity for their fellow men, they conduct their business altogether on the mercenary and skin-flint principle." The working-class

Kansas City Mail similarly asserted that since the church "had forgotten the simplicity and love of Jesus, its founder," the "church proper has almost entirely lost its hold upon the working people and the vast under-crust of society which has no visible means of earning a living." A contributor to the *Midland Mechanic* later in the decade argued that Jesus was murdered for his sympathies for the poor. Moreover, he argued, "any branch of the church that is not in the van of progressive reform movement has outlived its usefulness."[43]

Leading trade union leaders and third-party advocates directly challenged the authority of Protestant ministers in local communities. Fewer than half the people of Rochester, Toledo, Milwaukee, and Kansas City in 1890 were communicants in the various churches, and the outspoken criticisms now lodged against them demanded thoughtful responses. The percentage of communicants of the entire population ranged from a low in Kansas City (24 percent) to higher figures for Milwaukee (33 percent), Toledo (40 percent), and Rochester (44 percent). Moreover, in the latter three cities, Catholics, who emphasized church attendance more than Protestants, formed more than half of the communicants. While these were still overwhelmingly Protestant cities, new Catholic immigrant Poles and Italians in particular added to their religious diversity. Older Protestant churches, therefore, faced challenges from new immigrant populations as well as angry Protestant workers, setting the stage for the Social Gospel.[44]

Advocates of the Social Gospel in local cities tried to overcome a generation of hostility between workers and the Protestant churches in the 1890s. In Rochester prior to the 1890s, for example, "workingmen were more frequently admonished than defended" from the pulpit. Ministers often viewed labor unions as anarchist led and Devil inspired, and workers were often called drunkards. "The men who cry the hardest against capital are those who are beggared by profligacy," announced one Protestant minister in 1890. In 1894 a local Baptist agreed that workers were alienated from the church, but he nevertheless placed the burden on the workers to end their estrangement from God's messengers.[45]

The Social Gospel was an essential ingredient in Progressive reform, even though advocates of social Christianity were a minority among the clergy. The majority of ministers opposed innovations such as the "civic church" and the "institutional church" that aimed to bridge the gap between religious institutions and the working class. As Rauschenbusch himself recalled in *Christianizing the Social Order* in 1912, "We were few and we shouted in the wilderness." It was the exceptional minister indeed who emphasized the radical side of Christianity that stressed "the fatherhood of God and the brotherhood of man."[46]

Industrial workers, not the Protestant clergy, most vocally endorsed the Social Gospel. Hostile to churches but not religion, many radicals turned to the teachings of Christ and primitive Christianity as the depression of the 1890s added new uncertainties to working class life. Undoubtedly, the basic Christian values of brotherhood and justice for the poor held particular meaning to wage earners during this period of acute social tension, economic disorder, and dissatisfaction with the evolving political system.[47]

This was the social context in which "Golden Rule" Jones rose to power as the leading grassroots reformer in Toledo. A conservative businessman until the depression of 1893 reoriented his thought, Jones was one of the most popular figures in Toledo's history, a folk hero whose memory lived on for decades after his death in 1904. He was a catalyst for educational and social reform in Toledo, revered by the working classes as well as by women's groups that applauded his Christian activism. By the turn of the century one of the handful of radical mayors in the urban Midwest, Jones was the secular embodiment of the "new religion" and one of the most colorful municipal reformers of his generation.[48]

Jones's early life, a tale of rags to riches, obscured the qualities that would make him the leading Progressive critic of capitalism in Toledo in the 1890s. Born in Wales in 1846, Jones settled in New York with his parents as a young child and received thirty months' worth of public schooling. He worked in a sawmill and on a steamboat and then traveled to the boom oil fields of Pennsylvania to seek his fortune. He faced a labor system that exploited men with long hours of work for relatively short pay. Jones migrated from town to town searching for work, at one point sneaking out of a boardinghouse without paying his bill. His personal experiences with poverty did not initially cause him to question the legitimacy of the capitalist order. Yet he never forgot "the feeling of utter desolation that possessed me as I walked up the crowded street of the bustling town, with my grip in hand, not knowing how or where I was to pass the night."[49]

Luckily, he landed a mechanic's position in a local boom town, survived by living communally in a tent with several workers, and ultimately abandoned western Pennsylvania for a position in Lima, Ohio, the site of another oil boom. By this time, Jones had invented a device revolutionary in the oil industry called a sucker rod, which drew oil from the ground with great efficiency and ease. He moved to Toledo in the early 1890s, where he successfully mass produced his invention at the Acme Sucker Rod Plant. By the middle of the business depression, however, Jones was transformed from an ordinary manufacturer to one of the leading radical thinkers in the city.[50]

Instead of finding total happiness in Toledo, Jones was shocked when he confronted the basic contradiction of American society: progress and poverty. Jones had not lived a sheltered life. He had seen numerous men begging for work in the oil fields and had lived for weeks on little more than bread and beans. None of this seemed to prepare him for city life. Although his plant was relatively small, Jones received hundreds of pitiful appeals for work as the depression deepened across the city. An unlettered woman made a typical plea:

> having heard so much about you and your kindness to the poor I come to you . . . please don't think we are biggars [*sic*] for we are not but our father above tells me to lay this before you my husband has no work and has had a felon on his thumb for the last eight weeks and you know what that means for a poor man with three children to keep clothing almost gone back in our rent and hardly enough to eat some days now my husband is willing to work and is a good christian man but sickness and no work has brought us where we are.[51]

As Jones later recalled, "I think the first real shock to my social conscience came when the swarms of men swooped down upon us. . . . I never had seen anything like it; their piteous appeals and the very pathos of the looks of many of them stirred the deepest sentiments of compassion within me. I felt keenly the degradation and shame of the situation."[52]

Like the Socialist working-class poet of Milwaukee, Jones believed that something was fundamentally wrong. He therefore aggressively searched for explanations to the problems of unemployment and poverty. A regular church attendant, he rejected the usual belief that poverty resulted from the intemperance and indolence of the workers themselves, finding it a poor explanation for the plight of the hundreds of men who begged him for a job. He told Henry Demarest Lloyd in 1897 that perhaps ten thousand people were unemployed in Toledo alone. "The rather anomalous spectacle confronts us that, while the streets are full of idle men, our banks are full of idle money." "Poverty," he wrote, "is too widespread a disease to account for it by cataloguing a few individual frailties. . . . To blame the unfortunate creatures themselves, to pharisaically point to their lack of thrift, their large families, and so forth, is to treat a large subject in a trifling way."[53]

During the depression, Jones discovered answers to contemporary social problems in ancient Christian beliefs. He believed that the practice of the Golden Rule and the basic tenets of Jesus' teachings would establish a veritable Heaven on Earth. Soon after his arrival in Toledo, Jones led a study group formed by Toledo's most radical minister, the Reverend George D. Herron of the First Congregational Church, who later became

one of the nation's leading Christian Socialists and a member of the
Socialist Party. Jones turned to the Bible, to Marx, to Tolstoy, to Whitman,
and to a host of Social Gospel writers whose essays now appeared in
religious and lay periodicals. He invited feminists and radicals to Golden
Rule Hall to address the workers and interested citizens. He even visited
Chicago's Hull House, and Jane Addams claimed that he was the only
person ever to receive a standing ovation from a radical study group that
met there in the 1890s. His ideas were simple, but were ultimately endorsed by the labor unions and women's clubs across his adopted city.[54]

Besides corresponding with reform leaders and Socialists across the
country, Jones read and reread the Bible and particularly the Sermon on
the Mount, now his greatest source of inspiration. He became convinced
that the only solution to injustice was the application of the Golden Rule
and ideals of brotherhood to everyday experience. He came to agree with
trade union leaders, Populists, and Socialists who felt that Christianity
as expressed by Jesus' life was poorly represented in the modern church.
"It seems to me the Church, instead of getting a few out of the world
into a place of safety, needs to do as Jesus did: get himself into the world,
in order that it may save all." He repeatedly blamed the churches for
their failure to lead modern campaigns for social justice, and announced
that "I believe in Equality, my dear brother. . . . I believe that poverty and
crime are results of social injustice, and above all things, we ought not to
call our civilization a Christian civilization; for when we have a Christian
civilization according to Jesus, we shall have the Kingdom of Heaven
here upon earth."[55]

Jones first applied his new beliefs at his factory. Social service became
his chief concern. Unlike other Toledo manufacturers, he viewed industrial time discipline as dehumanizing and alienating. He therefore replaced the time clock with a tin sign that hung on the wall and read,
"Therefore Whatsoever Ye Would That Men Should Do Unto You, Do
Ye So Unto Them." The Golden Rule, this infamous crank argued, was
the only rule needed anywhere in society, including the factory. "My
belief in Equality," he asserted, "has led us to undertake the experiment
of running a shop without 'bosses,' 'rules,' or 'discipline.' I believe the
way to make people better is to believe them, to trust them, rather than
to 'boss,' 'rule,' 'govern,' or 'force' them."[56]

Jones was disillusioned with how factory life separated individuals
into employers and workers and how human beings loved Mammon
rather than one another. He repeatedly asserted that factories made profits
but "unmade" people by treating them as mere "hands." To undermine
class distinctions and industrial abuses, Jones established the city's first
industrial health plans for workers, paid vacations, profit sharing, higher

pay, and a shorter workweek; and he inaugurated picnics and excursions to the parks for workers and their families. Then this poorly schooled but highly educated man started to write weekly sermonettes to his workers, emphasizing the iniquities of capitalism and the importance of human brotherhood. Jones set up the Golden Rule Band and the Golden Rule Settlement House, and instead of expanding his factory, at one point established a free Golden Rule Park and playground for area children. Social service became the dominant note of his life.[57]

It is not surprising that several labor unions applauded Jones's emergence as a Christian businessman, something Jones himself regarded as a contradiction in terms in a capitalist society. The *Toledo Union* first urged Jones to run for public office. Here was a man who ate his meals with his workers, joined them in their singing society (and entertained them with his violin), and actually tried to practice the Golden Rule. Here was a man who would defy the ministers, manufacturers, Pastors' Union, chamber of commerce, major newspapers, and various institutional voices of respectability and still easily get elected to office. In 1899 he won nearly 70 percent of the vote for mayor even though all the above groups opposed him and he ran without the support of either major political party. He became a symbol of third-party, working-class, and Socialist-like protest in Toledo in the 1890s, a unique example of the forces that converged in urban grassroots Progressivism.[58]

Jones's desire for a kingdom of God on earth was only the most dramatic example of how religious enthusiasms motivated a number of reformers in the depression years of the 1890s. Jones and his Christian brethren told "the tale of a new time,"

> Of a world that surely will be,
> When men live [as] comrades and lovers
> All rancor and hate under ban,
> And the highest and holiest title
> Will be that you're known as a man.[59]

Continually affirming his faith in the dignity of all men and women, he championed a full program of municipal socialism during his tenure as mayor and in particular denounced nativist groups, racists, and antisuffrage organizations. As he told one minister, "I see in every human life a child of God, and as I look upon them, they all appear to me as People, just People, some of them have had opportunity, thousands and millions have never had any."[60]

Christian ethics, therefore, was a salient factor in the evolution of this important Progressive reformer. It was part of the exciting social developments that changed Rochester, Toledo, Milwaukee, and Kansas City in the 1890s, a contributing force to the social and intellectual milieu that ushered in an age of educational innovation and school reform. The groups that formed in the 1890s—the clubwomen, the Populists, the Socialists, the resurgent labor unions, and the Social Gospelers—provided much of the grassroots leadership found in these cities by the turn of the century. Individuals ranging from ordinary parents in school associations to articulate Socialist publicists such as Victor Berger of Milwaukee would interact on many school-related issues during the Progressive era, as third-party participation in school reform in local cities reached an all-time high. The precise way in which outsiders could become insiders was the unsolved riddle at the dawn of the new century.

Chapter 4

A "Better Class" of Men

I

By the end of the depression of 1893, numerous voluntary organizations had clearly assembled across urban America. Whether they were middle-class women or radical Populists, grassroots reformers with various political agendas for the schools enlivened policy debates throughout the 1890s. Political participation, as exemplified by voting turnout and civic activism, remained high in urban life during this decade, and these individuals raised serious questions about the nature of schooling and the larger social order. The folklore of Progressive era school officials was that public education, if entrusted to the benevolent care of professional elites, could be truly "non-partisan." However, thousands of men and women involved in municipal reform movements dismissed this as an ideological cloak of new political adversaries.[1]

Few citizens in Rochester, Toledo, Milwaukee, or Kansas City believed that schools could be apolitical. Women who were spat on at the polls and workers whose children sat in rickety school buildings realized that politics was the heartbeat of educational decision making. To understand the ties between politics and the schools, citizens simply had to observe the behavior of business and professional elites, who often lived in the "seal skin" districts and wanted exclusive control over educational policy. Economic elites, of course, had been enormously influential in the very creation of public schools in these cities. Building upon this tradition, a new generation of business and professional leaders surfaced in local communities in the 1890s. They categorically attacked the effort by some community leaders to draw schools closer to the people. Instead, elite reformers wanted to consolidate their influence over the economy and vital social institutions such as the public schools. For that reason, Victor Berger would argue years later that contradictory forces vied for mastery in the schools.[2]

The timing of movements to reorganize school boards was hardly fortuitous, and it is not surprising that those who benefited most from economic change championed particular school reforms. Monopoly capitalism slowly triumphed in industrial America in the late nineteenth century, as fewer and fewer citizens controlled the workplace or owned the means of production. In this context, schools became an important testing ground for this new wave of political leadership based on the rise of industrial capitalism. The most radical elements of the grassroots challenged the designs of these elite reformers, whose efforts to centralize and professionalize school administration provoked the first major educational conflicts in urban America during the Progressive era. In an age when a broad variety of competing interests believed that the state, through its schools, should increase its holding power over children by changes in the curriculum and the adoption of innovative social services, the question of who would rule the world of education was vitally important.[3]

Schools, therefore, were tugged in diametrically opposed directions during the late nineteenth and early twentieth century. Aware that schools shaped in an earlier phase of development were ill suited for an industrial age, urban elites actively endorsed more centralization and professionalization. Other reformers challenged this position, believing that schools should be brought ever closer to neighborhoods. Many of these community reformers—endorsing Progressive innovations such as playgrounds, social centers, free lectures, district high schools, and penny lunches— were hostile to school board reform, some were ambivalent, and others had good reasons to join in the assault on ward-based boards of education.[4]

Since school board centralization was triumphant across most of urban America during the early twentieth century, many historians have emphasized this aspect of educational change and ignored the persistent opposition it engendered throughout the period. Centralization augmented the power of school superintendents and led to changes in school board membership. Some writers have even argued that school boards before the 1890s represented "the poor and the disinherited." Ward systems of school governance did allow a minority of male citizens of middling status to serve on boards of education; centralized school boards, by contrast, favored the new business and professional leadership emerging in the city. But centralization, however important during the Progressive era, was never a monolithic force that crushed its opponents. Socialists, trade union members, organized parents, Progressive women, and other politically active citizens fought for community-based programs and school innovations in a sometimes hostile political environment. Rather than simply complain about the effects of centralization, coalitions of grassroots reformers elected their own representatives to the school board, lobbied for neighborhood improvements, and made the schools more responsive to local needs than they otherwise would have been.[5]

Like their successors, ward leaders on school boards before centralization could be illiberal, insular, petty, vindictive, and devious as well as fair,
thoughtful, and responsive to the citizenry. The ward system provided
avenues of social mobility and respectability for ethnic leaders as well as
for nativist bigots such as Guy Major of Toledo, the local champion of
the American Protective Association. Centralized school boards similarly
counted among their numbers narrow-minded efficiency experts as well
as outstanding Socialist women such as Meta Berger of Milwaukee, who
defended working-class and feminist interests on the school board for
three decades. Women of different ideological persuasions made strides
under the centralized structure that were impossible under the existing
ward system. Fewer cosmopolitan elites served on school boards in American cities under the ward system than was true of Progressive-era boards,
but the pre-1890s was hardly the golden age of urban school systems.[6]

Educational innovation and social welfare reform—from penny lunches
to playgrounds—cannot be understood apart from the constant tensions
between centralization and decentralization that increased over school
board reorganization in local cities in the late 1890s. To neighborhood
activists, the specter of centralized forms of school governance was a
new political problem that every would-be reformer would ultimately
confront. Centralization had the contradictory effect of opening avenues of
influence for women who previously lacked political rights while denying
other citizens inroads into the new power structure. Centralization also
had the unintended consequence of mobilizing Socialists, Populists, trade
union members, and many women who formed the earliest mothers'
clubs and permanent parent-teachers' association in America at the turn
of the twentieth century. The dialectics of school reform was a constant
exchange between those who would centralize and those who would
decentralize power.

II

The national trend toward school consolidation at the turn of the century
was clearly reflected in political developments in Rochester, Toledo, and
Milwaukee. In 1900, Rochester's elective, ward-based board was replaced
by a five-member board elected at large. Toledo's ward-based board
similarly fell from power in 1898. A year earlier, Milwaukee's unusually
large, council-appointed ward board was reduced to a twenty-one-member board; it was still ward-based, but was now appointed by a special
four-man committee chosen by the mayor. Unlike these cities, Kansas
City already had a small, citywide elected school board since the 1870s,

and its schools enjoyed a continuity of board structure and elite membership unknown in most American cities. The movements for reorganization
in Rochester, Toledo, and Milwaukee were typical of the period. They
produced new political alignments in the schools and naturally affected
the nature of school innovation and control for decades to come.[7]

In light of the obviously elite character of Progressive-era school
boards, historians often view nineteenth-century boards of education as
bulwarks of democracy, the poor, and the oppressed. While condemning
Progressive-era school boards for their elite backgrounds, many writers
equate educational governance before the new era of centralization with
representative democracy. By comparing and contrasting board membership in these four cities for three separate census years (1870, 1880, and
1890), however, one can highlight the atypical social backgrounds of
school board members even before the Progressive era. Examining board
membership at ten-year intervals misses non-census-year membership
but reveals long-range trends in the social composition of school representatives.

What is striking about board membership over this twenty-year
period in Rochester, Toledo, and Milwaukee is not the number of laborers
or ordinary citizens who served on school boards, but rather the prepon-
derance of businessmen, manufacturers, and professionals. A so-called
age of representative democracy was overrepresentative of the elite classes.
All these cities were becoming more industrial and, therefore, more working class during the period between 1870 and 1890. But school boards
did not include increased proportions of unskilled wage earners, skilled
artisans, or white-collar workers. In fact, unskilled laborers who constituted the bulk of the labor force never even served on these school boards.
In addition, before the 1890s women in these cities were disenfranchised
and blacks were never nominated for office. School boards were all male
and all white.[8]

Ward-based school boards were never made up of the poor or dispossessed. They were primarily the bastion of small entrepreneurs or established businessmen, professionals, or manufacturers who were active in
various civic affairs. President W. J. McKelvey of the Rochester school
board in 1892 characteristically asserted in his inaugural address that
"most of the members of this board are businessmen, or men of experience
in the management of affairs," whose private business talents were invaluable in public service. "Our policy can be stated in four words—business
on business principles," claimed one of McKelvey's contemporaries. "The
board contains successful and honorable business and professional members." Without benefit of detailed collective biographies of their peers,
these men still spoke with authority. In 1870 businessmen and profession-

als constituted 71 percent of the total board membership, a figure that increased to 87 percent in 1880 and 88 percent in 1890. Although several white-collar workers were found on some of these boards, they contained only two skilled workers: a carpenter and a machinist.[9]

The situation was remarkably similar in Toledo. The Rochester school board was elective and ward-based, and increased from fourteen members in 1870 to sixteen members in 1890; Toledo's school board was similarly constituted except that it grew in twenty years from eight to nine members. Toledo's business and professional representatives never constituted less than 87 percent of the total number of members at each census year. Toledoans who were fortunate enough to get nominated by the major parties and then elected to office were commonly referred to as "gentlemen" by contemporary writers. One biographer, applauding the decades-long presidency of Charles W. Hill, captured the essence of noblesse oblige in noting that Hill made the perfection of the schools "the great hobby of his life." It was indeed only one of Hill's many diversions, since he was a land speculator, lawyer, politician, and original founding father of the schools in the 1840s. Less subtle but equally telling was the appraisal of a wealthy German, Charles Zirwas, of Toledo's school board in 1890: "All the members at the present time are men who are themselves actively engaged in business affairs."[10]

The likelihood of broader public representation was only slightly improved on Milwaukee's school board, which grew from eighteen members in 1870 to twenty-six members in 1880 to thirty-six members ten years later. Milwaukee's boards were appointed by local aldermen rather than directly elected by the people. The size of the board, however, was somewhat deceiving, since most of the important educational policy decisions were made by the executive committee, which only included half the total membership for a given year. And even though Milwaukee had an estimated thirty-eight thousand wage earners by 1890, business and professional interests dominated on the school board; they constituted 77 percent of the total membership in 1870, 71 percent in 1880, and 75 percent in 1890. As in other cities, white-collar workers such as petty clerks, cashiers, and bookkeepers in small businesses, banks, and manufacturing plants were more likely to serve than were workers in less prestigious positions. Skilled workers were noticeably absent. The degree to which various working people sought election to the school board is unknown, but Milwaukee's system of representation clearly favored businessmen and professionals.[11]

The great virtue of the ward system in urban America was its geographically representative character, since all classes, races, and sexes were not proportionally represented. Local citizens occasionally expressed disgust and anger at the men who represented them (especially in Milwaukee, where the school board was not popularly elected). Still, the notion that each section of the city should have its own representative enjoyed wide popular support. In theory each ward was equally important in decision making. Yet the theory did not always match the realities of school politics. By the 1890s, Populists, Socialists, trade unionists, and liberal women together criticized the misappropriation of funds, condemned the poor physical conditions of working-class schools and neighborhoods, and in the process demonstrated that not every section of the town was treated equally. Giving credence to this position, for example, was the last report issued by Toledo's ward-based school board. Writing in 1896, a prominent board member complained that business districts had comfortable, well-lighted, and ventilated classrooms. Working-class children in the outlying wards, however, often held makeshift classes in "grocery rooms, empty stores, saloons, churches, cellars, and basements."[12]

A closer examination of those who served on ward-based school boards in Rochester, Toledo, and Milwaukee better explains why certain individuals took advantage of opportunities for educational leadership. Ward school boards well represented the small businessmen and professionals who had considerable visibility and prominence in local neighborhoods, ethnic leaders who were not laborers but entrepreneurs and champions of business enterprise, and neighborhood elites proud of their locale and in search of wider personal and social advancement. None of these cities ever had governing structures that permitted the industrial laboring classes to have much direct influence on official school policy. At-large elections simply ensured the continuation of this undemocratic condition in the twentieth century.[13]

The *Rochester Democratic and Chronicle* in 1898 cynically called the ward school board a "preparatory school for would-be aldermen." Cynicism aside, school board membership gave many political aspirants their first foothold in public life. Numerous mayors, aldermen, county supervisors, and other public officials used school positions as springboards to greater political influence. The German-born Emil Wallber, the mayor who called out the Wisconsin National Guard during Milwaukee's Bay View Riots in 1886, had earlier served on the school board. Milton Noyes, Rochester's school superintendent in the 1890s, was a lawyer who held the longest tenure on the ward school board. Guy Major, a candy manufacturer and linseed oil producer in Toledo, gained prominence as a nativist hero of the American Protective Association: his high visibility on the school board, where he attacked "Romanism" in the schools, helped usher him into the mayoralty in the mid-1890s. The examples for different cities can easily be extended. With short tenure, the typical school board member under the ward system often viewed his position as a way station, a temporary office that would promote future success in social and political life.[14]

For the majority of individuals, school board membership was often a badge of social distinction and an indication of ambition or aspiration. That is not to demean the motives of individuals who sought mobility for themselves or recognition for their ethnic group or social class in the larger political community. Like the men who had constructed these school systems, ward leaders were men of affairs—often neighborhood rather than cosmopolitan elites perhaps—but they were usually unrepresentative of the lower classes and exclusionary toward women and racial minorities. The businessmen who served on school boards prior to the onset of at-large elections were ordinarily not large manufacturers or major capitalists (though they were represented, too). Rather, they included the local jeweler, the grocer, the proprietor of the small cigar shop, even the local saloon keeper. They were not dispossessed men, but small capitalists and entrepreneurs who dispensed beer, candy, fruit, groceries, and news to their friends and neighbors; they were individuals whose businesses served as crossroad meeting places for neighborhood discussions on public subjects and whose visibility and material success made them natural candidates for political office.

In many ways, therefore, the early school boards reflected the social backgrounds of those who helped commercialize American life in the Gilded Age. These were not poor or disinherited men but the backbone of small-scale capitalism. By the same token, later school boards reflected not a nation of shopkeepers but the new wave of large-scale capitalist businessmen, industrialists, and professionals who increasingly dominated the nation's political economy. Men who had risen through the ranks of the ward system rightly saw centralization as a hindrance to their social mobility, an insult to their neighborhood, and a denial of opportunity and representative government.[15]

A definite shift in the types of representatives who served on urban school boards in Rochester, Toledo, and Milwaukee occurred after the turn of the century. The local florist, grocer, hardware store owner, drugstore cashier, machinist, or railroad clerk who might have successfully served on ward school boards earlier lacked the personal and organizational resources to succeed in at-large elections. Their personal contacts with voters were limited to a small geographical area and social group. Moreover, the support of the local ward heeler did little to influence the voters in cities with more than one hundred thousand citizens. This meant that white- and blue-collar workers, who had only modest success under the ward system, were even less successful in many cities in the Progressive era. Milwaukee was one exception, since the socialist working class ultimately controlled one-third of a fifteen-member board after 1910. In other places, such as Kansas City, which had at-large elections since the 1870s, workers had never served on school boards from the earliest days of the schools, and trade union efforts to change the situation in an age of administrative centralization produced negligible results.[16]

In many respects Kansas City's school board in the nineteenth century was a sign of things to come in mass education. On its small at-large elected board in 1870, 1880, and 1890, businessmen and professionals filled every position. While small numbers of white-collar and skilled workers served on ward-based school boards in many cities, Kansas City had an elite-dominated board from the very start. The first school board in 1867, for example, was composed of William Sheffield, a prominent attorney who with Robert T. Van Horn orchestrated several citizens' meetings on education; Edward H. Allen, the vice president of the First National Bank, the city's premier financial institution; Thomas B. Lester, a physician who became the president of the Missouri State Medical Association; Joachim A. Bachman, a wealthy merchant; and Ephriam Spaulding and Henry C. Kumpfh, prosperous realtors. Census data for 1870 indicate that the average total wealth of these men was more than twenty-five thousand dollars, a sizable fortune for these years. Moreover, their total wealth was slightly less than the average wealth of the first twenty-two members of the Kansas City school board.[17]

"No other city in the country has placed continually year after year first-class citizens on their school boards," exulted the Democratic *Times* in 1883. In 1891 the *Kansas City Star* applauded Superintendent James Greenwood's earlier role in convincing the Republican and Democratic Parties to divide the school board between them, resulting in a bipartisan board that was usually called "nonpartisan." "Kansas City took one of its occasionally wise steps when it raised its public schools above the arena of party strife," claimed the *Star*. The schools were not plagued "by the demands of saloon keepers or any particular brand of business industry, by lifelong Democrats or lifelong Republicans, or by pigheaded individuals whose only claim to consideration is that they have always voted the straight ticket, and probably never have read it." By the turn of the century, leading Kansas City citizens commonly wrote that the school board stood above "politics" and party strife and that only "the best and most honorable citizens" could serve. This was "an honor bestowed only upon men of the highest standing in the community."[18]

Working people and ordinary citizens often viewed this situation very critically. In 1894 the working-class *Mail* published its usual but ineffective plea for new blood on the school board, and trade unions throughout the Progressive era who were snubbed by the major parties and defeated in third-party bids aptly termed the school board the "Mutual Admiration Society." Their resentment was well founded. Only thirty-seven different individuals served on the Kansas City school board between 1867 and World War I. Many individuals on the board enjoyed decades-long tenure, and almost all the men were businessmen and professionals, with large-scale businessmen and financiers dominant. Only one white-collar worker, a railroad agent, served on the board during this half century.[19]

A collective biography of this Mutual Admiration Society for these decades demonstrates that the average board member was usually elected to office in his early forties, was often native born (but usually not born in Missouri), and was a man of considerable means and prominence. Even foreign-born members were wealthy and upper class. Several members of the board, such as Patrick Shannon, E. H. Allen, Henry C. Kumpfh, R. H. Hunt, E. L. Martin, and Charles P. Chace, were mayors of Kansas City in the late nineteenth century; many of the lawyers were presidents of the Kansas City Bar Association; and numerous merchants were presidents of the Board of Trade and the Commerce Club. Although the board was officially nonpartisan, it reflected as well as promoted the political ambitions and dominance of select individuals. Kansas City's school board members had considerable social standing and political influence within the major parties; they were a metropolitan elite who formed an inner circle of prestige and power.[20]

The elite status of the Kansas City school board over the decades was promoted by the early establishment of at-large elections and a small school board, and it anticipated future trends in urban school governance in the Progressive era. Who should rule has always been a central issue in the annals of history, and it was never more important than in cities during the Progressive era, when third-party, Socialist, and working-class supporters clamored at the schoolhouse door with a variety of educational and social demands. The end of the ward system in Rochester, Toledo, and Milwaukee was swift, decisive, and full of social import. Its demise and the changing character of school boards were ominous political developments during the early Progressive era.

III

Persistently critical of Good Government leaders throughout the 1890s, the *Rochester Democrat and Chronicle* finally admitted in 1899 that their plan for a small, citywide elected school board deserved popular support as well as encouragement from the major political parties. "Public sentiment will unquestionably approve any change which has for its object the divorce, so far as may be practical, of school management and politics. The system of ward representation now in vogue necessarily gives undue prominence to ward politics in educational matters." The ward boards were marred by "scandals" and were "cumbersome and ineffective," while the proposed reorganization would yield "a more capable class of men." In Toledo, both the Republican *Blade* and the more working-class, Democratic *Evening Bee* concluded a few years earlier that their city's ward-based school board had also outlived its usefulness. The Democratic organ repeatedly enumerated the multiple sins committed by the board. Particularly distressing were the machinations of the schoolbook monopoly, that "slimy octopus whose tentacles wind through and around all branches of our school system."[21]

Administrative change was also a pressing concern in Milwaukee. In 1897 a four-man commission appointed by the mayor sliced the existing school board in half. This reform produced a twenty-one-member board chosen along ward lines. Still, the selection process yielded administrative officers with more elite backgrounds. One critic argued in the *Educational Review* in 1900 that this new board, compared with the older ones, "fails to be in as close touch with the people at large; is self-sufficient with reference to its attitude towards some educational problems; and is composed of the 'better classes,' so-called, a somewhat flexible and indefinite term, but used here to express wealth and social and political prestige—as opposed to democratic methods and democratic ideas. A board which goes into power by virtue of appointment by and thru [*sic*] another board could scarcely be otherwise."[22]

Across urban America in the early twentieth century, traditional structures of school governance crumbled in an increasingly inhospitable atmosphere. The details surrounding school board reorganization naturally varied in different cities, but the pattern of social change was unmistakable. The ward system in the Rochester schools was dead by 1900. The same thing happened two years earlier in Toledo and, in 1897, Milwaukee's council-appointed system was similarly eliminated. Political scandals, financial corruption, and ineffective leadership by ward leaders, when coupled with the growing influence of administrative reformers, spelled doom for the old ways. A rising generation of professionals, businessmen, and especially manufacturers that was often linked to Good Government organizations ushered in a new age of school governance. They were aided by various grassroots Progressive women's clubs and even temporarily by political upstarts such as Samuel M. "Golden Rule"

Jones in Toledo. Most notably, women reformers remembered how rudely they had been treated by ward heelers, who spat at their feet when they tried to vote, ripped up their ballots, and ridiculed the new municipal housekeepers. The new woman soon learned that revenge was sweet.[23]

The actual amount of malfeasance in office by ward leaders prior to reorganization is notoriously difficult to estimate. Good Government leaders, known by critics as the "Goo-Goos," demanded "more efficiency and less politics" and corruption in the schools throughout the 1890s. The Goo-Goos certainly had their own axes to grind, but chicanery and corruption were not unknown under the old system. As David B. Tyack has written, "The 'corruption' so frequently charged should not be dismissed as simply a code word for anti-immigrant or anti-Catholic feeling—though sometimes it was just that." Construction contracts, teaching posts, janitor positions, textbook orders, and school supplies generally were a lucrative means of personal economic advance. In the 1880s, Rochester's school commissioners used pseudonyms on business contracts to line their pockets at the taxpayers' expense. Billing procedures were slipshod; teachers often paid for their jobs, lacked formal tenure, and were intimidated when they tried to vote after school suffrage bills were approved. Every city buzzed with the familiar tales of nieces and nephews of school commissioners unfit to teach who were appointed as teachers, or of businessmen who submitted the lowest bid to furnish school supplies but never received a contract. Dozens of school contracts in Rochester and other cities were vetoed by the mayor because boards refused to advertise or accept competitive bids.[24]

Conditions had so deteriorated in Rochester by 1890 that the city council condemned the school commissioners for "reckless extravagance and loose business methods." It then hired a special investigator to examine the commissioners' books to explore various charges of malfeasance. John Bowers, an attorney who later joined the Good Government League, found a total disregard for itemizing school accounts, numerous examples of fraudulent payments, and sworn testimony by teachers that they had paid for their positions. The president of the school board was Milton Noyes, the future superintendent and an ally of the city's powerful Republican boss. He shrugged off attacks on the ward system with a few profound words. "Intelligent criticism by the public and press is not so much against the system which renders peculation possible," he pointed out, "but rather against the selection of such Commissioners as would make such conditions probable."[25]

Quite mysteriously, nearly a thousand documents gathered by the prosecuting attorney disappeared right before the grand jury convened. Having won their first round against an incipient Goo-Goo, ward officials

enjoyed condemning those who only uncovered "petit larceny on a ten-
cent basis" and were now unable to prove their allegations in court. Ward
leaders refused to be "gibbeted at the crossroads of public opinion." To
demonstrate its keen sense of humor, the school board then resolved to
purchase a safe in which to store its precious documents! This symbolic
gesture of defiance, however, only steeled the resolve of the opposition.[26]

Contracts, teaching positions, and schoolhouse construction in Toledo
also provided lucrative sources for graft. By the late 1890s, normally
competitive Republican and Democratic newspapers assailed the ward
system as an anachronism. The most publicized scandal was in 1897 when
Superintendent A. A. McDonald, a married man, was seen in a Cleveland
hotel with a prostitute. He was supposedly on a "business" trip and she
was reportedly a gift from the American Book Company. When the school
board refused to censure, discipline, or remove McDonald from office, it
caused a scandal across Toledo, producing vitriolic speeches from the
pulpit and lurid headlines in the press. The ward aldermen even passed
a mock resolution that read: "Resolved, That as the board of education
has, by its action, lost the respect of all citizens and there is no further
reason for its existence, that the governor be requested to call out the
militia for the purpose of shooting all the members."[27]

Milwaukee's school board had a special way of handling its own
corrupt public servants, adding fuel to public discontent and legitimacy
to some of the Municipal League's criticisms of the ward system. Over
the decades, citizens had read occasional complaints in both English- and
foreign-language newspapers of graft and corruption in the schools. There
were charges of fraudulent billing practices, conflicts of interest among
businessmen on the board of education, and the perennial problem of
nepotism in teacher hiring and promotion. Nothing, however, matched
the Schattenburg affair, which began in the late 1880s.[28]

August Schattenburg was a well-respected German who served as
secretary of the school board. He was also a crook. In less than two years
he stole more than forty thousand dollars from the operating budget to
cover sizable gambling debts, money that was sorely needed for the
overcrowded schools. What infuriated many Milwaukeeans was not simply the discovery of malfeasance, but the response of the school board
to his behavior. Ward leaders exhibited notoriously bad taste when they
canceled classes and ordered school flags at half-mast on the day of
Schattenburg's funeral; he had committed suicide when his misdeeds
were uncovered, leaving no one for the district attorney to prosecute.
Parent and citizen groups held indignation meetings across the city, many
principals and teachers refused to cancel school, and the city council's
resolution to censure the school board failed by one vote. One educator,
in the *Wisconsin Journal of Education*, wryly noted that "the old story

is repeated—'a good fellow'—gambling—misuse of funds—'doctored' accounts—theft—forgery—suicide."[29]

Through such actions by the ward-based school board of Rochester, Toledo, and Milwaukee, advocates of school reorganization along the lines of "efficient" and "nonpartisan" administrative governance gathered additional strength. Paralleling the rise of the women's clubs, Socialist and Populist parties, resurgent trade unions, and Social Gospelers in the 1890s were Good Government Clubs that evolved in many cities. Dedicated to civil service reforms and business efficiency, these organizations were dominated by new business and professional interest groups. In Rochester, Toledo, Milwaukee, and other cities, they led the charge against ward leadership in the schools.[30]

Joseph T. Alling, a young liberal industrialist who ran Rochester's largest adult Bible class, helped form the local Good Government League in 1893. The league advocated efficiency and honesty in city government, especially in the schools. The same year saw the formation of the Good Government League of Toledo and the Milwaukee Municipal League, both of which fought for the principle of civil service in municipal hiring practices. As early as 1892, Kansas City also had its own Municipal Improvement Association, later renamed the Municipal Reform Committee. Although "ward politics" had never affected their schools, these Kansas City residents as well as their peers in other cities wanted to revolutionize municipal government, whether in the city council chambers or in local boards of education.[31]

As in so many other areas of social and political development in the 1890s, major changes occurred in the character of school administration. These reforms greatly affected the nature of educational innovation for the following two decades. While working-class, third-party, and female challenges against the existing social order echoed throughout the 1890s, business and professional interests reacted swiftly to the excesses of the ward system and possible political threats from below to consolidate their power in the schools and larger society. "Good government," "efficiency," and "nonpartisanship" were the slogans that these elite groups hurled against the ward bosses, but their underlying commitment to the preservation of a hierarchical social structure ultimately made them enemies of all urban radicals. Just where various grassroots forces would align on administrative reform was a critical historical issue on the local urban scene.

IV

Disillusioned Rochesterians suggested various ways to eliminate ward politics in the school in the early 1890s. In 1894 the Women's Educational and Industrial Union urged the election of a University of Rochester professor to the school board to help raise the standard of decision making. A recently revived Citizens' Educational Association, composed mostly of University of Rochester faculty members, returned the favor and proposed the establishment of a five-member board, with the stipulation that three members of the board would be elected at large, that two would be appointed by the mayor, and that at least two representatives would always be women.[32]

The *Rochester Herald*, in turn, offered the alternative conceived by the Republican boss and current mayor, George Aldridge. Aldridge agreed that the school board was too large and unwieldy, dispersing authority and undermining accountability. Attorney Bowers's investigation and the school board's response testified to the need for immediate action. In a spirit of public service, Aldridge favored a small board, which he would appoint! Since the Rochester school board was overwhelmingly Republican in the 1890s, Aldridge's apparent scheme was to reduce the size of the board, keep it Republican, and extend his personal control over his party. Aldridge never feared centralized administrations, for they were sometimes even easier to manipulate than larger ward-based bodies. For now, however, his Republican newspaper expressed the popular view that "upon one point all are agreed. The present board of education is too large for practical purposes, and radical changes are absolutely necessary."[33]

While the Republican boss, the Goo-Goos, the Women's Educational and Industrial Union, the Citizens' Educational Association, and the city council discussed ways to dismantle the ward-elected board, the school commissioners angrily dismissed any talk of reorganization and defended the centrality of geographical representation in democratic polity. When the city council called for a smaller board in 1894, ward leaders responded that this would only introduce "politics" in the schools. Pressure for change nevertheless mounted, from women's demands for new subjects to more threatening proposals for administrative reorganization. The ward board responded that the present system held "the affections of our citizens" and that a change from ward elections would constitute taxation without representation. President William G. Brownell added in 1895 that contrary to some reports, "there was no public demand for a change in our school system."[34]

By 1898, however, some form of administrative reorganization seemed imminent. Ward leaders contended that they were never consulted on any proposed reorganization plans when, in fact, prominent school board representatives vocally attacked various proposals for change and discredited some attempts within the board to fashion some political compromise. At times the ward board sent out contradictory messages to the citizenry. It usually asserted that the ward system was unassailable if democratic government continued, but sometimes took the opposite position. In 1898 the board president attacked reform legislation, then added that "all concede that a small board, consisting of three to five members, whether elective or appointive . . . might result to the city's benefit." While ward politicians failed to act consistently, their enemies struck quickly and decisively.[35]

Rochester's ward-based school board was the victim of a political agreement between Boss Aldridge and the Good Government League. By mid-decade the Goo-Goos had gathered sufficient strength to deny the Aldridge machine several municipal offices, including the mayoralty. The schools were a convenient and lucrative source of patronage for loyal Republicans, but Aldridge decided to cooperate with the Goo-Goos on school centralization in exchange for a free hand in other areas of municipal politics. Good Government workers drafted the Dow Bill in 1898, which provided for a five-member school board elected at large, to take effect in 1900, and Aldridge helped shepherd it through the state legislature. In May of 1898 Aldridge personally explained the virtues of the Dow Bill to Governor Theodore Roosevelt, who signed it into law.[36]

Aldridge's longevity as a political boss in Rochester in the Progressive era rested on his ability to adapt to changing social forces and shape them to his own ends. At the very time he helped destroy ward school representation, he increased this control over the Board of Estimate, which approved the educational budget. In that way, Aldridge gave to the Goo-Goos with one hand and stole power away from them with the other. Moreover, Aldridge deftly altered part of the Dow Bill when it reached the state printer. Without consulting the Good Government League, he added a clause that gave his old Republican crony, Milton Noyes, a guaranteed position as superintendent on the reorganized board. A master politician, Aldridge had eliminated a pack of fellow Republicans from the school board through his alliance with Good Government forces on centralization, but in the process he had actually dealt himself a new hand. The Goo-Goos were incensed by this political sting. Only after the new board demonstrated that Noyes had dipped into the school fund for personal uses was he forced to resign.[37]

Like Rochester, Toledo witnessed a fatal blow against ward representation in the schools late in the 1890s. During earlier years of the decade, various proposals surfaced on how to eliminate politics from the school board, which typically opposed administrative reforms and defended the existing system. Guy Major presented the first serious recommendation for political change in 1896. Like Aldridge of Rochester, Major was a local

Republican leader, but he built his support in Toledo on a somewhat narrow and ephemeral issue: anti-Catholicism. Nativism's electoral appeal reached its apogee in Toledo in the mid-1890s when the American Protective Association helped catapult Major to the mayoralty. Major hated Catholics as well as Progressive women who had meddled in school affairs during his earlier tenure on the school board. As a strategy to remove the few remaining Catholics from the school board, he proposed that henceforth the mayor would appoint a small board and eliminate the ward structure. Women's clubs, trade unions, Populists, and even the chamber of commerce united to prevent the passage of Major's "ripper bill" in Columbus.[38]

Within two years, however, Good Government reformers used the pretext of Superintendent McDonald's escapades in Cleveland and other forms of graft in the schools to crush the ward system. Like Rochester's reform movement, Toledo's effort at administrative reorganization ultimately enjoyed bipartisan support and approval from business, manufacturing, and professional interests. In the name of efficiency, progress, and educational advance, normally rival newspapers such as the Republican *Blade* and the Democratic *Evening Bee* endorsed administrative reform. "There have been jobs in schoolbooks; jobs in school buildings; jobs in furniture; jobs in everything that could be subject to jobbery," claimed the *Blade* in a typical denunciation of political logrolling and corruption in the schools. "Purify the schools. Dump the politicians. Fire out the books and supply companies. Get rid of bribers and men who want to be bribed. Wipe off the slate. Clean out both factions. Run the schools of Toledo in the interest of the scholars," added the *Evening Bee*.[39]

Through dozens of articles and editorials, these major newspapers vigorously assaulted ward leadership in the schools. They exposed the connections between powerful ward leaders and the American Book Company and featured stories on the low morale of teachers. All in all, the press cultivated a congenial climate for reform that enabled a handful of citizens to secure legislative approval of the Niles Bill in 1898. Named for the Democratic legislator who drafted the bill, it replaced the ward-based board with a five-member school board elected at large without party designations on the ballot. With the support of Good Government reformers and various Progressives, the Niles Bill was widely heralded as the turning point in the history of the schools and the beginning of a new era in educational administration.[40]

A number of prominent members of the Toledo Chamber of Commerce formed a delegation in Columbus to support the Niles Bill, including George W. Writner, a realtor who was its secretary, and W. H. Chase, a business executive with Aetna Insurance. Aiding the cause were a number of suffrage leaders and the new Christian Socialist mayor, Samuel M. "Golden Rule" Jones, who wanted to infuse the spirit of nonpartisanship throughout municipal government. Jones fully realized that none of the leading commercial organizations shared his larger concerns with social and educational reconstruction, and the chamber of commerce, wealthy congregations, both major parties, and many businessmen denounced his prolabor campaign platforms.[41]

For a variety of reasons, however, Jones also attacked the ward system and supported administrative reorganization. He believed deeply in the idea of direct nomination, which meant that any citizen with several hundred signatures on a petition could run for office. Jones was himself the dark-horse mayoral candidate of the Republicans in 1897, but he soon left the party and thereafter refused to run on any party ticket. In 1899, he captured every ward in Toledo without the endorsement of any newspaper or political party. Jones saw the removal of school offices from the clutches of the Republican and Democratic Party as an exercise in direct democracy and the only way by which women might gain election to the school board. Progressive women agreed with him. When the Niles Bill took effect in 1898, almost forty individuals ran for office, more than was true under the old ward system, and several of the candidates were women.[42]

The Central Labor Union was ambivalent about the reorganization plan. A vocal minority of the affiliates of the organization applauded the idea of direct nomination. More prescient workers declared in the *Toledo Union* that "organized labor can do more in individual wards toward the defeat of an enemy than in the city at large." When Golden Rule Jones endorsed the eight-hour day, the municipal ownership of utilities, the end of municipal contract labor, minimum-wage legislation, pensions, child-labor legislation, and public-works projects for the poor and the unemployed, the trade unions stood firmly by his side. Many letters in Jones's manuscript collection indicate widespread trade union endorsement for his political stands, and he was a hero of the laboring masses. But on the reorganization plan of 1898, labor leaders had more foresight than Jones. To his credit, he soon joined with parents' groups, women's organizations, and the Central Labor Union in 1904 and successfully petitioned the state legislature for some district representation on the school board.[43]

Many ward representatives in Toledo, like their counterparts in Rochester and Milwaukee, fought strenuously to preserve the old order. Some small businessmen rightly saw their personal avenues of political advancement blocked by the Niles Bill; others undoubtedly disliked the loss of patronage, kickbacks, and power; and still others opposed the reorganization scheme for democratic reasons. William Tucker, for example, denounced all the reformers as elitists and demanded the preservation of the ward-based school board. The president of the William McKinley Club, the president of the school board, a prosperous attorney, a banker and a philanthropist, Tucker resented the prevailing stereotype of ward leaders as grafters. "I believe that the nearer you can get to the people in the matter of selecting of members of our board, the better it will be, otherwise our American system of choosing officers is a failure," he contended in 1898 in a speech against school reorganization. Tucker favored district elections and warned that the rich would dominate on future school boards, "while the outlying districts and the districts containing the great laboring portion of our citizens would be neglected, and these sections are the ones that especially need representation . . . for the wealthy and well-to-do classes are able to secure proper educational advantages for their children, while the poor people are compelled to rely upon our public school system."[44]

Like the ward boards of Rochester and Toledo, the method of selecting school commissioners in Milwaukee that had prevailed since the 1840s ended because of Good Government reform in the late 1890s. With the aid of William Geuder, a prominent German and Republican school board leader, the Municipal League in 1897 convinced the Grand Old Party to endorse legislation that eliminated the system by which ward aldermen appointed school board members. In its place stood a twenty-one-member ward-based board that was appointed by a special four-man commission named by the mayor. Socialist trade unions as well as more moderate working-class groups and small entrepreneurs in the Populist Party assailed the reform. Both the German Socialist *Vorwarts* and the Populist *Daily News* offered readers caustic commentary on school centralization and elite reform.[45]

The aldermen-appointed, ward-based school board of Milwaukee long opposed any shift from the status quo, especially the popular election of its members. The board was insulated from public opinion in the sense that it was not directly elected by the people. In that way ward members were as distrustful of the electorate as were the Goo-Goos, and they opposed the persistent demands of working-class groups for an elective school board. From the 1870s to the early twentieth century, when it helped establish direct elections, the Socialist working class in particular rallied other grassroots organizations against all appointive schemes and in favor of more democratic structures.[46]

In 1872 the Milwaukee school board, dominated by small-scale businessmen and professionals, typically attacked working-class pressure for direct elections, claiming they would only draw education into the "political arena." In the late 1880s and early 1890s, the appointed board rejected similar suggestions for reorganization by external pressure groups. Still smarting from the popular backlash over the Schattenburg scandal, the ward board was implicated in a number of shady financial and real estate deals involving schoolhouse construction. Moreover, the board now had to deal with "faddists" and School Alliance women; the Municipal League, which wanted civil service reform; the *Daily News* and the *Vorwarts*, which wanted large, popularly elected ward-based boards; and the *Milwaukee Sentinel*, a particularly powerful voice for Republicans and Good Government.[47]

The ward-appointed board, already in a precarious political position, only aggravated the situation by refusing to compromise with various urban reformers. It regularly insulted members of the Woman's School Alliance for their meddling and soft pedagogical ideas; it rejected all the proposals of the Municipal League; it opposed suggestions for direct election; and it voted against a proposal to ban nepotism in teaching appointments. The board that refused to bend was broken in 1897, even though many grassroots Progressives opposed the appointive feature of the Municipal League's reorganization plan. The Socialist working class in Milwaukee spent the following several years trying to dismantle this reform and to provide direct election of the school board. Ultimately many women's organizations and parent groups, including the Woman's School Alliance, joined the Socialists in a powerful community movement for direct elections.[48]

The Populists and the Socialists, however, were the major and most consistent opponents of the Municipal League in Milwaukee in the 1890s. They attacked the alderman-appointed nature of the current board of education and questioned whether a four-man commission was anything but a capitalist reform. Drawn even closer together, the Populists and the Socialists often endorsed similar educational programs during these years: free lunches, textbooks, more district high schools, lecture programs, and the free and unrestricted use of neighborhood schools as community centers. These largely working-class groups wanted the schools closer to the people and accurately predicted that upper-class businessmen and professionals would dominate the mayoral commission.[49]

Upon learning of the commission plan in 1897, the Populist *Daily News* offered an alternative: the establishment of three separate, popularly elected district school boards and a larger, ward-based board to guide the educational affairs of the entire city. The Municipal League rejected the plan as inefficient; the school board also viewed such decentralized governance as impractical. The Socialist *Vorwarts* had less well developed proposals, but shared the Populists' contempt for the Goo-Goos. The

Socialists attacked the allegedly nonpartisan commission as a fraud, since the mayor packed the four-man commission with elite members of society as well as his own political partisans. "If we understand the facts correctly, the object of the law was to steer highly political people away from the school board," wrote Victor Berger in 1897. "But it's obvious that this 'capitalist reform' should be simply relegated to the manure heap of political life."[50]

Even earthy metaphors could not prevent school reorganization in Milwaukee. And, as in other cities, clubwomen whose supposedly nonpartisan and feminine qualities disqualified them from political participation helped topple established patterns of social governance. Women's clubs would often cooperate with trade unions, Socialists, Populists, and other political organizations on a wide range of social welfare reforms in the schools during the Progressive era, but in the 1890s they opposed these groups on the question of school board reorganization. Drawn from more comfortable classes, Progressive women often equated ward or district representation with antifeminist politics and, therefore, drove the stake deep within the heart of the ward system whenever possible. They never forgot that ward leaders had insulted them, ignored them at party caucuses, and intimidated them at the polls. The new woman had little to lose with the destruction of the ward system, which she rightly perceived as a bastion of maleness and a deterrent to the new housekeeping.

In Rochester the Women's Educational and Industrial Union, the Local Council of Women, and various suffrage leaders forcefully backed the Dow Bill in 1898, and Helen Montgomery in particular rallied support against the old system. Emily Bouton, a leader in the Women's Educational Club and other voluntary organizations in Toledo, joined Mary Law and other clubwomen in support of the Niles Bill. Shunned by the major parities in the 1890s, Toledo women shared the view of Golden Rule Jones that the direct-nomination features of school reorganization constituted their only hope for election to the school board. Bouton in particular compared the local struggle with Jane Addams's more famous clashes with ward politicos in Chicago. The Woman's School Alliance of Milwaukee, tired of its token position on the school board and cognizant that local aldermen opposed the women's movement, similarly cast its lot with the Municipal League. The Socialist working class would help radicalize many of the members of the Woman's Alliance over the years, finally encouraging them to push for an elective school board. In the 1890s, however, the Alliance and other Progressive women enjoyed their victory over the ward bosses.[51]

By the turn of the century, then, the new woman joined with more influential Good Government advocates to restructure school administrations in Rochester, Toledo, and Milwaukee. Together they built the political structure that parents, reformers, and radicals of all stripes encountered in the twentieth century. The question of who would formally rule in urban education in these cities was partially answered as the new century dawned. The ward-based school boards of the nineteenth century, dominated by small-scale commercial and business elites, never gave proportional representation to all classes, races, or sexes. They did ensure geographical representation of every ward, and their members fought valiantly against a coalition of reformers more attuned to a changing political economy. Ward boards were plagued with problems related to patronage, tyranny over teachers, and alliances with corrupt schoolbook monopolies. Centralized school boards, of course, were never immune from these ills, and many believed that mutual admiration societies were hardly an improvement upon their predecessors.

Chapter 5

An Age of Centralization and Grassroots Reform

I

School board centralization marked the first but not the last round of educational reform in the Progressive era. Reflecting larger economic trends toward consolidation and monopolistic practice, school board reorganization unmistakably altered the character of urban education for decades to come. But centralization often nurtured its opposite. Radicals such as Victor Berger of Milwaukee and wealthy ward leaders such as William Tucker of Toledo opposed centralization for different ideological reasons, but their criticisms of the new educational Pooh-Bahs were shared by many ordinary citizens. The movement toward centralization produced a shifting coalition of opponents, many of whom sought greater community participation in the schools and the inauguration of various innovations to serve neighborhood parents and children.[1]

It is easy to remember the victories of the new power elite within the schools and to forget the struggles of those who resisted elite domination throughout the Progressive era. Now the dominion of wealthy businessmen and professionals, individual boards of education tried to behave like a board of directors in a business, delegating authority to newly empowered experts such as superintendents. But schools were not factories, and even centralization could not silence a host of educational critics. Despite the illusions of educational rulers to establish a nonpartisan school system, politics remained a central feature of educational life. Ward leaders, Progressive trade unionists, Socialists, Populists, ethnic minorities, and even middle-class clubwomen in some cities who were excluded from reorganized school boards did everything possible to peacefully challenge centralized elites. Competing views of education and the state clashed throughout the early 1900s and enlivened the urban scene.[2]

Following the successful movements for school board centralization, an impressive assemblage of individuals in this age of intense citizen activism continued to view schools as a main vehicle for progress and social improvement. "This is a great age for the phenomenal growth of organizations," noted the *Rochester Democrat and Chronicle* in 1897, and the schools remained a prime concern of countless voluntary associations. Citizens often agreed on the value of schooling, as they had done in the antebellum period, but they disagreed markedly on who would direct social innovation in a rapidly changing society. Centralization often drove dissimilar groups into common cause against unresponsive school boards: socialists and workers who saw educational reform as integral to class conflict, feminists who viewed educational struggle as central to women's rights, and occasionally ward leaders who disliked innovations but disliked their school board successors even more.[3]

Tensions between those who advocated centralization and those who wanted to revitalize neighborhood schools through educational innovation were visible throughout the Progressive era. True to the days of their founding, public schools were the site of intense conflict. Some citizens, architects of a new economic and educational order, believed that schools could prepare youth to accept the existing industrial system and find their place within it. Other members of the community—virtually disenfranchised educationally by the centralization movement—were as passionate in their belief that, if they firmly resisted elite dominance, schools could still become more democratic and responsive institutions. "The thought of social service is in the air," claimed one observer in the *School Journal* in 1901, and this well described the alternative perspectives on the role of schools in the community nurtured by the grassroots.[4]

Indeed, the aim of expanding the social functions of the school often united many voluntary organizations throughout the first two decades of the twentieth century. Socialists and trade union members were usually more critical of school centralization than were women, largely because of their class position, yet all of these groups believed that state-sponsored welfare reforms could greatly improve the lives of children and youth. All these grassroots Progressives rejected the capitalist dicta that schools were factories and youth were raw materials. Rather, these citizen activists often resisted and challenged businessmen and their metaphors in an attempt to draw schools closer to local neighborhoods. The realities of centralization meant that critics did not live in a political world of their own choosing, but they nevertheless refused to cower before the power of the centralizers.

As they struggled to secure representation on centralized school boards and cooperated to force elites to adopt educational innovations, various members of the grass roots became an integral part of a movement to broaden the social mission of the schools. They fought for minority representation on the board of education, vacation schools, playgrounds, medical and dental inspection, breakfast and lunch programs, district high schools, special schools for the diseased and disabled, evening schools, public lecture series, and the use of the schools as social centers. Many of these innovations existed, to be sure, within a centralized framework that could undermine their effectiveness, yet local reformers actively challenged those who favored pinchpenny economies and the elimination of lay influence in education. School board centralization, therefore, only seemed to intensify the demands of those who wanted to increase the service role of urban schools.

The triumph of business reform in the schools was never complete during the Progressive era, largely because of the activist stance of Socialists, Progressive workers, liberal women, and other groups that had surfaced during the depression of the 1890s. These organizations often lacked the power and resources to dominate in local cities, yet they prevented total elite control as well. The grass roots refused to abandon political action after the initial triumph of centralization in the schools. In fact, the history of the Independents in Toledo and the Social Democrats in Milwaukee showed how third-party forces could link educational reform to broader community struggle. For various reasons, third-party activists had more trouble mobilizing against the system in Rochester and Kansas City, but even there educational reform remained embedded in wider community efforts at civic reconstruction. Fighting against more powerful foes, the grass roots nevertheless attempted to coalesce to build a new educational world and urban community.

II

During the Progressive era, Toledo became famous as the city of Golden Rule Jones. Milwaukee, by contrast, was renowned as the home of Victor Berger and a variety of Socialist leaders. Jones was one of the most famous municipal reformers of his day, a prominent peace advocate and champion of labor unions, women's rights, and Christian Socialism. Jones symbolized the social justice, religiously based orientation of grassroots Progressivism. At his death in 1904, fifty-five thousand mourners paid their respects to this charismatic crusader for the Golden Rule. Working-class poets penned eulogies in his memory, activist women applauded his Christian Socialism, and immigrant groups marched in line to pay homage to a colorful leader. "Toledo has become notorious as the city of Sam Jones, 'Golden Rule' Jones," wrote a Socialist who disliked him in 1905. "He died a few months ago before the expiration of his term and his name is revered by the thousands in this city."[5]

A similar outpouring of respect occurred at the funeral of Victor Berger in 1929. He was killed by a streetcar, owned appropriately enough by the private transit company he had long opposed. The nation's first Socialist congressman and the man who introduced Eugene Debs to the writings of Karl Marx, Berger was the leading Socialist in Milwaukee throughout the Progressive era. A former cattle puncher and school-teacher, Berger in the 1890s edited the *Wisconsin Vorwarts*, which was the official paper of the Socialists and the Wisconsin State Federation of Labor. Later he edited the *Social Democratic Herald* and the *Milwaukee Leader*, both nationally syndicated Socialist newspapers. Like Jones, Berger and the Social Democrats struggled for widespread social and political reform, making educational improvements one aspect of larger grassroots agitation. In both Toledo and Milwaukee, movements for social improvement were fashioned out of the various reform groups emerging out of the depression decade.[6]

Although Berger's Social Democratic Party ultimately had more far-reaching and long-lasting effects in municipal and educational reform, school reform remained integral to Toledo politics after the passage of the Niles Bill in 1898. The fight for school improvements was waged by Golden Rule Jones and his successor as mayor, Brand Whitlock, who assembled a loosely knit Independent movement that controlled Toledo from 1905 to 1913. Educational change in Toledo and Milwaukee was political Progressivism writ small, one significant aspect of broader political movements by men and women who either disliked or abandoned the Republican and Democratic parties. Grassroots Progressives—workers, club women, Social Gospelers, and third-party dissidents—occasionally formed significant voting blocks on local school boards after the turn of the century. More typically, however, they remained an issue-oriented coalition that pressured school boards to implement a variety of social welfare reforms.

Jones and Whitlock forged disparate voluntary groups into a cohesive movement for political and social change. Interaction between liberals, radicals, and utopians on school reforms was common throughout the Progressive era, and Toledo's mayors helped fashion a reform platform that appealed to the electorate. In fact, the Republicans and Democrats were excluded from the mayoralty from 1897 to 1913. Moreover, Whitlock's Independents controlled the city council for several terms, until the Republicans crushed them at the polls. Less Socialistic, flamboyant, and colorful than Jones, Whitlock nevertheless shared his mentor's support for women's suffrage, labor unions, and the legal rights of the poor. Through such leadership Toledo was nationally renowned as a city dedicated to human rights and social justice.[7]

Unlike Whitlock, who constructed a loosely organized political organization, Golden Rule Jones was successively elected to office on the basis of his personal appeal and social beliefs. He never formed a political party, with the result that conservative Republicans dominated the city council and often undermined his policies. Eugene Debs, a close friend, urged Jones in 1898 to become a member of the new Social Democratic Party. Jones responded that the Republicans and Democrats were "purely capitalistic," yet he eschewed all parties. His independent status often angered other partisans on the left as well as the chamber of commerce, the Pastor's Union, and others frightened by his socialist, feminist, prolabor ideology. After running as a dark horse candidate for mayor for the Republicans in 1897, Jones quickly broke with the party and ran as an independent until his death three terms later.[8]

Jones's ability to admit his mistakes in endorsing school board centralization in 1898 solidified his position within the labor movement. At the same time, he became a hero of local parent organizations and women's clubs. A number of these grassroots forces coalesced around him to agitate for political and educational reform, leading the way to the restoration of partial district representation on the school board in 1904. By the turn of the century, the reorganized, consolidated school board advanced the ethic of "business efficiency" and opposed "fads and frills" such as kindergartens, playgrounds, the extended use of the schools, and other innovations known locally as the "new education." J. Kent Hamilton, a prominent attorney and former mayor, dominated in the restructured board from 1898 to 1904 and opposed curricular innovations and anything associated with Golden Rule Jones. One of the sponsors of the Niles Bill, Hamilton was a regular Republican who resented Jones's bolt from the Grand Old Party and support for district representation.[9]

The election results for Toledo's new school board in 1898 revealed that neither women, the working classes, nor the advocates of the new education would find much support from the new educational establishment. The new board was hardly more congenial to school innovation than the now displaced ward heelers. All five new school board members were either attorneys or businessmen and were drawn from the central city business districts. As ward leaders and labor had predicted, the outlying working-class wards, particularly the populous East Side, were excluded from representation. The new school superintendent, William W. Chalmers, unlike his predecessor, avoided the lures of Cleveland prostitutes, but he, too, opposed innovations and disliked outside interference. Moreover, women who believed that direct nominations and at-large elections would promote their interests watched Mary E. Law run sixth in a field of nearly forty. The small size of the board effectively denied her office. By 1901 this prominent kindergarten instructor, suffrage leader, and clubwoman attacked the reorganized school board in the *Toledo Blade* as "a self perpetuating machine, which takes its form largely from the dominating mind, progressive or non-progressive, honest or corrupt."[10]

Criticisms of the new school board mounted in the early 1990s. In 1902 one citizen, who likened the board to the "Pooh Bah in the Mikado," complained that all of the representatives were from the "seal skin districts . . . while those districts most largely represented in attendance at the schools were obtaining absolutely no representation." "Your board does not represent the laboring classes of the city. You . . . are all businessmen," protested an angry labor leader. "You know you never are in touch with the poorer classes, whose children form four-fifths of the school children." Both women and working people as well as entire sections of the city lacked representation on the school board. Tempers flared and a grassroots coalition for administrative reorganization assembled.[11]

With cosmopolitan business and professional elites from the silk stocking districts ensconced on the school board, parent groups joined with Golden Rule Jones, the Central Labor Union, women's organizations, and older ward leaders such as William Tucker to demand a reorganization of the reorganized board. A group called the Broadway Civic Club formed in 1898 and included mothers and fathers from the South Side, a working-class area. These citizens strongly opposed at-large elections, favored district or ward representation, and called for the inauguration of the new education. First they demanded the end of cramming, overtesting, and the use of the rod. Then they planned to destroy the "oligarchy" in the school administration, to throttle the school superintendent, and to empower teachers to select texts and school materials. Another parent-citizens' group was the Complete Education League, which had citywide membership. The league was the brainchild of Golden Rule Jones and his followers, who lobbied for social welfare programs, district representation, and working-class members on the board of education. "Let us get nearer the people through district representation," wrote the league in 1902, "and Toledo will take her stand with cities which are placing the needs of the child first."[12]

The Complete Education League was the main vehicle through which Jones united various grassroots Progressives behind the new education and a new phase of school board reform. In his *Annual Reports*, given to the city council, as well as in countless activities, Jones supported the establishment of playgrounds, kindergartens, social centers, and other educational innovations. He viewed these reforms as an expression of Christian service and brotherhood, and his religious beliefs colored local

Progressive reform. Jones never sought accolades for social service reforms, since "the Christian law is service for service," a foundation of the Golden Rule. The service ethic appeared prominently in his 1901 *Annual Report*, which the local press lambasted for its utopian qualities. "The only justification that can be offered for the right of a government to exist and to levy taxes upon the people to pay its expenses is that it makes conditions of life easier and better for the people than they could possibly be without it. Its mission then is to *serve* rather than to rule by force."[13]

When the school board controlled by J. Kent Hamilton refused to move as rapidly as Jones and other critics desired, citizens quickly learned that nonpartisan school administrations were highly political creatures. Jones helped form the Toledo Playground Association in 1899, which collected private donations for the establishment of the first public playgrounds in Toledo. The success of the playground movement caused the organization to change its name in 1900 to the Complete Education League, which, it was argued, reflected "the new education movement" and the "progressive spirit" of the city. The new title indicated the organization's desire to "broaden the meaning of public education" to include play, recreation, relaxed learning environments, closer parent-teacher relations, and a more pleasant and harmonious environment for the child. By 1902 a contributor to *Complete Education* contended that education meant growth and required constant experimentation. The school board, unfortunately, brazenly defied this principle, "as if fully realizing the fact that they are removed away from the reach of the people; that they are responsible to nobody; that they are safe in their position; and so they keep on in their detrimental policy."[14]

In attacking the elite nature of the school board and in broadening their plans for social reform, Jones and his followers solidified their alliances with labor and especially with women. Many suffrage leaders, such as Rosa Segur, one of the oldest feminists in the city, were active in women's clubs and parent's organizations such as the Broadway Civic Club, which visited schools, published critical reports in the local newspapers, and became consumerlike watchdogs on educational policy. Jones was a recent convert to the women's suffrage movement, part of his larger transformation during the depression from conservative businessman to urban radical. His discovery of the Golden Rule as a cure for human misery led him to embrace the concept of equality between men and women. As he asserted in 1898, "(w)omen are people, and, in my opinion, their inferiority (?), real or imaginary, is due wholly to their economic dependence upon man; it is an artificial condition that will disappear with the better civilization that is coming."[15]

"I believe in Brotherhood," the Golden Rule mayor often argued, "and my belief in it includes every human being on the face of the earth—the scalawag, the president, the harlot, the social leader of the four hundred, the puny baby, the brutalized plug ugly; they are all a part of me and I am part of them." Jones spoke with such sincerity that many parents, women, and workers were attracted to the simplicity and beauty of his arguments. Rosa Segur, Pauline Steinem, Mary Law, and Kate B. Sherwood—all suffrage activists, advocates of labor unions, parent-teacher associations, and now district representation on the school board—joined the mayor as he marched in numerous Labor Day parades, listened to guest lecturers on contemporary problems at the Golden Rule Settlement House, and preached the gospel of Social Christianity.[16]

Pauline Steinem, the president of the Council of Jewish Women and a leader in the city's Federation of Women, pushed the latter organization until it formally adopted the principles of "complete education" in 1900. Steinem lectured throughout Toledo on the value of the new education before groups such as the Golden Rule Mothers' Club, which met at Golden Rule Hall. Elected to the school board between 1905 and 1909 on a Progressive platform, she was the president of the Ohio Woman's Suffrage Association and supported the local Independent movement, parent organizations, and many liberal political causes. Kate Sherwood, whose husband was the perennial choice of the Central Labor Union to Congress, where he served for many years, was herself a Christian Socialist and another prominent supporter of Jones and social welfare innovations. And, under the leadership of Rosa Segur, the Broadway Civic Club also endorsed Jones's candidacies for mayor. None of these women was ever able to cast a ballot for Samuel M. Jones, but together with the Complete Education League, the Central Labor Union, ward leaders, and other agitators, they successfully restored some district representation to the school board in 1904. During that year voters turned the entire Hamilton school board out of office.[17]

Emerging as a prominent political leader out of the depths of the economic depression, Jones probably filled multiple voids in the lives of many Toledoans while making educational reform part of his larger designs for social and political reconstruction. Jones actively endorsed the initiative, the referendum, the recall, and the direct election of senators; preferred popular referenda over the mayor's veto powers; and took guns away from the police. A teetotaler who regarded alcohol as "poison," he defended workers and immigrants who enjoyed their Sunday beer and refused to advance temperance in his allegedly "wide open" town. To Progressive women, Jones symbolized hope for social equality and voting rights. But the question remains how this Welsh immigrant with his stocky build, sandy hair, and freckled complexion captured the enthusiasm of voters for more than seven years, building the basis for a third-party movement that would continue his policies until 1913.[18]

Jones's popularity stemmed partially from his promotion of women's rights and labor organizations at a time when business was consolidating its control over the marketplace and its supporting institutions. By supporting the second reorganization of the school board, he represented several groups—parents, workers, and women—that were poorly served by the Niles Bill. More than that, however, Jones placed specific social justice issues within a larger religious framework still valued by many citizens who were alarmed by the "tainted money" accumulated by predatory wealth. What formal religion failed to provide for many troubled citizens was perhaps compensated for by their deeply religious mayor, who never went to church. He provided the comfort, solace, and hope for a better day that was absent in the typical Sunday sermon, which still relayed the assumption that poverty had personal rather than social roots.[19]

Brand Whitlock, Jones's close friend and successor as mayor, once wrote that support for the Golden Rule resulted from the fact that the working classes had abandoned the churches, but not religion. "The great mass of the people, the working people, the poor people, do not go to church," Whitlock observed, "they have no interest in the church and very little respect for it, and yet . . . I have discovered . . . among the working people [that] nothing so quickly interests them as the real gospel of Jesus, i.e., the ethics, the morals of Jesus." Whitlock viewed Jones more as a prophet than a politician, whose evangelical style enabled him to use his office as a "pulpit" to popularize "progressive and radical utterances." Indeed, the *Evening Bee* in 1903 described a typical Jones rally at Golden Rule Hall: "The crowd sang Jones's songs under the leadership of the mayor, until the meeting resembled a free Methodist revival." There was Jones, speaking from open carriages or at open-tent meetings, shouting the Gospel of the Golden Rule. Or there he was on the street corner, pleading for an end to capitalism, with his son Paul playing the saxophone in the background to help lure the inevitable crowds.[20]

Jones's death deprived the city of the most colorful mayor in its history. Progressive politics and grassroots school reform, however, continued under Whitlock. Greatly influenced by the politics of Illinois governor John Peter Altgeld, Whitlock drafted the famous pardon that freed the Haymarket Square bombers. He settled in Toledo at the turn of the century, where he formed a close bond with Golden Rule Jones and became a "poor man's lawyer." He opposed capital punishment, continued Jones's policy of replacing policemen's weapons with light canes, and favored Continental Sundays, women's suffrage, trade unions, home rule, and numerous democratic voting devices. He regularly stood on the side of labor unions, women's organizations, and parent groups. Whitlock championed the new education, refused to invoke injunctions against labor during prolonged strikes, and along with clubwomen rallied behind striking laundry workers in 1907. When these working women reached an amicable settlement, he received widespread support from suffrage leaders, women's organizations, and labor during his several terms as mayor.

Under Whitlock's tenure in office between 1905 and 1913, Progressive school reform remained only one phase of larger municipal reform. There were prolonged fights against boodlers in public office as well as struggles for cheap transit fares for consumers. With various women's groups, Whitlock promoted the Ohio Juvenile Court movement and sought enabling legislation to permit the use of municipal funds for social centers, penny lunches, and other innovations that were encouraged by women and Progressive trade unions. After coauthoring the home rule section of the Ohio Constitution in 1912, he considered his job completed and refused to run for reelection. He became a national hero for his role in evacuating refugees from Belgium during World War I and spent the remainder of his life fulfilling his ambitions as a journalist and writer. Republican rule returned to Toledo in 1913, but Whitlock and the Independents were influential for more than a decade in the city of the Golden Rule.[21]

III

While Toledo was nationally recognized for sixteen years of political independency under Jones and Whitlock, third-party dissent made Milwaukee notorious. Political crankism had grown to maturity. Trade unionism and Socialism were visible features of grassroots reform in Toledo, but few cities could match the political successes of the Socialist Party and the labor movement in this Wisconsin metropolis. The Social Democratic Party, firmly allied with the Federated Trades Council by the turn of the century, led a working-class revolt against Milwaukee Republicans and Democrats. While Jones skyrocketed to popularity, the Social Democrats built a well-oiled political machine in Milwaukee that slowly gained influence in the city council, the school board, and the state legislature. An article on the "rising tide of Socialism" in the *Journal of Political Economy* in 1911 accurately described Milwaukee as the key municipality in the Socialist movement.[22]

Milwaukee is an exceptional city, yet it nevertheless illustrates the power that unions and radicals could exercise in municipal politics early in this century. As in Toledo, school innovation was only one aspect of larger social justice campaigns and the product of interaction among women's clubs, parent groups, working-class organizations, and Socialists. Compared with Rochester and Kansas City and even Toledo, however, Milwaukee possessed a very successful third-party movement, based firmly upon thousands of Socialist workers. While Golden Rule Jones failed to organize any political organization and Whitlock's Independents

Victor and Meta Berger on a European Holiday, 1923

Courtesy: State Historical Society of Wisconsin, Negative (X3) 48960

never congealed into an actual party, Victor Berger and the Social Democrats slowly constructed a formal, stable, and growing political network to challenge the established parties.

During the Progressive era, Milwaukee had one of the nation's strongest and most politically astute labor movements. The Federated Trades Council had approximately thirty-five thousand members by 1920. In 1910, the Social Democratic Party (SDP), the political wing of the Federated Trades Council (FTC), won nationally acclaimed victories at the polls by electing a mayor and a majority of the members of the city council and the board of county supervisors. The first Socialist sweep in a large American city, it nurtured rising expectations in thousands of American Socialists. Toledo's Independent movement was moribund by 1913. In contrast, Milwaukee's Socialist tradition endured throughout the first half of this century, both in the schools where the SDP constituted a significant voting block and in city government generally. When Meta Berger, the wife of the Socialist editor and congressman, became president of the school board in 1915, she not only was the first Socialist in the nation to achieve this distinction, but she also symbolized the growing recognition of women and labor's political power.[23]

Socialist and trade union leadership in Milwaukee was not an accident of history, but the result of years of concerted effort. The Socialist working class grew by accretion; gradually increased its ideological sophistication; and ultimately represented diverse, shifting elements of workers. From their dismal entry into municipal politics in 1898 to their landslide victories more than a decade later, the Social Democrats increased their voting strength each election year. Over time, the nonsocialist unions within the FTC were silenced, the trade unions broadened their loyalty and financial support to the party, additional services and programs (which would appeal to other social classes) were added to the party platform, and a variety of new immigrant groups became attracted to Socialism. A multifaceted Socialist movement was in the making. When nine Social Democrats were elected to the city council in 1904, the Milwaukee *Sentinel* aptly noted that "a new element has come upon the field to assertively dispute the right of the democrats and republicans to dominate the politics of the city of Milwaukee."[24]

Contemporaries continually commented on the trade union foundation of Milwaukee Socialism. One reason for the success of the local Socialist party, claimed a partisan in the *International Socialist Review* in 1904, "is its proletarian character. The members of the organization are workingmen almost to a man, and there is no large city in the United States where the Socialist movement is so overwhelmingly trades unionist." Mayor David Rose, who was a formidable Democratic opponent, typically complained that the SDP was forever "prattling about the rights of labor, always appealing for the down-trodden laboring men." Similarly, the party chieftain, Victor Berger, asserted that "working-men, organized and unorganized, constitute the overwhelming bulk—more than 95 percent—of the [local] Socialist party." Little wonder, then, that he often proclaimed that nonpartisan workingmen were traitors to their class and that the Socialists were the "partisans of the proletariat."[25]

The evolution of an explicitly Socialist and working-class third-party movement that gained solid footholds in politics and the schools contrasts sharply with urban developments elsewhere. Socialists formed the majority within the Federated Trades Council by the turn of the century and remained dominant for several decades. This situation was not replicated either in Toledo, Rochester, or Kansas City. These cities had their share of pro-Socialist unions, but the majority of urban trade unions usually eschewed formal alliances with political parties or socialist leaders. Even in Toledo, where the Central Labor Union applauded many of the principles and programs of Golden Rule Jones and Brand Whitlock's Independents, organized labor essentially remained apolitical. Local unions backed certain individuals for office and passed numerous resolutions on sundry issues, but usually avoided direct political entanglement.[26]

Compared with the case in other cities, therefore, the creation of a long-term, successful, and explicitly Socialist third party in Wisconsin's leading city was somewhat unique. Golden Rule Jones, for example, believed that the two-party system buttressed capitalism, yet preferred the use of direct nominations by the people over political parties. Jones and other grassroots radicals often used the word *socialism* fluidly, sometimes as a synonym for social justice, social democracy, or brotherhood. "I am a Socialist," argued Jones in the *Social Gospel* in 1901. "I believe in Brotherhood and can only find peace in advocating those principles that will lead men to live more brotherly." Toledo's voters obviously were receptive to his beliefs, even though he was maligned by Republicans, Democrats, and party-oriented radicals. Neither Jones nor Whitlock joined the Socialist Party, though they publicly endorsed many of its programs and policies.[27]

Even the Milwaukee Socialists, attacked by more doctrinaire radicals as being right-wingers, understood that the realities of municipal politics required broad appeals to nonsocialists in the community. Victor and Meta Berger, Emil Seidel, Daniel Hoan, and the many men and women in the movement were nondoctrinaire though committed to the establishment of a Socialist state. Living in a city with immigrants and Catholics, liberal women's organizations, and a strong German trade union tradition, they tried peacefully to build a broadly based, multiethnic organization with genuine electoral appeal. In 1901 the FTC unanimously adopted the following resolution, which testified to the need for civic cooperation as well as a vision of the "cooperative commonwealth":

> Resolved, That we call upon all righteous and liberty-loving citizens to unite with us at the ballot-box in order that we may abolish the present system of exploitation and establish a new and higher order of civilization, where poverty, misery, and prostitution, and all the crime and insanity emanating therefrom shall be unknown.[28]

The emphasis by the Social Democrats on gradual, peaceful social action by all "righteous and liberty-loving citizens" earned them the epithet "slowcialists" in some quarters, but was an important factor in their emerging strength. They slowly built up their membership rolls, borrowed ideas from non-Socialists when they benefited workers, and discovered that social cooperation was the key to political strength. The *Social-Democratic Herald* summed up this perspective in 1901 by favoring "a policy of steady socialistic reforms" over violent revolution, even if party leaders sometimes warned that bullets might replace ballots if peaceful social activism failed. The Socialists soon carved their own ideological niche in city and national politics. They distinguished themselves from "reformers" with whom they often had to cooperate, but who saw reforms as ends in themselves; and they also separated themselves from more-left-wing Socialists and members of the Industrial Workers of the World who favored revolutionary struggle over political participation.[29]

By attempting to build a nonviolent reform coalition that transcended liberalism, the Milwaukee Socialists were attacked by the Left as well as by the ruling business elite. They often occupied the somewhat uncomfortable position of popularizing programs of non-Socialist origin. Longtime Socialist leader Emil Seidel, a wood-carver and former mayor, recalled in the 1930s that "some eastern smarties called ours a Sewer Socialism. Yes, we wanted sewers in the workers' homes; but we wanted much, oh—so very much more than sewers. We wanted our workers to have pure air; we wanted them to have sunshine" and "living wages," "recreation," and "a chance for every human being to be strong and live a life of happiness." Milwaukee's Socialists admittedly worked with liberals for immediate "reforms." Still, only the Socialists never forgot that "no mere reform can solve the social problems; that nothing can save them or us in the end but a complete transformation of our economic system and its method of production and distribution of wealth." Until then, however, "all possible advantages for the toilers are gained" through reform, which hopefully helped implant the "final goal and the notable ideal of Socialism . . . permanently in the minds of the workers."[30]

Contemporary political adversaries as well as later historians have been harsh critics of the Milwaukee Socialists. Like many white union leaders, Victor Berger often demonstrated a Neanderthal approach to race relations. His racism was tempered in the 1920s, when he supported a federal antilynching law. More typically, critics have condemned the Milwaukeeans as middle class and reformist: too interested in the daily problems of workers and not sufficiently concerned with actual revolution. Amid these criticisms one can easily forget that these Milwaukeeans continually linked their demands for social change with working-class struggle. So-called movements for gas-and-water socialism, so easily dismissed today, were often working-class challenges to the hegemony of monopoly capitalism. Moreover, to divide turn-of-the-century working-class activists into reformers and revolutionaries obscures rather than illuminates the past. Socialists and skilled workers in particular often "linked union struggles over job conditions to community reforms of desperate importance to workers. Nothing could be more misleading than to identify 'sewer socialism' with bourgeois influence upon the party. The bourgeoisie, and only they, already had good sewers."[31]

After 1898, the Milwaukee Socialist platform contained more and more social welfare and educational demands as radicals incorporated the popular ideas of other voluntary organizations. Education became integral to working-class struggle. Party leaders, for example, emphasized constructive social action, chastised doctrinal thinking, and urged all Socialists to "continually develop, learn, and study" while advancing the immediate interests of the workers. Although sensitive to the charge that they were "sewer socialists," organized labor increasingly welded educational reform to proletarian struggle and became more vocal in school affairs and more likely to flex its enlarged political muscle. By 1905, the *Social Democratic Herald* sensed that the working class had finally begun to strengthen its forces on all fronts. "The working class have a big stake in the public schools," wrote a local commentator, "and [they] are sufficiently awakening in Milwaukee to see from now on that the educational system is not abused and misdirected."[32]

Indeed, nowhere was the working-class nature of the movement better revealed than in the party's views on education. The SDP and FTC did not have any direct influence on educational policy until 1909, when they joined to elect representatives to the school board. Yet their concern with improved education for working-class children was recognized even by their most severe critics. Socialists and union members viewed educational reform as part of their larger movement to build a Socialist state.

Initial demands for free textbooks and easy access to school halls in the 1890s blossomed into much broader programs for school social services. Long, glowing statements on the power of education to cultivate working-class intellect and to nurture Socialist perspectives permeated the writings of prominent trade unionists and party leaders. Like Socialists elsewhere, some of the Milwaukeeans conducted Socialist Sunday schools to try to educate working-class children about the rights of labor and the principles of socialism. But mostly they focused their attention on the public schools. Through their mass character and compulsory features, the schools would presumably help advance socialism once the proletariat seized control over them.[33]

The *Social-Democratic Herald* and the *Milwaukee Leader*, which were the official newspapers of the Socialists, continually focused on the fortunes of public education. Editorial after editorial and resolution after resolution highlighted the centrality of education in working-class struggle. The Socialists were the "staunchest friends" of the public schools, "in fair weather and foul"; the schools were "the key with which the masses may unlock the storehouses of the world's accumulated knowledge"; hence the Social Democrats "stand for the public schools and the widest extension of their facilities, that every child may have the opportunity to get an education." In 1917, the *Milwaukee Leader* asserted that no class benefited as much from collective activities such as health programs or public education as "the proletariat. It is the only place . . . the working class exercises any real political function and from which it gets any benefits worth while."[34]

Socialists fought for decades for liberal reforms in school and society, making educational innovation a branch of their political movement just as the Independents had done in Toledo for more than a decade. Yet if the Socialists were willing to cooperate with liberals, they were not prepared to fuse with them ideologically. Poverty, they realized, could not be eradicated through social services, only through a redistribution of national wealth. The Socialists repeatedly emphasized this point, which was highlighted in an editorial in the *Milwaukee Leader* in 1913:

> Reformers are willing to amuse the poor, to educate the poor (on some things) . . . to do almost everything imaginable except to stop the causes of poverty. Socialists are willing to accept all these alleviations. They want good schools and social centers, and public parks, and pensions and unemployment relief and everything that can be devised to make more tolerable the condition of the workers while poverty remains.[35]

At the same time, however, "none of these things, nor all of these things added together is sufficient, nor fundamental to the Socialist."

By the early 1900s, Milwaukee's Socialist movement was not only surviving, but flourishing, gradually building into a force for political and educational change. The Socialists already had representatives on the city council and in the state legislature, a weekly newspaper to disseminate their ideas, and a splendid political organization. Their infamous "Bundle Brigade" greeted workers at the factory gate at every municipal election and within several hours could distribute thousands of party leaflets printed in several foreign languages. Socialist cells flourished across the city, tightly bound into the central body of its democratically elected ruling elite. By 1905, an industrialist and political analyst accurately predicted that the Republican and Democratic parties would soon field a single ticket to stop the growth of Socialism, reminiscent of the "Citizen's Ticket" that repelled the Socialists and the Union Labor Party in 1888.[36]

Near the middle of the first decade of the new century, the Socialists expanded their appeal beyond skilled laborers in the FTC. They spread their ideas to new segments of the working class and to the leaders of several voluntary groups. This process of expansion and dialectical change constituted the most exciting episode in the making of Milwaukee Socialism. A third-party movement became a viable entity in Milwaukee's political life and seriously threatened the two-party system. Perhaps most fascinating in this historical process was the attraction of substantial numbers of Poles to the Socialist cause. Milwaukee Socialism has always been associated, of course, with the predominantly German trade unions. By the turn of the century, however, the Germans were losing their historical predominance in the city's cultural and political life. Polish, largely unskilled working-class citizens who lived in the southern, industrial section of town were gradually replacing the Germans as the major ethnic group.[37]

Poles were used as strikebreakers in Milwaukee as early as the 1870s, and trade union prejudice against these new immigrants seemed to hinder any coalition of workers. When the Polish Educational Society petitioned for Polish language instruction in the public schools in the 1890s, the FTC failed to endorse the plan before the school board, and Polish classes only began when the Social Democrats and settlement workers on the school board championed this innovation more than a decade later. The individuals who were isolated from each other joined together behind this reform as German and Pole put their differences aside, at least temporarily, for mutual protection and welfare.[38]

The movement from isolation to cooperation was a difficult one. The Roman Catholic Church, an aggressive opponent of Socialism, was central to the lives of many Polish citizens. The church's influence among the Polish working classes was only partially overcome by the Socialists and this only with the greatest difficulty. The astonishing thing is that the

Social Democrats made *any* headway in the Catholic neighborhoods of Milwaukee, for the religious establishment vigorously denounced them. Parochial-school groups opposed the introduction of Polish in the public schools out of fear that this would undermine the attractiveness of church-based institutions. As late as 1915, they helped defeat Social Democratic resolutions in the state legislature for free textbooks and meals for children. Moreover, Catholics regularly condemned the Socialists and the public schools in the Sunday pulpit. The public schools allegedly bred Socialism, vice, and crime; they "have produced nothing but a Godless generation of thieves and blackguards." This was hardly surprising, since the Social Democrats who defended the public schools were "atheists," "beasts," "hell's lowest vomit," and "free lovers."[39]

Inured to such statements, the Socialists responded that they were good family men and women, temperate in eating and drinking, and supportive of reforms that would protect the nuclear family from the ravages of the profit system. The Catholic hierarchy remained skeptical. Archbishop Sebastian Mesmer, a lifelong foe of Socialism, denied the sacraments, church burial, and other Catholic benefits to those who joined the SDP. It is surprising, therefore, that so many Poles transcended their religious identities and risked their souls for a glimpse of a new social order as the SDP made significant inroads into Milwaukee's Polonia. When the Social Democrats swept into office in 1910, they convincingly triumphed in the city's famous Fourteenth Ward, which was predominantly Catholic and Polish working class, and they won pluralities in other Polish districts. Polish Social Democrats represented the city in the state legislature and, to highlight the long-term effects of Socialism, seven of the twenty-one Poles elected to the city council between 1910 and 1940 were Socialists.[40]

Diligent effort and mutual benefit sealed this unlikely alliance of German trade unionists and certain members of the Polish working class. The Polish Educational Society, defeated in its lone bid to force the adoption of Polish as a class subject before the board of education in the 1890s, reorganized after the turn of the century as the Polish School Society. Convinced that the masses suffered under the yoke of the clergy, the Society was intensely anticlerical and devoted to secular education; moreover, its members shared the cause of class struggle and school reform already promoted by the Socialists. The society was led by a Polish brewery worker, Martin Gorecki, who was elected Socialist alderman-at-large in 1910 and later became a state assemblyman. Aware of this split within the Polish community, the FTC launched a full-fledged effort to recruit more Poles to the party in 1907 to expand its power base, so the rise of Polish Socialism resulted from concentrated effort. The Socialists began to publish a Polish Socialist newspaper and to infiltrate the South Side with pamphleteers and speakers who were careful never to insult work- ingmen who were still church members. These efforts helped to counteract the influence of local priests and the archbishop. And by 1912, a few thousand Polish children received bilingual training in the public schools, where they read books donated by the Polish School Society.[41]

If the alliance of Poles and Germans was a somewhat surprising occurrence in the new century, the increased interaction of the Milwaukee Socialists and local women's clubs was a similarly unexpected yet impor- tant political development. The Socialists, of course, repeatedly empha- sized their differences with nonsocialists who were "merely" reformers. Still, both the women and the workers had tangible effects on each other's political development and reform strategies. The Socialists, for example, sensed the popularity of many of the social welfare programs already financed or suggested by these voluntary associations—the playgrounds, vacation schools, lunch programs, and social centers. The enlargement of the social functions of the public schools became the common goal of these ideologically dissimilar groups.

Civic associations such as women's groups never endorsed the revo- lutionary rhetoric and aims of the Socialist working class. These groups never embraced Socialism, but were nevertheless significant forces in shaping Milwaukee politics during the Progressive era. These civic groups, wrote a leading Social Democrat, "much prefer advancing the common good to being mere rubber stamps of big business." And, he added, they "have not only been an important force for the good, but often have provided the balance of power necessary to compel recalcitrant officials to stand on the side of civic decency and progress." The increased coopera- tion of Socialist and non-Socialist groups for educational reform was not foreordained in the 1890s, but like so many people in history, both soon learned that for better or worse they needed each other's support. The civic associations left their own imprint on the Socialist working class, which in turn radicalized many individual clubwomen who ultimately embraced Socialism. The histories of the Socialist working class and these civic groups became closely intertwined.[42]

The transit of ideas and influence between these groups did not follow a single path. Socialists adopted some of the social service programs of the women and incorporated them into their political platforms. The ideas of prominent Milwaukee clubwomen in turn were reshaped by the spirit of Social Democracy, just as the women in Toledo were influenced by the Golden Rule. Had they lived in a city without a Socialist working- class tradition, some Milwaukee women might never have shifted from liberal reform to a more radical perspective. The experience of living in a place, however, where laborers became more powerful through political organization served as a catalyst for a more systematic analysis of social issues such as poverty. In the 1890s, many clubwomen believed that poverty was a temporary condition remediable through charity and benevolence. A decade later, important voluntary association members, including some of the Woman's School Alliance (WSA), questioned this position.

By 1907, for example, a prominent member of the WSA proclaimed that school meals were a human right for all children, not a charity for the poor. The Social Democrats had already popularized this position for several years. Mrs. Charles B. Whitnall, one of the earliest WSA members, publicly announced her conversion to the SDP in 1908, shortly after her appointment to the school board as a nonsocialist reformer. Moreover, Meta Berger, a Socialist school board member from 1909 to 1939, had warm personal and political relationships with settlement workers and liberal reformers in various voluntary groups, ensuring a reliable voice for the expansion of social services and school innovations. During her three decades in office, Berger was often simultaneously an Alliance official, highlighting the compatibility of Socialism and service group participation. Hence the Social Democrats both reacted to as well as shaped the dominant reform coalitions that evolved in Milwaukee.[43]

The growing cooperation and interaction between previously isolated groups in the interest of social reform were most evident in the movement for the direct election of the school board and the school bond crisis of 1909. Golden Rule Jones had helped encourage women to support district representation in Toledo in 1904, and the public esteem and respectability of the Milwaukee Socialists also climbed dramatically because of their position on similar issues, paving the way for later electoral successes. Milwaukee Socialists would have preferred to work only with other Socialists, of course, and left-wing critics often attacked their "opportunism." In spite of this, the Milwaukeeans placed the immediate welfare of the city's schoolchildren above ideological purity. Reformers—both Socialist and non-Socialist, clubwoman and worker, German and Pole—practiced the art of cooperation.

Concerning the type of school board needed in Milwaukee, the Socialists put it bluntly in 1907: "Shall we have a Merchants and Manufacturers' Association school board or a people's school board?" Even though they vacillated on whether they wanted a school board elected at large or by wards, the Social Democrats called for direct elections over the commission and appointment plan engineered by the Goo-Goos in 1897. Many non-Socialists rallied to the Socialist side. The *Social-Democratic Herald* proclaimed:

We do not mean to say that if the old system of appointment of members of the board was in vogue that the board would be any less a nest of politicians and embryo politicians, but we do say that the present system is no improvement over the old and that besides it is in this sense worse. Because the directors get their appointment at the hands of a commission appointed by the mayor and it becomes a part of the old party spoils system.[44]

Whether the Socialists would have complained if their own members had been named to the school board either by ward aldermen or commission members is questionable. Throughout the early 1900s, however, Mayor David Rose, the chief enemy of the Socialists and the partisan of thousands of Catholics, appointed the commission's members and thereby shaped board membership. In opposing the direct election of the school board, in defiance of the Socialists and then most of Milwaukee's civic groups, Rose unintentionally drove these individuals together and helped topple his regime from power in 1910.

Not all of the appointees to the school board were unqualified foes of Socialism or outspoken champions of parochial schooling as was David Rose. But there were enough of them. Besides securing the appointments of a large number of Catholics to one particular board, Rose helped name some leading union-busting representatives of big business. For example, Thomas J. Neacy, a major industrialist in the metal trades and a leader in the Merchants and Manufacturers' Association, used his influence on the board after the turn of the century to seek parsimony in school expenses in the name of "business efficiency." The Social Democrats and the new Milwaukee Teachers Association, which sought higher salaries for teachers, condemned him as one of the largest tax dodgers in the city. Moreover, the Socialists unanimously denounced Neacy and his industrial cohorts in 1904 when they established a privately endowed trade school, which the Socialists simply labeled a "school for strike breakers." The *Vorwarts* summed up trade union sentiment when it stated, "Frankly, the 'people' have no respect for the workings of the Rose regime, any more than they have for a 'boodler and a pimp.'"[45]

Not all the members of the board were as intolerable as Neacy. Victor Berger and other Socialists agreed that settlement workers and other liberal members sympathized with the problems of the poor and advocated more school programs and social services. Still, it was obvious that the only way to secure Socialist representation in the schools was through direct elections—the same mechanism they were already using to place members on the city council and in the state legislature. After the turn of the century, therefore, the FTC presented bills in Madison for the at-large election of the school board, with little success. Realizing that the ward was their best geographical base of power, they increasingly backed a ward-based, elected board, "so that no matter what political party has the upper hand in the city, it cannot have complete control of the school board with no vestige of *minority representation*. That's the issue!"[46]

In some ways, ideological consistency would have mandated that Social Democrats simply argue that school board conflict was only one aspect of larger proletarian struggle. That, however, would have isolated them from numerous nonsocialists in Milwaukee who agreed on the need for reform and thus weakened their growing political power. City politics were shaped not only by formal political parties, but also by all kinds of voluntary interest groups, and a strict class interpretation of social change was hardly shared by many potential allies. The Milwaukee Socialists had little choice but to cooperate with other reform-minded groups if they wanted to make a difference or to advance working-class interests.

The Socialist-led movement to create an elective school board beautifully illustrates the so-called opportunism of the Milwaukee radicals. Neither the ward leaders of the 1890s nor later advocates of the commission plan generally endorsed the concept of direct elections. The behavior of the Rose-dominated boards nevertheless angered Milwaukeeans of many different classes and social positions. Many voluntary associations—the WSA, the Social Economics Club, and large groups of teachers and principals—vigorously opposed a proposal for direct election considered by the legislature in 1901. Women in particular feared the return of an older generation of sexist ward heelers. Yet almost every such visible group favored the elimination of the commission plan by 1909. Again, in a few short years, Socialists and non-Socialists united on a specific issue of crucial importance to many citizens: the direct election of the school board.[47]

Popular dissatisfaction with the appointment plan accelerated by 1907, when the Social Democrats and voluntary associations demanded direct elections. Even the Republican and conservative *Sentinel*, an enthusiastic lobbyist for the commission plan in the 1890s and a traditional opponent of direct election, reversed its stand after a series of polls of its readers revealed overwhelming support for change. Certainly the context of city politics early in the century helps explain why isolated groups coalesced over this issue. During these years dozens of city officials were indicted for graft and corruption, with many actually convicted of boodling. This legitimized Socialist attacks on the major parties. Moreover, the miserly allocation of school funds by these officials helped make the prospects of direct elections gradually more appealing over time. No school officials were indicted, for the abuse of power rested in the city council, which controlled the school's funds. For years, no new schools were constructed, as the mayor and his associates diverted funds initially earmarked for the schools to other pet projects and to their own pockets, leading to increased overcrowding and citizen complaint.[48]

The Social Democrats correctly sensed that the idea of the direct election of the school board had popular support in Milwaukee. This was a classic example of the political behavior of the Wisconsin Socialists that infuriated more radical comrades. Locally, citizens hotly debated the issue of taxation without representation (particularly minority representation for women and laborers) and worried about a possible slowdown in the inauguration and progress of school welfare programs. Individuals who disagreed on other public issues seemed for their own various reasons to prefer direct election over the commission plan. The Socialists were not fools: they realized that many people opposed the commission plan, favored direct election, and hated the SDP. One could easily hate corruption and tax-dodging as well as every tenet of Marxism. The Socialists, however, successfully channeled this discontent into a constructive struggle to secure one of labor's immediate demands: direct election. By opposing graft and promising honest government, the Social Democrats again widened their electoral base. David Rose, nicknamed David "Roach" and the "degenerate mayor" by labor for his reactionary school policies, used his influence in the council to block direct elections until 1909, but even he could not repel the new reform coalition.[49]

In addition to the direct election struggle, the key issue that then catalyzed a broadly based movement for reform was the city administration's slashing of school bonds. Besides opposing the direct election plan, the city council moved at a snail's pace in adequately funding the schools. Because only parochial-school partisans such as Mayor Rose denied that the schools were grossly overcrowded, school bond referenda passed with comfortable margins throughout the Progressive era. In 1908, voters routinely approved a $360,000 bond for new school buildings, receiving at the time the largest plurality in Milwaukee's history. Rose illegally slashed the appropriation to $120,000. The Social Democrats as well as the Federation of Civic Societies, an umbrella organization of grassroots voluntary associations, immediately sponsored indignation meetings across Milwaukee. Nearly two thousand people attended some sessions. A School Defense Committee was formed, petitions were drafted for the city council, and even competing newspapers condemned Rose for his actions. After well-publicized and lengthy court battles, an alliance of the Socialists and non-Socialists finally salvaged $245,000 of the original appropriation.[50]

It had been an unintended alliance, born of the circumstances of Milwaukee's political life. The clubwomen and dissident Poles emerging in the 1890s seemed the most unlikely people to seek common cause with the Socialist working class. But it had occurred all the same. Out of the unexpected twists and turns of urban politics, out of the growing realization that it was better to cooperate than to work at cross purposes, there emerged a multidimensional political movement whose influence would peak in the following decade. Between 1897 and 1909, a third-party movement arose that now threatened to transform city politics and the public schools.

In both Toledo and Milwaukee, educational change occurred in the context of the larger social and political developments that emerged out of the depression and continued to shape urban life in the new century. Jones, Whitlock, and the Independents fought for district representation, a larger role for women, and a school system that provided expanded social services and programs. Victor Berger and the Social Democrats in Milwaukee built a more durable political base and on certain issues provided political leadership for various community activists. Voluntary associations and third-party organizations remained viable if not always dominant forces for political and educational change in the Progressive era. Even in Rochester and Kansas City, where third parties never seriously threatened the two-party system, school reform reflected the shape of the larger political environment and was the product of interaction between many competing forces.

IV

The contours of the age of reform in Rochester and Kansas City were strikingly different from those of Toledo and Milwaukee. Under Golden Rule Jones and the Independents of Brand Whitlock, Toledo witnessed more than a decade of political revolt against the Republican and Democratic parties that included new directions in educational thought and school reform. An even stronger, more radical, and more working-class movement for Socialism raged in Milwaukee during the Progressive era, as the Social Democratic Party and the Federated Trades Council challenged the supremacy of the two-party system. The major elements of third-party revolt were also present in varying degrees in Rochester and Kansas City. What was missing, however, was a sustained movement on the left or by liberals who could control municipal politics for any notable period of time. The two-party system seemed invincible in Rochester and Kansas City, while elsewhere, politicians such as Jones, Whitlock, Mary Law, and Rosa Segur in Toledo, and Victor and Meta Berger, Emil Seidel, and Lizzie Black Kander in Milwaukee dissented from the established parties and actively shaped city politics and the schools.

That is not to say that significant changes in the curriculum and social services in the schools did not occur in either Rochester or Kansas City. On the contrary, various grassroots organizations still interacted with the political system and forced many new ideas upon the school system. Labor groups, Socialist organizations, women's groups, and other voluntary associations continued to agitate for change as they did in many other cities after the turn of the century. Reform movements in Rochester and Kansas City nevertheless lacked the cohesiveness and continuity of the efforts by the Toledo Independents and the Milwaukee Social Democrats. There was never any strong third-party organization or leader who united competing groups of people into a common cause, as, say, the Socialists had done in Milwaukee. As a result, working-class groups, Socialists, and women's organizations often lacked a focal point around which divergent community forces could challenge the dominant political system. School reform after 1900 in Rochester and Kansas City, therefore, was led not by cohesive third-party elements, as in Toledo and Milwaukee, but by more fragmented voluntary groups.

Despite recurrent efforts to rally organized workers to political action, Rochester's labor movement paled in significance compared with Milwaukee's Federated Trades Council. During and after the depression of the 1890s, Socialists and trade union radicals tried to ignite the laboring classes and other citizens. An Independent Political Labor League was formed in the early 1890s to challenge the hegemony of the two parties; its flame was bright but brief. When Socialists tried to convert the Monroe County Labor Congress in the mid-1890s into a third-party alternative, they were also repelled by the unions. The same difficulties marred the Socialist attempt to seize power within the Rochester Trades Assembly, still home to remnants of the Knights of Labor late in the decade. Socialists such as William Lippelt of the Tailor's Union as well as radical shoemakers, typesetters, and other skilled workers lobbied in vain for political action by their peers. At the end of the depression, third-party movements had failed to materialize as prominent trade unions eschewed political participation and continued to limit their organizations to the struggle for better wages and working conditions.[51]

In the early twentieth century, Rochester's most prominent trade union leaders still agitated for political action, but rarely enjoyed electoral success. After 1905, for example, labor groups engaged in serious political organizing. As usual, their political forays were unproductive. The labor presence in the city was certainly quite visible in the new century. Labor Day parades, for example, grew from five thousand marchers in 1901 to six thousand in 1906 and by 1907 expanded to fifteen thousand men and women. It was in that year, marked by an economic slowdown and a business panic, that the new Central Trades and Labor Council (which replaced the defunct Trades Assembly in 1900) made its only serious political bid.[52]

Early in the spring of 1906, the editor of the *Labor Journal* reported that the majority of Rochester's trade unions planned to join other independents in a third-party challenge to Boss George Aldridge. Aldridge's Republican Party was a tower of strength in Rochester and Monroe County politics. An Independent League was nevertheless formed in hopes to "cause anxiety to 'Uncle' George Aldridge." Urging the municipal ownership of utilities as well as the direct election of senators, the initiative, the referendum, and the recall, the League wanted to "break the bipartisan alliance existing in this city between political bossism and private monopoly." The platform was similar to that of third-party agitators in other cities, and the Central Trades and Labor Council overcame its usual political reticence and formally endorsed the Independent ticket.[53]

As the Rochester elections neared, the *Labor Journal* editorialized: "Despite frequent discouragements and the continual protesting of unprogressive and timid members, there is a strong sentiment among the trade unionists of the country in favor of united political action. The further the active unionist goes into the ever broadening field of labor legislation the deeper becomes his conviction that the labor giants should exert the power he possesses at the polls and cease to petition at the feet of lawmakers who neither respect nor fear him." This hope for more politically astute wageworkers had sprung eternal in the history of the local movement, but 1907 was not their year of destiny and achievement. After two years of campaigning, the Independent League only succeeded in electing a union worker as New York's new secretary of state.[54]

Rochester's labor press was filled with proposals for working-class entry into politics in the early 1900s. These were mostly veiled threats against the major parties, which might pay more attention to prolabor legislation such as factory inspection and child-labor-law enforcement. Socialists were well represented in the garment and clothing unions, a fertile ground historically for progressive trade unionism. Unfortunately for them, the Central Trades and Labor Council was controlled by men such as Martin Kovaleski, who vehemently opposed the Socialists. In spite of several Socialist Party efforts to improve its relations, it forged weak links with mainstream labor unions, links that were unlike the formal ties between the SDP and the FTC in Milwaukee. As the city became increasingly white collar due to the rise of Eastman Kodak and related industries in the twentieth century, the trade union base of the city weakened further. Third-party movements then faced even greater struggles against the dominant parties.[55]

All this directly impinged on the political development of the Socialists, who met at the city hall from the turn of the century to 1911 through
the good graces of Boss Aldridge and the Republicans. In their Labor
Lyceum, formed in 1896, the Socialists continually attacked their hosts,
told workers to abandon the major parties, and dreamed of the establishment of a new social order. The Lyceum kept dreams of political and
social reconstruction alive in an environment controlled by the Republican
party and the mediating influence of the Good Government forces. Socialists assailed the imperfections of the capitalist order, and Lyceum speakers
presented radical ideas for local debate. The Rochester Socialists were
better debaters than organizers: neither laborers nor many women rallied
to their cause.

Rochester's Socialists, as those elsewhere, felt a strong bond with
radicals around the world. The *Rochester Socialist* argued in 1907 that "the
socialists of Rochester are but a small part of the great international movement, which is the expression of a world-wide proletariat rising against
a condition which renders all workers wage slaves." Through their
speeches, writings, and occasional publications, the Rochester Socialists
spoke out against poverty, boss rule, and social injustice. While the Milwaukee Socialists were preparing to sweep into office, however, their
comrades in New York were subjected to police intimidation. Golden
Rule Jones removed the clubs from Toledo's policemen, but that policy
did not prevail in Aldridge's Rochester. In 1908 the members of the Italian
Socialist Federation (continually confused by the police as an anarchist
group) were harassed and then jailed for "alleged inflammatory speeches."
Polish Socialists faced the same tactics, and police in 1911 arrested a
number of Rochester's most prominent Socialists, including a University
of Rochester professor, for "obstructing the sidewalk."[56]

While Toledo's grassroots Progressives coalesced to secure district representation on the school board and the Milwaukee Socialists fought for
direct elections and sufficient educational funding, Rochester experienced
its first decade of school board reorganization. Liberal Goo-Goos and local
women had disproportionate representation on these school boards, since
Boss Aldridge and his Republican mayors placed them on the party ticket
in exchange for Good Government support in other areas of municipal politics. Occasionally a letter to the editor surfaced locally critical of the elite
membership of the school board—which included shoe manufacturers,
elite clubwomen, businessmen, attorneys, and University of Rochester professors—but there was no visible or consolidated effort by excluded grassroots forces to secure labor representation or district membership.[57]

Without an effective third-party mechanism to challenge administrative reforms supported by the Republican boss and local liberals, Socialists

and organized labor were unable to place representatives on the centralized board of education. Liberal men and women gained representation
after 1900 at the expense of some ward leaders as well as Socialist and
working-class populations. Lurking in the background was still George
Aldridge, who determined the board personnel even more than in the
1890s, when the ward caucuses controlled school nominations. Through
centralization, Aldridge had a streamlined board that he easily made
majority Republican—just as it had been in the previous decade. Nonpartisan school administration existed only in theory, not in practice, in Rochester and other urban areas. Moreover, in Rochester, school centralization
made the city boss more powerful than before, and even the Goo-Goos
were in a very precarious position even though they enjoyed his good
graces until roughly 1910, when he found them expendable. They served
at the pleasure of Boss Aldridge, who controlled the educational purse
strings through his influence on the board of estimate, and who with
other leading Republicans selected the nominees for public office. The
failure of prized community reforms such as the city's famous social center
experiment was almost foreordained by Aldridge's continuing power over
the schools during the Progressive era.[58]

James M. Greenwood's Kansas City similarly lacked a viable third-
party movement with the stature of Toledo's Independents or Milwaukee's
Social Democrats. It had all the materials for a united grassroots revolt:
competing Socialist parties, a stable German-language worker's paper, and
an articulate labor movement. With the largest network of parent-teacher
associations in the world and strong women's organizations, the elements
existed to seriously challenge the decades-long supremacy of Superintendent Greenwood and the school board. The Republicans and the Democrats,
however, frustrated all critics by controlling the nominations to the "bipartisan" school board, and social innovation and curricular change often occurred only through continual outside agitation.

The *Kansas City Star* claimed as early as 1891 that "the grievous
oppression of labor is no longer possible in America. . . . The whole trend
of public sentiment is in the direction of an enlargement of the rights and
privileges of labor, and regulations which favor the toiling masses." The
"toiling masses" found it virtually impossible to lead a meaningful assault
on the major parties that dominated the schools. Decades of struggle by
some critics for a representative on the school board yielded disappoint-
ment and failure, products of the apolitical stance of the unions in the
Industrial Council. Whenever dissenting unions pushed the council into
politics, they lacked the organizational strength to translate their sense
of political and educational injustice into victory at the polls. Many unions
in the council in 1893 endorsed a "workingmen's ticket," since "the work-

ing classes of the city had derived no benefits from voting the party ticket." The following year they briefly coalesced with Single Taxers, Socialists, and other dissidents in a labor reform movement, again with disappointing results.[59]

The official organ of Kansas City's trade unions, the *Midland Mechanic*, quite typically concluded, in this atmosphere in 1898, that "we do not believe it to be expedient for a union to take concerted action in politics. It is not a wise policy." At the same time, workers fully realized that "the absence of political power to back up the demands of trade unions is responsible for the deplorable condition of the toilers." The working-class, quasi-Socialist *Missouri Staats-Zeitung* warned in 1901 that industrial conditions would improve only if workers broke completely with the major parties. If workers lacked power, "it is their own fault," claimed one writer. "They can't blame the plutocrat for looking after his own interests." Two years later, the Industrial Council tried to follow this call for political organization. The majority of Kansas City's unions formed a Union Labor Party, which had the Declaration of Independence for its guiding principle and demanded democratic voting devices and munici-pal control of the street railway. By the end of 1904, the inability of the new party to undermine the existing party structure marked yet another dismal political effort by the labor movement.[60]

By failing to join with the trade unions in a strong third party, the Kansas City Socialists replicated the situation in Rochester and in other cities. Socialism was rarely taken seriously in Kansas City in the Progres-sive era, and "it had no measurable effect on the place of labor organization in public opinion." The *Midland Mechanic* did attempt to better relations with various Socialists. It praised the leadership of the SDP formed in Milwaukee, and it reported that Christian Socialism was commonly dis-cussed by labor leaders. Still, the paths of Socialist and labor organizers crossed, but did not often meet. The members of the Kansas City Socialist Labor Party were mostly skilled workers and union men, but the Industrial Council never endorsed it at the polls. In fact, when the Union Labor Party entered politics in 1904, its vote was divided by a competing Socialist ticket. The regular parties, noted the German language *Kansas City Presse*, therefore benefited by the split between these two grassroots forces. The Milwaukee trade unions and the Socialists had faced a similar situation, but had the leadership and conditions necessary for greater political unity. In contrast, this rare form of Labor-Socialist cooperation was absent in Kansas City throughout the Progressive era.[61]

Trade unions and Socialists in Kansas City separately, though consis-tently, condemned the centralized structure and elite membership of the local school board. Each called for representative democracy, but unfortu-nately, lacked the power to implement desired changes. The working-class *Evening Mail* called for new blood on the school board as early as 1894. The *Staats-Zeitung*, in turn, printed a typical critique in 1899, complaining that the board was "supposed to be non-partisan" but was actually a "close[d] combine." School members should be "public servants," added the editor, but "once warmly ensconced in their official positions, they defy public opinion" and conduct all their meetings in closed session. The Socialist Labor Party called the school board members "absolutely capitalistic" during its unsuccessful bid to elect its own members to office. Radicals recognized that educational reform was not a bourgeois undertaking, but part of working-class struggle, yet they lacked the power to transform Kansas City's political alignments.[62]

Even the Industrial Council had few good words for Kansas City's school board in the Progressive era. The board seemed to enjoy angering the council by employing nonunion labor in schoolhouse construction. In 1906 the *Labor Herald* claimed that the so-called nonpartisan plan had been "foisted" on the citizenry in 1880 and "has resulted in the buildup of a machine that has no respect for the rights of the citizens of Kansas City, the pupils or the teachers." Six years later, the *Herald* reiterated this claim, calling the school board "self perpetuating, autocratic, irresponsible . . . instead of the board being servants of the people they have become masters." In 1916 a member of the Tailor's Union reflected the pessimism of organized labor when he asserted that the Industrial Council should again nominate a laboring man of the school board. "Even if he is not elected, it will be a vote of protest against present conditions in that body which, as at present constituted, is an aristocratic body. You get less out of the Board of Education than you do of any other department of our municipal government."[63]

Neither labor unions nor Socialists, however, were able to form a common front. In 1919 the Industrial Council endorsed the first woman in Kansas City to run for the school board, Mrs. Henry Ess, a prominent clubwoman and civic activist since the 1890s. But without school suffrage for women, her friends were unable to help her on election day, and she perished at the pools despite union support. Women, like union laborers, Socialists, and other grassroots reformers, failed to join together sufficiently to gain representation on the school board. The two major parties kept party nominations tightly controlled and out of their reach. While women were increasingly found on the school boards in Rochester, Toledo, and Milwaukee after the turn of the century, in Kansas City they were primarily limited to agitating with other grassroots forces from outside the power structure. In that way much of their leadership potential was undermined, even if they succeeded in promoting a number of the programs of the new education in the city at the bend of the Missouri.[64]

In all these cities, therefore, school reform proceeded within a larger social and political environment. The shape of schooling is to an important degree always a product of its surrounding environment. Educational policy in the Progressive era, as in all periods before and after, reflected changes outside the school system. Without the rise of various competing sources of reform in the depression 1890s, schooling would not have been subjected to different personalities, social theories, and viewpoints. None of the important changes in the configurations of urban schooling at the turn of the century—from school board centralization to penny lunches—are explicable without reference to the social forces that give rise to movements for change. Women, organized labor, Socialists, and other reformers who first became visible critics of school and society in the 1890s remained in different degrees influential sources of social change in urban education through the early decades of the twentieth century.

Municipal reform clearly differed in dramatic ways in various cities. Toledo and Milwaukee had qualitatively different political environments from those of Rochester and Kansas City, and there was no mistaking the difference between a mayor who took clubs away from the police and one who didn't. Socialists met without fear of reprisal in Toledo and Milwaukee, but with expectations of reprisal in Rochester. Toledo's Independents and Milwaukee's Social Democrats partially overturned long traditions of third-party failure, while the established parties in Rochester and Kansas City made short work of several challenges by local political upstarts. All this provided contrasting environments in which school reform and curricular change would proceed in the early decades of this century.

The political environments of these two sets of cities therefore differed markedly. Now, however, one must turn from a political analysis of municipal reform to a social analysis of actual educational policy and practice. Only then can one determine the differences that varying environments made in the history of school innovation. For example, did the existence of viable third parties concerned with social and educational reconstruction guarantee the establishment of more widespread reforms than were possible in cities under regular party rule? How did different political developments affect the timing and pace of educational change and social service innovation? How close did specific schools come to the ideal of the school as a center of neighborhood life? How widespread, for example, were the various decentralized programs that were established under newly centralized systems? Only by moving away from the social and political context of reform, closer to the operations of different programs and services in varying environments, can one hope to answer such questions about the immediate and long-range effects of the age of municipal reform on the urban school.

Chapter 6

Vacation Schools, Playgrounds, and Educational Extension

I

"Recent years have demonstrated the need in this city of a new kind of education," wrote Charles L. Aarons, an attorney and the president of the Milwaukee school board in 1910. "The call of the persecuted and oppressed, of the weak and the delinquent has been listened to. Despite the fact that the funds of the Board were never originally contemplated to supply such needs—now so urgent—the School Board has attempted to come to the rescue of neglected and suffering humanity. There was no one else—no other institution or body which undertook to perform this duty—a duty which devolved upon society itself through some one of its agencies." While worried that the new education progressed too rapidly against the old and certain that the schools were not a panacea for every social ill, Aarons still applauded the rapid expansion of their social role in the early twentieth century. Innovations such as vacation schools; playgrounds; social centers; classes for stammerers, the blind, the deaf, and the "feeble-minded"; and extensive programs in manual training, domestic science, and even vocational education in a few short years had become the trademarks of a modern urban school system.[1]

Aarons nevertheless believed that "the tendency in this and other School Boards has been that anything new, appealing to the Board as inherently meritorious, must be adopted, without giving due thought to the proper relationships between such new ventures and the basic principles upon which the system should rest, and without proper consideration of the possible result of crowding out of the system certain of the old departments which were thereby injuriously affected." If new was not always better and sometimes miseducative, Aaron's belief that America's schools were undergoing massive change was shared by many citizens during the Progressive era. Whether one attended a union smoker, a parent-teacher meeting, a Socialist rally, or a businessmen's convention, school reforms were continually discussed and implemented throughout the Progressive era. "Ten years ago it was the fashion to call any man who worked for reform and helped to disclose corruption a knocker," argued the *Missouri Staats-Zeitung* in 1906. But now it was common knowledge that all cities and their social institutions were in the wake of a "general reform movement sweeping over the country."[2]

Three closely related educational reforms that reflected the new spirit of change were vacation schools, playgrounds, and the broader movement for "school extension." This last idea included a wealth of programs—school gardens, evening schools, and children's and adult's recreational classes—all commonly subsumed by many contemporaries under the title "social center." Together with vacation schools and playgrounds, the social centers became one of the most important reforms sought by many grassroots Progressives. Different elements of the grass roots, especially women who were not Socialists or tied to labor, quarreled among themselves about school board centralization and the end of ward representation in their cities. But these differences were put aside when it came to extending the social reach of neighborhood schools. Despite the obvious disagreements one would expect to find among Social Gospelers, middle-class women, skilled workers, Socialists, Populists, and assorted parent associations and voluntary groups, these organizations fought strenuously for school expansion.

The history of vacation schools, playgrounds, and social centers should not be divorced from the larger, often contradictory reform movements that swept American cities in the early twentieth century. These reforms were classic examples of how the state, through its supporting institutions, expanded its control over the lives of children during this period. Centralization never dampened the spirits of grassroots organizations, whose members realized that conflicts over play, leisure, and the public use of local schools reflected larger class, gender, and neighborhood struggles with a new generation of professional and business leaders in various cities.

When understood in this context, the evolution and establishment of innovations such as vacation schools and playgrounds become rooted in the broader movements for change that characterized the Progressive era. It is fruitless to ask whether these innovations were a product of some vague entity called "democracy" or some amorphous movement for "social control." Rather, the history of play and school extension was shaped by the dialectical forces that controlled all aspects of school innovation: the demands by capital and its professional allies to centralize, consolidate, and integrate everyone into a corporate America under its control, and the counterdemands by a wide range of civic activists to build decentralized, fluid, and responsive school systems across urban America.[3]

Because the school, as a vital social institution, had become the center of tremendous community conflict after the 1890s, every aspect of educational change became contentious. Reforms to secure safe places for children to play attracted individuals with competing worldviews, since children's leisure and socialization to adult mores were of concern not simply to their future employers, but also to their parents and labor unions. Just as radicals had to fight for sewers for working people, so too did they struggle over the right to drink beer on Sunday, to hold evening citizens' meetings at their local school, and to find safe and enjoyable entertainment and play spaces for their children. It may seem anomalous for self-proclaimed radicals in Progressive unions or the Socialist Party to join hands with nonsocialist reformers to build vacation schools, playgrounds, and social centers, but only if one ignores how citizens' groups linked these demands with broader protest movements against an emerging industrial state.

Over and over again, reformers of all stripes turned to the public school as a lever for social improvement in the lives of children. Often sensing that family control was undermined by capitalism and that church influence had waned in many workers' lives, radicals as well as efficiency reformers saw the school as a major agency of reform in local communities. As the twentieth century dawned, conflicts over play and leisure in urban life intensified, and only the future would determine whether schools would serve the interests of business, labor, socialism, or other elements of the grass roots. Could institutions that were increasingly controlled by elites on the school board innovate in ways that satisfied the diverse voluntary groups that challenged the status quo? Could schools serve rather than dominate neighborhoods when citizens had often been stripped of the power to place local representatives in office? The social history of vacation schools, playgrounds, and social centers in various communities provides some answers to these highly political questions raised by citizens throughout this age of municipal reform.

II

"Vacation schools have become an important part of our public school system," wrote Adele Marie Shaw in a popular series of articles on education in the *World's Work* in 1904. Operated for several weeks in the summer by Progressive women for the children of the poor, the vacation schools were one of the best publicized experimental programs of the period. They were the subject of numerous articles in educational and social work journals, popular magazines, and local newspapers. Initiated primarily by voluntary associations and women's clubs, vacation schools appeared in dozens of American cities at the turn of the century, and many of them ultimately received municipal funding. Like other famous "efficiency" reformers, Clarence A. Perry viewed the innovation as part of "the wider use of the school plant," an illustration of multifaceted movements to make schools better serve the community.[4]

The vacation school became one of the best known innovations of reform-minded women in the early Progressive era. A few vacation schools had operated in Newark and Boston before the 1890s, but their heyday was after the depression of 1893 and the birth of new women's organizations. Laypeople rather than professional educators, therefore, were the early catalysts for change. A well-known chronicler of the vacation schools and a national leader of the playground movement, Henry S. Curtis, wrote in 1905 that the "work was started in the first instance in nearly every case by philanthropic societies," mostly composed of women. The Women's Educational and Industrial Union in Rochester, the City Federation of Women's Clubs in Toledo, the Women's Club of Wisconsin in Milwaukee, and the Athenaeum in Kansas City funded and operated the first vacation schools in their respective cities, and their activism reflected the zeal of women's associations across the nation. With the creation of vacation schools, the new education had arrived in local cities through the perseverance and labor of reform-minded women.[5]

The vacation school was ultimately endorsed by labor unions, Socialists, Populists, and even many school officials in the early twentieth century. While suspicious of anyone who viewed educational innovations as ends in themselves, Socialists supported vacation schools as an immediate form of relief and welfare, less significant than a full-fledged assault on inequality on the shop floor, but nonetheless an integral aspect of community struggle. But in the 1890s, women above all other groups championed social experimentation through vacation schools. "One of the chief functions of vacation schools," argued a writer in the *Forum* in 1900, "is that of serving as experiment stations, so that these schools exert a positive influence upon regular school methods. . . . The instruction is, briefly, according to the laboratory method." Women in city after city emphasized the experimental nature of the innovation. They also privately funded these schools and, with the aid of diverse voluntary groups, lobbied for their permanent establishment.[6]

Miss Beulah Douglas, an extremely popular vacation school teacher in Milwaukee, sounded like a devotee of John Dewey when she asserted in 1902 that the "work is experimental; what is considered best one year may not be feasible the next. This elasticity is of great value, for when methods become cut and dried, growth ceases." In describing the vacation school in a slum neighborhood near the Sixth District School, the *Milwaukee Free Press* concurred with Douglas's viewpoint. The vacation schools were in reality "pedagogic experiment stations," wrote the paper during the same year. "The new ideas which are to be tried in this school may later be adopted in the grades of the public schools if they are found to be thoroughly practical and feasible. The idea of taking care of the children and keeping them off the streets in the hot summer is, to be sure, a philanthropic one, but it is not the primary object of the vacation school. Educators expect much of the vacation school in the way of solving problems which have disturbed teachers in the lower grades for years."[7]

With many of these objectives in mind, grassroots reformers established vacation schools in Rochester, Toledo, Milwaukee, and Kansas City at the turn of the century, initiating a similar pattern of change. Typically, women's organizations sought permission from the school board to use particular buildings in the summer months, usually for six weeks. Because regulations often prohibited the use of the schools for anything except regular instruction, women usually presented a round of petitions to school leaders until their proposal was finally accepted. The terms of agreement were fairly simple: the women paid for the teachers and the instructional materials, the school board provided the building for free. Under these conditions, women created vacation schools in Rochester and Milwaukee in 1899 and in Toledo and Kansas City in 1901.

Fiscal as well as pedagogical conservatives on boards of education were properly suspicious of the ulterior motives of the women who, they realized, wanted their own positions on the board and used the vacation schools to publicize their organizations and enhance their overall visibility. Although many groups claimed to be nonpartisan, everyone recognized that most people who used that phrase were highly political. As vacation schools grew in popularity during the Progressive era and voluntary associations gained more representation on the school board, public policy shifted from private to municipal funding. By 1910, all these cities had municipally funded vacation schools.[8]

Women reformers and other champions of vacation schools offered various justifications for the establishment of this innovation. They complained of the evil consequences of street life on youth, the common increase of juvenile crime in the summer months, and the potential of vacation schools to counter these conditions. "There are sections of the city where the streets fairly swarm with children," noted Rochester's Helen B. Montgomery in 1899. A leader in the Women's Union and a school board member from 1900 to 1909, she also added that many children "are near no park, the houses are small, the streets hot and dusty, the associations demoralizing."[9]

Vacation schools were expected to yield numerous outcomes. Progressive women in Toledo argued that the experimental schools would teach "the love of nature, consideration for each other, and wholesome recreation." In Milwaukee, the Woman's Club of Wisconsin and the Woman's School Alliance also promised to secure social order through the schools. The president of the Milwaukee school board, William Pieplow, a former Populist and associate of Victor Berger but now a steadfast Republican, wrote in 1909 that the incorporation of these schools into the public system promoted stability on the streets. The vacation schools, he argued, eliminated "habits of indolence and lawlessness" and the "destructive infection of evil associations and enforced idleness." Moreover, they taught "law and order without the discipline and pressure of the ordinary school."[10]

To accept these law-and-order statements at face value and presume that the vacation schools actually functioned as instruments of social control ignores the context of change and confuses the history of ideas with social reality. Many petitioners faced conservative, business-dominated, efficiency-conscious school boards that responded best to law-and-order ideology. Many women's groups assuredly believed that their experimental schools would retard juvenile crime in the summer months, but they were equally interested in using these schools for educational experimentation. Moreover, many parents disliked summer crime, juvenile delinquency, unsafe streets, lurid movies, cheap dance halls, and other city attractions. That is, many ordinary citizens preferred supervised education and recreation for their children over absolute freedom. Many Socialist parties wanted to change ownership of the means of production rather than to establish a capitalist welfare state, yet they also endorsed new social services and experimental programs despite their basic disagreements with liberal reformers on the ends of social policy.[11]

Liberal and radical reformers agreed that class differences greatly determined how children spent their summer months. Everyone agreed that "when summer comes, the rich leave for seashore or mountain; the poor remain [in the city], perforce of circumstances, to swelter in the heat." Numerous individuals with conflicting political philosophies believed that new programs offered children some immediate compensation for the larger inequalities in their lives. Hence the Women's Educational and Industrial Union created new educational experiences not for all children but for "the eighteen or twenty thousand who stay in town all summer long; who play up and down dirty streets, who hang about corners."[12]

Emily Bouton, a prominent new woman in Toledo who supported Golden Rule Jones, similarly argued that poverty trapped many little children in the city, forcing them into crime-ridden environments. Society, in turn, blamed the children for their summer pranks and petit larceny when in reality they had nowhere else to play but the city streets. Bouton believed that vacation schools and other social services were the Golden Rule in action and deepened public awareness of the effects of environment on character formation. Like other women who financed vacation schools, Bouton recognized that poverty prevented many children from enjoying such simple pleasures as an out-of-town vacation.[13]

Since attendance was voluntary, vacation schools could hardly function as a powerful agency of social control. Children and parents would have shunned these schools if they had not offered any worthwhile alternative to the city street. Emily Bouton, for example, noted that "if they do not like what they find there, these boys and girls can stay away" if they so desired. But reformers worked diligently to attract the young to the vacation schools. Everywhere demand outstripped supply. Many parents and children, often faced with few constructive alternatives, valued the six-week sessions during the hot, lazy summer months. Vacation schools should be criticized less for their tendencies toward social control and more for the fact that they only reached a small percentage of the total population and never achieved their goal: to notably alter the character of the public schools.[14]

The popularity of the vacation schools stemmed from their innovative qualities and relaxed environments. Programs differed in various cities. Chicago, for example, emphasized nature study. Others favored industrial subjects or a mixture of various programs. Common activities in many cities included field trips to the country, excursions to outlying parks, manual training and domestic science, museum visits, storytelling, plays, kindergarten work, and visits to local points of historical interest. Often the casual study of local history and geography was also pursued through invited lectures, library visits, and trips through the city. With a curriculum that mostly ignored textbooks and emphasized "learning by doing," the vacation schools offered a respite from boring afternoons and the singsong drills, recitations, and regular subjects in the classroom.[15]

In reference to the progress of the vacation schools in Milwaukee, *Charities*, a prominent social welfare journal, put forth the belief in 1902 that "if attendance is a straw showing which way the wind is blowing in educational methods, no greater endorsement is needed for the vacation school than the story of the past year." The experimental schools had a magnetic influence, drawing children from all parts of the city. "The idea of vacation schools for the children of the poor is now accepted by everyone," claimed an enthusiastic writer in the *Elementary School Teacher* in 1905. "The demand for them far exceeds the supply."[16]

Nearly all the earliest vacation schools originated in the poorest and often immigrant-populated sections of the city, in areas that lacked sufficient open spaces for play except for occasional vacant lots and the city street. Even though cities such as Rochester and Kansas City in particular were building nationally renowned park systems, these spots of green were often miles from tenement districts and accessible only to those with money for carfare. That made municipal responsibility for leisure pursuits, for young and old, partially a class issue. What was needed, according to various reformers, were more accessible programs for everyone, a position argued most strenuously by Socialist and labor leaders. And in neighborhood after neighborhood where vacation schools were founded, there was literally a rush for the limited places available, angry confrontations with parents whose children were denied admittance, and the very success that Progressive women in particular had long desired in child welfare and municipal reform.

The ward leaders in the Rochester schools attacked the Women's Educational and Industrial Union in the 1890s as meddlers, faddists, and socialists. With continual prodding by the Good Government League and Susan B. Anthony, Helen B. Montgomery, and their cohorts, the board of education finally permitted the Union to open one vacation school in 1899. Located at the No. 9 School in an area populated by Russian Jews and Italians, the innovation was a complete success. The principal of the school, Anna Van Marten Jones, wrote that "the eagerness of parents and children to obtain places in the school was beyond our expectations." Five hundred children vied for two hundred places, producing many disappointments. Children so enjoyed the activities, especially the excursions to the city's parks, that the *Union and Advertiser* repeatedly noted that annually more children were turned away than were allowed to enter the schools. "Pathetic were the appeals for admittance," noted the paper in 1903, "and so many children turned sadly away from the building." There were folk dances, storytelling, and other programs that appealed to different immigrant groups, and the Women's Union always had more children to teach than it could accommodate.[17]

Toledo's Federation of Women's Clubs began vacation schools in 1901 with support from Golden Rule Jones, the Complete Education League, and the Broadway Civic Club, a parents' club from the South Side. Like their Rochester counterparts, Toledo reformers established the first school in the poorest and most congested part of town: the East Side. Separated from the rest of the city culturally by its large Hungarian and ethnic populations and geographically by the Maumee River, the East Side was heavily industrial. Even the names of the neighborhood

schools—Ironville and Birmingham—perfectly reflected the world beyond the classroom door.[18]

Pauline Steinem, the liberal activist school board member (for 1905–9)
and advocate of the new education, spent countless hours with poor East
Side children during the long summer months. Merging ideology with
action, she was the chair of the vacation school committee of the women's
clubs. The Republican *Blade*, which was often skeptical of most social
welfare programs, claimed that the schools were "successful from every
point of view." For every hundred children who went on a field trip,
twice as many were turned away for lack of funds and space. Women
were usually unable to raise sufficient money to accommodate all the
children from the district.[19]

The situation was very similar in Milwaukee and Kansas City. In the
latter place the Athenaeum and the Council of Women's Clubs privately
operated vacation schools for more than a decade, starting in 1901. In
Milwaukee, the Women's Club of Wisconsin, aided by the ubiquitous
Woman's School Alliance, started them in 1899, sponsoring the schools
until the school board began to fund them five years later. In 1899 the
Milwaukee Journal, like so many other newspapers, noted the great demand
for these innovations. Many of the children at the vacation school were
exceedingly poor. When five hundred of them were taken to outlying
parks, one observer wrote, "the beauty of the woods was a revelation to
most of them, many never having been so far away from home before
. . . it was pathetic to hear their expressions of delight on all sides." Entire
Italian families went on popular excursions on Lake Michigan, as the
philosophy of social service and wider use of the schools found expression
in Milwaukee.[20]

By the turn of the century, even the Republican *Sentinel* publicized
how "one school conducted last summer was filled to overflowing, demonstrating the great desire both on the part of children and parents to
avail themselves of the advantages to be had at these schools." Again,
their popularity emanated from the relaxed environments, the stimulating
activities, and the enthusiasm of particular teachers. Miss Beulah Douglas,
for example, was an extremely popular teacher in the Milwaukee vacation
schools, and all the available accounts of her teaching point to her talents
and love for children. Douglas taught in Minneapolis during the regular
year. When she visited Milwaukee, children routinely tagged behind her,
hoping for a guarantee that their name would be included on the vacation
school roster.[21]

In 1902 more than seven hundred children stood in line for admittance
to the vacation school in the Sixth District neighborhood. Many of the

children were poor and ragged, and as the *Sentinel* reported, "the young-sters came from all quarters of the city in twos and threes and in squads of a dozen or more." For those who were turned away, "big tears that ran down their disappointed faces told in epitome the whole story of Miss Douglas' success in her vacation school work." Such poignant scenes melted even the sternest heart. School board member Jeremiah Quin, who dismissed vacation schools as a fad in the 1890s, visited the local experimental classes, was impressed by their popularity and utility, and then led the movement for municipal funding of the vacation schools after the turn of the century.[22]

Old-fashioned discipline was never a major concern at the vacation schools. As one writer contended, "The discipline in the schools was something remarkable. No children were sent away permanently for bad conduct, and there was but little need of reprimands." Many women's clubs in the 1890s, of course, petitioned unsuccessfully for the abolishment of corporal punishment in the pubic schools, and the Women's Education and Industrial Union of Rochester along with other groups hoped that the vacation schools would demonstrate the value of relaxed, informal learning environments and "gentle training." The principal of one school in Rochester contended that "the word discipline seemed unnecessary to speak" because children were so involved in new activities. Similarly, the Federation of Women's Clubs of Toledo took more than fifteen thousand children on excursions to the parks in 1902 without unpleasant incidents or so-called discipline problems.[23]

Vacation classes were often more exciting than the regular public schools. Heavy-handed discipline was not a problem in part because attendance was voluntary: children who disliked these schools probably stayed away from them. Hence, those children deemed by some reformers as potential juvenile and adult criminals probably avoided social manipu-lation. Given the intense competition for admittance, children ordinarily viewed attendance at the vacation schools as a privilege rather than an effort by elite women to manipulate and control them. The *Rochester Union and Advertiser* claimed that the No. 9 vacation school was popular because of "the character of the institution and work done" there. Some children so enjoyed the park excursions, manual training, domestic science, and storytelling that they attended these schools for six weeks in the summer without missing a single day! Children at No. 9 received prizes for a project in neighborhood beautification, which included destroying cater-pillars that were ravaging the city's trees. Little Ella Davis was given a copy of *Grimm's Fairy Tales* for eliminating seventy-seven hundred co-coons. "The boy's first prize was equally won by Isaac Cohen and Willie

Newsclaum, who destroyed so many cocoons that they could not be counted." For destroying an estimated fifty thousand cocoons, Isaac and Willie received a penknife and a baseball.[24]

Many parents, no doubt, used the vacation schools as a form of summer day care, especially when their children enjoyed the experience. In many of Milwaukee's ethnic neighborhoods, working-class parents often donated money to the vacation school fund, with the hope that more local children, including their own, would be served. In all cities, local women tried to reach the poorest children, whose families presumably could not afford a middle-class vacation out of town. Hence the children from Milwaukee's Jones Island, a poor fishing village of Poles and Germans, were usually given preference for attendance as well as the Italian children of the Third Ward. The "Bloody Third" was located near the downtown business district and had slumlike tenements, high rents, and few safe places for children to play.[25]

The *Milwaukee Daily News*, which was an outgrowth of the *Labor News* in the 1890s, claimed that the South Side Poles and the Third Ward Italians eagerly sent their children to the vacation schools. Unfortunately, many of the children were sent home because of overcrowding. For those who did attend the vacation schools, teachers received scores of letters from appreciative parents. Beulah Douglas received "pathetic" pleas from children "begging to be allowed to come to the school" and letters "from the parents who almost invariably write that they are living in a bad neighborhood for children." Every year numerous children were killed in all these cities while playing in the streets or on railroad tracks, and some parents preferred supervised instruction over complete freedom for their children during the summer months.[26]

Women's clubs in Rochester, Toledo, Milwaukee, and Kansas City gradually expanded their programs to at least a handful in response to rising demand in the early twentieth century. In the process of expanding and popularizing the vacation schools, women's clubs gathered support from other grassroots organizations and from the men who predominated on the school boards. One classic example of the continuing vitality of grassroots coalitions existed in Rochester, when a number of vacation schools were approved by the city council in 1907. The council's action was a direct response to a joint petition for social centers, playgrounds, and vacation schools from eleven community organizations, ranging from the trade unions to the Socialists to the Women's Union. The Socialist Labor Party (of all groups) and Mabel Kennon—a suffrage leader, clubwoman, and Socialist—promised to expand the schools to every neighborhood if elected to office. With such broad public support from labor, radical, and women's organizations, Rochester's various educational experiments ultimately became a national showcase through the activities of the local school extension director, Edward J. Ward.[27]

This shift from the private to the municipal control of vacation schools was common in many American cities. In Toledo, Pauline Steinem and a school board almost totally supportive of the new education were elected to office in 1904. They replaced the efficiency-minded school board that had been dominated by J. Kent Hamilton and had opposed the new education for six years. Within a year after her election, Steinem led the effort to establish vacation schools at municipal expense. The city solicitor, however, intervened, showing that the state school code did not currently permit the use of tax dollars for school gardens, lunches, social centers, or vacation schools. Undaunted, Steinem joined with the Independents and Brand Whitlock and changed the code. By 1910 roughly one-fourth of Toledo's schools had municipally funded vacation schools, located both in wealthy and in poor neighborhoods.[28]

Women's club members in Milwaukee and Kansas City also agitated for municipal control of vacation schools after the turn of the century. The Milwaukee women, as previously noted, were successful in 1904; the Kansas City women scored their victory in 1910, when state-enabling legislation finally permitted the use of tax monies for these projects. Because David Rose's regime in Milwaukee slashed the public school budget, local school boards that were sympathetic to the expansion of vacation schools were prevented from funding more than a few of them. By 1910 Kansas City had equipped a number of neighborhoods with these schools, while fewer were found in Milwaukee. By this time, however, the vacation schools had begun to lose their innovative qualities, compared with the situation in the 1890s. When vacation schools were adopted in the Rochester, Toledo, Milwaukee, and Kansas City schools, they gradually became less experimental and primarily aided children who had failed in their regular school lessons during the year or sought educational enrichment in particular classes.[29]

Vacation schools changed greatly after the first decade of their existence. This change has generally been ignored by historians, who have treated the vacation school as a static institution. By World War I, however, when all these cities had adopted vacation schools, they had lost much of their earlier strength as an instrument for reform and educational experimentation. Like many other new programs of the Progressive era, from school breakfasts to domestic science classes, the vacation schools lost their "experimental" character. Through the common movement from private to public control over innovations, experimentalism was often laid at the wayside. Clubwomen at the turn of the century often boasted of how unpredictable the work at the vacation schools might be from year to year. This was not the case two decades later. By then lay reformers had receded from public view, and the public schools had altered the original purpose and meaning of summer "vacation" schools.

Several factors help to explain the new functions of the vacation schools. In the first place, many of the innovative subjects popularized in the early vacation schools entered the regular schools at the turn of the century. In Rochester, Toledo, Milwaukee, and Kansas City, for example, complete programs in manual training and domestic science that had been promoted by women's organizations and various civic clubs were now established in the schools in part on the strength and popularity of vacation school experiments. As these innovations became linked to the public schools, however, experimentalism soon gave way to formalism.

By the early 1900s, nearly every child from the kindergarten to the high school participated in some classroom exercises in manual dexterity and related skills. In the newly formed kindergartens, there was paper folding, simple lessons in form and design, and work with colors and paints. All the boys and girls from the first to sixth grades in many cities then typically had occasional work in raffia, weaving, more paper construction, and the use of basic tools. By the sixth or seventh grades, sex-role socialization became even more pronounced: girls received lessons in cooking and sewing and boys went to shop class. Diverse programs of manual training and domestic science had entered the schools, and the vacation school made important contributions to these movements. And although some school board members, such as Charles Aarons of Milwaukee, believed that these programs threatened the old system of education, children met in these classes only for a few hours per week. They never dominated the curriculum or "crowded out" the older subjects, as some individuals feared.[30]

What was missing in the school systems that adopted these innovations was the flexibility that had been the sine qua non of earlier vacation schools. Innovative subjects increasingly found in the schools lacked the informal, relaxed environments of earlier private school experiments. Since the public schools were not voluntarily attended, neither were the domestic science and manual-training classes. One often attended these once "experimental" classes under compulsion, just as one would classes in the more textbook-oriented subjects that dominated in the schools. Field trips, museum visits, and informal learning experiences were adopted by the public schools in part because of the successes of the vacation schools, but they became an occasional, incidental part of the curriculum. The public schools absorbed many new areas of instruction in the Progressive era. They still lent to many of them their heavy emphasis on textbooks, traditional discipline, rote memorization, and teacher authority. In this respect, the more the schools changed, the more they stayed the same.

The vacation schools that existed in many urban systems after 1910 bore little resemblance to earlier programs except for the fact that they operated in the summer. Between 1910 and 1920, the vacation school became more synonymous with modern conceptions of "summer school": a place for students to repeat failed subjects or to do advanced work, and for regular teachers to augment their salary. Summer school attendance might enhance the rate of children promoted from grade to grade during the regular school year, a worthy goal and a passion of efficiency-minded educators. But such classes were not particularly the source of new ideas or experimentation. A special report to the National Education Association in 1917 titled *Kansas City and Its Schools* made little mention of the earlier experimental functions of the vacation schools, except to say that they had once been operated privately by women. These schools, the report argued, were useful for "backward children" who lagged behind in their regular work, and another study by the City Club of Toledo two years later emphasized the same general trend. In less than a generation, memories had so dimmed that the initial impetus behind vacation schools was lost to history. What had once been an experimental, evolving, nonformal alternative to the schools was now part of the system.[31]

Contrary to social control theorists, the privately funded vacation schools were immensely popular institutions whose greatest faults were that they reached too few children and failed to refashion the regular schools. In their earliest days, these experimental schools offered some children relief from the boredom of hot summer days. Parents applauded them and preferred their influence on their children over street gangs, loafing, and the many temptations in city streets and alleys. Vacation schools, of course, added some variety to the curriculum but never transformed the public schools. But, like its closely related reforms of the Progressive era—playgrounds and social centers—the vacation school was one of the best examples of school expansion and extension during the period. It demonstrated the complex ways in which laypeople contributed to the development of new educational ideas at the grass roots and tried to make centralized institutions open to changes that might benefit local neighborhoods.

III

The effects of urban poverty on children's lives were a constant concern of educational reformers during the Progressive era. Throughout works such as Jacob Riis's *How the Other Half Lives*, Robert Hunter's *Poverty*, and John Spargo's *The Bitter Cry of the Children*, ran a common interest in how poverty affected children's housing, nutrition, education, and overall care. The most famous muckraking photographs of the period show poor children huddling in dank rooms in tenements, laboring in notorious sweatshops, or stalking the city streets in search of recreational diversion. Famous reformers as well as many ordinary parents complained of children going to lurid movies, joining street gangs, and shooting craps on the corner. Like the vacation school movement, playground innovation was partially a reaction against commercial amusements and a response to fears of juvenile crime, especially dominant social concerns at the turn of the century. Always a key ingredient in social change in the Progressive era, voluntary associations once again became a prime force behind educational change.

As property values increased as a result of inflation, and growing populations placed demands on certain neighborhoods, local cities had an anomalous situation: more and more children but fewer and fewer safe places for them to play. Vacant lots and common ground often disappeared, and in many congested neighborhoods mortar and brick replaced spots of green. Some of today's streets are safer places for children to play than parks and playgrounds, but at the turn of the century reformers continued the long battle against the street that had characterized school reform throughout the nineteenth century.[32]

As one contemporary reformer argued in 1903, "The narrow streets become like ovens under the scorching rays of the sun, which beat down from above and reflect from the buildings at all sides." At the same time, the streets were filled not only with questionable characters who taught children to smoke, drink, and curse—the bane of children's existence for generations—but they also threatened children's health. "Each gust of wind raises a cloud of dust, which analysis proves to be 95 percent horse manure, to fill the eyes and lungs of the children." The beautiful parks of many cities gave little regular relief, since they were often miles from tenement districts and inaccessible to little children who lacked escorts or carfare. Once again, class differences that translated into housing differences created varying opportunities for play and leisure. Children born through no fault of their own in congested districts, according to reformers, lacked safe and desirable places to play.[33]

Playgrounds were not an invention of the Progressive era. They existed next to some local schools in the nineteenth century, but never before had they stirred so much controversy or plans for reform. Numerous organizations formed in American cities with the primary object of creating playgrounds. And, like so many other innovations, playgrounds became linked to the most accessible institution for each child: the neighborhood school. As one chronicler of the movement asserted in 1910, the "Playground movement in this country has been begun in nearly every case through private initiative. A Mothers' Club, A Civic Club, or some other private organization begins an agitation."[34]

Because individuals with diverse social backgrounds and political orientations became involved in reform, the history of playground development cannot be explained through a single explanatory device such as social control. A wide variety of groups ranging from women's clubs to parent organizations to trade unions and Socialist parties lobbied for school playgrounds. In addition to having the support of these voluntary groups that were interested in many social welfare reforms, the playground movement included more highly specialized organizations of laypeople who lobbied solely for this innovation. Examples included the Children's Playground Association of Toledo (formed in 1899 and the predecessor of the Complete Education League), the Children's Playground League of Rochester (1903), the Milwaukee Outdoor Art and Improvement Association (1903), and the Kansas City Public Playground Association (1908). With representatives from women's clubs, trade unions, Socialist organizations, and other interest groups, these lobbyists demanded more attention to organized play.[35]

One writer in the *Playground* who analyzed the proliferation of public play spaces during the Progressive era argued that women's activism was central to the wider recreational use of the schools. Even though women did not dominate in the playground movement as they did in the promotion of vacation schools, the generalization was basically sound. The Women's Educational and Industrial Union ran a popular playground in a congested part of Rochester as early as 1899 and with other voluntary groups firmly supported the expansion of municipal recreation. The Woman's Suffrage Association of Toledo also endorsed playground construction in petitions before the ward school board in 1895, when the modern playground movement was just growing in American cities. The association paved the way for later activist groups such as the City Federation of Women's Clubs and the Women's Educational Club.[36]

In Milwaukee, as elsewhere, women were prominent in the playground movement. The Woman's Club of Wisconsin, the Woman's School Alliance, the Social Economics Club, the Social Culture Club, and the Council of Jewish Women endorsed many child welfare reforms during the Progressive era, including playgrounds. And as in other cities, these women did not stand alone, for the local movement was championed by the men and women in the Children's Betterment League, the South Side Educational Association, the Westminster Civic Club, trade unions, and the Social Democratic Party. Citizens in the Kansas City Public Playground Association built upon the work of the Athenaeum, which had privately funded vacation schools and playgrounds with the aid of mothers' unions after the turn of the century. Women, therefore, continued to exert considerable influence on social policy related to children's welfare.[37]

Labor unions also contributed notable leadership in the playground movement in Rochester, Toledo, Milwaukee, and Kansas City. Winfred Smith, a leader in the Central Trades and Labor Council of Rochester, was an official of the Children's Playground League and nationally prominent in the Playground and Recreation Association of America. In 1907 the Rochester Labor Council "cheerfully" endorsed the work of local playground enthusiasts. The unions attacked proposals by elite officials who sought the expansion of Rochester's beautiful parks but ignored the needs of inner-city children. "We need breathing places for our little ones in the crowded centers of population far more than we need any addition to our large park system," grumbled the *Labor Journal* in 1907.[38]

The *Toledo Union* in 1897 similarly applauded the expansion of accessible parks and playgrounds for area children. It especially praised the pioneering work under way at Golden Rule Park and Golden Rule Playground, the brainchild of Samuel M. Jones. The *Toledo Union Leader*, founded in 1907, was also a staunch supporter of more parks and accessible playgrounds. The Industrial Council of Kansas City even had a working-class poet who conceived of lyrical paths to reform. Titled "Give Them Playgrounds," his poem read:

> How about the little children,
>   And a place for them to play;
> Will the Park Board keep them waiting
>   Until the Judgement Day?
>
> The children cannot raise a fund
>   To help their cause along,
> But public sentiment you'll find
>   In their behalf is strong.
>
> We all know that playgrounds
>   For the children are a boon,
> But the motto of the Park Board
>   Seems to be, "Not Yet, But Soon."[39]

Earlier, the ill-fated Labor Political League had included children's playgrounds in its municipal platform in 1904, and the labor and Socialist *Missouri Staats-Zeitung* gave total support to this phase of school extension.[40]

Socialists realized that parks, playgrounds, and other social programs would never eliminate crime or replace their basic goal of redistributing wealth and power in America. Still, they joined with liberal reformers and viewed the establishment of playgrounds as a form of social justice. Rochester's Socialist Labor Party, politically to the left of the Socialist Party, urged municipal playgrounds for children as early as 1899, and the Labor Lyceum banded together with almost a dozen other organizations to secure municipal funding for playgrounds, vacation schools, and social centers in 1907. Socialist clubwoman Mabel Kennon optimistically predicted that when private property was abolished in the future, local children would have many safe places in which to romp and play. Christian Socialists, such as Golden Rule Jones, and prominent Toledo clubwomen were very active in the Children's Playground Association. Over in Kansas City, the Socialist Party wrote a long diatribe in 1904 against the school board for lagging behind playground construction and ignoring the welfare of the working classes. According to the Socialists, the school board was "absolutely capitalistic, and the class it represents is not interested in taxing itself to give the children of the working class any further facilities for education."[41]

Thousands of members in Milwaukee's Federated Trades Council and in the Social Democratic Party strenuously endorsed playground expansion. As early as 1902, the party platform had playgrounds on its list of educational demands, which soon included lunches, social centers, the direct election of the school board, full funding for the schools, and other ideas that had increased appeal with the grassroots. The *Social Democratic Herald* and the *Milwaukee Leader* openly supported civic associations, parent groups, and women's clubs that led the local playground movement. The *Leader* published scathing indictments of the city's reluctance to provide safe places in which children could play. Editorial cartoons showed how children were forced to dodge trolley cars and automobiles and how they played on garbage dumps and on rooftops because capitalists refused to pay their fair share of taxes. Emil Seidel, the Socialist mayor in 1910 and alderman for many years, was long remembered locally as a friend of the children and of playground expansion.[42]

Like the vacation schools, urban playgrounds were often viewed as "experimental" programs, were initially funded privately, and became very popular with many local residents. The Women's Educational and Industrial Union of Rochester opened a playground in a principally Italian neighborhood in 1900. Located at the No. 18 School, it attracted foreign and native-born children from throughout the city. One day on the overcrowded and popular playground, a newspaper reporter found "all types of miniature humanity: Celtic eyes that twinkled with fun; swarthy little

Fourth of July Celebration, Rochester School No. 9 Playground, 1910

Source: *The Fifty-Fifth Report of the Board of Education of the City of Rochester, New York* (1910)

Hungarians; Fritz and Dorothea with florid complexions and round merry faces; Norse boys with blue eyes, flaxen hair and almost defiant look; and the clean-cut, classic features of the American girl."[43]

Ethnic stereotypes aside, the playgrounds of Rochester fairly swarmed with all kinds of children. After countering the opposition of some local neighbors, the Children's Playground League established a playground at Brown's Square in 1903. The square had a reputation for radicalism, since it was the traditional location for many labor rallies and Socialist agitation. But the Playground League competently established a supervised playground in the area. Literally thousands of children were also taken by league members on summer excursions to Rochester's beautiful outlying parks. Social Gospelers, trade union members, women, and other grassroots activists participated in the local efforts, which reportedly yielded splendid results. Commenting on the summer excursions, the Children's Playground League noted, "No one who witnessed the pleasure of the children had a shadow of a doubt of the success of the undertaking, nor did he fail to be personally interested."[44]

The Children's Playground League of Toledo, under the guidance of Golden Rule Jones and assorted liberal reformers, established the city's

Samuel M. "Golden Rule" Jones and the Art of the High Kick, 1902

Courtesy: Toledo-Lucas County Public Library

first supervised playground in 1899. Located on Canton Avenue, a few blocks from downtown in a poor and congested area, the playground rested upon a former garbage dump. Jones and other volunteers removed "102 loads of old tin cans, bottles, and like rubbish" from the site to give children another place to play. The *Toledo Blade* reported that this "experimental playground" had children "swarming on the lot ever since the work was started" and concluded that it was a good antidote to associations in "the streets and gutters" that often fostered "strong dispositions toward vice and crime."[45]

A large number of social welfare associations contributed to playground development in Milwaukee, and here, too, the popularity of the innovation was equally striking. Both the *Daily News* and the *Free Press*, for example, commented on the popularity of supervised playgrounds, and the *Sentinel* added the conservative idea that they would help combat vice and crime. One of the first supervised playgrounds established by the Milwaukee Outdoor Art and Improvement Association was on the corner of Greenbush and Mitchell on the Polish South Side. On opening day in 1906, children anxiously awaited their chance to play, and "in rushed hundreds of grimy-faced, ragged youngsters to take possession of the swings, see-saws, and other attractions." "My littlest brother wouldn't eat no dinner, he was so anxious for the playground to open," stated one little girl, who strained her voice trying vainly to coax her brother home. But why eat when one could play that popular game, mumble-the-peg?[46]

Municipal governments spent more than $100 million on the construction and operation of playgrounds during the Progressive era, but not everyone was equally pleased with this development. There was often a wide gap between the promises of some reformers and the actual activities that occurred on the neighborhood playgrounds. Some playground enthusiasts promised law and order, but only contributed to the creation of play spaces that were occasionally noisy and socially disruptive. Some playgrounds were simply too popular, with the result that they seemed to do everything *but* control youth. Overcrowding and boisterous activity at some play sites demonstrated that children were active folk not easily beguiled by the lofty plans of adult reformers of whatever persuasion.[47]

Parks and playgrounds were indeed touted from time to time by various reformers as breeding grounds of good citizenship, morality, and civic virtue. They offered alternatives to the street and to environments that presumably nurtured impure thoughts and questionable socialization. "Play is instrumental and helpful indeed in making Americans of foreigners," added a confident writer in the *Playground* in 1912, and tons of paper and ink were sacrificed to prove that organized play hindered crime. Few reformers demonstrated whether the playgrounds produced any of these outcomes. Fewer still explained whether these popular innovations were viewed in similar ideological terms by their clientele, neighborhood parents and children, who may have liked this form of municipal welfare but viewed safe play spaces as summer relief for youth and nothing more.[48]

No matter what the intent of the different advocates of school playgrounds, the innovations sometimes became a convenient place for children to learn to smoke, drink, fight, and curse. By allowing larger numbers of children to congregate into a smaller space than was possible on many city streets, playgrounds in some instances became centers for social disorder. Undoubtedly many children were socialized to orderly values, some were Americanized, and others were taught discipline, cooperation, and respect for public property. However, the children who in the eyes of reformers most needed socialization and discipline could easily stay away from the playground, since attendance was voluntary. When playgrounds were regularly supervised—increasingly an aim in the schools—the most unruly children probably avoided them. Loafers and gang leaders always had more attractive pursuits than playing in a pile of sand. When poorly supervised, playgrounds were more attractive to these young people, who could turn a "reform" into personal vehicles of social disorder.

Isolated forms of dissent against school playgrounds surfaced in many cities. Newspaper editors occasionally likened them to new forms of state socialism, like penny lunches and vacation schools, which improperly relieved parents of their responsibilities for caring for their children. In 1908 the Rochester Federation of Catholic Societies, whose members realized that some groups hostile to organized religion favored playgrounds and school extension, attacked these innovations as socialistic, expensive, and conducive to mass pauperization. More typical was the complaint that poor children were wild and could not be tamed. When the Children's Playground League of Rochester promoted a playground for Brown's Square, action was delayed for a year until local residents were assured that the grounds would be supervised and would not become a haven for thugs and criminals. Civic clubs attached to neighborhood school social centers after 1907 repeatedly had to defend poor children, who were sometimes accused by other neighbors of low morals, vile habits, and disregard for private property. The playground at the No. 9 School in an Italian neighborhood was attacked by some fervent Catholics who disliked Sunday baseball. They told the local alderman that "there was so much noise at the playground that the peace of the entire neighborhood was disturbed."[49]

Republican newspaper editors in Toledo, who preferred business "efficiency" and vocational education above all other reforms, claimed that all play and no work was the underlying philosophy of the new education. Playgrounds would not only make Jack a dull boy but also an "idle shirk." Some teachers at the Erie School, located in an impoverished neighborhood north of downtown, feared in 1906 that a proposed playground there would only increase crime and become a hangout for "drunkards and toughs." Only after the Toledo Federation of Women's Clubs and the school board, which jointly sponsored the playground, assured teachers that there would be sufficient supervision did they approve the plan. Exactly how much "vice" or "crime" were promoted by (or, conversely, prevented by) local playgrounds in various cities is difficult to assess. More than once, however, Emil Seidel and Milwaukee's trade union leaders repudiated charges that "Nightly Orgies" abounded at the local playgrounds. From time to time local residents attacked the evening behavior of many immigrant and working-class children.[50]

In Milwaukee as elsewhere there were the usual problems of children breaking windows, trespassing on neighbors' lawns, and trampling vegetable patches while searching for that missing baseball. Some citizens occasionally complained that the local playgrounds teemed with children who reveled into the dark night. When neighbors chastised local children for their rudeness or questioned their activities, children often replied with "impertinent answers" and foul language. Because of these activities, residents of some neighborhoods feared that playgrounds would lower property values. Delegations of citizens sometimes appeared before various school boards and opposed playgrounds in the interests of peace and tranquility, but they generally swam against the current of the times. Additional playgrounds, increased tax support for municipal recreation, and the continual expansion of related welfare characterized city life in the Progressive era, even though a defiant minority of citizens realized that playgrounds were not necessarily a cure for the ills of the city street.

School playgrounds, therefore, like the reform movements that sponsored them, had contradictory features. Far from constituting an agency for domination or liberation, playgrounds never reached enough children to attain either end. Dozens of voluntary groups enthusiastically lobbied for playgrounds to serve every child in their municipality. Standing on the threshold of a new era in public recreation, many reformers had bountiful visions that were never translated into living reality. When the Children's Playground League assembled in 1903, it promised "a spot for every child in Rochester to play." When the Children's Playground Association of Toledo opened its second public playground before hundreds of appreciative residents, Golden Rule Jones told the audience: "When your children grow old, there will be hundreds of them. There will be playgrounds for everybody."[51]

Economic problems often thwarted the plans of voluntary groups and sympathetic school board members who constructed the first municipal playgrounds at the turn of the century. School enrollments increased rapidly during these years, causing a shortage of funds at times for basic school construction. Playgrounds also competed with every other innovation for an appropriation. Moreover, class considerations greatly determined which neighborhoods received new playgrounds. Various reformers—whether Socialist workers or capitalist employers—argued that, as in the case of vacation schools, children in the most congested sections of town especially needed playgrounds and more spots of green. Even this problem was further complicated, since these areas had the most children per acre but frequently very expensive and scarce real estate. One observer also noted that a playground in some instances used land needed for more housing; the price of buying land for a playground was dear and could effectively force rents higher than before.[52]

The class bias in school playground policy was extensive and difficult to overcome. For example, the native elite on Milwaukee's East Side had larger homes, more spacious yards, and easier access to the parks. The working-class South Side, by contrast, had smaller homes and yards, larger families, and less money for transportation for children. Hence many local reformers, believing playgrounds would equalize opportunities for the poor, centered their efforts in the most congested, working-class areas. Such logic meant that the voluntary associations of Rochester placed their earliest playgrounds in the Italian and immigrant neighborhoods and at Brown's Square. Toledo's were placed in poorer areas near downtown and on the industrial East Side. And, in Kansas City, reformers tried to center their attention on the North End and the First Ward, the area's most crime-ridden and poverty-stricken districts. Playground associations publicly called for playgrounds everywhere, for all children; privately they began their efforts in selected neighborhoods, making the playgrounds in part a form of municipal charity.

Gradually, of course, playgrounds fanned out across the city, and many wealthier wards that had single dwelling housing with convenient yards also received more public play spaces. This eliminated some of the class determinants of public play for children. By 1912, Toledo had playgrounds for approximately one-third of its schools and Rochester had a slightly lower proportion, followed closely by Milwaukee and Kansas City. Comparative statistics on the number and public use of playgrounds are often misleading or notoriously difficult to assemble, since the information was gathered irregularly, calculated by different methods, and printed with conscious political intent. Some reformers undoubtedly emphasized the bright side of life when praising "hundreds" of children for their behavior on a particular afternoon. Everyone counted with particular goals in mind. When newspapers, for example, reported in 1902 that fifteen thousand children went on school excursions run by Toledo's City Federation of Women, they failed to explain who gathered the statistic; how many children participated one, two, or three times; whether there were limits on attendance; and whether the statistic was an estimate or carefully determined.[53]

Information on the size of playgrounds from city to city and neighborhood to neighborhood is also difficult to collect and of limited value. More important, it is virtually impossible to state precisely which children of particular neighborhoods or sections of the city attended various play-grounds. Newspapers regularly noted that children would often travel from different districts to use a popular play spot, and one cannot presume that playgrounds in a predominately Italian neighborhood were only used by Italians. Rochesterians, it will be recalled, found all forms of "miniature humanity" at the No. 19 school: swarthy immigrants as well as genteel Americans. But exactly which children attended the playgrounds? Certainly gang leaders or "street gamins" would have found supervised play unattractive, meaning that those youth whom reformers wanted to influence probably slipped through the educational net.

If available statistics are unsatisfactory indicators of popular use, there are many other types of materials that illuminate the social role of playgrounds in different communities during the Progressive era. Numerous local studies, for example, were published near the end of the period in an attempt to assess the influence of different public amusements and recreational facilities on the quality of urban life. Quite consistently, reformers discovered that playgrounds, vacation schools, and social centers rarely competed effectively against the wide range of amusements and activities provided by private enterprise and the city street. In the battle between the street and the school, the street usually emerged victorious.

A special report by the Milwaukee City Club in 1914 discovered what everyone already knew: more children played on streets than on playgrounds. To highlight this phenomenon, the cover of the report had a photograph of a street gamin who, according to the caption, had "No Place to Play." Actually there were many places to play, but the playground was only one place of diversion and entertainment after the turn of the century. At best, Milwaukee's playgrounds could handle one-third of the city's children between the ages of four and nineteen, and that assumed that three hundred children could fit comfortably on every acre of playground space. At least two-thirds of the childhood population, therefore, played elsewhere. When asked by the expert in charge of a school board survey where they played, many children quickly responded: "We play in the alley, that's our yard."[54]

Children in Milwaukee were in little danger of being unduly controlled or excessively reformed by the playground, though some undoubtedly were. As in most cities, the poorer districts had smaller private yards in which to play but also proportionally fewer open spaces and playgrounds. And there were many other sources of recreation besides the playground for every child with even a few cents to spend. The Milwaukee City Club survey estimated that although thirty-two thousand children between four and nineteen years old were within a reasonable

distance from a supervised playground, three-fourths of the total childhood population were not, so they "spend their playtime in streets, alleys,
and vacant lots." There were also pool halls, cheap theaters, dance halls,
gangs, and many other sources of diversion with which the schools could
never adequately compete and certainly never supplant. There was the
Avery Street Gang, which usually fought with the Patrick Avenue Gang,
or anyone else who stepped into their territory. And there was reportedly
a colorful gang of seven-year-olds whose chief activity, according to its
leader, was in "beatin' up de fellars on de next street."[55]

A massive survey of Kansas City's recreational resources by the Board
of Public Welfare at the same time similarly found that playgrounds
were a small aspect of public recreation for the majority of children. An
examination of the northwestern part of the city showed the situation at
its worst extreme. This district included mostly the First Ward, near
the bend in the Missouri River. With approximately twelve thousand
residents, who were mostly poor native whites and others of more than
a dozen foreign nationalities, the ward had one of the highest crime rates
in Kansas City. Of the 1,238 dwellings in the area, more than half were
inspected by the city for this survey. They included 48 lodging houses,
47 "bawdy" houses, and 203 tenement houses. At least four thousand
homeless men roamed through the streets, constituting most of the potential tenants for the lodging houses. Some of these people included "capable
working men displaced by industrial depressions, disturbances, or labor-
saving inventions; all classes of casual or seasonal laborers between jobs;
boys out on a lark or seeking their fortunes; the inefficient on account of
sickness, age, and disability, victims of drugs or strong drink; vagrants,
beggars, and occasional strays from the ranks of professional criminals."[56]

The area had infamous gangs of every variety, dozens of saloons, and
for the nearly three thousand parochial and public school children—one
playground. The playground competed with the largest number of commercial entertainments in all of Kansas City. These included 19 motion
picture shows, 60 pool halls, 10 dance halls, 6 penny arcades, 4 shows
for "men only," 2 "medical museums," and shooting galleries, bowling
alleys, and theaters. In addition to these attractions, of course, there were
countless activities for free on the city streets and alleys. Conditions were
less extreme in other parts of Kansas City, but the northwest area was
where reformers tried to search for alternatives to street education and
recreation provided by private enterprise, all with dismal results.[57]

To some degree, the class stigma associated with playgrounds disappeared over time, since few people today regard municipal funds for
recreation as desirable solely for the poor. But playgrounds and many
other social services were initially established primarily for the poorer

classes, for immigrants as well as the native born. Progressive voluntary organizations, motivated by diverse aims and expectations, fought numerous battles against the temptations and lures of the city street and made the first inroads into the area of public responsibility for organized play. Radical third parties and Socialists saw struggles over leisure, play, and recreation as part of larger political and community struggles against capital, and women used the issue of school extension to popularize their organizations, to grow in political importance, and hence to expand women's rights.

The popularity of many of the new playgrounds demonstrates that many parents endorsed this new alternative to the alley and the street, preferring supervised play at the neighborhood school to their children's potential membership in street gangs or slumming at local dives. Perhaps, like a number of the radical voluntary groups, some parents appreciated neighborhood social services in an era when centralization stripped them of power in the political economy and its supporting institutions. Whatever the case, playgrounds served as an important illustration of school extension during the Progressive era. Playgrounds became, however, only one of the many alternatives available for leisure activities, a single option to sometimes more-alluring attractions found on many city streets.

Chapter 7

The Spirit of the
Little Red Schoolhouse

I

From the hot and dusty city streets, with their many lures and temptations, the story of school extension shifts to the more alluring shores of Lake Mendota on the University of Wisconsin campus. The year was 1911. In Madison, in a large fortresslike building that still stands today, hundreds of citizens from across the country convened to discuss one of the era's most fascinating educational reforms: the social center. Sponsored by the university's famous extension division and inspired by Edward J. Ward of Rochester, the conference attracted many distinguished visitors. Those in attendance included the new Socialist working-class mayor of Milwaukee, Emil Seidel; the next president of the United States, Woodrow Wilson; Kansas City's industrial relations expert, Frank P. Walsh; and the New York religious divine Josiah Strong.

Delegates from rural and urban areas debated the fine points of social centers for several days. In the end, however, enough agreement was reached that a constitution was drafted and a new organization formed: the Social Center Association of America. "A spirit akin to the fervor of a great religious revival actuated the whole conference," wrote an observer in *Survey* magazine. "It seemed to those present that America was at least about to develop a true democracy." The spirit of the meetings was intense, reaching a crescendo when several hundred people broke out into song on the final day:

> Come close and let us know the joy
>   Our Fathers used to know,
> When to the little old school house
>   Together they would go.

> Then neighbor's heart to neighbor warmed
>   In thought for common good;

We'll strike that fine old chord again –
    A song of neighborhood.[1]

The conference will never be remembered for its memorable song lyrics. Still, the meetings symbolized that the social center movement had reached national proportions. Cities such as Rochester, Toledo, Milwaukee, and Kansas City represented only a handful of the hundreds of communities across the nation that established these centers. By 1910, the social center concept was endorsed for various reasons by educators of the stature of John Dewey, G. Stanley Hall, and Charles W. Eliot and by politicians ranging from Theodore Roosevelt to Robert M. La Follette. Supported by a wide range of national welfare and educational organizations, the movement produced a national association, a short-lived journal, and numerous informational bulletins from the federal government and private foundations. And on the local level, educational reformers ranging from the Socialists to middle-class clubwomen to efficiency advocates championed wider school use.[2]

School extension and the general idea of wider school use in the Progressive era found their greatest expression in the social center movement. The desire to utilize schools for broader public purposes than in the past through programs such as vacation schools, playgrounds, and use of local facilities for meeting places first appealed to many Americans during the social upheaval of the 1890s. Responding directly to the overall trends toward centralization, many citizens in the new century struggled to make schools more accessible for local residents. While school boards were controlled by more elite individuals who increased the power of superintendents, numerous voluntary groups tried to counter their moves through their own movements for change from outside the system. Educators, of course, ultimately endorsed social centers with different degrees of enthusiasm. Yet the earliest, primary thrust for the innovation came from the grass roots, from men and women who ordinarily lacked power in policy decisions, who believed that educational control had drifted too far from parents, and who disliked the "better class" of individuals who dominated urban school governance.

Like many Progressive school innovations, the social center movement had complex origins and was supported by individuals representing a broad social and political spectrum. Some activists rooted the idea in the town meetings of colonial New England, others pointed to the previous educational aims of evening schools, lyceums, and chautauquas, and some even viewed the Roman forum as the real antecedent of this phase of Progressive reform. The concept of efficiency sometimes figured in the writings of Edward Ward, the leader of Rochester's social centers; however, like other reformers, he often pitched his arguments to the character of his audiences: to businessmen, fuller use of the schools meant dollars-and-cents economy; to physicians, a way to curry favor in the neighborhood; to conservatives, a way to reduce delinquency by offering children alternatives to street gangs; to democrats, a free forum for public debate of timely subjects to increase civic intelligence and general knowledge.[3]

Rural imagery infused the writings of social center advocates. Ward, for example, occasionally made nostalgic appeals for the spirit of the little red schoolhouse. "The real ancestor of the public school social center is not the social settlement," Ward claimed in *Survey* magazine in 1909, "but the little red schoolhouse back home, which, in the evenings, was used for a common meeting place for the neighborhood." An ordained Presbyterian clergyman, Ward had once ministered to rural folk, from whom he absorbed an enduring love of small-town simplicity. A correspondent in *American Education* in 1912 similarly invoked rural imagery in asserting that "the little red schoolhouse of our fathers and mothers' day with its spelling matches, singing schools, and Sunday services blazed the trail which was lost for a time but which recently has been rediscovered."[4]

Other observers disagreed that revived memories of the rural past explained the nation's current fascination with the social center. An Anglophile such as Woodrow Wilson, for example, saw the centers as a manifestation of our Teutonic flair for organization and representative government, and many reformers hoped that social centers would become the focal point of the neighborhood, similar to the town-meeting venues of colonial New England. Others more commonly believed that the movement was a response to the isolation of urban life and the deprivations caused by industrial capitalism, with their ill effects on family life, income distribution, and general social welfare. "The root of the movement lies deep down in the growing realization that those upon whom falls the heat and burden of the day have a right to more than mere existence," claimed a representative of this position in the *American Review of Reviews.*[5]

Surprisingly few advocates of the social centers argued that they were trying to reestablish a form of community life that once existed in the city. Ward, for example, had lived in cities as well as in rural areas, but evinced little understanding of how the "community" interacted with city schools prior to school board reform movements in the late nineteenth century. The leaders of the ward system were not especially enthusiastic about the use of schools as community centers either for adults or children, and political machines placed easy access to local schools low on their social agenda.

Indeed, rules and regulations often expressly forbade the community use of urban schools in the nineteenth century. The architecture of the schools was designed for children, not adults, and the addition of auditoriums and other meeting places was an early-twentieth-century phenomenon. Certainly many civic organizations, including various women's clubs, working-class groups, and radical third parties labored diligently in the 1890s to open the schools for wider use, often in an effort to blunt some of the effects of centralization. Late-nineteenth-century schools were used for graduation exercises and special occasions, but Rule 32 of the Milwaukee school board, written in the 1860s, remained in force throughout the Victorian era: "Scholars shall not assemble about the school building exceeding thirty minutes before school, and then they must enter their respective rooms, take their seats, and pursue their studies. . . . NO PLAYING MUST EVER BE ALLOWED IN THE SCHOOL BUILDING." Such rules militated against the idea of school extension yet prevailed in many American cities.[6]

Strictures against adult use were common and lapses from such rules usually temporary, though they did occur. In Toledo in the 1860s, President Charles W. Hill persuaded his peers on the board of education to allow high school cadets the use of the schools for military drills. Teachers were also occasionally allowed to use the schools for free in the summer to operate "select" schools to supplement their meager incomes. In the 1840s, the Rochester schools, later the preeminent leader in the social center movement, had gone even further by allowing religious services in the local schools on weekends because of a shortage of available buildings. Neighborhood use proved to be short-lived. Other segments of the community demanded the separation of church and state, and the schools were then sealed from religious as well as nonreligious groups for several decades.[7]

Clarence Perry, the efficiency expert of the Russell Sage Foundation, who rivaled Edward Ward as a major promoter of wider use, aptly described the prevailing state of affairs: "The children who went to school back in the eighties," he wrote, "skipped out of the school house door at half past three and scampered down the street shouting with glee. Instruction was finished for the day and the building turned over to the janitor for sweeping." In response to a many-sided grassroots movement for school extension, this narrower conception of education slowly changed in the 1890s. The quality and extensiveness of new evening schools, recreational programs, and social centers varied from city to city. As in the case of vacation schools and playgrounds, the realities of the social centers often fell far below many people's expectations. Still, the social center movement—whether it was called school extension, school socialization, the Rochester movement, or the wider use of the school plant—remained a heated political concern of competing voluntary groups, school boards, and superintendents throughout the early twentieth century.[8]

II

Urban social centers were rooted less in the rural past than in the dynamism of women's and parents' organizations beginning in the 1890s. Edward Ward and many local activists always recognized this aspect of urban reform. "Wherever, as at many of the schools of Rochester, there is a flourishing Parent-Teachers' Association," Ward believed, one found "the germ of the development of a Social Center." Indeed, perhaps the most important early forces behind the wider use of the schools were mothers' unions and parent-teacher associations that first permanently organized in American cities in the 1890s. These local agencies for reform became visible nationally in 1897 with the formation of the National Congress of Mothers.[9]

By actively supporting innovative educational programs and school social services, parent organizations helped reduce the isolation of institutions whose increasingly professionalized and centralized nature separated them from the life of the average citizen. Vacation schools, playgrounds, social centers, school lunches, domestic science and manual-training programs, as well as other innovations, received much of their impetus and strength from these organizations. In fact, this effort by voluntary groups to restructure education upon a foundation of activity, experimentation, and social welfare reflected changing popular perceptions of the social functions of schools and constituted a forgotten grass-roots expression of Progressive education.

As women's clubs expanded in the 1890s, the parlor rooms of gracious hosts became unsuitable for regular interaction. As a result, women turned to one of the most convenient and accessible institutions: the neighborhood school. By the late 1890s, many women's organizations had forced male ward leaders to open the schools for their meetings, whether on a weekly, biweekly, or monthly basis. This was true of the Women's Educational and Industrial Union of Rochester, the Women's Educational Club and affiliates of the City Federation of Women in Toledo, the Woman's School Alliance in Milwaukee, and the Athenaeum of Kansas City. By acquiescing to women's demands, school officials unintentionally contributed to a broader movement for even wider school use.

In addition to women's clubs, which contained mothers as well as some single and childless women, another catalyst of wider use in the 1890s were mothers' unions and related parent-teacher organizations. The years from the depression of 1893 through World War I witnessed the proliferation of parent organizations. The historical timing was hardly accidental, since the elimination of ward representation in the schools only encouraged more direct community participation. Ephemeral parent groups had existed in the nineteenth century, but without the popular enthusiasms of the Progressive era. "The Parents' Association," wrote one university professor in 1908, "seems to be a veritable exception of the general statement that 'there is nothing new under the sun.'" Mary Beard, the historian, also noted in 1915 that citizen activism was central to municipal reform movements and that "today there exists an incredible number of organizations whose main aim is cooperation with the schools in one way or another."[10]

Cooperation, of course, had been a nominal goal of the original common-school movement in Rochester, Toledo, Milwaukee, and Kansas City. Professional educators, school board members, and other citizens had routinely urged parents to support teachers and to applaud the evolving system. This new drive for cooperation between home and school in the 1890s produced an array of parent organizations. Clubwomen, many of whom were former teachers and currently mothers, not only met in the schools but often belonged to parent-teacher organizations and actively supported their formation.

Prominent clubwomen and school activists such as Helen B. Montgomery of Rochester, Pauline Steinem of Toledo, Lizzie Black Kander of Milwaukee, and Ruth Weeks of Kansas City all supported cooperation between home and school and every association that promoted that end. Urging more-frequent visits by parents to local schools, a subcommittee of the education division of the Women's Union in Rochester in 1897 wanted to make citizens "fully acquainted with their school system and to bring about a closer, more friendly relation between teacher and patron." Helen Montgomery claimed that parent organizations fostered that "intelligent cooperation" between parent and teacher that would "bring to bear on the child the strongest possible influence for good." Her sisters in other cities, like the members of Milwaukee's School Alliance, viewed "intimate and cordial relations between teachers and parents" as a prerequisite to all educational progress. Often mothers and former teachers, Alliance members understood how conflicts could divide home and school. The parent-teacher organization seemed like the ideal way to advance the best interests of the child.[11]

While local women's clubs encouraged parent-teacher associations in the 1890s, kindergarten teachers also emphasized the need for better home and school relations. In that way they also indirectly popularized the idea of wider school use and, ultimately, the social center. Kindergarten teachers continually promoted the establishment of mothers' clubs. Inspired by the writings of Friedrich Froebel, who desired a mystical unity of humankind, these teachers formed many of the nation's first permanent mothers' clubs in Rochester, Toledo, Milwaukee, Kansas City, and other

cities. The main thrust of professional teachers' organizations in the Progressive era was job security and economic well-being, but kindergarten
teachers and early childhood educators above all remained leading parent-
oriented enthusiasts in the early twentieth century. Froebel's call—"Come,
let us live with our children"—was expanded to include parents as well.[12]

Kindergarten instructors in the late nineteenth century often taught
in the poorest, immigrant-populated sections of the city. In Rochester,
however, the earliest mothers' meetings sponsored by a kindergarten
teacher met at the No. 14 School, located in a middle-class residential
area. The *Democrat and Chronicle* noted in 1896 that "these meetings are
for the purpose of bringing the teachers and mothers of children together
for a better understanding of the work" of schools. The success of mothers'
unions, as well as parent organizations that often evolved from them,
obviously depended on the mutual respect of teachers and parents. Miss
Adele Brooks, a kindergarten teacher described as "the mother of Mother's
Clubs" for her organizational talents, struggled with clubwomen and
others until mothers' unions appeared at nearly every Rochester school
after the turn of the century. In addition to the monthly meetings held by
local organizations, an annual mass meeting of several thousand mothers
convened in June. Brooks reportedly organized people from very different
social backgrounds. "Poor mothers, rich mothers, old mothers, young
mothers, white mothers, and black mothers attended the mass meeting"
in 1901, according to the *Union and Advertiser*. Little wonder, then, that one
observer in 1905 asserted that the mothers' unions were "in a flourishing
condition."[13]

Parent groups also flourished in Toledo in the early twentieth century.
Foremost among them was the Golden Rule Mothers' Club, which met
at Golden Rule Hall and promoted the Christian Socialism of Samuel M.
Jones. Occasionally a sympathetic newspaper editor would also encourage
more parental organizations, and grassroots representatives on the board
of education solidly endorsed such activism. For example, Pauline
Steinem, a grassroots reformer on the board from 1905 to 1909, rose to
power through her aggressive struggle to help establish some district
representation on the school board. Her faith in localism led her to sponsor
parent rallies in nearly every district school after her election to office.
She also held receptions for parents, who came and talked and criticized
every conceivable educational idea with her and with Progressive teachers
every Wednesday evening. These meetings, she contended, gave "the
teachers a better insight into the character of the pupils, and the parents
an unprejudiced opinion of the teachers." By 1910, one Toledo principal
remarked that although "there was a time when parents seldom entered

a schoolhouse except that they were angry and went there to scold . . . we are getting away from that very rapidly."[14]

In both Milwaukee and Kansas City, mothers' unions and parent associations similarly gained access to the schools for their meetings and thereby encouraged their wider use. In the working-class Jones Island neighborhood in Milwaukee in 1897, Principal Mary F. Flanders and kindergarten teachers organized poor German and Polish mothers "in order to awaken the interests of parents" in the schools in well-attended meetings. In Kansas City, as in many cities, kindergarten instructors formed the first mothers' unions during the depression of the 1890s, and by 1901 the *Daily Journal* wrote that "scarcely a month passes without the organization of some new union." Soon it was "not an uncommon thing for three or four hundred parents to visit one of the ward schools" on Patron's Day to demonstrate their concern for their children. This flurry of activity made Kansas City's parent-teacher associations, an outgrowth of these mothers' unions, the largest parent network in the world in 1919.[15]

For cities such as Rochester, Toledo, and Milwaukee, where local representation on the school board had suffered a decisive setback during the Progressive era, these organizations provided mechanisms by which parents advanced neighborhood interests. In Toledo, for example, parent associations throughout this period actively lobbied for new and improved school facilities as well as for various social welfare programs. After 1910 in particular, when a rural-controlled state legislature placed spending limits on Ohio cities, numerous parent organizations routinely appeared at the school board meetings and demanded new facilities and improvements for local neighborhoods. Very often, the most persistent parental lobbyists locally received new schools. In 1913, an indefatigable Ironville delegation from the working-class East Side, as well as many other parents, petitioned for and received notable building improvements for their schools as a result of their persistence.[16]

In a place such as Kansas City, with a long history of elite control of education, parent organizations brought the local schools and teachers into closer affiliation with parents and children. The often impersonal ways of the administration were not altered by new parents' groups, but mothers and fathers continued to work outside the system for local and citywide educational improvements. It is not surprising, of course, that the school system that was one of the most centralized led the world in parent organizations.

Parent groups had diverse goals in the Progressive era. Their basic aim, however, was to improve home and school relations and to make the schools more serviceable to the community. Along with other civic groups, they championed the funding of penny lunches, playgrounds, school gardens, medical and dental inspection, free eyeglasses for children, better sanitary conditions, and any number of improvements. In many ways, they contributed to the civic activism of the period. Instead of letting the schools drift further away from their control, many parent organizations tried to draw the schools closer to local neighborhoods. In the process, they popularized the idea of wider school use that ultimately nourished the social center movement. Often hostile to centralization, parents and other grassroots forces fought for innovations that might establish what local cities had never really experienced: the spirit of the little red schoolhouse that, as the song said, "our fathers used to know."

III

As new social services and programs entered the public schools after the turn of the century, many reformers soon endorsed the establishment of "social centers" in neighborhood schools. The simple notion that many innovations could be centered in the school encouraged the belief that the school could become the center of the community: the nucleus of varied social activities. In 1904, Rochester's new school superintendent discovered that every grammar school with an assembly hall was evolving as a center for community activities. The halls, he wrote, "are in constant use and become the center of the life of the school. They are used as assembly rooms; for classes in music and gymnastics and free games."[17]

Social centers—like vacation schools and playgrounds—were advocated by competing groups for different, often contradictory reasons, and the reform was therefore a many-sided phenomenon. To many people, the concept included the use of the schools as reading rooms, branch libraries, gyms, meeting places, polling places, and all forms of extension. Playgrounds, at least, can be counted, but it is impossible to say exactly when enough programs existed simultaneously to satisfy every reformer, or when schools had actually become a center of social life in the community. Did this occur, for example, when parent or women's groups simply gained access to the schools for their meetings in the 1890s? How many programs constituted a true center?

Even though the activities at playgrounds and vacation schools varied, these innovations lacked the complex nature of the "social center," which was usually a shorthand expression for a hodgepodge of different programs or cluster of ideas rather than a single entity. Even the delegates at the national social center conference held in Madison vigorously quarreled over what constituted a social center, or when a school had become one. Carroll Pearse, the superintendent of the Milwaukee schools during much of the Progressive era, recognized as much in 1909, stating, "Different cities are working out the Social Center idea along different lines. . . . The term Social Center does not as yet mean any one thing; no 'type' has been developed."[18]

The lack of precision in the phrase *social center* does not preclude analyzing the effects of wider use in education if one carefully preserves its different meanings in various contexts. For most people, *social center* meant the after-hours use of the schools in several nontraditional areas for children and adults. Since nearly every schoolhouse in Rochester, Toledo, Milwaukee, and Kansas City was regularly used as a meeting place for mothers' unions, parent associations, and women's clubs after the 1890s, they were all in a sense social centers. Some cities emphasized evening recreational programs for the community; others operated evening schools and stressed academic study. The Rochester centers, at least during their formative years under the guidance of Edward J. Ward, were very distinctive and demand special scrutiny.

The unique character of the Rochester social centers captured national attention between 1907 and 1911. "There is hardly a city in the United States but what is unfamiliar with the work of the Rochester social centers," claimed an author in the magazine the *Playground* in 1910. Under the leadership of Edward J. Ward, the city basked in the light of national recognition. The centers were featured in articles in lay periodicals such as the *Outlook* and the *Independent*; in professional magazines such as *American Education*, the *Journal of Education*, and the *American School Board Journal*; and in such welfare journals as the *Child-Welfare Magazine*, *Survey*, and *Charities and Correction*. Progressives such as Judge Ben Lindsey, Lincoln Steffens, and Brand Whitlock praised Ward's experiments in glowing terms and publicized them across the country.[19]

Rochester's social centers were not significant for being the first ones established in the United States. Several cities operated so-called social centers for a few years before the Rochester plan was approved by the city council and the board of education in 1907. Even the circumstances surrounding social center development in Rochester were not especially noteworthy, since centers across the nation owed their existence to the cooperative spirit binding civic organizations. Yet the circumstances certainly seemed unique and dramatic to the people of this city. More than a decade of civic struggle in Rochester for various social and school reforms culminated in 1907 with the creation of a School Extension Committee. "The Board of Education had absolutely nothing to do with the organization of this movement," claimed the president of the school board in 1910 in a disclaimer when opponents attacked the centers as un-American.[20]

President George Forbes was a professor at the University of Rochester, a Good Government leader, and a supporter of Ward and the social centers. He was also correct in stating that the demand for social centers came not from within the schools but from without. The School Extension Committee represented diverse segments of the community and claimed to represent the views of fifty thousand citizens. The eleven organizations that composed the group were hardly monolithic. They included the Playground League, the College Women's Club, the Daughters of the American Revolution, the Local Council of Women, the Officers' Association of the Mothers' Club, the Political Equality Club, the Social Settlement Association, the Women's Educational and Industrial Union, the Humane Society, the Central Trades and Labor Council, and the Labor Lyceum, who were better known locally as the Socialists. Social Gospel ministers also aided the cause.[21]

The *Labor Journal* summed up the local feeling in 1907 when it wrote: "The schools should be the people's clubs. The city's money is the people's money." This impressive display of civic cooperation between grassroots forces that had first gained public recognition in the 1890s culminated more than a decade of reform efforts in Rochester. Under the new centralized school board, which took power in 1900 through the combined support of Good Government leaders and Boss Aldridge, the first decade of the twentieth century witnessed more school reforms than any other comparable period in the city's educational history. The contradictions of trying to build locally oriented schools under a centralized school administration became as central to social center development as to all facets of grassroots innovation.[22]

Under the leadership of Susan B. Anthony and other Progressive women, the Women's Educational and Industrial Union had already locked horns with ward leaders in the 1890s and agitated for sewing classes, domestic science and manual-training programs, vacation schools, penny lunches, and other innovations. After the turn of the century, these women joined community interest groups such as the Children's Playground League and the Central Trades and Labor Council to demand the expansion of these service programs. This heightened concern with social welfare in the city schools led to the February 1907 meeting that produced the social center proposal. Under continual pressure from grassroots voluntary groups, the city council and board of estimate steadily increased the social center budget from 1907 to 1910, though many realized that Boss Aldridge's political influence made the centers extremely vulnerable.[23]

Even though the Rochester centers, like those elsewhere, resulted from intense voluntary group effort, their operations were nevertheless quite distinctive because of the influence of Edward J. Ward, who was the local supervisor between 1907 and 1910. Ward has been fundamentally misunderstood by many historians. Called everything from a rural romantic to a social engineer, from an elitist to an opponent of Socialism, Ward has become the personification of the paternalistic reformer.[24]

Critics of Ward and the social center movement properly note that advocates of the broader use of the schools often employed factory metaphors in their prose. In capitalist America, it could hardly be otherwise. Even educational luminaries such as Charles W. Eliot of Harvard University claimed that businessmen would not permit *their* physical plant to remain idle so many hours a day. *School plant* became synonymous with *schoolhouse*, an easy enough mistake in an era when capitalist consolidation affected every sphere of life. "When the public pays for schools, it pays for institutions that lie, as a rule . . . in profitless idleness eighteen hours out of every twenty four," claimed a writer in the *World's Work* in 1903. Locking up schools was "a waste of investment that private capital would not tolerate for a moment," and as Clarence Perry asserted, businessmen on school boards were finally "beginning to see that the utilization of the expensive school plant less than half the time . . . does not jibe with the policy followed in their places of business."[25]

During the Progressive era, "efficiency" often became an irresistible idea to many reformers and public school leaders. It was, however, only one of the many concepts social center advocates employed. Considering the social composition of school boards at the time, it would have been surprising if "efficiency" was not widely enunciated. But the range of groups that endorsed school extension was such that numerous, sometimes contradictory aims informed the movement. Writers in magazines and petitioners before school boards praised social centers for promoting citizenship, democracy, socialism, neighborhood solidarity, equality of opportunity, and social control. There was something in it for everyone.[26]

Edward J. Ward was one grassroots Progressive who could distinguish between pig iron and people, and between narrow and broad methods of argumentation. In his widely read volume *The Social Center* (1914), as well as in other writings, one is impressed not by the occasional interjection of *efficiency* in the analysis but by his broadly conceived views on education and numerous justifications for wider use. Writing in the *American City* in 1914, Ward asserted that an economic-efficiency argument was the "least" important justification for community centers; more important in his writings were family and home metaphors, since he wanted to connect the primary bonds of familial association to the entire neighborhood through the local schools. In *The Social Center* he titled one chapter "Like Home" (not "Like a Factory"), where he hoped that neighborhood families and citizens would meet at the schools to discuss significant social issues and make them a "homelike institution."[27]

Details of Ward's social philosophy that might present him in a more favorable light have been downplayed by some historians. For example, pacifists might be drawn to his belief in social cooperation and arbitration as a legitimate consideration in an interdependent world; historians of academic freedom might be interested in the circumstances surrounding his dismissal from a college teaching post for his allegedly radical views; women's rights advocates might be attracted to his full support for women's suffrage; and critics of the competition spawned by a capitalist social structure might perceive in his writings more than some narrow efficiency rationale.

Ward believed that modern society was based on the laws "of the brute—pretense, suspicion, fear, deception, exploitation, dog-eat-dog, caveat emptor." In condemning self-centered individualism, the abuse of public rights by private corporations, and the stranglehold of "political and economic bosses" over the citizenry, Ward exhibited a sense of moral outrage shared by many local Progressives. Undoubtedly these various elements of his social thinking caused this Social Gospel minister to leave the clergy, to join the Socialist Party as a young man, and to seek other avenues of public service. To describe him as an efficiency expert is to force his ideas and behavior into an ill-fitting straitjacket.[28]

In the context of his times, Ward was fairly democratic in his perspectives. After the Rochester school board hired him as social center director in 1907, he proceeded to translate his novel ideas into public policy. In many cities, community use of the schools reflected a philosophy of school uplift, which meant that the poorest neighborhood schools (often those also targeted for vacation schools and playgrounds) first became social centers. Ward, however, wanted to establish centers without any hint of class, ethnic, or racial bias. He was deeply critical of social-uplift theories that were specifically aimed at the poor. In a general sense, Ward believed that social centers "uplifted" the community by spreading democratic ideals. He accepted the belief that poor people "need the wholesome entertainment, the opportunities for physical and literary culture, and the inspiration which comes through club association." But poor people were not the only individuals who could benefit from the wider use of the schools: all people could profit from the social centers. Ward emphasized that "the Social Center, according to the Rochester idea, is not a municipal substitute for a social settlement. There is no taint of 'charity,' no paternalistic spirit of philanthropy about it."[29]

Ward firmly believed that the social centers as he conceived them promoted good citizenship, but citizenship training was a participatory process, not something the better class of people or the schools did to others. To Ward, charity organizations were condescending in their treatment of the poor, and he did not want Rochester's social centers to suffer from "the stigma of class service" or become "a sort of municipal charity institution." For that reason Ward established the first center at the No. 14 School, located in a middle-class area, before additional centers spread across the city. As he argued in *Survey* magazine, every city should establish its first center in a "relatively well-to-do neighborhood" and not in a section where one paternalistically attempted to "uplift the submerged, the poor."[30]

The Rochester centers were also distinctive because they followed Ward's emphasis on adult civic clubs over community recreational activities that were common elsewhere. This was the heart of the Rochester social center movement and what made Ward's contributions to schooling and to democratic theory so engaging. Historians who equate these clubs with the high school civics classes that generations of Americans have sometimes suffered through greatly exaggerate the comparison. Ward supported self-government for the adult clubs, a position that was strongly opposed by some members of the school administration. Ward claimed in the *Independent* in 1909 that "from the beginning there has been absolutely no limitation upon freedom of discussion, and the clubs have uniformly shown a desire to have every question fairly presented from both sides." To condemn Ward as a "social engineer" is to overlook his reluctance to interfere with the internal operations of the clubs. His defense of self-government ultimately helped destroy the local experiment.[31]

The only requirement that Ward levied on the adult civic clubs was that everyone in the city could join them and that everyone must have a chance to participate in the meetings. The meetings must not simply be nonexclusive, he argued, they must positively be "all-inclusive." School superintendent Herbert Weet later reminisced in a history of the centers that Ward's extreme views were simply unacceptable. The adult clubs, Weet complained, were "self-directing organizations. The only restriction placed upon them was that they could not be partisan or exclusive either in meetings or discussion. Any adult, therefore, was eligible to attend and to participate in the discussions, subject only to such rules as the club itself might see fit to make." As a result, he continued, these clubs "had in them a full quota of extremists for one cause or another." Anarchist and Socialist "extremists" would monopolize discussions, spread their heretical though false doctrines, and "give expression to extravagant and poorly timed views on public questions. These things are, of course, inherent in the open forum."[32]

Weet disliked open, unrestricted discussions, and he surely exaggerated the radicalism of local social center participants. Yet Weet understood that the relatively autonomous position of the adult clubs was the novelty of the Rochester experiment. Ward likened social center directors to hired clerks: they scheduled meetings, contacted potential speakers, and helped organize various affairs. If this was social engineering, he was all for it. Ward repeatedly argued that it was absurd either for social center employees or school board members to tell adults and taxpayers what subjects to discuss and how to analyze them at their meetings. Addressing the National Education Association in 1912, Ward asserted that the social center director and "his assistants in the various neighborhoods are not teachers, but servants of these neighborhood civic clubs, aiding in the preparation of programs, the work of publicity, and otherwise serving the owners of the building." Ideally, good citizenship in a democracy meant not simply obeying laws and voting, but also fully participating in the formulation of public policy through debates and citizen interaction.[33]

Ward's support for free speech and for autonomous adult participation was widely applauded by progressive members of the school board and the various community groups that initiated the movement. Under his guidance the social centers and civic clubs evolved in representative parts of the city along with the establishment of vacation schools and playgrounds for children. Within two years, the civic clubs multiplied from a single club to sixteen with fifteen hundred members; a League of Civic Clubs united these diverse groups to press for increased appropriations for the centers. Besides men's and women's civic clubs, junior clubs of adolescent girls and boys were formed. These clubs usually met on alternate weekday evenings, free of charge, followed by a general neighborhood meeting of all interested people on Saturday night.[34]

The civic organizations became reasonably all-inclusive, and the adult civic clubs were often highly representative of Rochester's class, ethnic, ideological, and racial interests. Besides Jews, Catholics, Protestants, and atheists, organized labor and business representatives often served on the steering committees of the local clubs. While Kansas City in particular followed the color line in its "community" centers, the Rochester clubs were racially integrated and prominently publicized as such in social center publications. The centers gained a reputation locally for radicalism and intense criticism of various municipal policies, and they were reportedly utilized by "people of all creeds, parties, and incomes." Italians and Swedes predominated in a few of the civic clubs, reflecting the local ethnic makeup of their neighborhood, as many different segments of Rochester found value in the concept of wider use.[35]

Free speech, debate, and interaction were the heartbeat of the adult clubs. Socialists argued with capitalists, atheists criticized the church, and the Turnverein debated the Prohibitionist Party. A broad range of subjects that affected the life of the average citizen captured the attention of participants. During the first year, for example, speakers led discussions under the titles "Duties of an Alderman," "Rochester's Milk," "Trusts," the "Tax Levy," "Socialist Policies," and the "Problems of This Community." Increasingly, however, the city boss looked askance at such discussions, which often condemned him as a dictator. By 1908, the chief Aldridge organ, the *Rochester Times*, began to claim that Socialists controlled the centers and threatened public order and morality. While supporting the idea of wider use in theory, the editor condemned the fact that "citizens other than Socialists" permitted them to "have the right of way" in discussions. Unless a "representative audience" regularly attended the centers, "persons whom we call cranks and faddists form the majority and crowd others aside." When that occurred the centers should be closed.[36]

Within the next several months, the city's five major newspapers followed the lead of the *Times* and demanded the end of the centers or at least a radical departure from past policies, namely, the firing of Ward, the purging of Socialist influence, and the end of free speech for adults. The pretext for the dissolution of the Rochester experiment was provided not by Ward as much as by the actions of his friend Kendrick Shedd, a

An Evening at Rochester's No. 9 Social Center

Source: *The Fifty-fifth Report of the Board of Education of the City of Rochester, New York* (1910)

University of Rochester professor who was the director of the No. 9 center. Shedd, who was forced to resign from the university for his radical views, was also the director of the Rochester Socialist Sunday Schools and the Young People's Socialist League. An extremely popular speaker, he had once lectured to the Labor Lyceum on the fallacies of radicalism but somehow became attracted to Socialism before 1910.[37]

The entire fate of the local movement publicly hinged on the No. 9 center, which had a reputation for radicalism because of Shedd's presence and the school's location in an immigrant neighborhood. One Sunday afternoon in 1909, Shedd sponsored a masquerade ball in which children reportedly dressed in costumes of the opposite sex, which caused a furor in the city. Catholic priests and various Protestants in the Minister's Association condemned the desecration of the Sabbath and hinted at sexual permissiveness that was headlined in the local newspapers. The speeches of any radicals or Socialists who talked at the centers were increasingly dramatized in the press, while milder discussions were often ignored. Conditions ripened for Boss Aldridge, who could point to these criticisms as just cause for the end of the experiment. The *Times* denounced the centers as the "hotbeds of Socialists" and the home of the "Ferrerists, Socialists, Anarchists, and other ists"; the *Post Express* claimed that "Mr. Ward's organization is a sort of socialist hatchery supported at the expense of the taxpayers"; and the *Union and Advertiser* called the centers "a fungus growth on the school system that should be got rid of."[38]

Ward and Shedd tried to undermine mounting criticism by pointing to the innocence of the masquerade ball. New rumors, however, surfaced, especially when Ward left the city on short trips. Ward's greatest clerical opponent, Father A. M. O'Neill (who labeled the centers Socialist centers) attacked the clubs for increasing class, ethnic, and religious conflict through the policy of unregulated discussions, and he accused Ward in the *Immaculate Conception Magazine* of falsifying his statistical reports to prove that the centers were popular. Then a minister reported that Ward, who had left the church, had approvingly written that the social centers would replace modern religion, which had outlived its usefulness. Ward denied this charge, but newspapers continued to assail the "unregulated and irresponsible utterances" at the centers. The Bill of Rights protected everyone's free speech, Ward responded, and adults in a democracy were capable of making up their own minds on public issues.[39]

Letters to the editor and editorials on the social center controversy filled the local newspapers in late 1909 and early 1910. The Shedd incident, the O'Neill accusations, and the Ward rebuttals made tremendous news stories but undermined the movement for wider use. Since the annual center appropriation would be determined in February 1910, delegations of citizens sensed the strength of the opposition and, therefore, flooded the mayor's office with petitions and personal appeals. The *Union and Advertiser* helped ensure that the debates would be heated when, in a joint effort with the other newspapers to throttle the local movement, it called Ward a radical and his associates a "motley array of Socialists, free thinkers, and apostles of discontent." Ward's admission that he was indeed a Christian Socialist only inflamed local debate, since it seemed to confirm the charge that "the social center idea as advocated by Mr. Ward and his friends is the thin edge of the socialistic wedge." The No. 9 civic club reaffirmed its commitment to free speech if not Shedd's political views and further intensified the debate: "Our movement has been started upon the proper basis—Free Discussion. Anything short of that spells failure."[40]

The community groups that had initially supported the Rochester experiment did not desert the cause. Women's club members marched on city hall. So did the delegates of the Central Trades and Labor Council, who "unanimously" passed a resolution favoring full funding for the center. They were joined by the Turnverein, settlement workers, mothers' clubs, parent-teacher organizations, and other associations that lobbied in vain for the survival of free speech and adult use of the schools. The centers, which had gained a national reputation, were all but eliminated by the city boss, who used Catholic opposition and major editorials from the press as proof of the unpopularity of the local innovation. Ward and his associates were dismissed, to the regret of grassroots community groups and sympathetic school board members. Rochester's centers after 1910 were almost indistinguishable from those in many parts of the nation, as they increasingly emphasized recreational programs to the virtual exclusion of adult civic participation. Ward viewed the failure of the Rochester movement as a failure of democracy. "Blinded by prejudice, narrowed by partisanship, made cowardly by suspicions, we have been kept back from the joy of human fellowship, we have let the government get out of our hands, we have failed of great achievement."[41]

Thanks to Professor Shedd, however, the No. 9 center, which was given a tiny appropriation by the school board to carry on its work, was able to provide one final example of how political bosses could crush efforts at free speech, especially when discussions led to somewhat radical and threatening positions on capitalist rule. The Rochester Socialists continually gained in electoral strength in these years and constituted a possible threat to boss rule. They were always quick to publicly denounce George Aldridge as an enemy of the people and Socialism. In 1911, however, the city administration was finally able to help eliminate Socialist speeches in the schools when Shedd gave a speech at No. 9 that praised

the red flag as the true international symbol of peace and human brotherhood; the stars and stripes, he argued, were limited to the love of a
particular country and did not represent humankind.

Shedd's words were twisted out of context by the mayor and the
city press and termed by the *Democrat and Chronicle* as "radical and revolutionary propagandism." The mayor actually barred Shedd from speaking
in any municipal building. Shedd nevertheless accepted an invitation
from the Labor Lyceum to speak on the subject "Free Speech," but the
Socialists, who had met for years on Sunday evenings at city hall, were
refused admittance. Once again, the Republican machine seized the opportunity to consolidate its power and defeat its opponents, whether they
were the Good Government forces or the Socialists. "Political" speeches
were thereafter banned in the schools and the Socialists were locked out
of City Hall. After being arrested with other Socialists for "obstructing
the sidewalk" at one protest rally, Shedd was forced to resign from the
University of Rochester after many years of teaching and service. Thus
ended the most famous effort of the Progressive era to adapt the spirit
of the little red schoolhouse to an urban setting.[42]

IV

By 1914 Edward Ward had become the leading social center advocate in
the nation. Forced to leave Rochester when Boss Aldridge's board of
estimates slashed the social center appropriation, Ward gained new visibility as an advisor in social center development in the extension division
of the University of Wisconsin. There he worked for several years, until
finally finishing his career decades later in the Justice Department in
Washington. After 1910, Ward continued to publicize the value of neighborhood civic clubs, the wider use of the schools, and general education
extension. He never let his failures in Rochester dim his optimism. Writing
in 1914 in Rochester's leading social welfare journal, *The Common Good*,
Ward criticized local individuals who feared that perhaps Aldridge and
others were correct in believing that the centers were a bad idea. "Cheer
up, old pal," he responded, "*your* Rochester may be stuck in the mud,
but—there are other Rochesters."[43]

There were indeed many other potential Rochesters across the nation
that tried to emulate some of the best features of Ward's ideas from the
city on the Genesee. For years after Ward and his staff were fired in New
York, local newspapers such as the now independent *Toledo News-Bee* and
the Socialist *Social Democratic Herald* and *Milwaukee Leader* publicized the
activities that brought fame to the Rochester centers. In fact, one of the

first acts of the new Socialist working-class administration elected to office in Milwaukee in 1910 was to hire Ward, a fellow Socialist, as an advisor on civic club development. Hence there were indications of other Rochesters, and Ward personally helped organize hundreds of social centers in small towns and villages throughout Wisconsin. And in city after city, from Toledo to Milwaukee to Kansas City, local reformers worked with different degrees of success to capture that elusive spirit of the little red schoolhouse.[44]

Like so many other urban areas, Toledo had a rule against community use of the schools except for special occasions. Women's clubs and parent organizations, however, gained permission to use the schools during the late 1890s. The idea of broader community use of the schools also constituted a central concern of the mayoral administration of Samuel M. Jones and Brand Whitlock between 1897 and 1913. Jones's *Annual Reports* to the city council always contained glowing statements on the value of new social services and school extension. With the support of female leaders, including Mary Law and Pauline Steinem, he and Whitlock agitated for the use of the schools as community meeting places. While the Republican-dominated, centralized school board that seized power in 1898 opposed local control and the social center concept, the Democratic *Evening Bee* endorsed grassroots efforts at school extension. "If Toledo were to build public halls or meeting houses in every ward in the city," speculated the *Bee* in 1898, "the people would probably get together once in a while to discuss matters of public interest. As it is they think there is no place to meet. . . . What's the matter with the school buildings for public meetings? They belong to the people."[45]

Although the wider-use concept in Toledo did not exactly follow the neighborhood civic club plan of Edward Ward, by the turn of the century Golden Rule Jones and the Complete Education League petitioned the school board to use neighborhood schools for weekly neighborhood meetings and entertainments. An outgrowth of the Children's Playground Association, the Complete Education League was formed in 1900 and, as will be recalled, fought for a wide range of school social services and programs. Despite the personal animosity of many school board members, such as J. Kent Hamilton, towards Jones, women's groups, unionists, and fellow Christian Socialists helped to secure approval of the league's petitions. With the help of the Complete Education branch of the City Federation of Women's Clubs, Jones and his followers ran various community programs in the local schools between 1900 and 1904, the year of the mayor's death.

At first the school board only let the Complete Education League meet in a few schools, especially those with an auditorium. In early 1900, the Lagrange School, located in a Polish neighborhood north of central city, was opened for weekly entertainments. Jones himself performed with local singing groups and played some tunes on his violin. The response to these entertainments was overwhelming, and foreign and native-born citizens flocked to these performances. Racially mixed audiences, reportedly containing individuals with a wide range of economic backgrounds, gave them a strong community feeling. More than thirteen hundred people packed into the Lagrange auditorium on one occasion, leading Jones to request the school board to fully endorse the concept of wider use. The *Evening Bee* noted that Jones was a bit of a crank, but agreed that few innovations in the city's history had gained such rapid popular support. "Why not bring the parents into closer association with the schools?" asked Negley Cochran of the *Bee*, for then the schools could become "a club for the people at night."[46]

Between 1900 and 1902, the Complete Education League expanded its work across the city to poor as well as wealthy neighborhoods, to the elite sections on Collingwood as well as the East Side. Complete Education Leagues that organized in several of the ward schools aided the effort. Some of the entertainments and invited speakers at local centers were so popular that every seat in the meeting rooms was occupied by seven o'clock, an hour before the festivities, and Jones routinely dispatched policemen to the schools to help people safely find a seat. While popular support developed for this aspect of the new education, J. Kent Hamilton and fellow Republicans rejected petitions from the league to expand these programs and to construct an auditorium in every school. In a dramatic confrontation between the school board and Jones's followers, the school board in 1902 limited the league to a handful of schools. While petitioners claimed that "the tendency of the times is to provide assembly rooms in school buildings, for the use of teachers, pupils, and their parents," businessmen called the reformers faddists who would lead the schools to economic ruin.[47]

"The public school buildings belong to the people," argued the *News-Bee* in 1904 in an effort to stir additional support for the wider use of the schools. "They are paid for with money taken from the people by taxation. Yet every night in the year the buildings are dark and closed, while the owners of the buildings are hunting for small halls in which to hold public gatherings." By closing almost all the schools for evening use, the Hamilton school board contributed to its own downfall; it was replaced in 1905 by a more Progressive membership generally supportive of the new education and especially social centers. Nine new auditoria were constructed in the city by 1909, and additional ones were planned by the school board and its new superintendent, William B. Guitteau (from 1909 to 1921). Guitteau was a dynamic individual who had once been an activist among the younger teachers and was dedicated to school expansion. He was a personal friend of Pauline Steinem and Brand Whitlock, two of Toledo's leading grassroots reformers, and he wrote long articles in praise of Rochester's social centers for local newspapers.[48]

Despite the favorable local atmosphere for wider use, however, Toledo's social center movement died a quick death after 1912. The Smith Law, passed by a rural-controlled state legislature, placed severe tax limitations on Ohio's cities by prohibiting school boards from increasing annual budgets in excess of one percent of the previous year's. While school boards were often sympathetic to the social center movement by this time, they were strapped economically and were unable to extend many programs such as social centers, since other needs, particularly new schools for a growing population, took precedence. The citywide parent-teacher federation called for the use of the schools "for all purposes of an education[al] nature" in 1912, and women's clubs, neighborhood groups, and the Young Men's Progressive League (a group of recent high school graduates) all petitioned for easy access to the schools. Groups were allowed to meet in schools with an auditorium, as long as no expenses were incurred by the school board, but the paucity of public funds limited the range of activities, prevented the hiring of special staff members to help coordinate activities, and greatly weakened local efforts at social center development.[49]

If there were other Rochesters, as Edward Ward believed, Toledo was not one of them. The neighborhood civic idea that briefly existed in Rochester never fully matured in the city of the Golden Rule, primarily for economic reasons peculiar to Ohio's financial system. As a result, Toledo received very little national recognition for its efforts at school extension, even less than Milwaukee, which had a very strong reputation as a Progressive city devoted to social services, child welfare, and of course Socialism. The Woman's School Alliance and the South Side Educational Association first opened the Milwaukee schools for wider use in the 1890s by gaining permission to meet regularly at the neighborhood schools. The Populists and Socialists, however, contended that the ward-based, council-appointed school board failed to go far enough in school extension, and after the turn of the century the Social Democrats attacked the commission-appointed and then court-appointed school boards that also moved haltingly toward wider use.[50]

The Socialists saw wider school use as a vehicle of democracy to educate citizens on the problems of municipal government and capitalism. The 1902 municipal platform of the Social Democratic Party demanded the free and unlimited use of the schools by all neighborhood groups. As usual, the Socialists linked educational reform to a larger class struggle. "The unions, thanks to the plucking process of the present industrial system, are composed of poor men," claimed the *Social Democratic Herald* in 1902. "The halls they meet in are at present dingy and mean, and badly ventilated, because they cannot afford to hire better ones." Additionally, Socialist politicians and later their representatives on the school board emphasized the need for free speech in the schools and attacked the state social center law of 1911 that permitted school access only to "non-partisan" and "non-religious" groups.[51]

Socialist Meta Berger, together with fellow school board member Lizzie Kander, tried to delete the restrictive clauses on social center use in 1914, but they failed, because Social Democrats composed only roughly one-third of the fifteen-member board during the war years. Kander was not a Socialist but a liberal settlement house leader, yet her support for social innovations, pacifism, and trade unionism led her into the Socialist camp in most areas of educational policy. As in Rochester, free speech at the social centers was a burning issue locally. Kander, Berger, and the Socialists believed that "fathers and mothers should be free to use [the schools] for the consideration of anything that affects their homes or the community life," but the businessmen on the school board opposed the unregulated use of the schools, fearing this would promote socialism. Victor Berger quipped that having social centers without free discussion— the heart of the Rochester idea—was like telling children they could go swimming as long as they avoided the water. Writing in the *Milwaukee Leader* in 1916, he further dissented from capitalist views by asserting that "for parents and children alike, the questions of light, transportation, wages, housing, and all the other important issues . . . are certainly of as great importance as the Three Rs."[52]

With Socialist support, the movement for easier access and wider use of the schools nevertheless accelerated in the early twentieth century. Socialist aldermen first elected to office in 1904 championed the cause for several years before a liberal women's group, the Social Economics Club, petitioned the city council in 1906 for several thousand dollars for recreational programs for congested areas. In 1908 a coalition of community organizations finally helped open an actual center in the Sixth Street School, a poor district and the earlier site of the first publicly supervised playground. The Federation of Civic Societies, which represented the majority of the local voluntary associations, advanced the idea as well as the Socialists, who promised a comprehensive plan of wider use for every school when they attained political hegemony.[53]

Heavily influenced by their fellow socialist advisor, Edward Ward, the Milwaukee Social Democrats helped promote the establishment of social centers, and nearly one-fourth of Milwaukee's neighborhood schools had adult neighborhood civic clubs by 1912. Schools were now also routinely used as polling places for municipal elections, and the voters easily approved a special tax for social centers, playgrounds, and vacation schools. Hence, Milwaukee went far beyond Toledo in social center reform. There were still numerous problems with the widespread establishment of all these programs because of inflation, growing enrollments, and increased school construction demands. Perennial conflicts over the aims of the social centers between community reformers and school officials also hindered their progress. The school board and the superintendents after 1904, Carroll G. Pearse (1904–13) and Milton Potter (1914–43), all endorsed social centers, but they officially opposed permitting all types of meetings in the schools. The social center director was no Edward Ward, and he diligently fulfilled the letter of the law by screening partisan and religious groups out of the schools. Moreover, Harold Berg of the extension division hoped to Americanize Milwaukee's many immigrant groups through the centers and claimed that extended use of the schools would lure children away from street gangs and civilize them.[54]

Similar to every educational change during the Progressive era, there was genuine ideological conflict in Milwaukee over the main objectives of the social center. School board president William Pieplow, a former Populist, argued in 1909 that the centers should be "a place for study and congenial occupation during the evening, for those less fortunate in home surroundings." In essence, he saw them as charity institutions, the very things that Ward and many Socialists abhorred. Many businessmen on the school board were only interested in the centers because in their minds schools resembled a "plant," which, like any factory, should run continuously to ensure maximum production and efficiency. Like many publicists on the national level, local businessmen often narrowly equated the schoolhouse with a factory. "Consider the school house a business plant. The greatest return from such a plant is secured by running it to its capacity," argued John H. Puelicher, a banker and the president of the Milwaukee school board in 1911.[55]

Just as the intellectual history of social centers in Milwaukee reflected the conflicts between efficiency and democracy, so too was their social history shaped by competing, contradictory forces. The Social Democrats never regarded themselves as nonpartisan, but they were very active in many neighborhood civic clubs, where they often railed against capitalism. Many school officials, however, wanted schools that promoted Americanization and patriotism. Some newcomers undoubtedly learned enough in the naturalization classes at the social centers to earn their citizenship papers, yet it is also clear that voluntary attendance meant that neighborhood residents could ignore programs and activities that were demeaning or insulting. Finns, Poles, Swedes, and Russians all petitioned successfully for the free use of the schools for community meetings, formed cohesive neighborhood civic clubs, and found value in the concept of wider use even if they did not desire full Americanization or to learn to become efficient.[56]

The *Milwaukee Free Press*, one of the most volatile anti-Socialist papers in the city, sent reporters to investigate the progress of Milwaukee's first social center in 1909. Since the neighborhood was a hodgepodge of different nationalities, they found numerous immigrants reading books in Yiddish, German, Polish, and Bohemian. Most were newcomers who could not speak any English and were only able to communicate with the young librarian at the branch library. The librarian was a remarkable man who had mastered five different languages. Congregating all these people under a single roof might seem like an ideal means of Americanization, but the *Free Press* complained that these adults would perhaps listen attentively (or so it seemed) to a lecture on sanitation, but "in religion and race loyalty they were immovable." By the same token, Italian-Americans whose children attended extension activities at the Detroit Street School kept an inordinately close watch on their offspring, undoubtedly to keep a firm hand in their children's socialization. "They come in crowds to all meetings, either to take part in social activities or to look on what their children take part in school activities."[57]

Even Americanizers who praised the good work of the naturalization classes that was found in some social centers admitted that the "prevailing foreign language of the neighborhood is catered to through books and periodicals," there being otherwise a distinct possibility that no one would attend them. Moreover, ethnic groups occasionally formulated social center activities with the expressed intent of preserving their ethnic culture and retarding Americanization. More than a thousand Jews from the Ninth Street School neighborhood successfully petitioned the school board in 1915 for their own class in Yiddish history, literature, and poetry. "We seek to establish this school," they argued, "to perpetuate the Jewish race."[58]

Milwaukeeans were, therefore, not simply clay that was molded at will by the social center directors or the board of education. In an age of elite, centralized control over school administration, Milwaukee's citizens often used the schools as best they could for their own intellectual, cultural, and social ends. They did this despite the fact that school leaders did not always have flattering notions of their culture or view them as more than mere material for school production. Even children and young adults to some degree nevertheless shaped recreational programs to fit some of their own needs. "The working boys of Milwaukee are not found to be particularly fond of formal gymnastics after a hard day's work, so athletic games are featured," wrote one social center director. "The girls have shown a distinct inclination for club, wand, and dumb-bell drills, aesthetic dancing, and folk dancing." School clientele voluntarily attended the vacation schools, playgrounds, and social centers. As a result they often became a force of their own in these situations.[59]

The Milwaukee schools were never transformed into ideal community centers in the Progressive era. Overcrowding in some neighborhoods and a lack of funds meant that some auditoriums were converted into makeshift classrooms, thereby hurting adult access to the local school. The schools' restrictions that activities be nonpartisan and "nonreligious" remained on the books despite Socialist opposition. Moreover, school board officials used the social centers to propagandize and justify American involvement in World War I, again in spite of Socialist and pacifist criticism. Free speech, a key issue in the social center movement in some cities, was sacrificed to further the war effort. Yet the Milwaukee schools to some degree had become another Rochester, as Ward had hoped to see when he first helped the Socialist administration in Milwaukee in 1910. The neighborhood civic clubs lasted longer than they had in Rochester, and in the 1920s the Milwaukee social centers were regarded as some of the best and most innovative in the nation. Rochester's, on the other hand, were mostly remembered for the short if glorious reign of Edward J. Ward.[60]

In a pamphlet titled *The Social Center in Kansas City* (1913), the Board of Public Welfare demonstrated that even James M. Greenwood's Kansas City was not untouched by the national movement for the wider use of the schools. Emphasizing the importance of cities such as Rochester, Milwaukee, Chicago, and New York in social center development, its author traced the slow maturation of the idea in Kansas City. First came the mothers' unions, the forerunners of the parent-teacher associations, which pounded on the schoolhouse door seeking admission for their meetings and thereby setting the basis for wider use. Then, by the turn of the century, came women's groups and some civic associations, also viewing the schools as the center of the local neighborhood. However, unlike other cities, Kansas City's groups faced not ward bosses, a penurious legislature, or anti-Socialists per se, but an extremely conservative school administration that only seemed to respond to calls for business efficiency.[61]

James M. Greenwood first demonstrated an interest in social center ideas in his 1904 *Annual Report*, noting that "the school houses lie idle

165 days out of every 365. There is no other business institution in which there is so much money invested, that shuts up its doors for three-sevenths of its time and does not operate." Greenwood's ideas, of course, were not original, and different segments of the community pushed for wider use while rejecting the language and logic of business efficiency. The Industrial Council, for example, resolved in 1911 that the school administration and Greenwood had not "at times in the past given to organized labor that consideration that its intelligence and good citizenship should command." Labor now demanded free and widespread community access to the schools to foster public discussions among those "who work in the factory, in the workshop, in the field, in the mine."[62]

The local social center movement typically was sponsored by grass-roots organizations: mothers' unions, labor unions, women's clubs, and the Socialist Party. Parent-teacher associations, however, which contributed greatly to the wider use concept across the nation, were particularly vital to the social centers of Kansas City. No doubt, organized parents gave special attention to the centers because of their lack of direct political power. The city had an entrenched school board dominated by cosmopolitan elites and a single, powerful individual who served as superintendent from 1874 to 1913. In this context, parent associations quite naturally tried to bring the schools closer to local neighborhoods, to improve relations with teachers, and to make the schools more serviceable to the community.

By 1914, nearly every one of the fifty-nine schools of Kansas City, in both African American and white as well as native and foreign-born neighborhoods, had active parent-teacher organizations. Because of mounting citizen pressure, the school board designated a few white and African-American schools as "social centers" after 1910 where, in these segregated settings, neighborhoods received popular lectures and different entertainments in the schools. While the Rochester and Toledo social centers were definitely integrated, the Kansas City centers, like the local parent organizations, were not. In their own separate spheres, white and African American parents endeavored to increase their civic intelligence through public lecture series, to decrease their boredom through civic discussions, and overall, to use the schools for personal and social improvement. As in most cities, partisan and religious organizations were prohibited from using the schools, but organized parents did their best to keep the idea of wider use alive. The several thousand parent-teacher association members utilized the schools on a monthly or bimonthly basis, forming the largest group locally that engaged in after-hours attendance in the local schools.[63]

The social center movement, as it was variously conceived in the grass roots in different urban contexts, was in many ways a reaction against the centralizing tendencies of the age. The thousands of parents in Kansas City who regularly met at their schools were only part of the larger effort nationally to make schools more serviceable, closer to the people, and relevant. To many grassroots Progressives—whether they were in parents' organizations, labor unions, women's clubs, or Socialist parties—the social center symbolized a growing belief that schools could help improve the quality of urban life. Like so many other innovations, social centers became a battleground between many individuals who were critical of the movement away from local control and the Mutual Admiration Societies that had swept into power at the turn of the century.

Because of conflicts between community groups and school leaders, the centers were not merely effective instruments of social manipulation and repression, as historians have occasionally argued, but like all voluntarily attended institutions a product of contradictory forces, with the schools clearly in a position of power though not complete dominance. Socialists, immigrants, and many other citizens fought against the restrictions on free speech and the efficiency aims of the school managers and to the best of their ability tried to keep the spirit of democratic revolt and social interaction alive in local cities.

Like the vacation schools, playgrounds, and other innovations, the social centers suffered from a basic lack of funding, class biases, and ideological conflict. Many people easily agreed on the virtues of wider use, but strenuously disagreed over its implementation. And, compared to the many other social institutions that still existed in local neighborhoods—such as saloons, pool halls, and other sources of amusement and general education—school social centers were never widespread enough to challenge these more accessible institutions. One did not have to petition the saloon keeper for permission to discuss public issues at his bar, nor did one have to ask him whether partisan and religious issues were taboo. Saloons were undoubtedly more the people's club than the schools could ever hope to be. For many, beer and free sandwiches were better than red tape. As far as Edward Ward and many grassroots Progressives were concerned, the heart of the real social center idea was free speech, for if individuals were limited in public discussions, the schools could not possibly contribute to the intelligent formulation of public policy in a representative democracy. The so-called spirit of the little red schoolhouse remained more an image of an irretrievable rural past than a reality of the urban school.

Chapter 8

The School Health Movement

I

The school health movement illuminated well the contradictory social forces that clashed in America's cities throughout the early twentieth century. The drive to broaden the school's responsibility for children's health emanated from narrow-minded advocates of scientific management and business efficiency as well as from grassroots Socialists and liberal reformers. From these school health crusades came the first systematic efforts to establish breakfast, lunch, and nutritional programs for the children of the poor. They also led to medical and dental inspection programs, special classes for anemic and tubercular children, increased emphasis on sanitation and hygiene, and the attempted vaccination of every child. Men and women who often had sharply contrasting personal backgrounds and social goals once again competed for state favor to secure the best interests of the child.

In the eyes of many grassroots reformers, these various programs had the potential to improve the quality of urban life, to strengthen the ability of poor children to excel in their studies, and to compensate them for the substandard home and school environments spawned by a competitive, inequitable social order. At the same time, however, many school superintendents, elite school board members, and other powerful, well-placed individuals viewed better health among children as everything *but* a matter of democracy or social justice. Instead, these individuals, so interested in transforming social institutions through business principles, saw these innovations as a form of capital investment, a response to the allegedly inferior biological makeup of the native poor and certain ethnic groups.

The concept of a healthy mind in a healthy body was a time-honored one in educational theory by the turn of the century. Only then, however, were specific programs established to improve children's health and, it was argued, to give them an equal chance to learn. Explaining exactly why many individuals suddenly embraced the ancient notion of *in corpore sano* at this particular time remains central to understanding the evolution of new urban social services in the Progressive era. Educators had long argued that sanitation, hygiene, and the overall health of children and the physical quality of their home and school environments directly affected educational achievement. For example, nineteenth-century common-school reformers in Rochester, Toledo, Milwaukee, and Kansas City frequently emphasized that proper ventilation, heating, and sanitation could make school buildings comfortable and healthy for children. But the thought of routinely feeding children, even if they were starving, or of examining their bodies for dental caries, adenoids, or heart disease was alien to that age. Schools only touched young people for a few years of their lives, and the boundaries between home and school responsibilities remained sharply drawn.[1]

All this changed amid considerable controversy and debate in the early 1900s. Scientific research had now convinced many people of the accuracy of the germ theory of disease. Most important, prominent leaders of science popularized the work of Edward Jenner and other pioneers in the treatment of communicable diseases. Inoculation, however, was never accepted as legitimate by every urban citizen or by all physicians. Many people still viewed diseases such as tuberculosis as hereditary or saw them as a sign of God's displeasure with the supposedly immoral ways of the poor. Others violently opposed placing any foreign matter in the human bloodstream.[2]

Previously, health officers and school officials had excluded individuals with infectious diseases from the general population through quarantine. Nineteenth-century school reports often described outbreaks of various diseases that forced the temporary closing of various neighborhood schools. Now, however, reformers increasingly sought to diagnose many noncommunicable ailments and to eliminate medical impediments that presumably produced "dull" and "backward" children. Science at last offered the hope that healthy bodies would indeed produce healthy minds—or at least children who could properly recite their lessons, compute their sums, and better compete in the classroom.

There was more behind the school health movement than some simple though humane desire to improve the lives of children or to enhance personal development. Physicians and educators who wrote the leading books and journal articles on school health during the Progressive era often agreed on the wonders of science in improving human comforts. They often simultaneously agreed on the inferiority of the new immigrant populations and the poor who formed majorities in many urban neighborhoods. Poverty-stricken neighborhoods, wrote one professor of public health, had "a concentration of tuberculosis stock, of alcoholic stock, of feeble minded stock—poor protoplasm and a bad environment supplementing each other in a vicious cycle." Of all groups, the urban poor were, therefore, most in need of inspection and care. Men of science were often not value free, responsive to cultural pluralism, or critical of an economic system that fostered the ailments they tried to cure. As a result, the wider use of the schools for health reform were often efforts to perfect a stronger race and to promote personal and social efficiency.[3]

"The children of today must be viewed as the raw material of the State," wrote Lewis Terman in 1914. "To conserve this raw material is as logical a function of the State as to conserve the natural resources of coal, iron, and water power." A nationally prominent supporter of eugenics, efficiency, psychological testing, and scientific management in education, Terman represented a new wave of educational thinkers who likened the schoolhouse to a school plant and who favored medical inspection as a panacea for most educational ills. School failure, he believed, was produced by the health problems of specific social classes and immigrant groups, and he rarely discussed the environmental determinants of personal maladies or appreciated the cultural gaps that separated many immigrants from the public schools. Yet he had little quarrel with the idea that better school health promoted "race betterment" and "the production of greater efficiency" in school and society.[4]

Leaders of the efficiency movement for school health scoffed at the "sentimentalists" whose desire for healthy children was a moral end in itself. "The movement to save human life is not alone a matter of mere sentiment. It pays to keep people alive," wrote an educator in 1912 in the *Pedagogical Seminary*, a journal that soon evolved into the *Journal of Genetic Psychology*. Although human life was often reduced to dollars and cents and interpreted from the perspective of cost accounting, this dominant perspective was not unchallenged. Many people concerned with the improvement of public health believed that efficiency was a narrow and unacceptable rationale for social reform. Radicals in particular linked health reform to larger class struggles in local communities. Conflicts between efficiency and democracy and human capital and humane reform characterized many of the ideological debates of the Progressive era, from the playground movement to social center experiments. Nowhere was the conflict better dramatized than in multifaceted efforts to feed malnourished poor children, as competing ideas once again vied for dominance in the urban school.[5]

II

The French statesman Georges-Jacques Danton once noted that "after Bread, Education is the first need of a people." Like many writers before him, he believed that sufficient food and education should be the corner-stones of a strong national state. Yet it was not until the late nineteenth and early twentieth centuries that numerous educators, physicians, political activists, and grassroots citizens seriously examined the exact relationship between nutrition and learning. These reformers publicly debated the connection between nutritional development and educational attainment and its possible impact on social policy. At every turn, the possibility of feeding starving or poorly nourished children at public expense raised a host of competing ideas: parental versus school responsibilities, socialist versus capitalist perspectives on the social order, and the rights of the child and the state.[6]

Municipal and state funding of school meals were volatile political issues in Europe and America in the late nineteenth and early twentieth centuries. Meals for the urban poor in France, Germany, and other European nations predated American efforts in the early 1900s, and the Socialist trade unions were often in the forefront of state intervention. The Social Democratic Federation of England, for example, denounced the role of privately sponsored soup kitchens and charity meals given to undernour-ished street waifs. Formed in 1884, the federation included in its platform one free meal per day for every child, not as a charity but as a human right. The Fabian Society, organized in the same year, also endorsed this position. From the very start, therefore, the issue of feeding children at state expense was a highly political one, certain to polarize those forces that competed for the control of mass education and public welfare in the twentieth century. What was at stake in many Western nations was the control and political power of the dependent classes and the urban poor.[7]

Socialist and working-class groups in America, just as those overseas, strenuously fought for government intervention to feed hungry children as a matter of justice. When it came to that most fundamental duty and pleasure—to feed their children, and to feed them well—the laborers who produced the world's wealth were often unable to provide adequate care for their families. Radicals argued that class dominance placed work-ing-class families in a precarious nutritional state. Before leaving the ministry to become an organizer for the Socialist Party, the Reverend William Brown of Rochester asserted in 1902 that workers had to sell themselves to the lowest bidder on the marketplace or else starve along with their dependents. A few years later, the *Rochester Socialist* complained that millionaires conspicuously consumed goods while "little babies" sometimes suffered from inadequate nutrition.[8]

Socialists and segments of Toledo's working class similarly believed that insufficient or inadequate food was an unjust reward for their labor. But as a representative of the Central Labor Union argued in 1897, an acceptance of social Christianity would mean that "men are not born to hunger and die in the midst of plenty." Perceived contradictions of progress and poverty that became apparent in the depression 1890s made such reanalysis of Christian faith and everyday life commonplace among working groups and urban radicals. In 1905, Toledo's Socialists sought election to the school board on a platform calling for free clothes and food "for children requiring the same." Their newspaper, the *Socialist*, repeatedly featured exposés of hungry children locally and across the nation. "If I am elected to the school board, I will do all in my power to secure the feeding of hungry school children, and the clothing of them, if necessary," argued Josephine Bates, a Socialist, during an unsuccessful bid to office in 1909.[9]

Milwaukee's Social Democratic Party and the Federated Trades Council warmly endorsed publicly financed meals programs for school children—for all of them, not just for the poor, and as a human right, not as a charity. "The hungry child cries out for food, and we give him a book," claimed the leading Socialist clubwoman and school board member, Meta Berger. According to the Socialists, starvation and malnutrition helped the wealthier classes retain their stranglehold over the working classes. Moreover, the Socialists continually demanded free meals as a "human gesture" of the citizenry, not as a way to promote "efficiency" or "race betterment." In a self-styled "humanitarian resolution" in 1909, the Federated Trades Council urged immediate aid for the "many children who are suffering from an insufficiency of food." It resolved that "a civilized community should hold itself responsible for the welfare of its rising generation, and unless it takes practical measures for their proper care and protection it will be punished for its cruel indifference."[10]

The contradictions of living in a nation that extolled the virtues of industry, application, and labor and yet permitted hunger among many hardworking citizens also infuriated many Kansas City residents. The editor of the *People's Advocate* in 1902 expressed his disgust through simple rhyme in "A Modern Business Sermon."

> I know a bold and honest man,
> Who strives to live on a Christian plan;
> But poor is he and poor will he be,
> At home a starving wife, soon
> A wreck is she.[11]

"Labor is the source of all wealth. Without it the wheels of commerce would cease to move and chaos and starvation would immediately follow," argued the *Labor Herald* in 1904. But the wheels of commerce reeled and men, women, and children still hungered, as urban radicals repeatedly testified. "Capitalism is slavery," contended the editor of the *Missouri Staats-Zeitung* in 1909. The industrialists "have the masses under their control. They can starve them to death, or freeze them to death, or work them to death." Certainly not all workers were hungry, freezing, or starving, but the denial of the promise of American life to many citizens led concerned individuals to espouse reform.[12]

Progressive working-class leaders and Socialist agitators repeatedly championed the cause of underfed and malnourished schoolchildren. Their newspapers featured muckraking exposés of tenement life that emphasized the problems of hunger and human want. Photographs of hungry children with peering eyes and desperate appearance touched the hearts of many readers. Moreover, Americans discovered the underside of social life through a variety of printed sources. In his classic volume *Poverty*, the moderate Socialist Robert Hunter sympathetically described the millions of Americans who were "underfed, underclothed, and badly housed," all the while emphasizing that "the great majority are children who have neither violated social laws nor committed any sin." John Spargo, the author of *The Bitter Cry of the Children*, similarly inspired social action when he discovered thousands of children trapped in a "heritage of poverty."[13]

The nation's first systematic efforts to feed the children of the urban poor during the Progressive era did not simply arise from working-class and Socialist agitation. Social change was an interactive process that pitted dominant forces against a variety of opponents. Initial state involvement in meals for urban children in the early 1900s never meant widespread public acceptance of a full-blown welfare state. Rather, this was a transitional period in which the ethic of personal responsibility and individualism clashed with newer theories of public intervention for private welfare. Many citizens retained traditional theories concerning the causes of poverty and the value of philanthropy in uplifting the poor. Strong ideological and class perceptions on education, nutrition, and state involvement discouraged the creation of comprehensive, equitable school meal programs, despite considerable evidence that meals helped improve the health and well-being of urban school children.

Policies related to school breakfast and lunch programs evolved within a specific political framework and foreign-policy orientation during the Progressive era. Beginning in the 1890s with the annexation of Hawaii and culminating with the war with Spain, American foreign policy shifted from a strategy of internal acquisition of contiguous territory between the Atlantic and the Pacific to a growing interest in markets abroad and competition with other Western nations. This led to control over islands such as the Philippines and Puerto Rico and an aggressive "big stick" diplomacy that characterized the administrations of Theodore Roosevelt, William Howard Taft, and Woodrow Wilson. During these decades there were numerous military interventions in the affairs of Caribbean and South and Central American nations, including intervention during the Mexican Revolution. All these activities were nurtured by a concern for national strength and hemispheric dominance and, as it was openly stated, racial superiority.[14]

An aggressive foreign policy that sought new markets and colonies decidedly shaped the school health movement at the turn of the century, even though school meals might seem unrelated to imperialism. Efficiency reformers and activist physicians, however, continually dismissed "sentimentalists" who simply wanted to feed hungry children because they were starving, might fail in their studies, or die prematurely. These matters interested them, but so did fear of racial decline and support for national strength. Leonard P. Ayres, coauthor of the most important book on health care in education, *Medical Inspection of Schools* (1908), was well versed in imperialist thought, in the so-called genetic basis of intelligence, and in theories of racial superiority. For several years he was the general superintendent of the schools of Puerto Rico before joining the Russell Sage Foundation as an expert in child care and hygiene. In the beginning of their famous book, Ayres and his medical associate, Luther Gulick, emphasized that health care in the schools was largely a response to changing patterns of immigration, especially from Central and Southern Europe. By the end of their volume, Ayres and Gulick highlighted the importance not of helping children as a moral end in itself, but of maximizing efficiency and saving money by establishing a healthier racial stock.[15]

Accelerated interest in school meals rested upon elite fears of a deteriorating race and a quest for national development. Children were perceived as "raw material" akin to "natural resources" such as water and oil. Even with "poor protoplasm," they represented the potential manpower for the workforce and a strong foreign policy. Influential individuals such as Ayres condemned the existence of malnourished populations and understood that poorer classes suffered from more disease and illness than wealthier citizens. Yet he and others refused to criticize the economic system that caused inadequate housing, low wages, deteriorating neighborhoods, and subsequent disease. Often attracted to eugenics, these efficiency reformers concluded that health problems came from personal or group origins and not, as radicals contended, from an unequal, immoral social order. Rather, illness stemmed from defective and inferior racial stocks, and better health care protected the citizenry from these individuals and increased national strength.

Whether one believed in the power of eugenics or in the environment, in bolstering or altering the prevailing economic system, numerous individuals at the turn of the century nevertheless concluded that starving children made poor scholars. This thesis pervaded the contemporary literature on education and nutrition. "Is it possible with empty stomachs to pay attention to the multiplication tables?" asked Jonathan Taylor, a prominent English Socialist, as early as 1884. After visiting poverty-stricken sections in England in the 1890s, William T. Stead, the Christian Socialist author of the bestseller *If Christ Came to Chicago*, concluded: "To drive children into school in order to fill their heads when they have nothing in their stomachs is like pouring water into a sieve."[16]

Studies proliferated on the importance of early childhood nutrition in scholastic achievement and later physical and mental growth, and they (perhaps incorrectly) inferred a causal effect between the high correlation between malnutrition and school failure among working-class groups. The moderate Socialist Robert Hunter wrote that "learning is difficult [for the poor] because hungry brains and languid bodies and thin blood are not able to feed the brain." Or, as another analyst contended in 1905, "A poorly fed child, it is quite plain, is unable to prosecute his studies with zest; he cannot prepare for the coming battle of life."[17]

Citizens in various cities concluded that malnutrition seriously impaired children's scholarship. "Undernourished children are especially susceptible to all diseases," claimed a Rochester woman's club leader, adding that medical problems hindered many children's academic progress. One school principal in a poor neighborhood told the *Toledo Blade* in 1908 that "it is as inhuman as it is impossible to compel a child to sit and study and recite with its stomach empty." Toledo's school superintendent similarly argued that many children were "so emaciated and hungry that it is a crime to expect them to be active, either mentally or physically," and one grassroots Progressive asserted in 1912, "The brain cannot gnaw on problems while the stomach is gnawing on its empty self."[18]

Similar testimonies on the perceived connections between school failure and human hunger appeared in Milwaukee and Kansas City. "With children, being properly fed, is half the battle," asserted the *Milwaukee Free Press* in 1906. "In many cases it makes the difference between the fretful, ailing child, in no condition for study, and the bodily comfort which promotes good temper and alert attention." A survey of numerous teachers in Milwaukee in 1911 concluded that proper nutrition made children who were "restless, dull, and difficult to manage . . . studious, tractable, and bright" scholars. Even if all citizens did not accept the alleged racial superiority of old stock immigrants or endorse theories of human capital formation, they often still believed that proper nutrition better equipped children for their studies.[19]

School Lunch in Kansas City, 1914

Courtesy: Special Collections, Kansas City Public Library, Kansas City, Missouri

Many individuals accepted the claim of the Kansas City protestors who wrote in 1906 that "in our large cities many thousands are shelterless, thinly clad, and starving." There were always some local residents who denied that anyone in America was hungry, but a wide variety of citizens argued that children often lacked proper nourishment. What citizens really disputed was whether local governments had any responsibility for this personal distress and whether state intervention would cause parents to "shirk" their responsibilities. "Who hesitates to take advantage of the State?" asked a worried member of the Ohio Board of State Charities, who feared a loss of "individual duty and responsibility" through such capricious actions. Or, as the *New York Times* editorialized in 1909: "Anything that enables the family provider to shift his burdens upon the State tends directly to State Socialism. . . . The home has been regarded as the cradle of religion, intelligence, industry, and patriotism. Can the State, which sprung from the family, supersede it, or even exist without it?"[20]

Despite such opposition, women's groups, labor organizations, Socialist parties, liberals, and many educators after the turn of the century began the nation's first programs to feed impoverished schoolchildren. By 1913, nearly three dozen cities had some form of meal service, besides many programs in towns and rural communities. Affiliates of the General Federation of Women's Clubs, the Council of Jewish Women, and the National Congress of Mothers privately funded many programs with the hopes that "the School Board . . . will inaugurate the system in all public schools as part of their work and not as a charity." Like many other social service reforms of the Progressive era such as vacation schools, playgrounds, and social centers, school meals were nevertheless initially targeted for the native and immigrant poor. However much humanitarian impulses guided some advocates of school meals, this innovation became a municipal charity for the poor and was caught between the tensions of efficiency and "race betterment" and a more humane response to the plight of unhealthy children.[21]

Ellen Richards, the famous domestic science advocate, agitated for at-cost lunch programs in the Boston high schools as early as 1894, and similar programs also began in the secondary schools of Milwaukee, Rochester, and other cities later in that decade. More commonly, however, contemporary women's clubs were concerned with the masses of children in the elementary grades. Rochester's ward school board leaders in the 1890s, however, usually equated school meals with "state paternalism" and "socialism." The only children to receive municipally financed meals were the juvenile delinquents and street waifs who stayed at the State Industrial School, a residential facility that provided "mush, milk, and beans." Representatives of the Women's Educational and Industrial Union nevertheless argued in 1897 that all children "need sufficient nourishing food, comfortable homelike surroundings, plenty of exercise and sunlight." At the turn of the century, the Union operated inexpensive luncheons for working girls in local factories and served free milk at their vacation schools between 1899 and 1906. Between 1911 and 1913, they operated a handful of school lunchrooms for poor children, until they finally convinced the local school board of the value of nutrition and school progress.[22]

A wide range of reformers advocated school lunches in Rochester as well as in Toledo. One of the first experiments with at-cost lunches in Toledo was at Golden Rule Jones's Acme Sucker Rod Company, where the mayor regularly dined with his employees. Increasingly, however, local reformers turned to the problems of hungry schoolchildren. As early as 1899, the Democratic *Evening Bee* argued that children "have a right to have enough to eat and to have food that the system needs." By 1904, the *Bee* had published several sensationalist articles concerning school failure among undernourished children. Soon Toledo's women's clubs, Independents, unionists, and Socialists agitated for more attention to the nutrition of the poor. The Republican *Toledo Blade* accused parents of "negligence" in this area, but that failed to deter the many grassroots reformers who demanded municipal innovations.[23]

As in all aspects of social welfare during this period, clubwomen and parents' groups were prominent in nutritional reform. An invited speaker before the Toledo Women's Educational Club in 1906 emphasized the poor quality of the food eaten by "the working classes" and underscored the plight of "the struggling poor, who eat only the lightest kind of a breakfast, go to work with a dinner bucket containing anything but nutritious food, and their children, no better fed." Pauline Steinem, the liberal school board member and ally of Golden Rule Jones and Brand Whitlock, endorsed free clothes, shoes, and food for any disadvantaged child. Even Superintendent Charles Van Cleve soon developed a strong personal interest in underfed children. "The child is not responsible for being in the world, nor for his condition in the world," wrote Van Cleve in 1908. "This is the only justification I ask for feeding children when they are hungry."[24]

In 1907 the Women's Educational Club established midmorning luncheons in some of Toledo's poorest neighborhoods. It first served meals to the Polish children in the Lagrange School (the site of the popular social center entertainments earlier conducted by Golden Rule Jones and the Complete Education League). A sympathetic school board in turn installed gas stoves in several schools on the industrial East Side—at Birmingham, Ironville, and neighboring buildings that housed large working-class populations. Superintendent Van Cleve was overwhelmed by the conditions at the Birmingham school, near the steel mills. "I noticed scholars whose faces were covered with heavy watery scabs, and who appeared to be suffering to such an extent that attention to study could not be expected. I believe that the disease, whatever it is, is largely if not altogether, due to malnutrition." Moved by such scenes, school officials and local women's groups jointly operated breakfasts and lunches in the poorest Toledo neighborhoods throughout the Progressive era.[25]

Milwaukee had the most extensive meals program of all of these cities. With the firm support of local trade unions, several voluntary associations, and the Social Democratic Party, the Woman's School Alliance established the first free lunches for poor children in 1904. In that year, a non-Socialist alderman who was moved by the spectacle of hungry children reported that malnutrition hindered their school performance. The Alliance discussed the issue at its October meeting and then unanimously resolved to fund luncheons in several schools. The women announced that "it has always been the aim of the Woman's School Alliance to support any measure tending to the betterment of existing conditions of children attending the public schools." Since 1891 the Alliance had dispensed free clothes and shoes to deserving children, aided the vacation school experiments, formed parent-teacher associations, lobbied for manual training and domestic science programs, and attacked corporal punishment. Year after year they fought for more money for the public schools, and now they took the major responsibility for funding yet another social service.[26]

Because of severe overcrowding in many Milwaukee schools, between 1904 and 1907, Alliance members served soup and crackers to hungry children at noontime in their own homes! Only when adequate space was found at local schools did the luncheons finally move out of members' homes. By 1908 the Alliance operated approximately eleven luncheons that served an astonishing fifty thousand hot meals annually. It was clearly an enormous undertaking. School plays generated operating revenue, supplemented by contributions from organizations such as the Social Culture Club, the South Side Women's Club, the Social Economics Club, and neighborhood parent and civic organizations. Mrs. Charles B. Whitnall, a Socialist school board member, was the chairwoman of the Alliance's penny lunch division and consistently championed the rights of the poor. The president of the Alliance was also an activist, and she told the working-class *Daily News* in 1909 that "we believe it is the right of every child that is born into the world to have enough to eat and suitable clothes to wear." Inspired by such ideals, the Alliance joined with Socialists and liberals on the Milwaukee school board to demand more attention to nutritional services. Together they pressured public officials until the board of education finally funded school meals in 1917.[27]

In many cities, therefore, local women's organizations initially operated the earliest school meals. They served them at the vacation schools, in poor neighborhood schools during the regular year, or as demonstrated by the Woman's School Alliance, in their own homes when necessary. Activist women then pressured the efficiency-minded business and professional elites on local school boards to fund programs in selected schools, achieving success roughly by World War I. By then, approximately one hundred cities in the United States had school meals for the poor, variously funded by voluntary organizations, charity groups, and local municipalities.[28]

Despite all the conservative fears of racial deterioration and progressive desires to help children overcome nutritional handicaps, America as well as many European nations failed to establish equitable and comprehensive nutrition programs for urban schoolchildren. Only one-third of the school districts of England, for example, created state-supported meal plans, since even its famous Meals Act of 1906 was permissive rather than mandatory legislation. Like the playgrounds, vacation schools, social centers, and other social service reforms of the turn of the century, school meals in America never reached the majority of children, including many poor youth in desperate need. Resistance to the expansion of these programs surfaced from many different sources to blunt the effectiveness of this new social reform.[29]

Since it was the Socialists who very early and very consistently championed free meals, Catholic organizations in Rochester, Toledo, Milwaukee, and Kansas City denounced the idea as an example of state paternalism that would lead to a Socialistic and atheistic government. The Rochester Federation of Catholic Societies, it will be recalled, attacked social centers, vacation schools, and playgrounds and criticized the Christian Socialist Edward J. Ward. It also adamantly opposed social services such as free meals. When liberal school board members and clubwomen secured municipal funding for school meals in Toledo, the Lucas County Federation of Catholic Societies in 1909 similarly condemned this new educational policy. Distributing free food was "unsound and most harmful to the spirit of American liberty, American independence, and American self help." Catholics typically called for more parental responsibility, urged parents to feed their own children, and warned the citizenry of further state encroachment. The Smith Law more than Catholic opposition paralyzed Toledo's meal program, but Catholic influence clearly undermined greater efforts at reform.[30]

In Milwaukee, where Socialists increasingly served in all levels of government, including the school board, Catholics also intensively opposed new school services. After the turn of the century the *Social Democratic Herald* wrote glowing articles on state maintenance in Europe, endorsed the labors of the Woman's School Alliance, and promised comprehensive nutritional programs for all children at municipal expense in the forthcoming Socialist state. The Federated Trades Council attacked those who claimed that intemperance among the working classes caused child hunger, and Meta Berger asserted that the causes of hunger were assuredly complex but essentially economic in nature. Still, Catholic organizations in 1915 effectively blocked permissive legislation for free textbooks and meals, berating the idea as socialistic. Besides denouncing labor unions, Archbishop Sebastian Messmer claimed that free textbooks, meals, and other services would destroy the family, establish "state paternalism, and . . . lead to advanced socialism." Because of Catholic political influence, the Milwaukee school board did not adopt the work of the Woman's School Alliance until 1917, culminating nearly two decades of grassroots struggle.[31]

While Catholic opposition to social services generally took organized form, advocates of school meals faced an equally potent though less visibly united opposition by citizens who viewed nutrition as a private

rather than a public responsibility. Some people endorsed parent education over the feeding of children, suggesting that it was not poverty but
ignorance that caused parents to underfeed or misfeed their offspring.
Other people denied that anyone was starving and argued that Socialists,
women, and other reformers were sensationalists and municipal busy-
bodies. When the Socialist trade unions and the Woman's School Alliance
unsuccessfully lobbied for an appropriation for school meals from the
Board of County Supervisors in 1909, a Democrat responded that "women
would go out loafing if their children were fed in school." A Republican
at the same meeting asserted that "all mothers could easily provide meals
for their children if they really loved them." Such critics could not be
swayed, by appeals to either efficiency or conscience, to vote in favor of
a county appropriation for meals for the poor.[32]

One of the biggest stumbling blocks to comprehensive nutritional
programs in every city was the widespread belief that parents were responsible for their own children. A leading advocate of lunch programs
summed up this feeling accurately in the *Psychological Clinic* in 1912:
"No one doubts that there is a close relationship between poverty and
underfeeding—the terms are practically synonymous. Many persons,
however, insist that the immediate cause of most of the underfeeding
among the school children in American cities is not poverty but ignorance—that if the majority of incomes, slender as they are, were expended
wisely, the children might be properly fed." Many well-educated individuals blamed the poor for their own predicament. One physician, for
example, informed the American Medical Association that "in the majority
of families among the poorer classes the food is poorly chosen, poorly
cooked, and poorly served." Other members of that organization throughout the Progressive era often asserted that the poor bought unsuitable
food "not because these people have not enough money, but that they
have no idea of what constitutes nutritious food."[33]

With often limited political support and this type of opposition, grassroots reformers had to work diligently to feed the maximum number of
children. Like playgrounds, vacation schools, and other innovations, the
meals were often popular with local parents and children even if they
did not reach everyone in need. While chastising those who feared that
municipally supported meals would lessen the child's initiative, the Central Labor Union of Toledo publicly applauded the work of women's
clubs and the school board. "School authorities in this city are fully alive
to conditions among working people," claimed the *Toledo Union Leader*
in 1908. "The authorities are battling with hunger versus pride, and are
attempting to solve the question of feeding children and at the same time
not have them stamped as receivers of charity."[34]

Nutrition advocates in Europe and America devised intricate methods to prevent children from feeling that they were objects of charity. In France, children separately entered booths, where they gave teachers a nominal sum to defray the costs of their meal if they were so able; those children without money still received a ticket for a meal, and presumably no one but the teacher knew which particular children could afford the price of a breakfast or lunch. Toledo and other cities employed different methods to try to protect children's pride, but undoubtedly many ragged youngsters were teased by other children and suspected of not having a penny for their lunch.

Because class prejudices were so potent, according to municipal Socialists, only a comprehensive and free meal program for all children would have eliminated the class stigmas that remained attached to school meals in the Progressive era. Yet the clubwomen, urban radicals, and other grassroots reformers who claimed that all children had a right to sufficient and nourishing food—and that the state should provide it— were voices in the wilderness, far ahead of public opinion and unable to alter class biases in nutritional policy. The members of the Woman's School Alliance, the Women's Educational Club, the Women's Educational and Industrial Union, and the Athenaeum nevertheless tried to aid all children in distress. More children came to their meals than they could possibly feed every year, and women again demonstrated their central role in Progressive school reform. Conflict among Catholics, efficiency advocates, Socialists, and other interest groups at the grassroots and national level guaranteed that the issue of perfecting children's health through the schools remained a pressing contemporary issue. If meals alone could not improve children's health, perhaps medical inspection and other measures might bring relief to unhealthy and hungry scholars.

III

"Whatever else may be added to the three Rs of the public schools," wrote the editor of *Charities* in 1906, "medical supervision is bound to be looked upon as fundamental." The editor dismissed critics who viewed medical inspection as an infringement of personal liberty by responding that "these people seem to overlook the spirit of our entire educational system, and that it is nothing more than reasonable, after forcing a boy to go to school, to see that he does the work with no serious handicap, and thus close one of the greatest doors to discouragement and dissatisfaction, leading to truancy." Medical inspection became one of the most highly touted panaceas of the Progressive era. It was variously endorsed as a way to eliminate "backward" and "dull" students, to ensure all children equal educational opportunities, to promote the vitality of the "race," and to make parents more responsible citizens. Because it had relatively weak links to grassroots organizations compared with innovations such as social centers or even penny lunches, however, medical inspection became one of the most unpopular social services of the early twentieth century, producing extensive civil disobedience including school boycotts and occasional riots.[35]

Despite considerable popular opposition to medical inspection, the health movement flourished in American city schools after the turn of the century. Boston established the first medical inspection program in the United States in 1894, and by 1900 eight other cities had followed its example. The greatest rate of growth of medical inspection, however, was between 1905 and 1910, when the number of urban school systems with medical inspection mushroomed from 44 to 312. As divisions of medical inspection and school hygiene organized in local schools, additional health personnel besides physicians joined the school staff. By 1910, dozens of nurses worked in the public schools, especially in the industrial Northeast. Roughly fifty cities had school dentists. Noting these trends, a writer in *American Education* in 1911 stated that "there are now but few progressive cities in the country which have not established at least the nucleus of a system of medical inspection."[36]

The justifications for medical inspection resembled those popularized for the closely related school meals movement. Poor health, it was argued, caused children to fail in their lessons. "The examination of school children with reference to their physical condition," argued a contributor to *Education* in 1905, "has led to the discovery of mental and physical ills which prevent the victims from making normal progress, and unfit them for classification with children sound and healthy." According to the skeptical editor of the *Nation*, medical inspectors unanimously believed that poor health was "the real trouble in most cases which we inaccurately call stupidity, inattention, indifference to study, ill-temper, sullenness, malicious disobedience, and truancy." Or, as one physician told a national charity organization in 1910: "What can a child learn who is constantly annoyed by blurring in reading, by headaches, by sensitiveness to light or who is always fatigued by close attention of any kind? What can one accomplish whose blood is impoverished by deficient oxygenation and whose brain is anemic or inundated with unoxidized products?"[37]

While assuming that sound minds could not coexist with unhealthy bodies and that wellness furthered academic excellence, school health advocates interpreted medical inspection as an educational and social cure-all. A physician in the *Review of Reviews* in 1907 claimed that since poor health led to truancy as well as "moral obliquity," health inspection would eliminate both maladies. Speakers at professional educational meetings asserted that poverty and paupers would disappear if all diseases were diagnosed and then eliminated through proper treatment; perfect health produced hardworking citizens and maximized efficiency. And numerous writers repeatedly emphasized the basic need to elevate the "physical standard of the race," to improve "the efficiency of the race," and, as one elite reformer claimed in 1915, "to move in the direction of race betterment."[38]

Advocates of medical and dental inspection of urban school children emphasized genetic rather than environmental interpretations of human development. Many of them believed in the superiority of the so-called Teutonic race and in the inferiority of the new wave of "swarthy" immigrants who migrated to America's shores. Medical inspectors and health officers were often attracted to Theodore Roosevelt's theory of "race suicide"—the fear that new immigrant families had disproportionately large families compared with those of the older immigrant stock. Selective breeding, health reformers believed, might reverse the trend, but some also argued that even old-stock citizens should have smaller families. As one author argued, a "few perfect children" of any ethnic origin were better than "a dozen unkempt degenerates, who add pathos to the struggle for existence, and who sink under the inflexible law of the survival of the fittest." Such logic helped promote eugenics-based sterilization laws for the poor in many states in the Progressive era, since it gave scientific legitimacy to the racist acts of legislators who discriminated against the lower classes.[39]

Since health reformers often believed in the supremacy of genetics as well as ethnic determinants of school failure and success, they usually placed the blame for unhealthy children on the shoulders of immigrants and the poor. It was commonly stated that "children are allowed to suffer, not so much because medical treatment is costly, as because parents are ignorant," and some medical reformers longed for the day when the state would actively prosecute parents who chose to ignore the orders of local medical inspectors. Since poor parents were so ignorant of hygiene, sanitation, and the elementary principles of child care, according to a writer in *American Education*, the state had to intervene in family life to rescue children from "ignorance on the part of parents. It becomes, therefore, the duty of the school authorities to see to it that such children are protected against influences that will seriously handicap them through life, often making them an economic burden to society."[40]

Armed with a set of questionable genetic theories and convinced of parental ignorance of medical knowledge, elite health reformers built a national network of information through dozens of articles, books, and pamphlets on the subject of medical inspection. Urban school systems gave increased attention to health care, and new medical personnel joined the school bureaucracy. The problem with the medical inspection movement was not that it overemphasized the existence of disease, for poor children still experience inadequate health care, considerable illness, and disproportionate school failure. Unfortunately, health reformers smugly assumed that health was the primary determinant of school success and that dental caries and adenoids produced problems such as truancy, boredom, inattentiveness, and immorality. Filling cavities, announced one writer, cured children's dullness. Certainly many children with poor teeth, adenoids, scabies, scarlet fever, and diphtheria had an unequal chance to learn, as the health leaders claimed. They ignored the fact, however, that good health is only one factor in whether children excel in their studies and that many children who were hungry did well at school. Although the medical knowledge of the health reformers was limited, as viewed from a modern perspective, they condemned parents and other citizens who opposed them as ignorant, narrow-minded, and superstitious.[41]

Medical inspection began in very similar ways in cities such as Rochester, Toledo, Milwaukee, and Kansas City. Leading figures in local boards of health, medical societies, and dental associations typically pressured urban school boards to adopt systematic health inspection. Although some health reformers gave random examinations of schoolchildren in different kinds of neighborhoods, investigations usually centered in congested areas inhabited by the poorest working-class populations. George Goler of the Rochester Health Department, for example, joined with the Rochester Academy of Medicine in 1901 and petitioned the board of education for permission to examine children in the poorest neighborhoods. The board initially rejected the program as exceeding its jurisdiction, but several years later, nurses and other health staff were employed in the poorest Rochester schools. The Rochester Dental Society inspected poor children's teeth for the first time in 1905, giving free exams and basic care to the "worthy poor." Four years later the Women's Educational and Industrial Union also contributed to the health movement by funding several school nurses. Soon toothbrush drills and modern lectures on hygiene and sanitation supplemented the school health program.[42]

Members of local boards of health, together with philanthropic physicians and dentists, also inaugurated medical inspection in Toledo, Milwaukee, and Kansas City after the turn of the century. Toledo's dentists examined poor children's teeth for free as early as 1901, and women's clubs, liberals, and health advocates pressured the school board to hire its first medical inspector in 1910. By then some altruistic Toledo dentists

Medical Inspection in Toledo, 1911

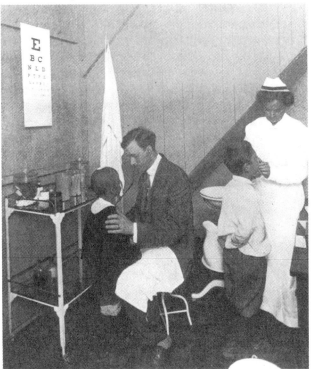

Source: *Annual Report of the Toledo, Ohio Schools* (1911)

already operated a free dental clinic for poor children, and school nurses soon ministered to their medical needs. The process of school health reform in Milwaukee and Kansas City was almost identical. As a result of agitation by boards of health, physicians, dentists, and some women's organizations, these cities joined the hundreds of municipalities that established programs of medical inspection. And as the health staff grew in size, children in every school received annual physical and dental exams by nurses and physicians, who kept extensive records on the physical development of thousands of individuals in these urban systems.[43]

As they had predicted, medical inspectors often uncovered numerous diseases and physical defects that impaired the health and schooling of individual children. Even if one acknowledged that health reformers worked to publicize the "widespread" existence of disease, there was still considerable evidence that serious health problems afflicted many children. When contemporaries asserted that three out of ten children had serious, uncorrected vision problems and that seven out of ten needed dental work, few people disagreed with them. Careful investigation demonstrated that almost half of Rochester's public school children in 1912 required dental attention. Thousands more had various communicable diseases, enlarged tonsils, adenoids, and poor nutrition. One observer in Rochester asserted that almost thirteen hundred children out of fifteen thousand examined in one study had some form of anemia. An examination of Toledo's schoolchildren in 1911 similarly found thousands of children who needed glasses, dental work, and special nutritional care.[44]

Detailed statistics gathered on children's health in many cities often underscored the power of social class in everyday life. Consider, for example, the Italian children at the Third Street School in Milwaukee, living in the impoverished "Bloody Third." Their school had the dubious honor of leading in the number of cases of impetigo, eczema, and other maladies, even though lice, scabies, and ringworm appeared in virtually every Milwaukee school. In 1912, Milwaukee physicians discovered more than 1,200 different cases of infectious diseases, including measles, mumps, and chicken pox; they found 239 cases of diphtheria and 317 cases of scarlet fever. Eye and skin diseases were very common. Nearly 3,000 cases of lice were also identified that year, along with ringworm, scabies, and other sources of children's discomfort. According to published reports in all these cities, children's teeth were also in a deteriorating state. School dentists found plenty of diseased gums, various forms of pyorrhea, and hundreds of thousands of cases of dental caries.[45]

Parental opposition to different aspects of medical inspection expressed itself in several ways. There were angry letters to the editor and to the school board and boycotts of the neighborhood schools. Parents often resented the insults hurled at them by health reformers, who primarily came from the ranks of an elite, professional class. Parents took pride in their own cures for children's diseases and sometimes denounced the treatment their children received at school. Too often, medical inspectors characterized all opponents as ignorant, narrow-minded people who interfered with those who wanted to perfect children's health. One reformer in 1914 encountered "a fusillade of prejudice, tradition and superstition, ignorance, distrust, apprehension, indifference, irresponsibility, poverty, and antagonism." Lewis Terman equated anyone who condemned school health work with "'sectarian' physicians, quacks, and patent-medicine vendors." He accepted the principled opposition of Christian Scientists to medical treatment, but like other health advocates, Terman believed that the uninformed public generally hindered medical progress.[46]

Many parents distrusted the claims of health officers that medical inspection would cure every social ill, and they opposed any treatment of their children without their written permission. A school riot began in a Jewish neighborhood in New York City in 1906 when school physicians removed adenoids from the children. A rumor spread through the neighborhoods that children's throats were being cut, and "an excited mob demolished several windows and doors before the children could be dismissed." During the same year, fifteen hundred angry Italian mothers in Brooklyn fought police, pelted the local school with stones and other objects, and prevented any medical treatments. School inspectors lacked the legal power to force parents to provide their children with medical care or operations, but many parents disliked the notes children brought home urging specific treatments. When a health inspector in one city complained to a mother about her son's body odors, she quickly told his instructor: "Teacher, Johnny ain't no rose. Learn him; don't smell him." School baths only reached a tiny fraction of the school population in any city, and parents often rejected school interference in what they considered private family matters.[47]

Even though parents were always ridiculed for opposing medical inspection and for endorsing Old World treatments for various illnesses, they often possessed a more complex understanding of social and educational problems than did better-schooled health officials. It must have raised more than a few eyebrows when Toledo's health commissioner proclaimed in 1907 that poor eyesight caused insanity. The head of Rochester's health department called for "selective breeding" and confidently told one community group that most criminals had adenoids as children and breathed through the mouth, causing their abnormal social behavior. And school boycotts and popular opposition to modern "science" were almost predictable when local physicians on the school staff urged the teaching of eugenics in the classroom to educate everyone on the alleged inferiority of Poles, Italians, Slovaks, and other ethnic and racial groups.[48]

School inspectors scoffed at the "traditionalism" of immigrant groups, who ironically often had a more basic understanding of why some children disliked school or had health problems. School physicians were always certain that good health almost guaranteed academic excellence; they incorrectly believed that truancy, misbehaving, poor scholarship, and all the other ancient evils of the schools would suddenly disappear if everyone followed their lead. Parents remained skeptical. One leading health advocate, Walter S. Cornell, reprinted the following letter from a parent in his seminal volume, *Health and Medical Inspection of School Children* (1912):

> We received the note from the Doctor and will say that we give [our son] medical attention when he needs it. We know that George has headaches

> but when he comes home from school he complains of a boy in the 3rd grade
> by the name of Andrew Aimeck who knocks him down and jomps [*sic*] on
> him. I wish you would give this your attention. I know boys are all alike
> but this boy is mutch [*sic*] bigger.[49]

Similar letters supposedly proved that parents were incompetent guardians, but perhaps they only showed that a wallop from Andrew Aimeck could make anyone ill.

Some officials in Rochester, Toledo, Milwaukee, and Kansas City faced numerous challenges to their authority. School physicians and nurses often received letters from parents that lambasted them for their arrogance, their snide remarks on children's physical states, and their cocksure belief that all problems stemmed from physical imperfections. One child in Rochester was sent home by the school nurse in 1913 because he had a severe case of acne. His angry mother secured little Fred's immediate readmission:

> I don't see why he should stay at home all the pimples he has are on his
> face and I want them left just as they are if all the children and teachers that
> have pimples were send [*sic*] home there would be only a few left in school.
> Yours truly his mother.[50]

Christian Scientists in city after city took school boards to court, boycotted classes, and demanded medical freedom. And when medical inspection staffs and health reformers tried to vaccinate every child, it virtually guaranteed additional cultural and social divisiveness.

"The vaccinator," wrote an author in the *Arena* in 1907, "cares nothing for individuality, idiosyncracy, temperament, condition of life or age of his subjects." As a result, the vaccinator became one of the most hated individuals in American cities in the Progressive era. While some members of the medical community accepted the validity of Jenner's work with inoculation and the germ theory of disease, many physicians, healers, and urban citizens strongly opposed compulsory vaccination. Some parents might endorse checking children's teeth or inspecting their eyes, ears, nose, and throat, but antivaccination crusades united many citizens of different backgrounds and political persuasions. As one poet of the opposition proclaimed:

> Hail, O Shade of once great Jenner!
> Stalk forth from thy place awhile,
> And kindly take the witness stand,
> Vaccination is on trial.[51]

The history of school vaccination is not a saga of how heroic physicians used the tools of modern science to rescue little children from disease and premature death. It is largely a tale of conflict between the school and the home, one of the most striking controversies of the Progressive era. Strong popular resistance to vaccination had been registered in America since the seventeenth century. Resistance in the twentieth century continued to hamper efforts by urban boards of health to establish basic school inspection programs. The working-class *Kansas City Mail* warned as early as 1893 that "a large number of people, respectable people, see that much evil results from vaccination. They see the state like a giant seize the little trembling babe and instill into its young life the germ of many diseases. These people see all around them persons afflicted with scrofulous and syphilitic diseases, the result of vaccination with impure virus." Many citizens opposed vaccination on religious grounds, viewing the body as a pure vessel that should be free from all foreign matter. Still others believed that vaccination caused tuberculosis, syphilis, and other diseases and that no rational person would willingly let a physician put smallpox vaccine into the human bloodstream.[52]

A compulsory school vaccination law in New York in the 1890s faced considerable dissent in the Rochester schools. The school board unanimously opposed the law, noting that it was impossible to enforce. According to optimistic estimates, perhaps half the city's children were already vaccinated, but thousands refused to comply with the law. The *Democrat and Chronicle*, which opposed compulsory but not voluntary vaccination, claimed that many parents feared that the virus "arouses diseases that have been lying dormant in the body." George Goler and the health board threatened various legal actions against noncompliant parents and the school board. Opposition to the law nevertheless continued throughout the Progressive era. In 1912 the parents of a twelve-year-old girl even defeated the school board in a court case. The girl had been inoculated in compliance with the law; however, the vaccination did not "take." Her parents pointed out that technically, children only had to be inoculated: the law did not require that it be successful. Thousands of Rochester's parents refused to submit their children to the vaccinator, no matter what the law stated.[53]

A similar compulsory law existed in Ohio in the 1890s, producing considerable parental and ethnic opposition. The Turnverein passed a resolution against the law in 1897, and parents and children routinely boycotted neighborhood schools after the turn of the century. The health department had pitched battles in local Polish neighborhoods, where opposition to vaccination flourished on religious grounds. There was a "police riot" in the Lagrange school district in 1902 when local officers protected physicians from residents who pelted the detested vaccinators. Golden Rule Jones, who basically subsisted on rye bread, nuts, and "natural" foods, opposed vaccination, and he was very popular with the Poles. He attacked the health department and defended the rights of immigrants to medical freedom. Jones said "plainly that he did not believe in kicking in doors . . . and did not approve of the rough handling" of local citizens. Toledo's health commissioner called Jones and the Poles "ignorant" and vainly tried to make Catholic priests alter the medical beliefs of their parishioners.[54]

The *Toledo Evening Bee* routinely asserted in 1903 that "the controversy over vaccination has lost nothing in bitterness in years, and that a great many very intelligent persons sincerely believe that it is worse than the disease." Improper inoculations and unpredictable viral strains caused deaths in many cities, which only fueled popular resistance. Local chapters of the League for Medical Freedom formed in Toledo, as elsewhere, and a citywide school boycott against vaccination crippled the school system in 1914. In January the children held what the *Toledo Blade* called an "anti-vaccination strike." Approximately 50 percent of the high school class and 65 percent of the elementary students boycotted classes rather than submit to vaccination. Once again, popular resistance made the law requiring vaccination unenforceable. At the Waite School, children followed their parents' orders and refused to leave their seats when school inspectors ordered them home. Meanwhile, parents from the Detroit district "accompanied their children to school and waited for inspectors to make their appearance." Only when local authorities agreed to accede to parental wishes did classes across the city resume their regular schedule—with the majority of children still unvaccinated.[55]

Through boycotts, occasional riots, and threats of legal action, therefore, parents often intervened effectively in health work in the schools and confounded the efforts of many school health reformers. Parents continued to wield considerable influence in health education and care for their children. Parents were less successful, however, in preventing the use of psychological tests, which were often promoted by health officers and other educational experts. Historians have demonstrated that these tests, which were used to track children into classes for the "feeble-minded," "exceptional," or "sub-normal" as well as into vocational classes, were culturally biased against immigrants and the poor. They had a profound influence on the treatment and education of urban school children. Tests went hand in hand with the eugenic theories on which much of the health movement rested, and they reflected the power of efficiency and scientific-management theories in schooling after 1910. Like all innovations, tests accented cultural and class divisions in the urban schools, providing further examples of the conflictive basis of educational policy.[56]

Not all the health services that entered the urban schools had inhumane or undemocratic results. Parents adamantly opposed many aspects of the school health movement, but undoubtedly many children benefited from medical and dental inspection in terms of personal comfort if not always in terms of academic success. Many children who could not afford glasses, who unknowingly had hearing problems, and who suffered from maladies ranging from heart ailments to skin diseases profited from greater attention to their health. In Rochester, Toledo, Milwaukee, Kansas City, and other places, school officials established classes for tubercular and anemic children. Here children were given (with their parents' permission) a special diet, individual attention, and adequate exercise. In "open air" facilities for tubercularly prone youngsters, children dressed in Eskimo suits and held their classes in open tents or in park pavilions. There teachers nurtured many children back to health, added stamina to bodies weakened by disease, and helped children return within a few months to the regular classroom. These experimental schools were extremely popular in many cities. Toledo's program had a long waiting list

An Open-Air Classroom in Rochester, 1910

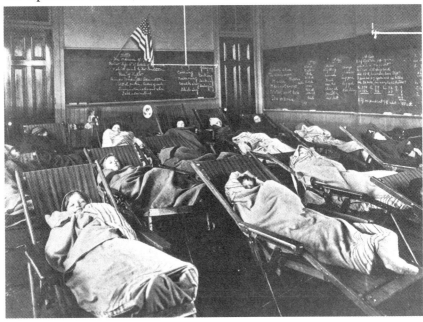

Source: *The Fifty-fifth Report of the Board of Education of the City of Rochester, New York* (1910)

of poor, unhealthy children whose parents believed that the open air, rest, and exercise might cure their disease.

Study after study by laypersons and experts alike demonstrated the value of these programs in improving the health and at times the academic progress of individual pupils. It is easy to dismiss all the efforts of medical reformers as self-serving, ill conceived, and unpopular, though undoubtedly many of their programs were so perceived by community groups. School health advocates promised too much, too soon, and with too little respect for the rights of many individuals. Their belief that proper health care would eliminate any "dull" and "backward" and "retarded" children was a simplistic assessment of the causes of school failure among the poor. By labeling children through biased psychological tests as backward, dull, feeble-minded, exceptional, or retarded, these reformers often created entire student populations who suffered under the stigma of being inferior, an enormous price for any child to pay for the advancement of "science."[57]

"Scientific authority is, in the nature of things, a most powerful instrument, whether it be established in error or in truth," asserted an opponent of vaccination in 1890. "Once established, the authority of science will be apt to secure absolute deference and obedience, most of all from the class who like to express their opinions in all matters non-scientific." Parents did not always defer to the presumed wisdom of the health reformers, who continually regarded their own logic and theories as unimpeachable products of scientific research. Many citizens properly distrusted the eugenics and efficiency theories of these men of science, preferring Old World cures for their ailments and traditionalism over modernity. Incidences of tuberculosis in America declined by about 30 percent in the Progressive era, but this did not result from vaccination or other medical intentions, as far as historians of medicine can determine. And more medical inspection did not cause a reduction in truancy or dropout rates or end listlessness, boredom, "moral obliquity," or the other evils perceived by the new medical mandarins.[58]

Elite health reformers, like all people who try to improve the world, believed that the problem really rested with a lack of power, resources, and will. If only more money, more staff, and better methods of examining and treating children were found, they argued, surely many problems of the classroom would be solved. Like other social services in the Progressive era, however, health reforms were expensive and competed with all the other new programs that simultaneously entered the schools. Not every citizen or policy maker accepted the theories of health reformers, and neither did taxpayers desire even heavier economic burdens. As a result, the basis for school inspection was laid in the Progressive era, but school hygiene departments were understaffed and small compared with the rest of the school bureaucracy. Toledo, for example, had only five physicians and one nurse for thousands of students in 1917. The City Club of Milwaukee estimated in 1919 that the local hygiene department would have to double in size to be effective. And, in Kansas City, four nurses in the same year ministered to the needs of forty thousand children.[59]

Still, the testers and medical and psychological examiners had power disproportionate to their numbers. Just as new avenues in recreation, play, vacation activities, and community use of the schools opened in the Progressive era, so too did urban systems expand into other areas of social welfare. Like many social reforms of this period, health innovations were initially targeted for the children of the poor, competed for scarce funds, and contributed to enlarging the social functions of education. And, like every other innovation during these years, these programs became enmeshed in struggles between efficiency advocates and local interests that respected parental rights and community interests in formulating educational policy. Efficiency and democracy once again struggled for mastery in the schools.

Chapter 9

World War I and the
Contradictions of School Reform

I

All social movements have historical antecedents and political ramifications, but the heyday and immediate impact of grassroots Progressivism in American education occurred during the period that spanned the depression of 1893 and the onset of World War I. During the 1890s, a number of new organizations and rising political leaders were forced to respond to the imperatives of economic crisis. Within a few short years, reformers such as Victor Berger, Golden Rule Jones, and Edward Ward contributed noticeably to the creation of a new social spirit and made a visible difference in the nature of schooling in local cities. Helen Montgomery, Meta Berger, Lizzie Black Kander, and Pauline Steinem—to name only a few of the prominent activists on the urban scene—similarly organized with thousands of women across the nation to champion programs of social amelioration.

These reform-minded men and women, who were anything but apologists for a corporate structure that threatened educational localism, made the Progressive era one of the most exciting and distinctive periods in the nation's history. What made the period so fascinating was not simply the clash between capital and these reform-minded individuals but the ways in which lesser-known socialists, populists, feminists, liberals, and other forgotten citizens shaped the world of mass schooling: the working-class poets who wanted playgrounds and school lunches for the poor; the parents who questioned the value of vaccination; the children who boycotted school; the immigrants who participated at the social centers; the men and women who marched in labor parades and demanded political equality and justice in the market place.

How to improve public education often became an all-consuming idea for this generation, for not only businessmen and corporate leaders, but for virtually all citizens. Struggles for playgrounds, free breakfasts, social centers, and other welfare reforms as well as for fair community representation on the school board were an integral part of larger community activism by working-class, socialist, and neighborhood interests hostile to business rule and centralized decision making. These groups ensured that the Progressive era never witnessed any monolithic capitalist mastery of the schools. Instead, school innovation and reform were produced by interaction, resistance, adaptation, and accommodation, with the power of capital clearly in a dominant though never unchallenged position. Liberals, Socialists, and business efficiency advocates all agreed that schools would be important social institutions in the twentieth century, and for that reason many of the period's most radical thinkers understood that educational improvement was an integral aspect of a better society. Schools could not build a new social order, but neither should they be delivered without a struggle to well-placed and more powerful urban elites.

By the time of America's involvement in World War I, a number of important social service innovations had already entered the public schools. Although these programs initially received meager funding and never reached every child, school lunches, social centers, playgrounds, vacation schools, manual training and domestic science, medical and dental inspection, and other reforms gradually affected urban education. Endorsed by a wide range of activists for numerous, often competing reasons, these reforms were joined by innovations that included psychological testing, vocational education, and special programs for the blind, deaf, physically disabled, and intellectually impaired. Educational expansion and extension were the trademarks of the Progressive era, as the schools broadened their influence in local neighborhoods and in the lives of the children.

The war did not eliminate any of these programs. Indeed, in the case of psychological testing and vocational testing, the war actually accelerated the movement toward change. The widespread use of psychological tests for military recruits and the passage of the Smith-Hughes Act brought more attention to the value of scientific evaluation and some financial support for vocational education. On the local level, however, the war was less important immediately for its effects on the pace of innovation than for its pernicious impact upon grassroots voluntary groups. Since the 1890s voluntary organizations had often cooperated to support community-oriented educational reforms. The war splintered many activist associations into hostile camps.[1]

Grassroots Progressivism had never been a single, static entity in urban life, but embodied shifting coalitions of community-based groups. Political and cultural traditions and the quality of community leadership differed remarkably from city to city, yet the trends of the day were clear. Beginning in the 1890s, Progressive women agitated for vacation schools, playgrounds, and other social services as a way to expand their power beyond the home. Socialists often criticized the aims of these liberals, but they, too, endorsed similar forms of municipal and state intervention whenever they seemed to benefit workers and their children. And countless other organizations such as parent associations, civic leagues, and neighborhood groups contributed time, money, and effort to expand the social functions of their local schools.

Reform movements in the Progressive era were ever dynamic, and their leaders refused to remain frozen in time. Activist men and women were shaped and reshaped through interaction with one another and with the powerful forces for change that went into the making of a new economic and industrial state. Through the years, liberals and radicals had often been forced by political circumstances not of their choosing to cooperate for reforms of mutual interest. To fund schools more generously or to expand programs such as social centers was often a common goal that transcended ideological viewpoints and dictated the formation of alliances against efficiency experts and fiscal conservatives. School board centralization often split voluntary organizations that had different perspectives on the value of ward-based political machines in the schools, but even community battles over how to elect school board representatives produced less stress and rancor among the grassroots than did the war in Europe. A spirit of cooperation and mutual respect almost vanished under the impact of militarism.

Progressive trade unionists often warned that war inevitably undermined the popularity of movements for domestic reform. Laboring groups, therefore, in particular dissented against attempts to link school policy with the prosecution of the war. Throughout the Progressive era, labor unions passed resolutions against American militarism and argued that all wars were inimical to workers. A member of the Central Labor Union in Toledo in 1897 warned that "the jingoism which causes men to orate on Fourths of July and picture a condition of liberty and happiness which does not exist, is misleading to say the least. To blind the people to the abuses which exist is no panacea for the ills of humanity, and is the most cruel deception which can be practiced upon a people." Unions repeatedly attacked the "Flag Idiots" who waved the national banner on every patriotic holiday but who then failed to improve social conditions for working people. According to many Socialist as well as non-Socialist working people, military conflicts made poor men fight a rich man's war.[2]

After 1914, many trade union newspapers attacked the preparedness movement, which, they feared, would draw America into the war in Europe. Working-class critics asserted that Wall Street and munitions manufacturers who sought profits through war-making posed a greater danger to

American freedom and liberty than the Kaiser or any European despot. No group, however, so criticized preparedness as Milwaukee's Socialist working class, which vehemently denounced preparedness movements in the schools. The Federated Trades Council proclaimed that wars primarily benefited the world's capitalist ruling classes, who by necessity sought new markets for their goods while they simultaneously made working people enemies on the battlefield. The burdens of war, resolved the council, "fall heaviest upon the working class, who have no interest in any such hostilities."[3]

Socialist trade union members joined the Social Democrats in a large antiwar rally in Milwaukee in 1914. When the ultraconservative National Security League then asked the Milwaukee unions to march in a preparedness parade, the Federated Trades Council bluntly responded:

> We do not desire to lend ourselves to a movement to weaken democracy and enthrone plutocracy. Industrial plutocracy is as oppressive as the autocracy of kings. . . . We are for the preparedness of a work day that will not exhaust the worker's vitality and a wage that will enable him to rear his children in comfort, without depriving his children of their childhood. We would prepare our nation's defense by keeping its children from being stunted in mine and mill and factory.[4]

Workers in other cities passed similar resolutions against the preparedness measures of Woodrow Wilson's administration, of local business leaders, and of elite members of the school board. At a time when numerous citizens tried to utilize the schools for military preparedness, Socialist and working-class groups that opposed the war and militarism in the schools engaged in one final battle over educational policy during the Progressive era.

Unlike grassroots radicals, the federal government and many prowar Americans viewed the public schools as an instrument of national defense and preparedness. "Federal agencies, scores of patriotic societies, and many school systems proceeded to formulate courses in patriotism and to initiate war activities," noted one observer. Schools increased their efforts to Americanize aliens through special evening schools and Americanization classes, thereby promoting "one hundred percent Americanism." Children sold millions of dollars' worth of war bonds and Thrift Stamps, marched in patriotic parades, and knitted clothes for the wounded. School gardens flourished and alleviated food shortages in many communities. And to ensure that the entire school staff firmly supported the Allies, teachers were forced to sign loyalty oaths to testify to their patriotism. What a writer in the *Toledo Union Leader* called flag idiocy seemed to overwhelm public education.[5]

War-related activities were common in the public schools in Rochester, Toledo, Milwaukee, and Kansas City after 1914. Labor unions and Socialists in particular opposed these preparedness activities, while women's organizations and liberal organizations in contrast endorsed greater attention to national defense. The Women's Educational and Industrial Union of Rochester, the City Federation of Women's Clubs of Toledo, the Woman's School Alliance of Milwaukee, and the Athenaeum of Kansas City all contributed to war garden work, knitted clothes for civilian casualties in Europe, and together with many parent organizations supported preparedness. When America finally entered the war, many women who believed that Wilson would one day press for full suffrage gravitated toward Red Cross work and other patriotic activities, thereby strengthening the home front. Local communities simultaneously witnessed vicious attacks on German Americans and on antiwar activists, whose civil liberties almost vanished in the "war for democracy."[6]

The Toledo and Kansas City high schools operated training programs for military cadets that infuriated many unions and working people. Toledo's labor leaders in particular vigorously attacked the preparedness movement as well as military training. The *Toledo Union Leader*, the official organ of the Central Labor Union, had long opposed jingoism and American imperialism. When several school board members of 1916 endorsed the Wyoming Plan, a voluntary military cadet program funded by the federal government, the union vocally attacked the idea as undemocratic and contrary to working-class interests. "We union men are the ones who will have to go out and shoulder the guns," claimed a labor leader who attacked the business elites on the Toledo school board. Unions also criticized preparedness parades, urged neutrality in foreign policy, and opposed the war and military training in the schools. As late as the spring of 1917, representatives of the twenty-four hundred members of the Toledo Machinists Union unanimously opposed the military draft.[7]

Unlike organized labor in Kansas City, which also opposed local preparedness movements, Toledo's workers nevertheless continually enjoyed political representation by peace activists. Golden Rule Jones, for example, was a major proponent of arbitration and national peace organizations and denounced the Spanish-American War and imperialism. Laborers also elected a perennial peace activist to Congress, Isaac R. Sherwood. Himself a local Civil War hero, Sherwood became a major congressional opponent of World War I. Widely denounced by Toledo's Republican press and by business leaders as a coward and German sympathizer, he had considerable popular appeal in Toledo. For his principled stands, Sherwood received his largest electoral pluralities during the war years. The Central Labor Union had been influential in establishing a municipal school for workers as part of the University of Toledo, and one of its leading radical professors, Scott Nearing, was also one of labor's leading antiwar heroes.[8]

Nearing was a radical economist with Socialist and pacifist leanings. He became a national figure when the University of Pennsylvania reportedly fired him because of his political views. His move from Philadelphia did not soften his radicalism. While in Toledo he even wrote a seminal essay on the elite control of school boards by business interests. The Central Labor Union regarded Nearing as a special friend and defended him on numerous occasions for his pacifist and anticorporate beliefs. In 1916, Nearing addressed the Women's Educational Club, arguing that war is "uncivilized and must be abolished." "We need protection," he warned, "but not against Berlin, or London, or Paris, or Petrograd, but against Wall Street." Socialists and working men who opposed the war supported Nearing when several self-styled patriots and community leaders verbally attacked him and demanded his removal from the university. At one meeting of several hundred members of the Commercial Club in 1917, the Reverend Patrick O'Brien echoed some growing sentiments: "I feel tonight like taking him by the nape of the neck and hanging him to the nearest tree." Nearing was spared the rope. Instead, the university regents fired him.[9]

School officials and Toledoans generally treated antiwar activists harshly during these years. Superintendent William B. Guitteau, an Anglophile, promised citizens in 1914 that teachers would discuss the war "in a dignified, scholarly manner, just as we study the other great wars of history." Within a few years, however, the Commercial Club prodded Guitteau and the school board to establish military training as a high school elective, to distribute copies of Wilson's Fourteen Points to every classroom, and to force every teacher to sign a loyalty oath. Guitteau also applauded the elimination of German-language training. Numerous "war gardens" by the children increased the food supply, patriotic leagues gained almost exclusive access to the schools as community centers, and children were pressured to sell Liberty Bonds and Thrift Stamps and to march in patriotic parades. The superintendent also became active in the local Committee of One Hundred, which was dominated by businessmen and manufacturers and which informed the federal government of suspected spies and harassed war resisters and pacifists. Across the city, the *Toledo Blade* sensed a "growing demand for straight Americanism. . . . We are through in this man's town with hyphenated citizenship."[10]

The Toledo school board could never have transformed the schools into a domestic extension of the war without public support. Many trade unions, pacifist organizations, and German-American anti-war leagues firmly opposed the new militarism in the schools, but other community forces openly welcomed it. Toledo's large Polish community, for example, roundly supported the Allies, who presumably would guarantee the autonomy of Poland. Through the Nebraska and Lagrange neighborhoods marched thousands of Poles in loyalty parades in 1917. As the *Toledo News-Bee* asserted, "The spirits of Kosciusko and Pulaski, those Polish allies of our revolutionary forefathers, marched thru [*sic*] the streets of Toledo . . . as a new testimonial of their pledge of Poland's heart and hand in America's fight for democracy." A mob of one thousand Poles assembled in 1918 at the meeting house of local Polish Socialists, manhandled their opponents, and forced several of them to salute and kiss the American flag. The mayor vetoed the requests of pacifist groups to meet in public buildings, a Socialist council member was removed from office, and members of the Justice Department raided Scott Nearing's home, since he was regarded by the federal government as a German sympathizer and a spy.[11]

Socialists in many sections of the country were torn by whether or not to oppose the war, but the opposition against American involvement by Milwaukee's Socialist working class led to especially tense local conflicts and educational policy debates. Through their opposition to the war, the Milwaukee Socialists exposed themselves to an inordinate amount of criticism. They were denounced as "the local Bolsheviks" and "the trash of the world." With there being a plethora of ethnic groups that inhabited Milwaukee and whose homelands were involved in the war, any strong position on foreign policy was naturally destined to alienate specific groups of people. The Socialists paid a heavy toll for their antiwar stand. "Everyone wanted to be a 100 percent American, and 100 percent citizens usually resorted to abusive unsigned letters," recalled Meta Berger. She received a letter on school stationery that read: "Mrs. Berger, Why don't you hide your dirty head in shame and take your stinking sausage and go back to Germany." It mattered little that Meta Berger, while of German parentage, was a native Milwaukeean.[12]

War hysteria overwhelmed Milwaukee. The federal government banned the *Milwaukee Leader* from the mails for its antiwar stand, and Victor Berger was sentenced to twenty years in federal prison under the Espionage Act in a conviction that was later overturned by the Supreme Court. Paint was splashed on the homes of numerous pacifists; German-owned restaurants and businesses changed their names to indicate their loyalty; and innuendo and circumstantial evidence ruined many reputations. The City Club, composed of elite reformers of varying political stripes, stopped debating war-related topics to preserve its organization. More important, one radical remembered how the war erased much of the earlier progress the Social Democrats had made with the Milwaukee Poles: "The Poles of South Milwaukee, many of whom we had captured for the Socialist Party, were now fighting the battles of Poland in the twelfth and fourteenth wards." The Poles held huge loyalty parades and denounced the Socialists as traitors, atheists, and opponents of a free Poland. Numerous foreign-language branches of the Social Democratic Party also wrote angry letters to party leaders, expressing their displeasure with the official antiwar position of the Socialists.[13]

Socialists and pacifists on the Milwaukee school board valiantly defended free speech as well as foreign-language training during the war years. When it came to counting votes, however, theirs were cast on the losing side. Antiwar activists could not prevent the schools from becoming a tool of preparedness and war. Lizzie Kander (a pacifist settlement worker), several Social Democrats on the school board, and occasionally, the former Populist William Pieplow were the only school officials to exercise any genuine opposition or restraint when confronted by patriotic pressure groups. The first important crisis occurred in June 1916, when an anti-war non-Socialist member resolved that the board march in an upcoming preparedness parade. Meta Berger, ever tactful, divided the resolution into two sections; the board formally approved of the parade, but did not require members to participate. Morris Stern, a Hungarian-born Socialist on the board, angrily complained: "Our function is to administer the duties of the school board. No one can compel me to march in the parade. This is a personal matter." Heated debates continually flared between the Socialists and their opponents, and in the future the Socialists would not be so fortunate.[14]

By early 1917, Meta Berger joined the Milwaukee Emergency Peace Committee, which tried to prevent navy recruiters from speaking to high school students. "I know that to oppose a measure as this is to lay oneself liable to being called unpatriotic, but I do not believe that our schools should be used for such purposes," she claimed in the *Milwaukee Leader*. Lizzie Kander joined her Social Democratic friends, stating that "I wouldn't say anything against this if the whole thing of the navy wasn't to teach [children] to kill." Their mutual effort to deter war recruitment in the schools failed. So did a number of other joint recommendations. They lost in an attempt to increase the compulsory school age from fourteen to fifteen years old, to hold young people from joining the military for an extra year; they lost when the children of the city marched in numerous patriotic parades, sold and purchased Thrift Stamps and Liberty Bonds, and operated victory gardens. The social centers were declared "seditious and traitorous" by the non-Socialists because of antiwar speakers sometimes heard there, and the schools were closed to all but patriotic organizations, presumably to conserve fuel to aid in the prosecution of the war. The Socialists fought strenuously against these actions, won few victories, and were called traitors for their efforts.[15]

The movement against free speech in the social centers was coupled with the abolition of foreign languages and the approval of loyalty oaths for teachers and even children. Numerous ethnic groups, especially the Germans, protested against the elimination of foreign languages, but by the end of the war, every language except English was essentially eliminated. Ellen L. Minehan, a firebrand organizer of the Milwaukee teachers, had earlier joined the Federated Trades Council in denouncing Milwaukee's corporate tax-dodgers. Now she turned her sights from big business and attacked the German language and the Socialists. "The vigorous protests of Prussianized Germans against cutting down the teaching of the German language in the public schools . . . is a part and parcel of the pan-germanic scheme to Prussianize the world," she declared before the Westminster Civic Club. Like the Poles, she became an enemy of the Socialist working class.[16]

The Social Democrats read long petitions favoring the retention of all languages, a useless enterprise in this atmosphere. They also failed to halt an aggressive witch hunt for German sympathizers on the teaching staff undertaken by patriotic zealots on the school board and in the community at large. A fourth-grade teacher was dismissed for allegedly urging the kaiser to sabotage a local munitions plant. Arguing in her defense, the Socialists claimed that the teacher was indeed a pacifist and probably a single-taxer, yet had committed no crime. And there was no rule against the employment of pacifist teachers. As organized labor announced, "If so, under such a ruling Christ Himself would have been barred from our schools, for He was, without question, the first of the pacifists."[17]

One abuse of civil liberties in the school followed another in the atmosphere of the Red Scare. The rights of minorities and peaceful dissidents were consistently violated. Usually only the Socialists spoke out against these outrages. Aliens previously hired to teach in the schools were pressured to secure their citizenship papers immediately or face removal from their jobs. Loyalty oaths were passed from school to school for teachers and children to sign. Protests against such policies were consistently aired yet repeatedly ignored. One Socialist board member, Elizabeth Thomas, former secretary of the state party, complained of the ridicule heaped upon children who refused to sign a pledge because of parental wishes or personal desire. Also, there was tremendous pressure "to make each school a 100 percent Red Cross school," wrote a fellow Socialist, and this "made many a child's life miserable at the time. War hysteria is an awful thing." It was so awful, in fact, that the Socialists in

1918 pledged themselves "to support every effort designed to eliminate reactionary tendencies and to make our school system a democratic institution."[18]

Writing in this age of hysteria and patriotism, the Socialists proceeded with their resolution:

> Resolved, That we condemn the poisoning of the mind of the pupil with imperialism and militarism; the pernicious practice of using the school youth as a medium of spreading war propaganda; the practice of constantly begging for funds; the drilling of the youth to act like puppets; and the brutal practice of subjecting a pupil, indicating a dislike for these practices, to ostracism.[19]

Despite such adversity, the Social Democrats still continued to endorse the enlargement of school programs and facilities, higher pay for teachers, and more attention to areas such as public recreation. The abuses of civil liberties in Milwaukee also offended other Milwaukeeans. Later that year, the entire county ticket of the Socialists was elected, making it a strong minority party there. Victor Berger, already under indictment as an enemy of the state, was reelected to Congress, though officials in Washington refused to seat him. The Republican county chairman only groaned at the thought of radical resurgence when he lamented, "Socialism, Socialism seems to have taken hold of the people."[20]

The blatant abuse of power by the patriotic citizens on the school board and in the city may indeed have led to an unexpected backlash in the 1918 elections. But by and large, the war dealt the Socialists a heavy blow. The war years in Rochester, Toledo, Milwaukee, and Kansas City led to an intensification of community conflict, not cooperation, especially when school superintendents and school boards in each of these cities openly utilized the schools for patriotic ends that were popular with some, but not all, citizens. Conflict and debate had shaped educational policy from the earliest days of the schools, but the war polarized community groups tremendously. Since the early 1890s, different elements of the grass roots had struggled to initiate a number of educational innovations. Through civic alliances, they fought for changes that promised to increase the usefulness and service of the neighborhood school. The war destroyed this spirit of community activism and undermined popular faith in social cooperation, bringing an exciting and remarkable era of grassroots Progressivism to a close.

II

By the end of the war years, many of the grassroots Progressives who first became active in municipal reform in the 1890s took stock of their accomplishments. "The expansion of the school system has been remarkable and the improvements in many respects noteworthy," asserted Milwaukee's school board president William Pieplow, in 1919. "Forward—Wisconsin's motto—was the course followed by the directors and that is why Milwaukee is favorably recognized educationally today." A Populist and a protégé of Victor Berger in the 1890s, Pieplow became a conservative Republican after the turn of the century, when he began a seventeen-year tenure on the school board. Not every grassroots activist viewed the various innovations of the age so positively, of course, but Pieplow accurately sensed that his generation had initiated some momentous changes. In the 1890s the community activists fighting for the new education were outsiders, battling against an array of male ward politicians who disliked public meddling in their affairs. By the 1920s many innovations had been adopted in the schools, providing tangible proof that a new spirit of social reform had captured the attention of many urban citizens.[21]

Rochester, Toledo, Milwaukee, and Kansas City were only a handful of the dozens of cities that experienced profound social change in the early twentieth century, yet they may still illuminate some of the dark corners of our educational past. Clearly, the Progressive era was more than an age when "new middle class" school superintendents and centralized school boards dominated in the shaping of the urban school. Their power, of course, cannot be ignored or underestimated. Centralized administrative reforms were class inspired and benefited some citizens at the expense of others, as every working-class radical and Socialist at the turn of the century realized. At a time when the forces of centralization were seemingly irresistible throughout the political economy, every supporting social institution, including schools, was affected by the influence of elite reform.

Schools existed in a society rife with contradictions that expressed themselves as basic educational policy. To argue that schools were divorced from the masses of people and controlled exclusively by the forces of privilege captures only one aspect of Progressive era reform movements and misses the dialectical nature of social innovation. Numerous voluntary organizations, often dedicated to localism, lay control, and neighborhood service, fought strenuously against the tide of centralization and made schools more responsive than they otherwise would have been at certain historical moments. Efforts at centralization promoted resistance, new strategies to promote neighborhood interests, and a civic will to unite diverse citizens in opposition to the evils of elite rule. Socialists, Progressive women, and working-class representatives occasionally gained election to urban school boards, attacked the values of business efficiency, and promoted many programs to make schools serviceable and meaningful to neighborhood parents and their children.

Grassroots Progressivism was a multifaceted phenomenon in different cities, and a wide range of dedicated individuals brought complexity and diversity to the urban scene. Unwilling to leave the world of educational politics to the well-to-do, but often unable to seize power from old and newly entrenched political elites, grassroots reformers linked school reforms to broader social struggles that had significance in the lives of many turn-of-the-century Americans. Women fought in a traditional arena, education, yet expanded female participation beyond the home into the larger world. At a time when capitalists across the nation were consolidating their influence and power, workers and Socialists rejected the beliefs of those who viewed children as human resources. Instead, they called for equality in a land that simultaneously exalted labor in Fourth of July speeches but viewed workers as unfit to serve on school boards. And at a time when the charge of "tainted money" still had meaning to many Americans, Social Gospelers and Christian Socialists reminded many citizens that schools were for everyone, especially the poor and ignorant, who above all groups deserved to feel the spirit of human solidarity and social justice at work in everyday life.

Certain clichés, unfortunately, now dominate our understanding of the Progressive era, since education for the purposes of "social control" or "efficiency" was so popular at the turn of the century. Another side to the Progressive era is revealed in this study, one that documents how the Sermon on the Mount, the writings of Marx, and the teachings of domestic feminists shaped school policy in the early twentieth century. People were moved by more than the calculations of efficiency engineers and by the beliefs of certain reformers who mistakenly viewed pig iron and people as synonymous. Schools never escaped the more powerful influences of businessmen and capitalists or of their professional allies on the school board or in the school administration, but education was also influenced by a wide range of competing citizen groups who valued more than dollar-and-cents economy.

One can easily document the sometimes inhumane, prejudicial, and narrow opinions of the dominant socioeconomic, political, and educational interests of the age: the elite school superintendents, the efficiency experts, the vaccinators, and the superpatriots who ran roughshod over the rights of less powerful citizens. There was always resistance to them, however, and the actions of dominant groups are always shaped to an important degree by threats against the established system of power. Historians have often called for a more "dialectical" interpretation of social change in education, but they have nevertheless tended to emphasize the ideas and actions of dominant groups, acting as if no one else shaped the past, affected elite activity, or protested against undesirable social policy.

Because the elite figures in history leave more literary records of their thoughts and activities than do common folk, historians are often forced to depend on their opinions and appraisals of social life in the past. But reconstructing the views of ordinary parents who sent angry notes to the school nurse, of children who boycotted classes, and of neighbors who met at the local social center fleshes out a side of our educational past often forgotten when only the powerful and successful capture our interest. The clash of competing interests was apparent in every school innovation initiated at the turn of the century; to emphasize one group at the expense of opposing forces oversimplifies the past and drains history of its dynamism.

It is clear, of course, that dominant interests often triumphed in the establishment of social service such as nutritional programs in the Progressive era: only when efficiency advocates saw school lunches as a form of capital investment and race betterment did they become interested in these Socialist-inspired programs to aid the poor. By establishing school meals as a form of municipal charity, school leaders reinforced class stigmas in social welfare and undermined radical objectives. Yet this is only part of the history of nutritional innovation. It is important to remember that some children undoubtedly benefited from a school meal—or a dental examination, or a summer class, or a safe place to play—just as it is important to recall that some people were dissatisfied with theories of human capital investment and proclaimed that all children had a right to sufficient food as a matter of social justice.

Progressive school reforms such as these were not simply imposed on the so-called unsuspecting masses, a position often implied in social-control models of education. Some people opposed the existence of obvious inequalities in the schools and in the larger social order and vigorously demanded many improvements. Social change in the schools was a product of accommodation and adaptation: there was widespread cooperation within communities on some issues but widespread disagreement on others. Radicals wanted free school meals for all children, while the subsequent policy created by elite interests meant that Socialists never shaped educational innovation exactly as they pleased. Neither did their opponents. Programs were created, but not for every child; and they were never free, except for the very poor. Socialists and Progressive women were hardly complete failures, and elite school boards were forced to make concessions to specific working-class populations. The nature of almost every social service innovation that entered the schools was determined by the tensions that divided different community groups and that divided their representatives and elected school officials. To leave either dominant or subordinate forces out of the history of social change in education, therefore, ignores the contradictory forces that competed for state favor at crucial moments in our educational past.

Opposing influences continually shaped the social history of urban education in the Progressive era. On the one hand, large numbers of men and women believed in the efficacy of reform at the turn of the century, agitated for school innovations as well as other changes to achieve social progress, and made the neighborhood school a central institution in larger social reconstruction. Through its supporting institutions, the state seemed to offer relief and social amelioration. On the other hand, certainly not all reformers agreed on which specific educational changes were desirable, who should control public education, and whether educational reform by itself would cure most of society's ills. After the depression of the 1890s, for example, many liberal women wanted to increase their influence over children's welfare and to augment their power generally in the city. That almost inevitably led them to the schoolhouse door. Once there, however, they encountered numerous other reformers who also saw schooling as a mechanism for social improvements and a way to help maximize their influence in the community.

There were visionaries such as Samuel M. Jones, who believed that school playgrounds and other innovations would teach human solidarity and cooperation and help institutionalize the Golden Rule. There were parent groups and kindergarten teachers who tried to bridge the gaps that separated home and school. And there were trade unions and Socialists such as those in Milwaukee, who saw schooling as a potential aid in social amelioration but also as currently often a capitalist prop. Instead of a community chorus for reform there sometimes seemed to be a babble of voices.

What all these grassroots forces contributed to the twentieth century, however, was a spirit of civic activism and faith in the power of men and women to change institutions peacefully for human betterment. They realized that public apathy led to social paralysis. Whether they quoted Marx or Jesus, many community-oriented Progressives spoke out against social injustice even when they realized that the road to social improvement was winding, hazardous, and filled with unexpected impediments. None of the most radical reformers ever witnessed the establishment of a society based on the Golden Rule or saw the redistribution of national power and resources among all citizens. Victor Berger's prediction in the mid-1890s that Milwaukeeans in 1945 would be living in a Socialist state was unfulfilled. Yet such faith and hope typified the Progressive generation, and men and women such as Victor and Meta Berger, for all their faults, held out the prospect of a more just social order. By the end of the war, elites dominated on the school boards of many cities. Still, that never deterred radical reformers from continuing their struggle against the powerful in the name of the powerless.

Schooling in Rochester, Toledo, Milwaukee, and Kansas City in the Progressive era was the product of intense conflict over contradictory trends: the movement of administrative centralization and the call for local representation, the rise of expert supervision versus the interest of parents and laypeople in schooling, the existence of male educational leadership and the challenge of the new woman, and the widespread struggles between proponents of efficiency and democracy. Business efficiency interests often triumphed in the schools, but not without a fight, and never totally. School boards indeed became mutual admiration societies because of school board centralization, but liberal women and Socialist representatives in some cities exemplified the spirit of dissent against the status quo common for the times.

Similarly, voluntary associations forced many new social service programs onto the schools, programs that were once privately funded, "experimental" innovations, including playgrounds and penny lunches. Dominant political interests that controlled the schools, of course, heavily influenced these and other programs and blunted their potential as a way to transform education. Hence social centers were created, just as numerous grassroots agitators desired, but free speech was denied. Cities increasingly funded lunch programs, playgrounds, and other welfare reforms, but they failed to reach every child in need. And, during the war years in particular, conservative business and professional leaders on urban school boards encouraged war hysteria, denied civil liberties to teachers and other citizens, and demonstrated how centralization greatly empowered those in office.

More effective community control over urban educational policy would have required a more democratic governing structure. That, however, was impossible after Good Government forces and some liberal Progressives had centralized school boards after the turn of the century. A ward-based structure would not have guaranteed that all classes, sexes, races, and ethnic groups would have fair representation on the school board. This never existed before the elimination of ward-based school boards in many cities, and many ward leaders resisted school innovation, endorsed hard-line pedagogical ideas, disliked meddling women and parents, and gave little power to teachers, who lacked tenure and served at the pleasure of local elites. But if the ward structure never guaranteed enlightened leadership, the at-large structure almost guaranteed elite dominance. Many local neighborhood interests suffered when the business efficiency wing of municipal reform movements ushered "a better class of men" into power.

Radical reformers at the turn of the century realized that the actions of the centralizers were not irreversible. History, they believed, would be shaped by those who organized most effectively and offered the people relief from the prevailing social order. Groups such as the Milwaukee Socialists, for example, understood that at-large elections denied many citizens adequate political representation; that nonpartisanship was impossible, since society was divided into social classes; and that centralization benefited the most wealthy and influential citizens. Efficiency, they realized, would have to be sacrificed if power shifted back closer to local neighborhoods, for representative democracy could only be achieved if citizen participation and parental input into the educational process became widely accepted and the power of school officials thereby reduced. The failure of decentralization plans in large cities in the recent past highlights many of the problems that communities will face in future struggles. It remains uncertain whether localism will receive serious attention in a society dominated by corporate interests and centralized power.

One legacy of radical thinking during the Progressive era was the belief that the contradictions of progress and poverty at key points in history would inspire large numbers of people to unite for social reconstruction. Although it was of little immediate consolation to the victims of various forms of discrimination, the Milwaukee Socialists in particular placed their struggles against corporate capitalism in broad historical perspective. By the 1920s, they realized that their early bouts against the prevailing economic, political, and educational system were necessary and worthwhile activities and provided a foundation for more community action in the future. The spirit of hope and struggle never really died in Milwaukee and in other cities, and many radical reformers attempted to remind contemporaries that the struggle for social justice transcended their own age.

When the Great Depression sent the nation into near chaos, the Socialist working class of Milwaukee pointed with pride to their activism in the past and remained confident of the future. "Our influence has created a real civic heart and consciousness," claimed the local radicals in their municipal campaign of 1932. "The period since the election of the first Socialist mayor has been the era of Milwaukee's greatest progress." And, they added, the partisans of the proletariat must aid the age-old struggle "in meeting oppression, wiping out poverty, and establishing industrial democracy, in place of the selfish, inhuman capitalist system of exploitation." Written at a time of economic and political despair, these words captured the activist spirit of many grassroots reformers.[22]

The Progressive era and the Great Depression seem so very far away, yet it is crucial to remember the collective struggles of grassroots reformers who led the charge against privilege in their own time. How to mobilize women, workers, radical political leaders, and other reform-minded citizens in the best interests of the child was a crucial concern of the early twentieth century. Domestic feminists, Socialists, Social Gospelers, and trade unionists—the backbone of grassroots Progressivism—were a diverse lot, but for many years they sacrificed parts of their own political agenda to unite against common enemies who regarded laypeople with hostility and viewed children as a human resource and little else. Whether new generations of grassroots agitators can overlook their own special concerns and coalesce into collective movements for educational and social reform remains one of the pressing issues of our own times. At the very least, community-oriented Progressive reformers of the early 1900s provided a legacy of activism and civic spirit for men and women of goodwill in their future crusades for social justice.

Notes

Preface

1. "Slave Factory or School," *Milwaukee Leader*, 6 March 1915.
2. The most influential interpretations of the administrative Progressives include David B. Tyack, *The One Best System: A History of American Urban Education* (Cambridge: Harvard University Press, 1974); and David B. Tyack and Elisabeth Hansot, *Managers of Virtue: Public School Leadership in America, 1820–1980* (New York: Basic Books, 1982), part 3. This book is a revised version of William J. Reese, *Case Studies of Social Services in the Schools of Selected Cities* (Washington, D.C., Final Report to the National Institute of Education, 1981). For more extensive documentation of the major arguments in this volume, please consult this earlier work.
3. See Michael B. Katz, *The Irony of Early School Reform: Educational Innovation in Mid-Nineteenth Century Massachusetts*, Second Edition (New York: Teachers College Press, 2001); and Joel H. Spring, *Education and the Rise of the Corporate State* (Boston: Beacon Press, 1972).
4. The phrase is, of course, borrowed from Richard Edwards, *Contested Terrain: The Transformation of the Workplace in the Twentieth Century* (New York: Basic Books, 1979).
5. On economic change, see Gabriel Kolko, *The Triumph of Conservatism: A Reinterpretation of American History, 1900–1916* (Chicago: Quadrangle Books, 1963). On changes in school administration, see Tyack, *The One Best System*.
6. Carl F. Kaestle, *The Evolution of an Urban School System: New York City, 1750–1850* (Cambridge: Harvard University Press, 1973); Stanley K. Schultz, *The Culture Factory: Boston Public Schools, 1789–1860* (New York: Oxford University Press, 1973); and Katz, *The Irony*.

Chapter 1

1. *Toledo Blade*, 9 May 1854, and *Toledo Board of Education Minutes*, 16 May 1865. Basic sources on time discipline include Edward P. Thompson, "Time, Work-Discipline, and Industrial Capitalism," *Past and Present* 38 (December 1967): 56–97; and Herbert G. Gutman, "Work, Culture, and Society in Industrializing America, 1815–1919," *American Historical Review* 78 (June 1973): 531–87.
2. Whig ideology and school reform are analyzed in Robert L. Church and Michael W. Sedlak, *Education in the United States* (New York: Free Press, 1976), chap. 3; and David Nasaw, *Schooled to Order: A Social History of Public Schooling*

in the United States (New York: Oxford University Press, 1979), 31–32, 40–43. On the salient role of the Whigs in public school development, see Daniel W. Howe, *The Political Culture of the American Whigs* (Chicago: University of Chicago Press, 1979). Although I have tried to write a more dialectical analysis of the origins of mass education, I am indebted to Michael B. Katz, *The Irony*.

3. *Toledo Blade*, 15 June 1849, 16 June 1849, and 12 September 1849; *Rochester School Report*, 1849, 3–4; *Rochester School Report*, 1855, 6, 15–16; *Milwaukee Sentinel*, 10 June 1845; and *Kansas City Journal of Commerce*, 22 December 1869.

4. Blake McKelvey, *Rochester: The Water-Power City, 1812–1854* (Cambridge: Harvard University Press, 1945), 264–66; and A. Laura MacGregor, "An Early History of Rochester Public Schools," in Blake McKelvey, ed., *The History of Education in Rochester* (Rochester: Rochester Historical Society, 1939), 45, 50.

5. *Toledo Blade*, 12 May 1849.

6. Quoted in Bayrd Still, *Milwaukee: The History of a City* (Madison: State Historical Society of Wisconsin, 1948), 108. "No city in the Union offers better, safer, or more remunerative employment for capital, than Milwaukee," claimed a booster in Milwaukee, Wisconsin. *Hunt's Merchant Magazine* 41 (September 1859): 314. During these years, Jesup W. Scott, a prominent booster, predicted that Toledo would be the largest city in the world by the year 2000. See Randolph C. Downes, *Lake Port* (Toledo: Toledo Printing Company, 1951), 5; J. H. Doyle, *A Story of Early Toledo: Historical Facts and Incidents of the Early Days and Environs* (Bowling Green: C. S. Van Tassell, 1919), 105; J. W. Scott, "Our Cities in 1862 and 1962," *Hunt's Merchant Magazine* 47 (November 1862): 404–8; and Still, *Milwaukee*, 84–85, 216–17. Useful sketches of King are provided in Frank A. Flower, *History of Milwaukee, Wisconsin* (Chicago: Western Historical Company, 1881), 1:623. C. King, "Rufus King: Soldier, Editor, and Statesman," *Wisconsin Magazine of History* 4 (1920–1): 371–81; and Joseph Schafer, "Origins of Wisconsin's Free School System," *Wisconsin Magazine of History* 9 (1925–26): 39.

7. *Journal of Commerce*, 8 October 1869. On Van Horn, see Frank A. Fitzpatrick, "James M. Greenwood: An Appreciation," *Educational Review* 48 (October 1914): 289; R. Richard Wohl and A. Theodore Brown, "The Useable Past: A Study of Historical Traditions in Kansas City," *Huntington Library Quarterly* 23 (May 1960): 239–40; and A. Theodore Brown and Lyle W. Dorsett, *K.C.: History of Kansas City* (Boulder: Pruett, 1978), 11–16.

8. *Kansas City Journal of Commerce*, 19 April 1867.

9. *Toledo Blade*, 28 March 1853. The same myth was perpetrated in the 1840s by the *Milwaukee Sentinel*, as evidence demonstrates in C. E. Patzer, *Public Education in Wisconsin* (Madison: Issued by the State Superintendent, 1924), 45. Also see Blake McKelvey, *The Water-Power City*, 263–66; Downes, *Lake Port*, 239; William G. Bruce, ed., *History of Milwaukee City and County* (Chicago: S. J. Clarke, 1922), Vol. 1, chap. 36; W. H. Miller, *The History of Kansas City* (Kansas City: Birdsall and Miller, 1881), 235–36; and William G. Parish, *Missouri under Radical Rule, 1865–1870* (Columbia: University of Missouri Press, 1965), 148.

10. Blake McKelvey, *The Water-Power City*, 263–66; and Blake McKelvey, "Rochester's Public Schools," *Rochester History* 31 (April 1969): 2–3.

11. The significance of these men was underscored in D. F. DeWolf, "Toledo,"

in *Historical Sketches of Public Schools in Cities, Villages, and Townships in the State of Ohio* (Columbus: Ohio State Centennial Education Committee, 1876), 4; in *A History of Education in the State of Ohio* (Columbus: General Assembly, 1876), 178; and in John M. Killits, ed., *Toledo and Lucas County, Ohio, 1623–1923* (Chicago: S. J. Clarke, 1923), 1:379. The activities of these school reformers can be traced in a massive volume by Clark Waggoner, ed., *The History of Toledo and Lucas County, Ohio* (New York: Munsell, 1888).

12. J. S. Buck, *Pioneer History of Milwaukee* (Milwaukee: Milwaukee News, 1876), 214; Still, *Milwaukee*, 114, 170, 179, 183, 248–49; Patrick Donnelly, "The Milwaukee Public Schools," in J. W. Stearns, ed., *The Columbian History of Education in Wisconsin* (Milwaukee: Press of the Evening Wisconsin Company, 1893), 439–40; Howard Louis Canard, ed., *History of Milwaukee* (Chicago: American Biographical Publishing, 1896), 1:456–57; 2:386–87; J. A. Watrous, ed., *Memoirs of Milwaukee County* (Madison, Western Historical Association, 1909), 1:183–84, 277–78; Still, *Milwaukee*, 76, 134; and Patrick Donnelly, "The Milwaukee Public Schools," in J. W. Stearns, ed., *The Columbian History of Education in Wisconsin* (Milwaukee: Press of the Evening Wisconsin Company, 1893), 439–40.

13. *First Annual Report of the City of Kansas* (Kansas City: Bulletin Steam Book and Job Printing House and Book Bindery, 1871), 4; Roy Ellis, *A Civic History of Kansas City, Missouri* (Springfield, Mo.: Press of Elkins-Swyers Company, 1930), 192; Glen Lester Hanks, "The Development of Public School Finance in the Kansas City School District" (Ph.D. diss., University of Missouri, 1953), 38; and Brown and Dorsett, *K.C.: History of Kansas City* (Boulder: Pruett, 1978), 84–85. Similarly, praise was bestowed upon those "influential citizens" who helped establish a centralized school system; see the *Toledo Blade*, 1 December 1848.

14. *Milwaukee School Report*, 1849, 10.

15. *Toledo Blade*, 24 May 1855; McEwen & Dillenback, *Kansas City in 1879* (Kansas City: Press of Kamseg, Millett, & Hudson, 1879), 51. On the ties between economic prosperity and educational growth, also see the *Kansas City Times*, 10 January 1875; *Kansas City School Report*, 1880, 7; *Kansas City School Report*, 1887, 6; and *Kansas City Times*, 21 October 1884. A Milwaukeean argued that schools "serve as an index of the growth and prosperity of the city" in *Milwaukee School Report*, 1874, 54.

16. *American Industry and Manufactures in the Nineteenth Century* (Elmsford, N.Y.: Maxwell Reprint, 1970), 16: 996–1003. On local commercial development, consult Blake McKelvey, *The Water-Power City*, chaps. 4, 8; Blake McKelvey, *Rochester: The Flower City, 1855–1890* (Cambridge: Harvard University Press, 1949), chaps. 4, 8; Paul E. Johnson, *A Shopkeeper's Millennium: Society and Revivals in Rochester, New York, 1815–1837* (New York: Hill & Wang, 1978), chap. 1; Randolph C. Downes, *Canal Days* (Toledo: Toledo Printing Company, 1949), chaps. 1, 2, 8, 11; Randolph C. Downes, *Lake Port*, chaps. 3–7; Still, *Milwaukee*, chap. 3; William G. Bruce, ed., *History of Milwaukee City and County* (Chicago: S. J. Clarke, 1922), Vol. 1, chaps. 17–21; and Dorsett and Brown, *K.C.: History of Kansas City* (Boulder: Pruett, 1978), chap. 3.

17. *Kansas City Times*, 7 September 1879.

18. *Toledo Blade*, 5 June 1855.

19. David B. Tyack, "The Spread of Public Schooling in Victorian America: In Search of an Interpretation," *History of Education* 7 (1978): 174; *Rochester School Report*, 1884, 83; *Milwaukee Sentinel*, 6 February 1871; and *Kansas City School Report*, 1884, 75–76. Slurs on the poor and on "vicious" children and parents were common in school reports, newspaper articles, and public speeches. See A. D. Lord, "Education in Ohio," *Ohio Journal of Education* 3 (September 1854): 258.

20. *Rochester School Report*, 1847, 19; and *Rochester School Report*, 1859, 32–33; *Rochester School Report*, 1862, 43; *Rochester School Report*, 1845, 18; and *Toledo School Report*, 1888, 48. Examples on the failure of school visitation fill the school reports. See *Rochester School Report*, 1852, 31–32; *Milwaukee School Report*, 1872, 21–22; *Milwaukee School Report*, 1874, 87; and J. L. F., "A Word to Parents," *School Monthly* 1 (August 1868): 98.

21. *Rochester School Report*, 1844, 16. The phrase "She [the teacher] has a grudge against my boy" was constantly pressed into service by parents, according to Toledo's superintendent, who said that parents were usually ignorant of the facts in school disputes; see the *Toledo School Report*, 1888, 48–49. Also read the *Rochester School Report*, 1867, 35; *Rochester School Report*, 1870, 38; and *Kansas City School Report*, 1877, 50.

22. *Kansas City School Report*, 1876, 18. Greenwood later argued that "everyone is sparing of time except the hopelessly ignorant. 'Punctuality' has passed into a proverb as 'the politeness of the great.'" Consult the *Kansas City Report*, 1889, 77. Details of Greenwood's life are in Wilfred R. Holister and Harry Norman, *Five Famous Missourians* (Kansas City: Hudson-Kimberly, 1900), 265–33; Carrie Westlock Whitney, *Kansas City, Missouri, Its History and People, 1808–1909* (Chicago: S. J. Clarke, 1908), 2:238–43; "Dr. J. M. Greenwood," *Missouri School Journal* 31 (September 1914): 401–6; and James M. Greenwood, "How I Became a 'School-Keeper,'" *Journal of Education* 25 (10 March 1887): 148. Details of Greenwood's death are in the *Kansas City Star*, 1 August 1914; and the *Kansas City Post*, 1 August 1914.

23. *Toledo School Report*, 1882, 25.

24. *Milwaukee School Report*, 1861, 32. Conflict over textbooks in Rochester is examined in D. S. Truesdale, "The Three Rs in Rochester, 1850–1900," in McKelvey, *The History of Education in Rochester*, 193.

25. *Rochester School Report*, 1845, 25; and *Toledo Blade*, 5 September 1849.

26. *Kansas City School Report*, 1881, 53. Also see James M. Greenwood, *Principles of Education Practically Applied* (New York: D. Appleton, 1887); and *Kansas City Journal of Commerce*, 24 December 1869.

27. *Rochester School Report*, 1843, 19; *Rochester School Report*, 1845, 19; *Rochester School Report*, 1859, 34; and *Ohio Journal of Education* 2 (March 1853): 198. Smyth's background is sketched in J. J. Burns, *Educational History of Ohio* (Columbus: Historical Publishing Company, 1905), 441–42; and in Killits, *Toledo and Lucas County*, 1:380. Toledo's school board early resolved: "Good morals being of the first importance and essential to the Scholars in their progress in useful knowledge, the pupils are strictly enjoined to avoid idleness and profanity, falsehood and deceit, and to conduct themselves in a sober, orderly, and decent manner both

in and out of School, and to be punctual and constant in daily attendance." See the *Toledo Board of Education Minutes*, 20 February 1850.

28. Randolph C. Downes, *Lake Port*, 287–88; J. Burns, *The Growth and Development of the Catholic School System of the United States* (New York: Arno Press, 1969), 40.

29. Frederick J. Zwierlein, *The Life and Letters of Bishop McQuaid* (Rochester: Art Print Shop, 1925), 2: 133. Also see Blake McKelvey, *The Flower City*, 151–52; J. B. L., "Rochester," *New England Journal of Education* 7 (4 April 1878): 219; Rev. Bishop McQuaid, "The Other Side of the Story," *Journal of Education* 17 (January 18, 1883): 35–36; A. D. Mayo, "Reply to Bishop McQuaid," *Journal of Education* 17 (19 March 1883): 195–96; and E. D. Mead, "Bishop McQuaid's Impeachment of the Public Schools," *Journal of Education* 17 (15 February 1883): 99–101.

30. S. A. Ellis, "Bishop McQuaid and Our Public Schools," *Journal of Education* 17 (17 May 1883): 307; and *Rochester School Report*, 1883, 83–85, 97–98.

31. Ninth Census, *The Statistics of the Population of the United States* (Washington D.C.: Government Printing Office, 1872), Vol. 1, table 8; and Ellis, "Bishop McQuaid," 82. In 1881 the Kansas City German Educational Society petitioned for the introduction of German, but it was refused by the school board, presumably for financial reasons.

32. *Milwaukee School Report*, 1899, 94; and Donnelly, "Milwaukee Public Schools," 60. On the Americanizing features of the teaching of German, see R. C. Spencer, "German in the Public Schools," *Wisconsin Journal of Education* 11 (May 1881): 210–11. Also consult Randolph C. Downes, *History of Lake Shore Ohio* (New York: Lewis Historical Publishing, 1952), 2:448. Selwyn Troen describes similar motivations and social policies in the St. Louis school system in *The Public and the Schools: Shaping the St. Louis System* (Columbia: University of Missouri Press, 1975), chap. 3. Also see *Ein Souvenir an die Milwaukee Industrie-Ausstellung, der Wisconsiner Staats-Ausstellung und des Nationalen Sangerfestes* (Milwaukee: Casper & Zahn, Herasgeberg, 1886), 61.

33. *American Industry and Manufactures in the Nineteenth Century*, 16: 998–99; and *Occupations at the Twelfth Census* (Washington, D.C.: Government Printing Office, 1904), 453–55.

34. Gerd Korman, *Industrialization, Immigrants, and Americanizers: The View from Milwaukee, 1866–1921* (Madison: State Historical Society of Wisconsin, 1967), chap. 2; Still, *Milwaukee*, 269–73; W. J. Anderson, ed., *Milwaukee's Great Industries* (Milwaukee: Association for the Advancement of Milwaukee, 1892); *American Industry and Manufactures in the Nineteenth Century*, 16:998–99, 1000–1001.

35. *Occupations at the Twelfth Census*, 466. Economic developments are analyzed in *The Industries of Rochester* (Rochester: Eltstner, 1912); Blake McKelvey, *Rochester: The Quest for Quality, 1890–1925* (Cambridge: Harvard University Press, 1956), 46–53; Blake McKelvey, "A History of Rochester Shoe Industry," *Rochester History* 15 (April 1953), 1–28; and W. F. Peck, *History of Rochester and Monroe County, New York* (New York: Pioneer, 1908), 130–31. Peck estimated that there were "between sixty and seventy factories" for boots and shoes in 1908.

36. Quoted in David Montgomery, *Workers' Control in America: Studies in the*

History of Work, Technology, and Labor Struggles (Cambridge: Cambridge University Press, 1979), 69. Also see Harry Braverman, *Labor and Monopoly Control: The Degradation of Work in the Twentieth Century* (New York: Monthly Review Press, 1974); Melvin Dubofsky, *Industrialism and the American Worker, 1865–1920* (New York: Thomas Y. Crowell, 1975); and James R. Green, *The World of the Worker: Labor in Twentieth Century America* (New York: Hill and Wang, 1980). On Debs, see Nick Salvatore, *Eugene V. Debs: Citizen and Socialist* (Urbana: University of Illinois Press, 1982).

37. *The Industries of Rochester*, 65; Blake McKelvey, "Organized Labor in Rochester before 1914," *Rochester History* 25 (January 1963): 16–20; Edward W. Stevens, "The Political Education of Children in the Rochester Public Schools, 1899–1917: An Historical Perspective on Social Control in Public Education" (Ph.D. diss., University of Rochester, 1971), 95; and J. L. Brewer, "Centennial History of Organized Labor in Rochester," in E. R. Foreman, ed., *Centennial History of Rochester, New York* (Rochester: John P. Smith, 1934), 4:425–27, which highlights the city's open-shop character.

38. *American Industry and Manufactures in the Nineteenth Century*, 16: 1002–3; *Occupations at the Twelfth Census*, 473–5; *Bramble's Views: Toledo, Ohio, Diamond Anniversary, 1837–1912* (Toledo: Bramble, 1912); Randolph C. Downes, *Industrial Beginnings* (Toledo: Historical Society of Northwestern Ohio, 1954), chaps. 5–9; and Randolph C. Downes, *History of Lake Shore, Ohio*, 1:228–99.

39. John M. Hrivnyak, "Birmingham: Toledo's Hungarian Community" (master's thesis, University of Toledo, 1975).

40. *Occupations at the Twelfth Census*, 448–50. On the significance of commerce and trade, see Brown and Dorsett, *K.C.*, chap. 2; also examine *The Commerce of Kansas City in 1886* (Kansas City: S. Ferd. Howe, 1886); *Kansas City: Its Resources and Development* (Kansas City: Kansas City Times, 1902); and *American Industry and Manufactures in the Nineteenth Century*, 16:996–97, 1000–1001.

41. *Occupations at the Twelfth Census*, 448; Brown and Dorsett, *K.C.*, 50–53; and Whitney, *Kansas City*, 1: 481–93.

42. All these statistics are readily available in the 1880, 1890, and 1900 *Census* materials.

43. Kathleen Neils Conzen, *Immigrant Milwaukee, 1836–1860* (Cambridge: Harvard University Press, 1976); Korman, *Industrialization, Immigrants, and Americanizers*, chap. 2; William G. Bruce, *I Was Born in America* (Milwaukee: Bruce, 1937); William G. Bruce, *History of Milwaukee City and County*, 1:174–82; 768–69; Still, *Milwaukee*, 259–67; T. Mueller, "Milwaukee's German Heritage," *Historical Messenger* 22 (September 1966): 112–19; and *Report on the Social Statistics of Cities in the United States at the Eleventh Census: 1890* (Washington, D.C.: Government Printing Office, 1895), 112.

44. G. La Piana, *The Italians in Milwaukee, Wisconsin* (Milwaukee: Associated Charities, 1915); Still, *Milwaukee*, 276–77; and A. C. Meloni, "Italy Invades the Bloody Third-Milwaukee Italians, 1900–1910," *Historical Messenger* 25 (March 1969): 35–46; Rev. B. E. Goral, "The Poles in Milwaukee," in Watrous, *Memoirs*, 1:612–13; *Report on Population of the United States at the Eleventh Census: 1890* (Washington, D.C.: Government Printing Office, 1895), 672.

45. Blake McKelvey, *The Quest for Quality*, 146; and *Report on Population of the United States at the Eleventh Census*, 671–72. The Irish and Germans of Rochester are examined in two essays by Blake McKelvey, "The Irish of Rochester: An Historical Perspective," *Rochester History* 19 (October 1957): 1–16; and "The Germans of Rochester: Their Traditions and Contributions," *Rochester History* 20 (January 1958): 1–28.

46. Hrivnyak, "Birmingham"; Stephen J. Bartha, "A History of Immigrant Groups in Toledo" (master's thesis, Ohio State University, 1945); and Marvin Jay Glockner, "Assimilation of the Immigrant in the United States As Characterized by the Poles in Toledo" (master's thesis, University of Toledo, 1966), 56.

47. *Report on Population of the United States at the Eleventh Census*, 670–73.

48. *Rochester Democrat and Chronicle*, 15 January 1898; *Kansas City Star*, 6 May 1894 and 20 February 1895. The Italians of Utica, Rochester, and Kansas City are studied in John W. Briggs, *An Italian Passage* (New Haven: Yale University Press, 1978).

49. *Kansas City Journal of Commerce*, 19 June 1875.

50. *Kansas City Mail*, 26 August 1893. *Toledo Evening Bee*, 27 March 1894, similarly editorialized: "The panic had its effect upon nearly all classes of society. It produced a fright that permeated everywhere, and from it sprung up a crop of calamity howlers that only increased its intensity."

51. The *Star*'s position is seen in the editorials and news reports for 20 May 1893, 6 June 1893, 10 June 1893, 13 June 1893, 20 June 1893, 1 July 1893, and 15 July 1893. Details on local bank failures are from the *Kansas City Mail*, 14 July 1893 and 17 July 1893.

52. *Toledo Evening Bee*, 27 September 1893. The question was how long the workers could continue to support the social system, claimed the worried editor. On the 1890s and the effects of the depression, consult A. C. Stevens, "Phenomenal Aspects of the Financial Crisis," *Forum* 16 (September 1893): 23; E. Atkinson, "The Benefits of Hard Times," *Forum* 20 (Summer 1895): 79–90; W. E. Russell, "Political Causes of the Business Depression," *North American Review* 157 (December 1893); Samuel Rezneck, "Unemployment, Unrest, and Relief in the United States during the Depression of 1893–1897," *Journal of Political Economy* 61 (August 1953); D. W. Steeples, "The Panic of 1893: Contemporary Reflections and Reactions," *Mid-America* 48 (July 1965): 155–75; and David P. Thelen, *The New Citizenship: Origins of Progressivism in Wisconsin* (Columbia: University of Missouri Press, 1973).

53. *Rochester Democrat and Chronicle*, 3 November 1893, 11 December 1893, and 19 February 1894; Blake McKelvey, *The Quest for Quality*, chap. 3; and P. E. Fisler, "The Depression of 1893 in Rochester," *Rochester History* 15 (June 1952): 1–24.

54. *Toledo Evening Bee*, 17 November 1893; Thelen, *The New Citizenship*, 58–59; and Emil Seidel, *Sketches from My Life*, unpublished autobiography, 2:14 (Emil Seidel Papers, State Historical Society of Wisconsin).

55. *Kansas City Mail*, 11 August 1893; and *Kansas City Star*, 18 August 1893.

56. *Kansas City Star*, 5 July 1894. Brown and Dorsett, in *K.C.*, argue that unemployment was already high before the onset of the depression. Also see the *Kansas City Labor*, 7 December 1895.

57. *Rochester Democrat and Chronicle,* 14 August 1897; and *Kansas City Mail,* 9 April 1895.

Chapter 2

1. Lizzie Black Kander, "The Evolution of the Husband," a paper presented to the Wednesday Afternoon Club, November 28, 1902 (Lizzie Black Kander Papers, State Historical Society of Wisconsin, Madison, Wisconsin).

2. Sheila Rothman, *Woman's Proper Place: A History of Changing Ideals and Practices, 1870 to the Present* (New York: Basic Books, 1978), 4. More generally, Morton Keller writes in *Affairs of State: Public Life in Late Nineteenth Century America,* (Cambridge: Harvard University Press, Belknap Press, 1977), 517: "Voluntary associations, always significant American institutions, took on increasing importance in the late nineteenth century." The women's club movement is discussed in Gerda Lerner, *The Woman in American History* (Menlo Park, Calif.: Addison-Wesley, 1971); Lois W. Banner, *Women in Modern America: A Brief History* (New York: Harcourt Brace Jovanovich, 1974); and Mary P. Ryan, *Womanhood in America: From Colonial Times to the Present* (New York: New Viewpoints, 1975).

3. Samuel T. Dutton and David Snedden, *The Administration of Public Education in the United States* (New York: Macmillan, 1908), 592.

4. My initial investigation on the role of women in Progressive school reform was "Between Home and School: Organized Parents, Clubwomen, and Urban Education in the Progressive Era," *School Review* 87 (November 1978): 3–28. For the standard study of Progressive intellectuals, see Lawrence A. Cremin, *The Transformation of the School* (New York: Random House, 1961). The literature on the feminization of teaching is immense, but at least see the following: Michael B. Katz, *The Irony of Early School Reform* (Boston: Beacon Press, 1968), 56–57, 193; David B. Tyack, *The One Best System* (Cambridge: Harvard University Press, 1974), 59–64; and R. S. Sugg, *Mother-Teacher: The Feminization of American Education* (Charlottesville: University Press of Virginia, 1978). On the importance of women in urban Progressivism, see David P. Thelen, *The New Citizenship: Origins of Progressivism in Wisconsin, 1885–1900* (Columbia: University of Missouri Press, 1972), chap. 5; Mary R. Beard, *Women's Work in Municipalities* (New York: D. Appleton, 1915); Jill Conway, "Women Reformers and American Culture, 1870–1930," *Journal of Social History* 5 (Winter 1971–72): 164–82; and Estelle Freedman, "Separatism as Strategy: Female Institution Building and American Feminism, 1870–1930," *Feminist Studies* 5 (Fall 1979): 512–29.

5. The best studies on the new middle class in the Progressive era are by Robert Wiebe, *The Search for Order, 1877–1920* (New York: Hill & Wang, 1967); and by Tyack, *One Best System.*

6. *Milwaukee School Report,* 1878, 78. Cf. Mary Jo Buhle, *Women and American Socialism, 1870–1920* (Urbana: University of Illinois Press, 1981), 56.

7. *Milwaukee Sentinel,* 13 December 1891; *Toledo Blade,* 14 November 1890; and *Kansas City Star,* 19 February 1891.

8. *Toledo Blade,* 13 January 1894. Also see the *Toledo Evening Bee* for 9 January

1898, where it was argued that "never in the history of Toledo have women taken such interest in civic affairs as at present." In addition, *Rochester Democrat and Chronicle* 6 February 1898 and 2 February 1899.

9. *Kansas City Mail*, 7 December 1892.

10. *Rochester Democrat and Chronicle*, 11 April 1893 and 8 December 1893; and *Toledo Blade*, 13 February 1909. Also examine Mrs. Harriet Dow, "The Influence of Women in the Life of Rochester," in E. R. Foreman, ed., *Centennial History of Rochester, New York* (Rochester: Printed by John P. Smith, 1933), 2:189–207; J. W. Huntington, *Women's Educational and Industrial Union* (Rochester: Written for the Fiftieth Anniversary Celebration, 1943), 1–11; "Minutes of the Women's Educational and Industrial Union," Volume for 1893–96, 83–89 (Women's Educational and Industrial Union [WEIU] Papers, Rochester Public Library, Rochester, New York); and Blake McKelvey, *Rochester: The Quest for Quality, 1890–1920* (Cambridge: Harvard University Press, 1956), 11–12.

11. Helen, *The New Citizenship*, 69, 93–94; J. A. Watrous, ed., *Memoirs of Milwaukee County* (Madison: Western Historical Association, 1909), 1:403–4; *Proceedings of the First Annual Meeting of the Wisconsin State Federation of Women's Clubs* (Berlin, Wis.: Printed by George C. Hicks, 1897), 28–35; *Kansas City Star*, 23 May 1894 and 26 May 1894; *Child-Welfare Magazine* 13 (August 1919), 330; Carrie Westlake Whitney, *Kansas City, Missouri, Its History and People, 1808–1908* (Chicago: S. J. Clarke, 1908), 1:627–30; and *Kansas City and Its Schools* (Kansas City: Prepared for the Department of Superintendence of the National Education Association, 1917), 89–90.

12. See, for example, *Constitution, By-Laws, and Standing Rules of the Woman's School Alliance of Wisconsin* (Milwaukee, 1897), 8–10, for a primary source. The widespread activities of the women's clubs are well documented in the fine study by Karen J. Blair, "The Clubwoman as Feminist: The Woman's Culture Club Movement in the United States, 1868–1914" (Ph.D. diss., State University of New York-Buffalo, 1976). See the revised version, published as *The Clubwoman as Feminist: True Womanhood Redefined, 1869–1914* (New York: Holmes & Maier, 1980). A useful study of Ohio clubwomen is by Annie Laws, ed., *History of the Ohio Federation of Women's Clubs* (Cincinnati: Ebbert & Richardson, 1924).

13. Whitney, *Kansas City*, 1:629; and Reese, "Between Home and School," 8–9.

14. Lizzie Black Kander, "Graduating Essay," 1878 (Kander Papers). A valuable study of Kander's life is by Ann Shirley Waligorski, "Social Action and Women: The Experience of Lizzie Black Kander" (master's thesis, University of Wisconsin-Madison, 1970).

15. Kander pointed out that the reputations of assimilated Jews were at stake as thousands of impoverished immigrants came to America. She was not surprised that at first many recent arrivals were suspicious of the motives of settlement workers. "They cannot conceive how anyone can devote time and money to a cause, without some expectation of gain," Kander wrote in 1900, and she added that personal gain was obviously one product of philanthropic effort. See "The President's Annual Report," Milwaukee Jewish Mission, 1900 (Kander Papers).

Part of Kander's early life is set to song in "My Sewing Society," and in an undated address before the Milwaukee Girls' Trade School, 1–6 (Kander Papers).

16. "The President's Annual Report," Milwaukee Jewish Mission, 1900 (Kander Papers).

17. See especially Kander's essay "Is the Saloon an Evil, and If So What Is the Remedy?" n.d.; and "Diary of a Trip Down South," 1895 (Kander Papers).

18. McKelvey, *Quest for Quality*, 11–12; and W. F. Peck, *History of Rochester and Monroe County, New York* (New York: Pioneer, 1908), 232–33.

19. Blake McKelvey, *Rochester: The Flower City, 1855–1890* (Cambridge: Harvard University Press, 1949), 158. The literature on Susan B. Anthony is extensive. Several older volumes are still valuable: I. H. Harper, *The Life and Work of Susan B. Anthony* (Indianapolis: Hollenbeck Press, 1908); Rhea Childe Door, *Susan B. Anthony* (New York: Frederick A. Stokes, 1928); *Toledo Blade*, 26 April 1894 and 18 May 1894. A short biography of Segur is provided in the *Toledo Evening Bee*, 25 February 1895.

20. The literature is cited in Reese, "Between Home and School," 5.

21. The *Herald*, a conservative organ of the Republican machine, had red-baited Montgomery in January 1897. Philip Jackson, a leading Socialist, promptly corrected the editor and defended Montgomery in a letter to the editor. Both sources are in WEIU's "Scrapbook, 1896–1901," 137–38 (WEIU Papers). Montgomery's activities can be traced in the *Rochester Democrat and Chronicle*, 8 December 1893, 9 April 1896, 4 February 1897; and through her addresses in the annual reports of the WEIU in the organization's manuscript collection.

22. *Yearbook of the Woman's Educational and Industrial Union, 1896–97* (Rochester, 1897), 13–14 (WEIU Papers); and *Rochester Democrat and Chronicle*, 9 April 1896 and 18 January 1895. Her lecture in the *Democrat and Chronicle* was appropriately titled "The New Woman."

23. *Toledo Evening Bee*, 11 November 1898. The address was before the City Federation of Women's Clubs on the subject of school extension.

24. *Kansas City Mail*, 7 December 1892.

25. *Toledo Blade*, 4 February 1897. The *Blade* later asserted (27 January 1899) the "the club idea is making great headway among women. What it is doing in Toledo is but an index of the progress along this line all over Ohio—and in fact all over the West."

26. *Tenth Biennial Convention of the General Federation of Women's Clubs* (Newark, N.J.: General Federation of Women's Clubs, 1910), 65, notes, "Woman is the mother of the race: she is the conserver and preserver of the world. Organized womanhood is a civic force of unlimited power." Richard Jenson, in a study of the backgrounds of several thousand female leaders of the Progressive era, has discovered that no variable explains civic participation in certain types of reform activities more strongly than "Motherhood." Mothers in clubs and other organizations demonstrated a greater interest in humanitarian reforms than childless wives in these clubs. See "Family, Career, and Reform: Women Leaders of the Progressive Era," in Milton Gordon, ed., *The American Family in Social-Historical Perspective* (New York: St. Martin's Press, 1973), 276–78. The grassroots nature of the club movement is described in William L. O'Neill, *Everyone Was Brave: A History of*

Feminism in America (New York: Quadrangle Books, 1969), 85. Also see *Toledo Blade*, 4 February 1897; and *The Works and Words of the National Congress of Mothers* (New York: D. Appleton, 1897). On the rise of parent-teacher associations, see Steven L. Schlossman, "Before Home Start: Notes toward a History of Parent Education in America: 1897–1929," *Harvard Educational Review* 46 (1976): 436–67; Julian Butterwork, *The Parent-Teacher Association and Its Work* (New York: Macmillan, 1928); and the various sources listed in Reese, "Between Home and School," 23–28.

27. *The West Side Mothers' Club, Milwaukee, Wisconsin, 1912–13* (Milwaukee, 1913), 1 (West Side Mothers' Club Papers, Milwaukee County Historical Society, Milwaukee, Wisconsin); and *Proceedings of the Fourth Annual Convention of the Wisconsin State Federation of Women's Clubs*, 1900, 7. R. C. Door, in a widely read account of organized women and social reform in the Progressive era, invoked numerous familial and domestic metaphors to explain women's civic activism. See *What Eight Million Women Want* (Boston: Small, Maynard, 1910), 327.

28. *Rochester Democrat and Chronicle*, 14 February 1896 and 8 March 1895. This club was the leading suffrage organization in the city.

29. *Toledo Blade*, 24 October 1894.

30. *Toledo Blade,* 30 November 1895. Miss Emily Bouton continued: "Dangers there always are in the process of taking a step forward involving so much that is vital to the home, and thus to the child's welfare. And . . . there was never a time when woman's responsibility was greater than it is today. . . . The increased responsibility does not rest alone upon the few who have gained the higher education, or upon the many who, from choice or necessity stand outside of that home life in which woman is the center, but upon each and all alike."

31. *Milwaukee Sentinel*, 1 October 1898; Dorr, *What Eight Million Women Want*, 57; and Beard, *Women's Work*, chap. 1, where the author insightfully noted that women's interest in schooling came about "partly because of their intimate family relation through little children and partly because of the fact that women teachers formed an easy bond of cooperation. Today there exists an incredible number of organizations whose main purpose is cooperation with the schools in one way or another" (38–39).

32. *Toledo Blade*, 24 October 1894.

33. *Constitution, By-Laws, and Standing Rules of the Woman's School Alliance of Wisconsin*, 1897, 2. When the Alliance formed, "the ladies felt that there were many things in school life which are apparent to *mothers* that are unnoticed by *fathers*," as quoted by Mrs. Harriet Holton Robertson, "Women's School Alliance of Wisconsin," in W. J. Anderson and J. Bleyer, eds., *Milwaukee's Great Industries* (Milwaukee: Association for the Advancement of Milwaukee, 1892), 36. Also see the *Toledo Blade*, 27 February 1892 and 24 October 1894.

34. Though superintendent's reports have been extensively used by historians who have emphasized the importance of the new middle class, school proceedings, newspapers, and the original records of local women's groups demonstrate the importance of voluntary associations in school reform in the entire Progressive era.

35. While teachers have been depicted in a very critical fashion in contempo-

rary literature on schooling, particularly on urban education, a more sympathetic appraisal is available in Tyack, *One Best System*, 97–104. A useful examination of the powerlessness of the teacher in one city is by Mark Van Pelt, "The Teacher and the Urban Community: Milwaukee, 1860–1900" (master's thesis, University of Wisconsin-Madison, 1978).

36. *Rochester Democrat and Chronicle*, 23 September 1898; and *Yearbook of the Woman's Educational and Industrial Union, 1896–97* (Rochester, 1897), 3 (WEIU Papers).

37. *Constitution, By-Laws, and Standing Rules of the Woman's School Alliance*, 1897, 2; and *Proceedings of the First Annual Meeting of the Wisconsin State Federation of Women's Clubs*, 28–29.

38. The names were drawn from the Alliance document cited above, 11–15.

39. Flanders was an energetic woman. She was involved in settlement work with Lizzie Kander and had considerable success with mothers' meetings and parent-teacher associations. On the popularity of the mother's meetings, see the *Milwaukee Sentinel*, 22 January 1897; on the settlement work, see Lizzie Black Kander, "President's Report," The Settlement, 1905 (Kander Papers).

40. Jones Island is described in Still's *Milwaukee*, 363; and by William G. Bruce, *A Short History of Milwaukee* (Milwaukee: Bruce, 1936), 139.

41. *Rochester Democrat and Chronicle*, 22 February 1896.

42. In 1896, Helen Montgomery argued that parents and others had often criticized the teachers, but never visited the schools enough. See Huntington, *Women's Educational and Industrial Union*, 3.

43. *Rochester Democrat and Chronicle*, 4 April 1890. This organization had been formed a year earlier and had a fitful existence in the early 1890s. Many professors from the University of Rochester were active in the group, which supported women for the school board and the application of Good Government reforms to the schools, namely, school board centralization and a greater attention to the professional development of the teaching staff. Also see the *Democrat and Chronicle* for 18 March 1890, 3 April 1891, and 8 February 1894.

44. *Toledo Blade*, 1 February 1895.

45. Reese, "Between Home and School," 3–28; Thelen, *The New Citizenship*, chap. 5; Beard, *Women's Work*, chap. 1; and Door, *What Eight Million Women Want*, chap. 2.

46. The best sources for the evolution of Progressive ideas on the local level are the grassroots petitions and original writings of the women and parents themselves. Helen Montgomery, for example, delivered an address in 1896 on the "new education," a term which was later used interchangeably with "progressive education," just as the "new woman" was often referred to as a "progressive woman." See Montgomery's speech in the *Rochester Democrat and Chronicle*, 30 January 1896. In Toledo, as in the other cities in this study, clubwomen in the 1890s attacked corporal punishment, cramming, overtesting, and other aspects of what they called the "old system of education." Many were familiar with Froebel's writings, which emphasized motherhood themes, since they were teachers them- selves.

47. *Rochester Democrat and Chronicle*, 19 March 1898. This phenomenon is noted by Steven L. Schlossman, in *Love and the American Delinquent: The Theory and Practice of "Progressive" Juvenile Justice, 1825–1920* (Chicago: University of Chicago Press, 1977), 76.

48. Numerous letters to the editor appeared in the *Kansas City Journal of Commerce* from the last half of December 1892 through the middle of January, 1893.

49. *Kansas City Journal of Commerce*, 21 December 1892 and 25 December 1892. These sorts of criticisms were made famous by Joseph Mayer Rice in his famous articles in the *Forum* in 1892 and 1893, and gathered in *The Public School System of the United States* (New York: Arno Press, c. 1969).

50. James M. Greenwood to J. Heermans, 10 August 1904. (James M. Greenwood Papers, Kansas City Public Library, Kansas City, Missouri). Here Greenwood wrote: "John Dewey, like most of those Chicago folks, is striving after something he hardly knows what. Should he decide to turn his attention to Greek mythology for the purpose of ascertaining what the hierarchy of Gods thought of Jupiter's thoughts, he possibly might dig up something not heretofore known." Since Greenwood was at one time the president of the National Education Association (NEA) and a prolific contributor of essays to educational journals on the state and national level, he was well known across the country. There are many short studies of his long career, but the most accessible analysis for most readers is Wilfred Rand Hollister and Harry Norman, *Five Famous Missourians* (Kansas City: Hudson-Kimberly, 1908), 265–333; and the eulogy titled "Dr. J. M. Greenwood," *Missouri School Journal* 31 (September 1914): 401–6. Also see the *Kansas City Journal of Commerce*, 25 December 1892.

51. *Kansas City Journal of Commerce*, 26 December 1892. The principal of the Karnes School also wrote a series of rebuttals against the "unfair critics" of the school system.

52. *Kansas City Journal of Commerce*, 28 December 1892; and 31 December 1892, where the writer asserted, "As a class, teachers are kindly conscientious—a true teacher always so. But pressure from above changes maternal promptings toward helpless into self-preservative methods against the martinet marker into whose hands is committed her financial fate, as shown to the school board on an ascending scale from 0 to 10 plus." Also see the *Kansas City Journal*, 3 January 1893. The teacher claimed that pedagogues stood in constant fear for their positions. "Military order is quite as objectionable to many teachers as to parents. But if it is not maintained, the assistant superintendent will have a *billet doux* on your desk to the effect that 'dignity of position' is essential to effective work. If a teacher, more daring than her colleagues, ever asserts her rights or individuality, she is speedily transferred to a school on the outskirts or beyond the city limits, where she can cool down and repent at leisure."

53. Dorothy Galloway, "James Mickleborough Greenwood: An Evaluation of His Services as an Educator and His Contributions to Educational Thought" (master's thesis, Washington University, 1931), 16–17. Galloway erred in dating this event but otherwise accurately assessed the social effects of this plan on

school board membership. In addition, read *Kansas City Mail*, 7 December 1892, 19 December 1892, 4 January 1893, 10 January 1893, 20 January 1893, 9 October 1893, and 21 February 1894. In the initial editorial cited, the *Mail* stated: "Kansas City people indulge in a pleasant little fiction that their own public schools are the best in the country, and embrace in their curriculum all the broad and progressive ideas which can be picked up anywhere. . . . Some of the mothers of the city, however, who are not upon the school board, are rapidly waking up."

54. *Kansas City Star*, 30 December 1892.

55. This is based on a close reading of Milwaukee's newspapers and the petitions of the Alliance presented to the school board. See especially the following dates in the *Proceedings of the Milwaukee School Board*: 2 June 1891, 6 October 1891, 1 December 1891, 3 July 1893, 5 February 1895, 3 March 1896, 7 April 1896, and 11 April 1899.

56. *Milwaukee Sentinel*, 8 April 1891.

57. *Proceedings of the Milwaukee School Board*, 11 April 1899.

58. The president's quote is from the *Proceedings of the Milwaukee School Board*, 5 May 1896; the committee's rejoinder follows on 7 May 1896. A typical list of Alliance demands is found in the *Proceedings of the Milwaukee School Board*, 5 February 1895.

59. On the appointment of the woman, see the *Milwaukee Daily News*, 4 March 1896; *Milwaukee Sentinel*, 4 March 1896; Still, *Milwaukee*, 416; and Watrous, *Memoirs*, 1:405, who argued that the female school board member's appointment to the visiting committee "was regarded in the nature of a joke, as the visiting committee was more theoretical than practical. But Mrs. Merrill [the alliance representative] infused new life into it and made it of some utility. Cellars and garrets of school buildings were visited by her direction, sanitary conditions were improved, and reforms in ventilation, heating, etc., were instituted."

60. *Milwaukee Sentinel*, 14 March 1895. In Toledo, a German on the school board simply said, "*We don't vant no vomen aroundt*," according to the *Toledo Blade*, 2 March 1892.

61. *Milwaukee Sentinel*, 14 March 1895 and 3 May 1895, which provides some commentary on the stand of the German newspaper. Of the thirteen members of the council who voted against the appointment of a woman, nine were German.

62. The controversy between the women and the school board is easily traced in the *Toledo Blade* on 16 February 1892, 1 March 1892, and 2 March 1892. On the anti-Catholic feelings of the American Protective Association regarding Law's candidacy, see *Toledo Blade*, 6 March 1895.

63. *Toledo Blade*, 18 May 1894.

64. On ballot irregularities and political intimidation tactics, see the *Toledo Evening Bee*, 16 March 1895; and the *Toledo Blade*, 20 March 1895.

65. *Rochester Democrat and Chronicle*, 17 August 1897.

66. *Rochester School Report*, 1890, 54. He continued his attacks on "faddism" in the *Rochester School Report*, 1897, 5, where he favored "fundamentals" over "showy experiments." Also see the *Rochester Democrat and Chronicle*, 11 November 1894.

67. *Yearbook of the Woman's Educational and Industrial Union, 1896–97,* 13; and WEIU, "Scrapbook, 1893–1896," 152–53. (WEIU Papers).

68. *Rochester School Report,* 1897, 93–95.

69. *Rochester School Report,* 1897, 94.

70. Quoted in Schlossman, *Love,* 76.

71. Richard T. Ely, *The Coming City* (New York: Thomas Y. Crowell, 1902), 63.

Chapter 3

1. The role of the "new middle class" has been brilliantly surveyed in Robert H. Wiebe, *The Search for Order, 1877–1920* (New York: Hill & Wang, 1967); and in David B. Tyack, *The One Best System: A History of American Urban Education* (Cambridge: Harvard University Press, 1974).

2. *Toledo Blade,* 15 November 1895.

3. I. Kugler, "The Trade Union Career of Susan B. Anthony," *Labor History* 2 (Winter 1961): 90–100; Bayrd Still, *Milwaukee: The History of a City* (Madison: State Historical Society of Wisconsin, 1948), 284; and *Toledo Blade,* 16 February 1892.

4. This point was made earlier in William J. Reese, "'Partisans of the Proletariat': The Socialist Working Class and the Milwaukee Schools, 1890–1920," *History of Education Quarterly* 21 (Spring 1981): 3–50.

5. *American Industry and Manufactures in the Nineteenth Century* (Elmsford, N.Y.: Maxwell Reprint, c. 1970), 996–1003; and Alan Dawley, *Class and Community: The Industrial Revolution in Lynn* (Cambridge: Harvard University Press, 1976), 143.

6. *Rochester Democrat and Chronicle,* 18 November 1896.

7. *Rochester Democrat and Chronicle,* 2 September 1890 and 22 April 1894.

8. *Toledo Evening Bee,* 8 October 1899; *Kansas City Star,* 4 September 1893 and 5 September 1893. Under new ownership, the *Kansas City Mail* blamed workers for the depression and the radical tendencies of the times.

9. On labor organizations in these cities, see Blake McKelvey, "Organized Labor in Rochester before 1914," *Rochester History* 25 (January 1963): 1–24; Edward W. Stevens, Jr., "The Political Education of Children in the Rochester Public Schools, 1899–1917: An Historical Perspective on Social Control in Public Education" (Ed.D diss., University of Rochester, 1971), chap. 4; G. Maude Brown, "A History of Organized Labor in Toledo" (master's thesis, University of Toledo, 1924); Thomas W. Gavett, *Development of the Labor Movement in Milwaukee* (Madison: University of Wisconsin Press, 1965); and A. Theodore Brown and Lyle W. Dorsett, *K.C.: A History of Kansas City, Missouri* (Boulder: Pruett, 1978), 91–93.

10. Blake McKelvey, *Rochester: The Flower City, 1855–1890* (Cambridge: Harvard University Press, 1949), 75–77; and McKelvey, "Organized Labor," 6–7; *Toledo Blade,* 15 May 1863; and *Toledo Commercial,* 27 July 1870. Even Toledo's historian, Randolph C. Downes, in *History of Lake Shore Ohio* (New York: Lewis Historical

Publishing, 1952), 1:578, argued that in the depression of the 1870s organized and unorganized labor "struck blindly" against lower pay. Unlike McKelvey's volumes on Rochester, which are superior examples of the craft of local history, Downes's volumes are unsympathetic to the history of working-class struggle. Also see Brown, "A History," chap. 4; and R. Boryczka and Lorin Lee Carey, *No Strength Without Union: An Illustrated History of Ohio Workers, 1803–1980* (Columbus: Ohio Historical Society, 1982), 79–81.

11. *Kansas City Mail*, 24 July 1893. Religious metaphors, as will be shown throughout this essay, were common in working-class literature of protest.

12. *Rochester Democrat and Chronicle*, 8 February 1892 and 18 November 1896.

13. *Constitution, By-Laws, and Rules of Order of the Central Trades and Labor Council of Rochester and Vicinity* (Rochester: Labor Journal, 1904): 3; Randolph C. Downes, *Industrial Beginnings* (Toledo: Toledo Printing Company, 1954), 125–26; *Toledo Blade*, 10 March 1893; and *The People's Call*, 8 September 1894.

14. Attacks against Debs were long and severe. See the *Rochester Democrat and Chronicle*, 10 January 1895, which applauded Debs's imprisonment; the *Evening Bee*, 6, 12, and 16 July 1894, which did likewise; and the *Kansas City Star*, which ran a string of editorials against Debs during and after the Pullman Strike. Also see the *Kansas City Mail*, 15 November 1892; and the *Rochester Democrat and Chronicle*, 29 September 1896, the latter for a description of a labor rally of fifteen hundred workers.

15. *Rochester Labor*, 6 June 1896; *Kansas City Labor*, 7 December 1895; *Midland Mechanic*, 28 April 1898 and 14 July 1898.

16. *Rochester Democrat and Chronicle*, 2 January 1899 and 23 September 1897. Leopold engaged in a long harangue against plutocratic control of the press, the church, and the economy.

17. *The People's Call*, 25 August 1894.

18. Gavett, *Development*, 3.

19. R. Ogden, "The Great Goddess Prosperity," *Nation* 69 (14 December 1899): 442. In Chicago, the police force violently attacked peaceful Socialist marchers in labor parades. The *Kansas City Star* endorsed this police action on 12 November 1891 and 18 November 1891.

20. *Konstitution and Neben-Gasetze der Brauerei-Engineer and Fuerleute Lokal-Union* (Milwaukee, 1913), 3. Marx's famous words were common on banners and publications of the Federated Trades Council in the 1890s.

21. Lawrence Goodwyn, *Democratic Promise: The Populist Movement in America* (New York: Oxford University Press, 1976); David P. Thelen, *The New Citizenship: Origins of Progressivism in Wisconsin, 1885–1900* (Columbia: University of Missouri Press, 1972); and Herbert F. Margulies, *The Decline of the Progressive Movement in Wisconsin, 1890–1900* (Madison: State Historical Society of Wisconsin, 1968), 12. Because few original records of the urban Populists survive, I have relied on newspaper reports of their meetings in the regular press and accessible Populist newspapers for the period.

22. *Rochester Democrat and Chronicle*, 14 September 1894; and *Toledo Blade*, 4 February 1893. That the Populists succeeded was doubtful.

23. *Kansas City Star*, 2 May 1892, 19 July 1894, and 23 September 1894. The opposition *Mail* asserted on 11 October 1893, that "Mormons and Socialists should be scattered to the four winds." Also see *Kansas City Mail*, 22 February 1894; and Brown and Dorsett, *K.C.*, 90–91, 110.

24. Williams Jennings Bryan, of course, was nominated as a fusion candidate for president by the Democrats in 1896.

25. On the history of the Federated Trades Council, see especially its own writings, *The Federated Trades Council Directory of Milwaukee, Wisconsin* (Milwaukee: Published by the Trade and Labor Association, 1892); *Artisan Day Souvenir* (Milwaukee: Meyer-Rotier, 1894); *End of the Century Labor Day Souvenir* (Milwaukee: Germania Press, 1900), as well as its manuscript collection and minutes deposited at the State Historical Society of Wisconsin, Madison, Wisconsin (which will be later cited throughout this study). Excellent secondary treatments include Gavett, *Development*; Still, *Milwaukee*, chap. 12; and Gerd Korman, *Industrialization, Immigrants, and Americanizers: The View from Milwaukee, 1866–1921* (Madison: State Historical Society of Wisconsin, 1967), chap. 2.

26. Still, *Milwaukee*, 289; Gavett, *Development*, chap. 6; and J. M. Cooper, "The Wisconsin National Guard in the Milwaukee Riots of 1886," *Wisconsin Magazine of History* 55 (Autumn 1971). Also see the superb analysis by Leon Fink, *Workingmen's Democracy: The Knights of Labor and American Politics* (Urbana: University of Illinois Press, 1983).

27. Still, *Milwaukee*, chap. 12; and Gavett, *Development*, 72–77.

28. Federated Trades Council, *Artisan Day Souvenir*, n.p.

29. *Wisconsin Vorwarts*, 21 January 1894. This Milwaukee Socialist was quoted in the *Kansas City Labor*, 7 December 1895.

30. *Wisconsin Vorwarts*, 22 November 1893, 25 November 1893, and 21 January 1894.

31. *Wisconsin Vorwarts*, 30 April 1893, 13 November 1893, 10 February 1894, and 1 November 1896. See Frederick I. Olson, "Milwaukee's Socialist Mayors: End of an Era and Its Beginnings," *Historical Messenger* 16 (March 1960): 5; Frederick I. Olson, "The Milwaukee Socialists, 1897–1941" (Ph.D. diss., Harvard University, 1952), 7; and, for an examination of politics and athletics, F. P. Ziedler, "When Milwaukee Turners Were More Than Gymnasts," *Historical Messenger* 11 (March 1955): 11–15.

32. *Wisconsin Vorwarts*, 11 February 1896 and 13 November 1898; and also examine an important letter, "Secretary of Socialist Society to the Central Committee of the People's Party of Milwaukee, September 16, 1896" (William Pieplow Papers, Milwaukee County Historical Society, Milwaukee, Wisconsin, Box 1, File 1).

33. Milwaukee Socialist thought and action are best described in Gavett, *Development*; Still, *Milwaukee*, chap. 12; Olson, "The Milwaukee Socialists"; and Marvin Wachman, *The History of the Social-Democratic Party of Milwaukee* (Urbana: University of Illinois Press, 1945). A valuable biography of Victor Berger is Sally M. Miller, *Victor Berger and the Promise of Constructive Socialism, 1910–1920* (Westport, Conn.: Greenwood Press, 1973).

34. Scholars have repeatedly emphasized the importance of members of the "new middle class," such as urban superintendents, in school reform. Sufficient attention has not been given to the role of various community groups and labor unions in education in the Progressive era.

35. Federated Trades Council, *Minutes*, 19 December 1900 (Federated Trades Council of Milwaukee Papers); and *Die Munizipal-Platform der Sozial-Demokratischen von Milwaukee fur das Neujahr*, 1904, n.p.

36. *Wisconsin Vorwarts*, 16 October 1895.

37. *Constitution and By-Laws of the Federated Trades Council of Wisconsin* (Milwaukee: Edward Keough Press, 1900), 4; and *Wisconsin Vorwarts*, 24 December 1899.

38. Quoted in Rev. O. J. Price, "One Hundred Years of Protestantism in Rochester," in E. P. Foreman, ed., *Centennial History of Rochester, New York*, (Rochester: Printed by John P. Smith, 1933), 3:241.

39. Elizabeth Fones-Wolf and Kenneth Fones-Wolf, "Trade-Union Evangelism: Religion and the AFL in the Labor Forward Movement, 1912–1916," in Michael H. Frisch and Daniel J. Walkowitz, eds., *Working-Class America: Essays on Labor, Community, and American Society* (Urbana: University of Illinois Press, 1983), 165–66.

40. Henry F. May, *Protestant Churches and Industrial America* (New York: Harper & Row, 1949); A. M. Schlesinger, *A Critical Period in American Religion, 1875–1900* (Philadelphia: Fortress Press, c. 1967), 14. The literature on the rise of the Social Gospel is vast. See at least C. H. Hopkins, *The Rise of the Social Gospel in American Protestantism, 1865–1915* (New Haven: Yale University Press, 1940); A. I. Abell, *The Urban Impact on American Protestantism, 1865–1900* (Cambridge: Harvard University Press, 1943); and, more recently, R. C. White, Jr., and C. H. Hopkins, *The Social Gospel* (Philadelphia: Temple University Press, 1976).

41. *Rochester Democrat and Chronicle*, 18 December 1893 and 29 September 1894. The wage earners adopted a resolution that attacked charity and demanded that workers "enjoy equal rights and privileges in the pursuit of happiness and enjoyment with any other class of citizens."

42. *Evening Bee*, 26 October 1893. The *Bee*'s editorials urged workers to attend church, despite their differences with it.

43. Federated Trades Council, *Artisan Day Souvenir* (Milwaukee: Federated Trades Council, 1895), 50; and *Kansas City Mail*, 19 July 1892. In appraising different ways in which the church could end its estrangement with workers, the *Star* (24 February 1895) concluded that formal religion currently lacked the proper emphasis on delivering a "spiritual" message to wage earners. Also see the *Midland Mechanic*, 13 January 1898 and 26 January 1899.

44. *Report on Statistics of Churches in the United States at the Eleventh Census: 1890* (Washington, D.C.: Government Printing Office, 1894), 91.

45. Blake McKelvey, *The Flower City*, 312; McKelvey, "Walter Rauschenbusch's Rochester," 1–27; *Rochester Democrat and Chronicle*, 19 May 1890; and 6 October 1894.

46. Walter Rauschenbusch, *Christianizing the Social Order* (New York: Macmillan, 1912), 9; and Schlesinger, *Critical Period*, 26, who argued that "these attempts

to socialize Christian thought and practice, of course, represented the efforts of energetic minorities."

47. Herbert G. Gutman, *Work, Culture, and Society in Industrializing America* (New York: Vintage Books, 1977), chap. 2.

48. The interpretation that follows is based on Jones's original writings and correspondence, supplemented with useful information drawn from the following works: Harvey S. Ford, "The Life and Times of Golden Rule Jones" (Ph.D. diss., University of Michigan, 1953), George E. Mowry, *The Era of Theodore Roosevelt* (New York: Harper & Row, 1962); Melvyn G. Holli, "Urban Reform in the Progressive Era," in Lewis L. Gould, ed., *The Progressive Era* (Syracuse: Syracuse University Press, 1974); Russel B. Nye, *Midwestern Progressive Politics* (East Lansing: Michigan State University Press, 1951); and J. H. Rodabaugh, "Samuel M. Jones—Evangel of Equality," *Northwest Ohio Quarterly* 15 (January 1943): 17–46.

49. Samuel M. Jones, *The New Right: A Plea for Fair Play through a More Just Social Order* (New York: Eastern Book Concern, 1899), 43.

50. Ford, "Life and Times," chaps. 1–3.

51. Mrs. E. Hearth to Samuel M. Jones, 29 August 1897. (Samuel M. Jones Papers, Lucas County, Toledo Public Library, Toledo, Ohio). All the letters cited in the remainder of this chapter are from this manuscript collection.

52. Jones, *The New Right*, 61–62.

53. Jones to Henry D. Lloyd, 28 May 1897. In a letter to C. D. Wright, the United States Commissioner of Labor, on 15 June 1897, Jones argued that "the industrial depression is so great in this city and the surrounding country that I am lead [*sic*] to conclude that the number of men in enforced idleness at the present time is greater perhaps, as it seems to me, than at any other time in our history. I am something of a radical, and believe it is necessary to adopt radical measures to correct the unjust conditions that afflict us in many departments of our social life." Also see Jones, *The New Right*, 118–19.

54. *Toledo Blade*, 12 November 1895. Over and over again in his correspondence, Jones praised Herron and argued that Herron first impressed upon him that an acceptance of the Fatherhood of God logically led to an acceptance of the Brotherhood of Man. See Jones to Rev. Crafts, 28 October 1897; Jones to G. D. Herron, 11 February 1898; Jones to W. A. King, 15 February 1898; and Jones to W. R. Waddell, 12 October 1898. For a splendid reanalysis of Progressive reform, see Robert M. Crunden, *Ministers of Reform: The Progressive's Achievement in American Civilization, 1889–1920* (New York: Basic Books, 1982); and also see the reference in Jane Addams, *Twenty Years of Hull House* (New York: Signet Classics, c. 1961), 140.

55. Jones to F. H. Boke, 2 February 1898; and Jones to G. P. Waldorf, 11 October 1899.

56. Samuel M. Jones, *Letters of Labor and Love* (Indianapolis: Bobbs-Merrill, 1905), 59. See also Jones, *The New Right*, 121, 127–28, and 401; and Frank T. Carlton, "Golden-Rule Factory," *Arena* 32 (October 1904): 408–10, for an examination of Jones's ideas in action.

57. Jones, *The New Right*, 227–28. Here Jones went on to complain that in most factories "men are treated as impersonal 'hands,' not as brothers or human

beings." Also consult Carlton, *Golden Rule Factory*, 408–10; and Ernest Crosby, *Golden Rule Jones* (Chicago: Public Publishing, 1906), 12–15.

58. Ford, in "Life and Times," 90–91, notes that Jones "infuriated" many of Toledo's ministers when he took out subscriptions of the *Toledo Union* for all of them.

59. Samuel M. Jones, "No Title Is Higher Than Man," a song found in the Jones Papers.

60. Jones attacked the American Protective Association, racist bigots, and those who called immigrants "scum scrub." See Jones to Dr. J. T. Lee, 29 September 1898. To nativists, Jones simply responded: "I believe in Brotherhood, universal Brotherhood." Also see Jones to Rev. L. M. Fisk, 2 February 1898.

Chapter 4

1. There have been many important books written about educational reform during the Progressive era, but none matches the importance of David B. Tyack, *The One Best System: A History of American Urban Education* (Cambridge: Harvard University Press, 1974). Also read Lawrence A. Cremin's classic, *The Transformation of the School: Progressivism in American Education, 1876–1957* (New York: Alfred A. Knopf, 1962); Joel H. Spring, *Education and the Rise of the Corporate State* (Boston: Beacon Press, 1972); and Samuel Bowles and Herbert Gintis, *Schooling in Capitalist America* (New York: Basic Books, 1976).

2. Slave Factory or School," *Milwaukee Leader*, 6 March 1915.

3. On business consolidation, see Gabriel Kolko, *The Triumph of Conservatism: A Reinterpretation of American History, 1900–1916* (Glencoe, Ill.: Free Press, 1963); and James Weinstein, *The Corporate Ideal in the Liberal State* (Boston: Beacon Press, 1968).

4. I have been greatly influenced by Samuel P. Hays, particularly his influential essays available in *American Political History as Social Analysis* (Knoxville: University of Tennessee Press, 1980).

5. Clarence Karier, et al., *Roots of Crisis* (Chicago: Rand McNally, 1973), 109 n. 4. The literature on school board centralization, in addition to Tyack, *One Best System*, is massive. See especially Scott Nearing, "Who's Who on Our Boards of Education," *School and Society* (January 1917): 89–90; George S. Counts, *The Social Composition of Boards of Education: A Study in the Social Control of Public Education* (Chicago: University of Chicago Press, 1927): William Bullough, *Cities and Schools in the Gilded Age* (Port Washington, N.Y.: Kennikat Press, 1974); Samuel P. Hays, "The Politics of Reform in Municipal Government in the Progressive Era," *Pacific Northwest Quarterly* 55 (October 1964): 157–69; Hays, "The Social Analysis of American Political History, 1880–1920," *Political Science Quarterly* 80 (September 1965): 383–84; Eleanor M. Gersman, "Progressive Reform of the St. Louis School Board, 1897," *History of Education Quarterly* 10 (Spring 1970): 3–21; William H. Issel, "Modernization in Philadelphia School Reform, 1882–1905," *Pennsylvania Magazine of History and Biography* 94 (July 1970): 381–82; R. M. Johnson, "Politics and Pedagogy: The 1892 Cleveland School Reform," *Ohio History* 84 (August 1975): 196–206; and David C. Hammack, *Power and Society: Greater*

New York at the Turn of the Century (New York: Russell Sage Foundation, 1982), chap. 9.

6. For criticisms of the prevalent, class-oriented interpretations of school centralization, read V. L. Shardar, "Ethnicity, Religion, and Class: Progressive School Reform in San Francisco," *History of Education Quarterly* 20 (Winter 1980): 385–401; and David N. Plank and Paul E. Peterson, "Does Urban Reform Imply Class Conflict? The Case of Atlanta's Schools," *History of Education Quarterly* 23 (Summer 1983): 151–73.

7. Blake McKelvey, "Rochester's Public Schools: A Testing Ground for Community Policies," *Rochester History* 31 (April 1969): 9–13; William J. Reese, "The Control of Urban School Boards during the Progressive Era: A Reconsideration," *Pacific Northwest Quarterly* 68 (October 1977): 164–74; *Milwaukee School Report*, 1897, 58–64; and "Educational Organization and Progress in American Cities," *Annals of the American Academy of Political and Social Science* 25 (January 1905): 182.

8. Although Wisconsin had a school suffrage law for women, it was essentially a dead letter. City directories and school reports constituted the major source materials for the collective biographies in this chapter.

9. *Rochester Democrat and Chronicle*, 9 April 1892 and 10 January 1899. Again, the names and occupations of school board members were examined in local school reports and city directories.

10. The number of members on the school boards of different cities was usually identical with the number of established wards. Also see W. W. Chalmers, "Brief History of the Toledo Public Schools," in J. J. Burns, ed., *Educational History of Ohio* (Columbus: Historical Publishing, 1905), 395; and D. F. DeWolf, "Toledo," in *Historical Sketches of Public Schools in Cities, Villages, and Townships of the State of Ohio* (Columbus, Ohio: State Centennial Educational Committee, 1876), 5; C. S. Van Tassel, *Story of the Maumee Valley, Toledo, and the Sandusky Region* (Chicago: S. J. Clarke, 1929), 2:1560; *Toledo School Report*, 1890, 11; and Peter J. Mettler, *Chronik des Deutschen Pionier-Vereins von Toledo, Ohio* (Toledo: Gilsdorf, 1898), 108–9.

11. Patrick Donnelly, "The Milwaukee Public Schools," in J. W. Stearn, ed., *The Columbian History of Education in Wisconsin* (Milwaukee: Press of the Evening Wisconsin Company, 1893), 462–63; *American Industry and Manufacturers in the Nineteenth Century* (Elmsford, N.Y.: Maxwell Reprint, c. 1970), 988; and the appropriate table in the Appendix.

12. The best analysis of the ward system is in Tyack, *One Best System*. It is not as critical, however, as his interpretation of the Progressive era. Also see *Toledo School Report*, 1896, 14. For a similar complaint on the inequalities that existed under the ward system, also see the report in *Milwaukee School Proceedings*, 2 May 1893.

13. See, again, the appropriate literature on the social consequences of school board consolidation in preceding endnotes.

14. *Rochester Democrat and Chronicle*, 21 June 1898. On the Toledo A.P.A. and mayor's activities, see H. J. Desmond, *The APA Movement* (Washington: New Century Press, 1912), 25–26, 68–69; D. L. Kinzer, *An Episode in Anti-Americanism: The American Protective Association* (Seattle: University of Washington Press, 1964), 98–99; and Harvey S. Ford, "The Life and Times of Golden Rule Jones" (Ph.D. diss.: University of Michigan, 1953), 81–84.

15. For a detailed breakdown of the social origins of ward school board members in Toledo just prior to consolidation in 1898, see William J. Reese, "William Backus Guitteau and Educational Reform in Toledo during the Progressive Era." (master's thesis, Bowling Green State University, 1975), 36–61, 115–20.

16. The *Kansas City Labor Herald* was a persistent critic of the school board in the Progressive era. More will be said about Kansas City trade unions and educational reform in later chapters, but the *Herald*'s editorial on 8 March 1912 summarized a common complaint: "The dissatisfaction among the citizens of this city with the school board is becoming so strong as to command serious attention to the party representatives responsible for the situation. Instead of the board being servants of the people, they have become the masters."

17. Fourteen city, county, and state histories of Missouri were used in assembling this collective biography, along with census materials, the annual city directories, and the *Kansas City School Reports*. Space limitations prohibit the formal listing of the various sources.

18. *Kansas City Times*, 23 September 1883 and 10 March 1882; *Kansas City Star*, 21 October 1891; and *Pen and Sunlight Sketches of Kansas City and Environs* (Chicago: Phoenix, 1892), 64; Dorothy Galloway, "James Mickleborough Greenwood: An Evaluation of His Services as an Educator and His Contributions to Educational Thought" (master's thesis, Washington University, 1931), 16–17; A. J. D. Stewart, ed., *The History of the Bench and Bar of Missouri* (St. Louis: Legal Publishing, 1893), in its biography of perennial board member Ronald L. Yeager, 663–64; and "Educational Organization and Progress in American Cities," 182. Yeager's own business orientations are reflected in "School Boards, What and Why?" *National Education Association Addresses and Proceedings*, 1896, 973–79.

19. *Kansas City Mail*, 16 February 1894; and the *Labor Herald*, 20 July 1906; 15 March 1912; and 27 March 1914. Most popular historians and biographers of the Kansas City area viewed these developments uncritically. A characteristic view is by Carrie Westlake Whitney, *Kansas City, Missouri, Its History and People, 1808–1908* (Chicago: S. J. Clarke, 1908), 1:318. In reference to the bipartisan plan, she wrote: "The leading residents of Kansas City believed that the personnel of the school board should be free from the influences of politics and sectarianism." It was also free from ordinary people. A. Theodore Brown and Lyle W. Dorsett acknowledge the elite character of the board of education in *K.C.: A History of Kansas City, Missouri* (Boulder: Pruett, 1978), 84–85.

20. See "Educational Organization and Progress," 182–83.

21. *Rochester Democrat and Chronicle*, 7 January 1899. The paper ran procentralization editorials and articles throughout January and February. Also consult the *Toledo Evening Bee*, 25 January 1898; and William J. Reese, "Another Look," 165–66.

22. D. Mowry, "The Milwaukee School System," *Educational Review* 20 (Summer 1900): 147.

23. Although historians have often commented on the role of Good Government associations in centralization reform, not enough attention has been placed on women's influence in social change.

24. Tyack, *One Best System*, 95; D. S. Truesdale, "The Three Rs in Rochester, 1850–1900," in Blake McKelvey, ed., *The History of Education in Rochester* (Rochester:

Published by the Society, 1939), 120–21. Typical examples of scandals and poor business practices for simply a short period of time are given in the *Rochester Democrat and Chronicle*, 22 March 1890, 30 October 1890, 4 November 1890, 6 November 1890, 14 November 1890, 19 November 1890, and 12 January 1891.

25. *Rochester Democrat and Chronicle*, 19 November 1890; and *Rochester School Report*, 1891, 58.

26. *Rochester Democrat and Chronicle*, 12 January 1891, 13 January 1891, 20 January 1891, 3 February 1891, and 17 February 1891. The records were stolen from the Free Academy, the building that housed the city high school and the place where the board kept its official documents. The foxes poorly guarded the chicken house.

27. The *Toledo Blade* and *Toledo Evening Bee* had almost daily reports on the affairs of the school board and the progress of legislative reform from January through April 1898. See, for example, the *Bee* for at least the following important issues: 25 January 1898 through 2 February 1898, 7 February 1898, 9 February 1898, 17 February 1898 through 19 February 1898, 6 March 1898, and 23 March 1898. Besides William J. Reese, "Another Look," 164–74, also see William J. Reese "Progressive School Reform in Toledo, 1898–1921," *Northwest Ohio Quarterly* 47 (Spring 1975): 44–59; and quotation in Ford, "Life and Times," 178.

28. In the early 1870s, for example the *Seebote* attacked members of the school board for land swindles and backroom deals, as cited in the *Milwaukee Sentinel*, 17 February 1872. Also see Mowry, "Milwaukee," 141; William Lamers, *Our Roots Grow Deep* (Milwaukee: Milwaukee Public Schools, 1974), 84; and J. A. Watrous, ed., *Memoirs of Milwaukee County* (Madison: Western Historical Association, 1909), 1:406.

29. *Proceedings of the Common Council of the City of Milwaukee*, Milwaukee, 1890, 16 December 1890. The vote was 17 to 16. William Geuder, a prominent German school commissioner, mentions the scandal in the *Milwaukee School Proceedings*, 5 May 1891. Also see the *Milwaukee Daily News*, 7 May 1890 and 1 April 1892; *Milwaukee Sentinel*, 6 May 1891. Compare the assessment of one of Schattenburg's contemporaries, Watrous, *Memoirs*, 1:406; and "Milwaukee Letter," *Wisconsin Journal of Education* 20 (January 1890): 24.

30. An important analysis of mugwumpery and its relationship to Good Government reforms is by David P. Thelen, in *The New Citizenship: Origins of Progressivism in Wisconsin, 1885–1900* (Columbia: University of Missouri Press, 1974), chap. 8.

31. Blake McKelvey, *Rochester: Quest for Quality, 1890–1925* (Cambridge: Harvard University Press, 1956), chap. 4; Edward W. Stevens, Jr., "The Political Education of Children in the Rochester Public Schools, 1899–1917: An Historical Perspective on Social Controls in Public Education" (Ed.D diss., University of Rochester, 1971), 30–31; Randolph C. Downes, *Industrial Beginnings* (Toledo: Toledo Printing, 1954), 157–58; Bayrd Still, *Milwaukee: The History of a City* (Madison: State Historical Society of Wisconsin, 1948), 299–301; and *Kansas City Star*, 25 January 1892; and *Kansas City Mail*, 16 February 1894.

32. *Rochester Democrat and Chronicle*, 19 January 1894, and 8 February 1894.

33. The plan was described in the Rochester *Democrat and Chronicle*, 23 No-

vember 1894. On Aldridge, pertinent studies include Blake McKelvey, *The Quest for Quality*; McKelvey, "Rochester's Public School," 9; McKelvey, "The Mayors of Rochester's Mid Years: 1860–1900," *Rochester History* 27 (January 1966): 21–24; and McKelvey, "Rochester at the Turn of the Century," *Rochester History* 12 (January 1950): 8–9.

34. *Rochester School Report*, 1894, 49; *Rochester Democrat and Chronicle*, 10 March 1894; and *Rochester School Report*, 1895, 69, 93. Also see the reaction of the school commissioners to various proposals for reorganization in the *Rochester School Report*, 1898, 152–53.

35. *Rochester School Report*, 1898, 152–53. The usual comment was still added: "No persons familiar with school affairs or school management was [*sic*] consulted" in the preparation of the final bill.

36. *Rochester Democrat and Chronicle*, 1 May 1898. Also consult McKelvey, "Rochester's Public Schools," 9, where he argues: "Frustrated by continued bickering, the Good Government forces accepted the promise of Aldridge of a free hand in the schools if they would back his nominees for Council." Other relevant sources include "The Laws of 1898, As Amended by the Law of 1900 and 1901," in *Rochester School Report*, 1902, 5–33; A. Laura McGregor, "History of Public Schools of Rochester, New York," in George R. Foreman, ed., *Centennial History of Rochester, New York* (Rochester: Printed by John P. Smith, 1934), 4: 179; and Herbert S. Weet, "The Development of Public Education in Rochester, 1900–1910," in McKelvey, ed., *The History of Education in Rochester*, 183–86.

37. McKelvey, *The Quest for Quality*, 84–85. According to McKelvey, there was proof that the clause was added by the state printer at the request of Boss Aldridge and representatives of the American Book Company.

38. The *Toledo Evening Bee* (21 January 1896) wrote an incisive editorial on Major's plans in the heat of political debate. Also see this newspaper for 18 September 1895 and 25 September 1895; as well as the Republican *Blade* for 23 January through 25 January 1896; and Hoyt Landon Warner, *Progressivism in Ohio, 1897–1919* (Columbus: Ohio State University Press, 1964), 13, 25.

39. On the issue of bipartisanship, consult McKelvey, *The Quest for Quality*, 83. For the Toledo scene, see Reese, "Another Look," 165; *Toledo Blade*, 23 March 1895; and *Toledo Evening Bee*, 26 January 1898.

40. *Toledo Evening Bee*, 3 April 1898 and 19 April 1898; *Toledo Blade*, 18 April 1898; Downes, *Industrial Beginnings*, 207–12; Downes, "The People's Schools: Popular Foundations of Toledo's Public School System," *Northwest Ohio Quarterly* 29 (Winter 1956–57): 12–13; Chalmers, *Educational History*, 395; and Reese, "Progressive School Reform in Toledo," 44–59.

41. See Samuel M. Jones's mayoral addresses for some of his public positions on the Niles Bill, especially *Annual Statements of the Finances of Toledo* (Toledo, 1898), 22; *Annual Statements of the Finances of Toledo* (Toledo, 1901), 16; and *Annual Statements of the Finances of Toledo* (Toledo, 1902), 28.

42. *Toledo Evening Bee*, 26 March 1898. Jones's public life and activities have been well documented. See especially Wendell F. Johnson, *Toledo's Non-Partisan Movement* (Toledo: Press of H. J. Crittenden Company, 1922); Brand Whitlock, "'Golden Rule' Jones," *World's Work* 8 (September 1904): 5308–311; P. J. Frederick,

"European Influences on the Awakening of the American Social Conscience, 1886–1904" (Ph.D. diss., University of California-Berkeley, 1966), chap. 9; and Gary Bailey, "The Toledo Independent Movement: A Test of the Urban Liberalism Thesis" (master's thesis, Bowling Green State University, 1977).

43. *Toledo Union*, 19 March 1898; Downes, "The People's Schools," 13–14. For a small sampling, for example, see especially the Toledo Building Trades Council to Jones, 10 March 1899; Granite Cutters National Union to Jones, 17 March 1899; and Knights of Labor to Jones, 18 March 1899. (Samuel M. Jones Papers, Lucas County, Toledo Public Library, Toledo, Ohio.)

44. *Toledo Blade*, 28 January 1898. Tucker's life and activities in the schools are easily traced in Nevin O. Winter, *A History of Northwest Ohio* (Chicago: Lewis, 1917), 2:676; J. Hazard Perry and Mason Warner, *The Lincoln Club* (Toledo: Warner and Perry, 1899), 353–54; and Harvey Schribner, *Memoirs of Lucas County and the City of Toledo* (Madison: Western Historical Association, 1910), 2:518–19. Also see the *Toledo Blade*, 27 January 1898. Tucker's defense of the ward system was eloquent, but just two years earlier he had attacked the inequitable distribution of resources under that very system. See the *Toledo School Report*, 1896, 14–15.

45. J. A. Butler, "School Systems," *Annals of the American Academy* 25 (January 1905): 171–79. Butler was a Yale-educated attorney who was the leader of the Municipal League, and his background and activities are well described in Thelen, *New Citizenship*, chap. 7.

46. *Milwaukee School Report*, 1872, 70; *Milwaukee School Proceedings*, 14 February 1887, which has a good statement on the importance of geographical representation in democratic government; for reactions to other plans, see 7 February 1888, 5 February 1889, 20 February 1889, and 7 May 1889.

47. *Milwaukee School Report*, 1872, 70.

48. *Milwaukee School Proceedings*, 7 May 1889, 5 July 1892, and 19 March 1895.

49. Much of this analysis was documented in the preceding chapter.

50. *Milwaukee Daily News*, 20 April 1897. The *News* wrote a long anticommission editorial on 10 February 1897, which also attacked the present system of appointment by the ward aldermen. It called for the direct election of all boards of education by the people. Also read the *Wisconsin Vorwarts*, 20 April 1897.

51. *Rochester Democrat and Chronicle*, 15 February 1898 and 14 May 1898; "Minutes of the Women's Educational and Industrial Union," Volume for 1893–1896, 165 (Women's Educational and Industrial Union Papers, Rochester Public Library, Rochester, New York); Mrs. H. G. Danforth, "Rochester's Gay Nineties," *Rochester Historical Society Publications* 20 (1942): 47; *Toledo Evening Bee*, 15 March 1898; and *Toledo Blade*, 2 April 1898. The Woman's School Alliance support for the commission plan was documented in the *Proceedings of the First Annual Meeting of the Wisconsin State Federation of Women's Clubs* (Berlin, Wis.: Printed by George C. Hicks, 1897), 34–35.

Chapter 5

1. On the importance of "extra-party techniques of lobbying and coalition building" during the Progressive era, examine Daniel T. Rodgers, "In Search of

Progressivism," in Stanley I. Kutler and Stanley N. Katz, eds., *The Promise of American History* (Baltimore: Johns Hopkins University Press, 1982), 116.

2. The seminal interpretation of urban school reform during the Progressive era is by David B. Tyack, *The One Best System: A History of Urban Education in America* (Cambridge: Harvard University Press, 1974). Compare Lawrence A. Cremin, *The Transformation of the School: Progressivism in American Education, 1876–1957* (New York: Alfred A. Knopf, 1962); Edward A. Krug, *The Shaping of the American High School, 1880–1920* (Madison: University of Wisconsin Press, 1969); Joel H. Spring, *Education and the Rise of the Corporate State* (Boston, Beacon Press, 1972); Samuel Bowles and Herbert Gintis, *Schooling in Capitalist America* (New York: Basic Books, 1976); and Paul C. Violas, *Education and the Training of Urban Working Class* (Chicago: Rand McNally College Publishing, 1978).

3. Rochester *Democrat and Chronicle*, 28 December 1897.

4. "The School Community Plan," *School Journal* 62 (2 February 1901): 128.

5. "Men Like Sam Jones Do No Good," *Socialist*, 25 March 1905. Reactions to Jones's death and long descriptions of his funeral procession are available in the mid-July 1904 issues of the *Toledo News-Bee* and the *Blade*. Also see Brand Whitlock, *Forty Years of It* (New York: D. Appleton, 1914), 139; and Whitlock, "'Golden Rule' Jones," *World's Work* 8 (September 1904): 5308–11.

6. Besides Victor Berger's own *Broadsides* (Milwaukee: Social Democratic Press, 1913), and his many editorials in the local newspapers, the next best introduction to his life is the fine biography by Sally M. Miller, *Victor Berger and the Promise of Constructive Socialism* (Westport, Conn.: Greenwood Press, 1973). More generally, see Bayrd Still, *Milwaukee: The History of a City* (Madison: State Historical Society of Wisconsin, 1948); Thomas G. Gavett, *Development of the Labor Movement in Milwaukee* (Madison: University of Wisconsin Press, 1965); Gerd Korman, *Industrialization, Immigrants, and Americanizers: The View from Milwaukee, 1866–1921* (Madison: State Historical Society of Wisconsin, 1967); and Frederick I. Olson, "The Milwaukee Socialists, 1897–1941" (Ph.D. diss., Harvard University, 1952).

7. See, for example, H. N. Casson, "Draining a Political Swamp in Toledo," *Aena* 21 (June 1899): 768–71; Washington Gladden, "Mayor Jones of Toledo," *Outlook* 62 (6 May 1899): 17–21; "The Late Mayor Jones," *Independent* 42 (21 July 1904): 162–63; Frank T. Carlton, "Golden Rule Factory," *Arena* 32 (October 1904): 408–10; Ernest Crosby, *Golden Rule Jones* (Chicago: Public Publishing, 1906), and Wendell F. Johnson, *Toledo's Non-Partisan Movement* (Toledo: Press of the H. J. Chittenden Company, 1922). See also Hoyt Landen Warner, *Progressivism in Ohio, 1897–1917* (Columbus: Ohio State University Press, 1964); Harvey S. Ford, "The Life and Times of Golden Rule Jones" (Ph.D. diss., University of Michigan, 1953); and Gary Bailey, "The Toledo Independent Movement: A Test of the Urban Liberalism Thesis" (master's thesis, Bowling Green State University, 1977.)

8. Antipartyism was a mainstay in Jones's thinking after he bolted from the Republican Party in 1899. Typical viewpoints are found in Jones's "Government by the Golden Rule," *Munsey* 28 (January 1903): 506–9; and the Republican-dominated realities are documented in John M. Killits, *Toledo and Lucas County, Ohio, 1623–1923* (Chicago: S. J. Clarke, 1952), 2:578–79; and Randolph C. Downes, *Industrial Beginnings* (Toledo: Toledo Printing Company, 1954), 162–68; Eugene

Debs to Samuel M. Jones, 6 March 1899; Samuel M. Jones to Eugene Debs, 30 December 1898 (Jones Papers), and Gary Bailey, "Toledo Independent," 21, notes that Jones's popularity with the citizenry probably would have kept him in office indefinitely.

9. The context is described in William J. Reese, "The Control of Urban School Boards during the Progressive Era," *Pacific Northwest Quarterly* 68 (October 1977): 166–172.

10. *Toledo Blade*, 21 May 1901, where Law added: "Electing members at large is an improvement upon the old ward plan of representation, but the board, as at present constituted, is too small, and the term, five years is too long, and the plan of electing but one member a year is destructive of progress or change."

11. Quoted in Randolph C. Downes, "The People's Schools: Popular Foundation of Toledo's Public School System," *Northwest Ohio Quarterly* 29 (Winter 1956–1957): 13.

12. On the Broadway Civic Club, the most useful of dozens of available articles are in the *Toledo Evening Bee*, 7 February 1898, 7 March 1898, 16 March 1899, 17 September 1899, 15 March 1900, 13 May 1900, 15 February 1901, and 14 February 1905. See also *Toledo Bee*, 23 March 1902. Like the Broadway Civic Club, CEL activities were described in newspaper articles and in the minutes of the Toledo school board. Though the sources are extensive, see especially "Complete Education," in the *Toledo Blade*, 17 January 1900 and 6 February 1900; *Toledo Evening Bee*, 17 January 1900, 28 February 1900, 29 March 1900, 19 November 1901, 23 February 1902, and 23 March 1902. The struggles of the league with the school board can be traced in the *Toledo Board of Education Minutes*, 5 February 1900; 19 February 1900, 19 March 1900, 16 April 1900, 7 May 1900, 17 September 1900, 18 November 1901, 21 April 1902, and 15 December 1902 (Center for Archival Research, Bowling Green State University, Bowling Green, Ohio).

13. Samuel M. Jones to W. H. Rice, February 10, 1899. Also consult *First Annual Message of Mayor Samuel M. Jones to the Common Council of Toledo, Ohio* (Toledo, 1898), 14; *Second Annual Message of Samuel M. Jones, Mayor* (Toledo, 1899), 14–23; *Sixth Annual Message of Samuel M. Jones, Mayor of Toledo, Delivered to the Common Council, March 2, 1903* (Toledo, 1903), 13; and *Fifth Annual Message, Samuel M. Jones, Mayor of Toledo, Ohio, for the Year 1901* (Toledo, 1901), 4.

14. *Toledo Evening Bee*, 17 January 1900 and 24 May 1900; and *Toledo Blade*, 17 January 1900 and 8 February 1900; and *Complete Education*, February, 1902, quoted in the *Toledo Evening Bee*, 23 February 1902.

15. According to several newspaper reports, the club often met at Segur's house. Her involvement in the organization was traced in the *Toledo Evening Bee*, 12 October 1898, 6 March 1899, 15 February 1901, and in the *Toledo Blade*, 11 October 1900; 7 May 1901, 7 January 1902, and 11 January 1902. Also see Samuel Jones to J. H. Ferriss, December 16, 1898.

16. Samuel M. Jones to W. L. Young, 19 July 1899. Most of this information has been pieced together through newspaper reports on the lives of these women. Segur was very active in suffrage associations from after the time of the Civil War. Steinem's life is examined in E. S. Anderson, "Pauline Steinem, Dynamic

Immigrant," in M. Whitlock, ed., *Women in Ohio History* (Columbus: Ohio Historical Society, 1976), 13–19.

17. Anderson, *Women*, 13–19. Through the work of Sherwood and Steinem in particular, the City Federation of Women's Clubs had a Complete Education division by May 1901. See the *Toledo Blade*, 22 May 1901. Long eulogies were written on the death of Mrs. Sherwood in the *Toledo Union Leader*, 20 February 1914; in the *Toledo News-Bee*, 18 February 1914; and in the *Toledo Blade*, 16 February 1914. The *Blade* gave some solid reasons for her friendship to Jones when it argued that while technically a Presbyterian, in reality she practiced religious tolerance and love for all people. "She was a Christian Socialist in the broad meaning, or, as she said herself, 'a primitive Christian,' in that she took the teachings of Christ literally and gave to the needy to the limit of her means."

18. Warner, *Progressivism*, 10–11.

19. Like many Social Gospelers, Jones believed that the churches had veered from the primitive Christian perspectives of Jesus Christ. As a result, he argued that workers would only return to the fold in large numbers when the churches rediscovered their roots and became part of working-class life. See "Why Do Not People Go to Church?" in the *Evening Bee*, 28 May 1899. In addition consult Samuel M. Jones, *The New Right: A Plea for Fair Play through a More Just Social Order* (New York: Eastern Book Concern, 1899); and "American Workingmen and Religion," *Outlook* 65 (14 July 1900): 640–42.

20. Brand Whitlock to Rev. T. H. Campbell, 7 January 1905, in Allan Nevins, ed., *The Letters and Journal of Brand Whitlock* (New York: D. Appleton, 1936), 40; and Brand Whitlock, unpaginated introduction to Samuel M. Jones, *Letters of Labor and Love* (Indianapolis: Bobbs-Merrill, 1905). As Jones told Washington Gladden on 20 April 1897, "I seem to think of nothing better at present than to use my utmost endeavor, through progressive or radical utterances, if you please, to call the attention of the people to the conditions as they exist around us." Writing to H. V. Caton on 19 December 1898, he wrote: "You look upon the situation exactly as I do; this office is a pulpit, from which I am preaching the gospel of liberty for all people more effectively than I could do it in private life." *Toledo Evening Bee*, 3 April 1903.

21. Whitlock's life is well described in Jack Tager, *The Intellectual as Urban Reformer: Brand Whitlock and the Progressive Movement* (Cleveland: Press of Western Reserve, 1968); Robert M. Crunden, *A Hero in Spirit of Himself: Brand Whitlock in Art, Politics, and War* (New York: Alfred A. Knopf, 1969); Randolph C. Downes, *History of Lake Shore Ohio* (New York: Lewis Historical Publishing, 1952), 2:413–15; and Killits, *Toledo* 2: 580–84.

22. R. F. Hoxie, "The Rising Ride of Socialism," *Journal of Political Economy* 19 (October 1911): 609–31.

23. Gavett, *Development*, chaps. 10–11; F. Howe, "Milwaukee: A Socialist City," *Outlook* 95 (25 June 1910): 411–21; G. A. England, "Milwaukee's Socialist Government," *Review of Reviews* 42 (October 1910): 445–55; "A Socialist City in America," *World's Work* 20 (June 1910): 12995–96; and the Social Democrats' own *History of the Milwaukee Social Democratic Victories* (Milwaukee: Social Democratic Publishing Company, 1911). The importance of Milwaukee in the Socialist move-

ment in the Progressive era is undeniable. For a framework for Socialist development in Milwaukee in the nation, see the following: Howard Quint, *The Forging of American Socialism* (Indianapolis: Bobbs-Merrill, 1953); David Shannon, *The Socialist Party of America* (Chicago: Quadrangle Books, 1955); Daniel Bell, *Marxian Socialism in the United States* (Princeton: Princeton University Press, 1967); James Weinstein, *The Decline of Socialism in America, 1912–1925* (New York: Vintage Books, 1967); D. Herreshoff, *American Disciples of Marx: From the Age of Jackson to the Progressive Era* (Detroit: Wayne State University, 1967); the essays in Bruce M. Stave, ed., *Socialism and the Cities* (Port Washington, N.Y.: Kennikat Press, 1975), especially Sally M. Miller, "Milwaukee: Of Ethnicity and Labor," 41–47; and *Milwaukee Leader*, 7 July 1915.

24. Quoted in Still, *Milwaukee*, 312.

25. E. H. Thomas, "The Milwaukee Election," *International Socialist Review* 4 (March 1904): 520–21; and undated pamphlet titled *Rose on Socialism*, 1, in the Milwaukee pamphlet collection at the State Historical Society of Wisconsin. The close ties of working people and the SDP are highlighted in Carl D. Thompson, *Labor Measures of the Social-Democrats* (c. 1911), 3. Also see Victor Berger, "What Is the Matter with Milwaukee?" *Independent* 68 (21 April 1910): 841.

26. Maude G. Brown, "A History of Organized Labor in Toledo" (master's thesis, University of Toledo, 1924), 56. The Central Labor Union voted more than three to one in favor of supporting the State Socialist ticket, according to the *Toledo Union Leader*, 24 July 1908.

27. Jones told the *Toledo Blade* on 24 January 1899, that he did not belong to any Socialist party primarily because he feared that such a party would be based on class hatred, something which was incompatible with Jesus' law of love for all human beings. On many occasions Jones argued that he loved all men, even if he believed that the wealthy and powerful often erred and were misguided on social issues. According to the *Evening Bee* (11 December 1899), a Toledo Socialist Club was formed later that year, and the *Toledo Saturday Night*, a paper that was unofficially a Jones organ, noted that the Socialist Labor Party had attacked Jones for refusing to join a radical political party (10 June 1899). Also see the quotation from James Dombroski, *The Early Days of Christian Socialism in America* (New York: Columbia University Press, 1936), 137. Jones's refusal has already been substantiated in previous notes. Whitlock's refusal to join was indicated in a latter to the editor of the *Toledo News-Bee*, 25 January 1913.

28. Federated Trades Council, *Minutes*, 18 September 1901 (Federated Trades Council Papers). Also see Miller, "Milwaukee"; and Roderick Nash, "Victor L. Berger: Making Marx Respectable," *Wisconsin Magazine of History* 47 (Summer 1964): 301–8.

29. *Social Democratic Herald*, 7 December 1901. Other examples of S.P. preference for evolution over revolution were registered in its newspaper on 28 June 1902, 31 October 1903, 30 December 1905, and 23 May 1908; and in the *Milwaukee Leader*, 7 December 1911; Berger, *Broadsides*, 3, 29, 41–42, and 228–29; Miller, *Victor Berger*, chap. 2; and "Milwaukee's Socialist Mayer," *Current Literature* 48 (May 1910), 477–78.

30. Emil Seidel, *Sketches from My Life*, 2:79–80, unpublished autobiography written in 1938 (Emil Seidel Papers, State Historical Society of Wisconsin, Madison, Wisconsin); *History of the Milwaukee Social-Democratic Victories*, 16; *Social Democratic Herald*, 23 May 1908; and Miller, *Victor Berger*, chap. 1.

31. David Montgomery, *Workers' Control in America: Studies in the History of Work, Technology, and Labor Struggles* (Cambridge: Cambridge University Press, 1979), 70–72. See a similar argument in James R. Green, *The World of the Worker: Labor in Twentieth Century America* (New York: Hill & Wang, 1980), 80.

32. *Social Democratic Herald*, 1 July 1905. The increasing variety of social welfare and education services in the SDP platforms is easily traced in the *Milwaukee Vorwarts*, 1 April 1900, 4 February 1906, and 8 March 1908.

33. Kenneth Teitelbaum and William J. Reese, "American Socialist Pedagogy and Experimentation in the Progressive Era: The Socialist Sunday School," *History of Education Quarterly* 23 (Winter 1983): 429–54; and W. Bruce Leslie, "Coming of Age in Urban America: The Socialist Alternative, 1901–1920," *Teachers College Record* 85 (Spring 1984): 459–76.

34. See in particular the *Social Democratic Herald*, 1 July 1905, 6 April 1907, and the *Milwaukee Leader*, 22 March 1913, 22 January 1914, 9 March 1915, 5 January 1917, 10 March 1917, and 15 March 1917.

35. *Milwaukee Leader*, 14 October 1913. The Federated Trades Council, demonstrating the continuing power of Christian ethics among workers, argued: "Urge in the name of justice that everything be done before the dispensation of charity, for in the language of the proverbs be it said: 'Give us neither poverty nor riches'" (FTC *Minutes*, 17 December 1913).

36. *History of Milwaukee Social-Democratic Victories*, 9–10, 45–46; and Olson, "Milwaukee Socialists," 81–83. As the *History* stated (45): "Scores of hall meetings of all sizes were held in every nook and corner of the city, and the people addressed on issues of the campaign from a working class standpoint in whatever language the people of a given section could best understand." The industrialist referred to was George Bruce, quoted in the *Social Democratic Herald*, 13 May 1905.

37. See, for example, Korman, *Industrialization, Immigrants, and Americanizers*, 52–53. The literature is surveyed and analyzed in a seminal essay by D. Pienkos, "Politics, Religion, and Change in Polish Milwaukee, 1900–1930," *Wisconsin Magazine of History* 61 (Spring 1978): 179–209.

38. Gavett, *Development*, 24–26; and *History of the Social-Democratic Victories*, 14, 35–39. On the Germans and Poles in Milwaukee, see Kathleen Neils Conzen, *Immigrant Milwaukee, 1836–1880* (Cambridge: Harvard University Press, 1976); and Roger D. Simon, "The Expansion of an Industrial City: Milwaukee, 1880–1910." (Ph.D. diss., University of Wisconsin-Madison, 1971), chap. 2.

39. The Socialist concern with organizing the Poles is revealed in the FTC *Minutes*, 2 October 1907. On Catholic opposition to Socialism, see the *Social Democratic Herald*, 12 March 1904, 21 January 1905, 1 July 1905, 20 March 1909, and 25 March 1911; and the *Milwaukee Leader*, 29 September 1912, 16 November 1912, 28 January 1914, 16 March 1915, and 4 April 1917; as well as Rev. B. J. Blied, *Three Archbishops of Milwaukee* (Milwaukee, 1955), 132–33, 141; Olson, *Milwaukee*, 123; and Meta Berger, unpublished autobiography, 67 (Meta Berger Papers, State His-

torical Society of Wisconsin, Madison, Wisconsin). M. Karson's *American Labor Unions and Politics* (Carbondale: Southern Illinois University Press, 1958), underscores the tension between Catholicism and radicalism on the national level (chap. 9).

40. Pienkos, "Politics," 195.

41. Information on the Polish School Society is from the *Social Democratic Herald*, 29 May 1909; and the *Milwaukee Leader*, 23 January 1913, 21 March 1913, and 9 October 1913; FTC, *Minutes*, 2 October 1907; and the *History of the Social Democratic Victories*, 14, 35–39.

42. Daniel Hone, *City Government: The Record of the Milwaukee Experiment*, (Westport: Greenwood Press, c. 1974), 63.

43. *Social Democratic Herald*, 25 June 1904 and 4 September 1909. Whitnall, who converted from liberal to Socialist reformer, was married to one of the leading Social Democrats in Milwaukee, prominent in planning Milwaukee's modern playgrounds and parks. Because of the paucity of WSA records, the earliest citation discovered on Meta Berger's official membership in the organization was in the *Constitution, By-Laws, and Standing Rules of the Woman's School Alliance of Wisconsin* (Milwaukee, 1911), 11. See, as well, her unpublished autobiography previously cited, 53–59, 180. The Social Democratic position on free meals for school children is explained in Marvin Wachman, *History of the Social-Democratic Party of Wisconsin, 1897–1910* (Urbana: University of Illinois Press, 1945), 81.

44. *Social Democratic Herald*, 30 March 1907, and 6 September 1902. Socialist animosity toward any appointment plan and their ambivalence on ward versus at-large elections are documented in the *Herald* on 21 February 1903, 30 March 1906, 6 April 1907, and in a particularly heated editorial on 5 October 1907.

45. *Wisconsin Vorwarts*, 16 April 1905; and *Social Democratic Herald*, 10 December 1904.

46. *Social Democratic Herald*, 13 April 1907 and 21 February 1903.

47. *Milwaukee Sentinel*, 17 February 1901, 20 February 1901, 23 February 1901, 26 February 1901, 10 March 1901, and 30 March 1901; and the *Milwaukee Daily News*, 8 March 1901 and 22 March 1901.

48. *Milwaukee Sentinel*, 21 March and 30 March 1907. The Milwaukee newspapers were filled with commentary on the proposed reorganization of the school board in March, April, and May of that year. Other useful sources include R. Younger, "The Grand Jury That Made Milwaukee Quake," *History Messenger* 11 (March 1955): 7–9; and Hone, *City Government*, chap. 7.

49. *Social Democratic Herald*, 2 November 1907; and Still, *Milwaukee*, 309.

50. *Milwaukee School Report*, 1906, 73–75; *Milwaukee Sentinel*, 4 April 1906; and William Lamers, *Our Roots Grow Deep* (Milwaukee: Milwaukee Public Schools, 1974), 68. In reference to the upcoming bond proposal for more than $300,000, the *Milwaukee Free Press* (18 February 1906) noted: "There is likely to be little if any opposition on the part of the people who will pay the greater share of the taxes. . . . There should be no division of sentiment." On the emerging alliance, see the *Social Democratic Herald*, 23 January 1909, 30 January 1909, 6 February 1909, 13 February 1909, 6 March 1909, 27 March 1909, 1 May 1909, and 8 May 1909; the *Milwaukee Daily News*, 24 February 1909 and 26 February 1909; and *The*

Fight for the Rights of the Public Schools in Milwaukee; Being the Report of the School Defense Committee to the Federation of Civic Societies (Milwaukee: Fowle, 1909), 5–24.

51. *Rochester Democrat and Chronicle*, 24 February 1890 and 6 January 1891. On the broader social and political environment, see Blake McKelvey, *Rochester: The Quest for Quality, 1890–1925* (Cambridge: Harvard University Press, 1956), chap. 2; McKelvey, "The Lure of the City: Rochester in the 1890s," *Rochester History* 28 (October 1966): 1–24; McKelvey, "Turbulent but Constructive Decades in Civic Affairs: 1867–1900," *Rochester History* 7 (October 1945): 1–24; and McKelvey, "The Mayors of Rochester's Mid-Years: 1860–1900," *Rochester History* 28 (January 1966): 1–24. Also consult the *Rochester Democrat and Chronicle*, 1 July 1895, 10 July 1895, 3 August 1895, 17 August 1895, 23 November 1895, 17 January 1896, and 25 September 1897.

52. "Rochester's Mid-Years: 1860–1900," *Rochester History* 28 (January 1966): 1–24. Also consult the *Rochester Democrat and Chronicle*, 1 July 1895, 10 July 1895, 3 August 1895, 17 August 1895, 23 November 1895, 17 January 1896, and 25 September 1987.

53. *Labor Journal*, 27 April 1906, 4 May 1906, 18 May 1906, 17 August 1906, 31 August 1906, 14 September 1906, 28 September 1906, 6 November 1906, 23 November 1906, 25 October 1907, and 1 November 1907.

54. *Labor Journal*, 30 August 1907.

55. The *Labor Journal* (e.g., 23 January 1904) discussed how the problem of political action for workers had become a subject of national debate. Details on Kovaleski are in McKelvey, "Organized Labor in Rochester," 23; and McKelvey, *The Quest for Quality*, 289.

56. *Rochester Socialist*, 14 December 1907; *Rochester Union and Advertiser* (18 February 1908), in reference to the attack on the Italian Socialist Federation, wrote: "It is said that there are a number of anarchists in Rochester and that the police think it is best to keep them in control." In addition, examine the paper for 16 March 1908 and 30 June 1911.

57. Republicans dominated the school board as they did in Toledo. Critiques of the Republican and elite composition of the Progressive era school boards appear in the *Rochester Union and Advertiser*, 30 October 1903, 2 September 1905, and 2 November 1909.

58. The political context is well described in Blake McKelvey, "Rochester at the Turn of the Century," *Rochester History* 7 (January 1950): 8–12; and McKelvey, "Rochester's Public Schools: A Testing Ground for Community Policies," *Rochester History* 31 (April 1969): 9–13.

59. *Kansas City Star*, 5 May 1891, and 25 December 1893; *Kansas City Mail*, 14 September 1893, and 21 February 1894.

60. *Midland Mechanic*, 13 January 1898 and 17 February 1898. "Labor produces all wealth and provides the luxuries of the rich," noted the *Mechanic* on 14 July 1898, "but it clothes itself in rags, lives in hovels, is denied justice and ridiculed by plutocracy." Also read the *Missouri Staats-Zeitung*, 5 September 1901; *Kansas City Presse*, 2 November 1903, 24 February 1904, 9 March 1904, and 8 August 1904; and *Labor Herald*, 26 February 1904, 4 March 1904, 25 March 1904, and 8 April 1904.

61. A. Theodore Brown and Lyle W. Dorsett, *K.C.: A History of Kansas City, Missouri* (Boulder: Pruett, 1978), 93; *Midland Mechanic*, 3 March 1898, 17 March 1898, 25 May 1899, and 1 June 1899; and *Kansas City Presse*, 11 April 1904.

62. *Missouri Staats-Zeitung*, 18 August 1899, 1 September 1899, 24 November 1899, and 21 December 1900; *Kansas City Evening Mail*, 16 February 1894; and *Labor Herald*, 19 February 1904.

63. *Labor Herald*, 20 July 1906, 8 March 1912, 15 March 1912, 29 March 1914, and 31 March 1916. The most perplexing, unsolved problem in Kansas City politics and the schools is the relationship between the school board and the Pendergast brothers, Jim and Tom, two powerful and acknowledged city "bosses" during this era. Little mention is made of their role in the schools in contemporary literature or in the standard text by Lyle W. Dorsett, *The Pendergast Machine* (New York: Oxford University Press, 1968).

64. *Labor Herald*, 8 March 1918, 29 March 1918, and 5 April 1918; and *Kansas City and Its Schools* (Kansas City: Prepared for the Department of Superintendence of the National Education Association, 1917).

Chapter 6

1. *Proceedings of the Milwaukee School Board*, 30 June 1910.

2. *Proceedings of the Milwaukee School Board*, 30 June 1910; *Missouri Staats-Zeitung*, 20 April 1906; and *Toledo Blade*, 5 April 1906.

3. An earlier wave of revisionist writing has emphasized the social control features of the wider use of the schools. See, for example, Joel H. Spring, *Education and the Rise of the Corporate State* (Boston: Beacon Press, 1972); Clarence J. Karier, Paul C. Violas, and Joel H. Spring, *Roots of Crisis* (Chicago: Rand McNally College Publishing, 1973); and Paul C. Violas, *The Training of the Urban Working Class* (Chicago: Rand McNally College Publishing, 1978). Recent critics of this perspective have more properly placed movements for organized play in community, often labor-oriented struggles. They argue that social control theories are not only nondialectical, but portray workers and others as passive entities. See Gareth S. Jones, "Class Expression Versus Social Control? A Critique of Recent Trends in the Social History of 'Leisure,'" *History Workshop* 4 (Autumn 1977): 162–70; Roy Rosenzweig, "Middle Class Parks and Working Class Play: The Struggle Over Recreational Space in Worcester, Massachusetts, 1870–1910," *Radical History Review* 21 (Fall 1979): 31–46; Frances G. Couvares, "The Triumph of Commerce: Class Culture and Mass Culture in Pittsburgh," in Michael H. Frisch and Daniel J. Walkowitz, eds., *Working-Class America* (Urbana: University of Illinois Press, 1983), 123–52; and S. Hardy and A. G. Ingham, "Games, Structure, and Agency: Historians on the American Play Movement," *Journal of Social History* 17 (Winter 1983): 285–302. Other important works are by Paul Boyer, *Urban Masses and Moral Order in America, 1820–1920* (Cambridge: Harvard University Press, 1978); C. Goodman, *Choosing Sides: Playground and Street Life on the Lower East Side* (New York: Schocken Books, 1979); D. S. Kirschner, "The Perils of Pleasure: Commercial Recreation, Social Disorder, and Moral Reform in the Progressive Era," *American*

Studies 21 (Fall 1980): 27–42; Dominick Cavallo, *Muscles and Morals: Organized Playgrounds and Urban Reform* (Philadelphia: University of Pennsylvania Press, 1981); and the superb book by Bernard Mergen, *Play and Playthings: A Reference Guide* (Westport, Conn.: Greenwood Press, 1982).

4. A. M. Shaw, "Spread of Vacation Schools," *World's Work* 8 (October 1904): 5405. Of the extensive periodical literature, at least examine S. American, "The Movement for Vacation Schools," *American Journal of Sociology* 4 (November 1898): 309–25; K. A. Jones, "Vacation Schools in the United States," *Review of Reviews* 17 (June 1898): 710–16; "Vacation Schools," *Charities* 9 (September 6, 1902): 220–24; G. Blackwelder, "Chicago Vacation Schools," *Elementary School Teacher* 6 (December 1905): 211–14; League for Social Service, "Recreation Plus Education," *Municipal Affairs* 2 (September 1898): 433–48; and R. Waterman, "Vacation Schools," *Proceedings and Addresses of the National Educational Association* 37 (1898): 404–10. A good historical introduction to vacation schools is in Lawrence A. Finfer, "Leisure as Social Work in the Urban Community: The Progressive Recreation Movement, 1890–1920" (Ph.D. diss., Michigan State University, 1974), chap. 3. Certainly youth work with city children was older than the Progressive era, as Joseph F. Kett points out in *Rites of Passage: Adolescence in America 1790 to the Present* (New York: Basic Books, 1977). Also see Clarence A. Perry, *Wider Use of the School Plant* (New York: Charities Publication Committee, 1910), chap. 5.

5. Henry S. Curtis, "Vacation Schools, Playgrounds, and Settlements," in *Report of the Commissioner of Education for the Year 1903* (Washington, D.C.: Government Printing Office, 1905), 1:4.

6. H. C. Putnam, "Vacation Schools," *Forum* 30 (December 1900): 492.

7. *Milwaukee Sentinel*, 23 June 1902; and *Milwaukee Free Press*, 7 July 1902 and 11 August 1903. Curtis, in "Vacation," similarly argued: "The vacation schools have been experiment stations, and there has been little uniformity in the courses of study in the past" (5).

8. All the advocates of playgrounds, penny lunches, vacation schools, and other social service innovations assumed that the city should take over the experiments begun by private charity and philanthropy. See Henry S. Curtis, "Playground Revivals' Education to Playground Values," *Playground* 5 (May 1911): 72.

9. *Rochester Union and Advertiser*, 13 May 1899.

10. *Toledo Blade*, 22 October 1901; and *Proceedings of the Milwaukee School Board*, 30 June 1909.

11. See the long editorial on the differences between liberalism and socialism in the *Milwaukee Leader*, 14 October 1913.

12. See the long editorial on the differences between liberalism and socialism in the *Milwaukee Leader*, 14 October 1913.

13. The "rich and well to do," Bouton wrote, "for the most part, are taken by their parents in the summer to the mountains, the seashores, into the country, and the many resorts, where they are free to enjoy an out-of-door life and gather new ideas while gaining health and vigor." Quoted in the *Toledo Blade*, 30 July 1904. Also read Carrie Westlake Whitney, *Kansas City, Missouri, Its History and People, 1808–1908* (Chicago: S. J. Clarke, 1908), 1: 629–30; and *Kansas City and Its*

Schools (Kansas City: Prepared for the Members of the Department of Superinten-dence of the National Education Association, 1917), 10, 67.

14. *Toledo Blade*, 30 July 1904.

15. See especially O. J. Milliken, "Chicago Vacation Schools," *American Journal of Sociology* 4 (November 1898), 289–308; American, "The Movement," 309–25; and Jones, "Vacation Schools," 710–16

16. "Vacation Schools," *Charities*, 222; and C. M. Hill, "The Extension of the Vacation School Idea," *Elementary School Teacher* 5 (January 1905): 298.

17. *Rochester School Report*, 1899, 86; *Rochester Union and Advertiser*, 7 July 1903. Also see the same paper for 6 July 1901 and 9 July 1901, as well as most July issues of local newspapers after 1899. The schools usually ran in different cities from the first or second week of July through the middle of August.

18. *Toledo Blade*, 25 May 1901, 27 May 1901, 19 July 1901, 22 October 1901, 10 May 1902, 14 May 1902, 17 May 1902, and 9 June 1902.

19. *Toledo Blade*, 9 June 1902. On Steinem, examine the *Blade* for 14 May 1902, 7 November 1903, 30 July 1904, 4 April 1905, and 15 April 1905. Also see E. S. Anderson, "Pauline Steinem, Dynamic Immigrant," in M. Whitlock, ed., *Women in Ohio History* (Columbus: Ohio Historical Society, 1976), 13–19.

20. *Kansas City and Its Schools*, 10, 67; *Kansas City School Report*, 1913, 56; *Kansas City School Report*, 1914, 56–7; and *Milwaukee Journal*, 10 July 1899. See also the *Milwaukee School Report*, 1899, 88–89; *Proceedings of the Milwaukee School Board*, 1 May 1899, 6 June 1899, and 11 July 1899; *Milwaukee Sentinel*, 12 April 1899, 5 June 1899, and 24 March 1900; and *Milwaukee Daily News*, 11 April 1900.

21. *Milwaukee Sentinel*, 24 March 1900.

22. *Milwaukee Sentinel*, 8 July 1902 and 23 June 1902.

23. Milliken, "Chicago," 294; *Rochester School Report*, 1899, 87; *Decennial Yearbook* (Rochester: Women's Educational and Industrial Union of Rochester, New York, 1903), 29 (WEIU Papers); and *Toledo Blade*, 9 October 1902.

24. *Rochester Union and Advertiser*, 12 July 1904 and 20 August 1904.

25. The class and geographical determinants were documented in the *Milwaukee Sentinel*, 2 May 1900 and 8 July 1904. The Reverend H. H. Jacobs, who ran a vacation school in 1904, noted that the applications of the children from Jones Island were always accepted, since they were the most needy children of the city. See *Milwaukee School Proceedings*, 1 November 1904. On the Italian neighborhood, which was stigmatized in much of the English and also German press as a den of vice and crime, see G. LaPiana, *The Italian in Milwaukee, Wisconsin* (Milwaukee: Prepared under the Direction of the Associated Charities, 1915).

26. *Milwaukee Sentinel*, 8 July 1904; *Milwaukee Daily News*, 13 July 1907 and 6 July 1909.

27. Kennon told the *Rochester Union and Advertiser* on 28 October 1905, "If vacation schools are needed, the city should provide them, then they will not be provided by a society, but they will be 'our schools.'" Also see the *Rochester School Report*, 1907, 8, 122–23.

28. Steinem's effort to permit the use of public monies for the vacation schools

were traced in the *Toledo Blade*, 15 April 1905, 20 June 1905, and 24 January 1906; and in the *Toledo News-Bee*, 9 December 1905 and 10 May 1910.

29. *Kansas City School Report*, 1913, 56; *Kansas City School Report*, 1914, 56–57; 1915, 40–44; and the *Milwaukee Sentinel*, 2 June 1909, which reported that only three vacation schools would operate, a small faction of the dozens of schools in the city.

30. A study of the manual-training movement in all of these cities would require a separate and detailed chapter. The sources of the movement were complex and went back at least to the 1870s, as Lawrence A. Cremin noted in *The Transformation of the School: Progressivism in American Education, 1876–1957* (New York: Alfred A. Knopf, 1962); and as Bernice Fisher indicated in *Industrial Education: American Ideals and Institutions* (Madison: State Historical Society of Wisconsin, 1967).

31. *Kansas City and Its Schools*, 67; and "The Public School System of Toledo," *Commerce Club News* 4 (28 July 1919): 26.

32. Jane Jacobs, *The Death and Life of Great American Cities* (New York: Vintage Books, 1961), part 1. On playgrounds and recreational policies in the schools, see E. C. Preston, *Principles and Statutory Provisions Relating to Recreational, Medical, and Social Welfare Services of the Public Schools* (New York: Bureau of Publications, Teachers College, Columbia University, 1935).

33. Curtis, "Vacation Schools, Playgrounds, and Settlements," 3.

34. Henry S. Curtis, "The Playground Movement of Today," *Proceedings of the Fifty-seventh Annual Session of the Wisconsin Teachers' Association* (Madison: Democrat Printing Company, State Printer, 1910), 167. A similar argument was made in Perry, *Wider Use*, 168–70. Standard interpretations of the playground movement include C. E. Rainwater, *The Play Movement in the United States* (Chicago: University of Chicago Press, 1922); Henry S. Curtis, *The Practical Conduct of Play* (New York: Macmillan, 1915); Henry S. Curtis, *Education through Play* (New York: Macmillan, 1916); Henry S. Curtis, *The Play Movement and Its Significance* (New York: Macmillan, 1917); and Cavallo, *Muscles*, chap. 1.

35. Pertinent sources on local organizations include the following: Samuel M. Jones, *Third Annual Message of Samuel M. Jones, Mayor* (Toledo, 1899), 24–25; *Toledo Blade*, 23 June 1899 and 6 July 1899; *The Children's Playground League, 1903* (Rochester, 1903); *Milwaukee Daily News*, 14 March 1903 and 22 April 1903; *Milwaukee Sentinel*, 22 April 1903; and *Second Annual Report of the Board of Public Welfare* (Kansas City: Board of Public Welfare, 1911), 51. Rochester's playground movement has been especially well documented compared to these other cities. See, for example, Blake McKelvey, "Rochester Learns to Play: 1850–1900," *Rochester History* 8 (July 1946): 1–24; Blake McKelvey, "An Historical View of Rochester's Parks and Playgrounds," *Rochester History* 9 (January 1949): 1–24; W. F. Peck, *History of Rochester and Monroe County, New York* (New York: Pioneer, 1908), 233; and Edward Stevens, Jr., "The Political Education of Children in the Rochester Public Schools, 1899–1917: An Historical Perspective on Social Control in Public Education" (Ph.D. diss., University of Rochester, 1971), 245–46.

36. "Women in the Recreation Movement," *Playground* 11 (July 1917): 203–4;

undated newspaper clipping, c. 1899, *Minute Book, 1896–1901*, Women's Education and Industrial Union (WEIU Papers); and *Toledo Blade*, 9 October 1895.

37. *Milwaukee Sentinel*, 26 November 1898, 25 February 1899, 22 September 1899, 20 October 1899, 12 January 1906, 21 January 1906, 29 September 1906, 7 March 1908; *Proceedings of the Milwaukee School Board*, 8 May 1908; *Milwaukee Daily News*, 5 July 1902, 5 October 1904, 15 April 1905, 10 January 1906; and *Social Democratic Herald*, 22 February 1902, 19 July 1902, 12 March 1904, 27 March 1909; and Whitney, *Kansas City*, 1:629–30.

38. *Labor Journal*, 22 February 1907. The *Journal* gave wide coverage to the work of the Children's Playground League. See *Labor Journal*, 29 March 1907; *The Children's Playground League of Rochester, 1903*, 1; *The Children's Playground League, 1908* (Rochester, 1908), 2; *Proceedings of the Second Annual Playground Congress and Yearbook, 1908* (New York City: Published by the Playground Association of America, 1909), 365; and "The Yearbook of the Playground Recreation Association of America," reprinted in *Playground* 7 (January 1914): 399.

39. *Toledo Union*, 31 July 1897; *Toledo Saturday Night*, 6 May 1899 and 1 July 1899; and *Toledo Union Leader*, 1 May 1908 and 13 May 1910. The poem is from the *Labor Herald*, 24 January 1908.

40. *Missouri Staats-Zeitung*, 7 June 1907 and 29 April 1910.

41. *Rochester Union and Advertiser*, 6 November 1899 and 24 March 1902; Edward J. Ward, *The Social Center* (New York: D. Appleton, 1913), 179–80; and *Labor Herald*, 19 February 1904.

42. *Social Democratic Herald*, 22 February 1902, 19 July 1902, 12 March 1904, 3 February 1906, and 5 November 1910. See especially D. C. Enderis to Emil Seidel, 24 January 1944 (Seidel Papers), on the former mayor's influence. A typical cartoon appeared in the *Milwaukee Leader* on 6 April 1914.

43. Newspaper clipping, c. 1900, *Minute Book, 1896–1901* of the Women's Educational and Industrial Union (WEIU Papers).

44. *The Children's Playground League, 1903*, 3; and McKelvey, "An Historical View," 15–16.

45. *Toledo Blade*, 6 July 1899, 27 July 1899, 7 August 1899, 11 September 1899, and 21 November 1899.

46. *Milwaukee Daily News*, 1 August 1905; *Milwaukee Free Press*, 7 July 1906; and *Milwaukee Sentinel*, 2 December 1903. When the first public supervised playground was opened in 1905, the *News* (cited above) stated, "The parents and children of the neighborhood are delighted with the new playground and have been interested spectators of the improvements there." Also consult the *Milwaukee Free Press*, 7 July 1906.

47. Cavallo, *Muscles*, 2.

48. D. Blaustein, "The Schoolhouse Recreation Center as an Attempt to Aid Immigrants in Adjusting Themselves to American Conditions," *Playground* 6 (December 1912): 334. Another writer argued, "The Playground deals with race cleavage by Americanizing immigrants." See D. Becker, "Social Cleavage and the Playground," *Playground* 9 (June 1915): 87. In addition to the literature cited in the previous note, also see Finfer, "Leisure."

49. *Rochester Union and Advertiser*, 23 November 1908 and 21 December 1908. Also see same newspaper 10 March 1908, 14 April 1908, and the letter to the editor, 3 August 1911.

50. Quoted in the *Toledo News-Bee*, 18 October 1898, the Democratic rival and warm supporter of the playgrounds. Also see *Toledo News-Bee*, 18 September 1906; and the *Toledo Blade*, 18 September 1906. Allegations of vice, immorality, and urban disorder at the social centers, recreation centers, and playgrounds are in the *Milwaukee Sentinel*, 19 October 1911, 3 October 1913, and 5 January 1914; and in the *Milwaukee School Proceedings*, 3 September 1912, 5 August 1913, 2 September 1913, 6 October 1914, 3 December 1914, 4 May 1915, and 1 June 1915.

51. *Rochester Union and Advertiser*, 15 October 1903, in a description of speeches at the annual meeting of the organization. Also read the *Toledo Blade*, 19 October 1899.

52. Quoted in Finfer, "Leisure," 141–42, on the effects of the vacation and playground movements in one particular city.

53. *Toledo Blade*, 9 October 1902.

54. R. Haynes, "Recreation Survey, Milwaukee, Wisconsin," *Playground* 6 (1912): 44; and Milwaukee City Club, *Amusements and Recreation in Milwaukee* (Milwaukee: City Club of Milwaukee, 1914).

55. *Amusements and Recreation in Milwaukee*, 10, 37.

56. *Fourth Annual Report of the Board of Public Welfare of Kansas City, Missouri* (Kansas City, 1913), 57.

57. *Fourth Annual Report of the Board of Public Welfare*, 49–77; and *Third Annual Report of the Board of Public Welfare of Kansas City, Missouri* (Kansas City, 1912), 244–45.

Chapter 7

1. G. B. Ford, "Madison Conference on Social Centers," *Survey* 27 (18 November 1911): 1229, 1231. On regional and national meetings, see C. W. Holman, "Focusing Social Forces in the Southwest," *Survey* 26 (23 September 1911): 866–68; "The Social Center—Center of Democracy," *Survey* 30 (6 September 1913): 675–76; and "Echoes from the First National Conference of Social Centers," *The Common Good* 5 (December 1911): 21–27.

2. See, for example, John Dewey, "The School as a Center of Social Life," *Journal of the Proceedings and Addresses of the N.E.A.* (1902): 373–74; and Charles W. Eliot, "The Full Utilization of a Public School Plant" *Journal of the Proceedings and Addresses of the N.E.A.* (1903): 241–47. Several useful reports by Clarence A. Perry include the following: *The Extension of Public Education* (Washington, D.C.: Bulletin of the U.S. Bureau of Education, 1915); *School Extension Statistics* (Washington, D.C.: Bulletin of the U.S. Bureau of Education, 1917); and *Social Center Gazette, 1919–1920* (New York City: Russell Sage Foundation, 1920). Also see H. E. Jackson, *The Community Center* (Washington, D.C.: Bulletin of the U.S. Bureau of Education, 1927).

3. Edward J. Ward described the multiple explanations in "School Exten-

sion," *The Common Good* 5 (January 1911): 12–16. This magazine was Rochester's main social welfare journal in the Progressive era. Also see Ward, "Rochester Social Centers," *Proceedings of the Third Annual Playground Congress and Yearbook* 3 (1909): 387–88.

4. Edward J. Ward, "The Little Red Schoolhouse," *Survey* 22 (7 August 1909): 640; Ward, *The Social Center* (New York: D. Appleton, 1913), 38–39, where he admitted that the rural analogy was overdrawn; and L. F. Hanmer, "The Wider Use of the School Plant," *American Education* 15 (March 1912): 305.

5. M. J. Mayer, "Our Public Schools as Social Centers," *American Review of Reviews* 44 (August 1911): 201; *Independent* 54 (March 6, 1902): 583–84; and W. Wilson, "The Need of Citizenship Organization," *American City* 5 (November 1911): 265–68.

6. *Milwaukee School Report*, 1867, 78.

7. *Toledo Board of Education Minutes*, 30 July 1860, 25 February 1864, 17 June 1864, 26 November 1864, 28 January 1865, 26 June 1869, 1 June 1871, and 18 June 1871; A. L. McGregor, "The Early History of the Rochester Public Schools, 1813–1850," *Rochester Historical Society Publications* (Rochester: Published by the Society, 1939): 51–52; and Blake McKelvey, *Rochester: The Water-Power City 1812–1854* (Cambridge: Harvard University Press, 1945), 266–67.

8. Clarence Perry, *Wider Use of the School Plant* (New York: Charities Publication Committee, 1910), 3.

9. *Rochester School Report*, 1907, 129. On the importance of parent organizations, see H. Woolston, "Social Education in the Public Schools," *Charities and the Commons* 16 (1 September 1906): 574; and E. T. Glueck, *The Community Use of Schools* (Baltimore: Williams and Wilkins, 1927) who asserted, "The National Congress of Mothers and Parents-Teachers Associations is by far the most important and far-reaching of the private organizations in their influence upon the establishment of a closer relationship between the school and the neighborhood." The first important scholarly examination of organized parents was Steven L. Schlossman, "Before Home Start: Notes toward a History of Parent Education in America, 1897–1929," *Harvard Educational Review* 46 (1976): 436–67. From a different perspective, consult William J. Reese, "Between Home and School: Organized Parents, Clubwomen, and Urban Education in the Progressive Era," *School Review* 87 (November 1978): 3–28.

10. N. Butler, "Work of the Associations," *School Review* 16 (Fall 1908): 78; Mary R. Beard, *Women's Work in Municipalities* (New York: D. Appleton, 1915), 39.

11. *Yearbook of the Women's Educational and Industrial Union, Rochester, New York* (Rochester: H. D. Bryan, Printer, 1897), 4, 12 (WEIU Papers). Montgomery was active in the local mothers' unions as indicated by the *Rochester Democrat and Chronicle*, 6 April 1898; and by the *Rochester Union and Advertiser*, 5 June 1901. Also see *Proceedings of the Second Annual Convention of the Wisconsin State Federation of Women's Clubs* (1898), 23.

12. See especially Wayne Urban, "Organized Teachers and Educational Reform during the Progressive Era: 1890–1920," *History of Education Quarterly* 16

(Spring 1976): 35–52; and Wayne Urban, *Why Teachers Organized* (Detroit: Wayne State University Press, 1982).

13. *Rochester Democrat and Chronicle*, 28 October 1896; *Rochester Union and Advertiser*, 12 June 1901. Brooks's activities can also be traced in 6 June 1900, 11 June 1901, and 5 March 1902. See also *Rochester Union*, 2 June 1905 and 5 October 1905.

14. *Toledo Blade*, 3 January 1905. Steinem's activism with parents can be easily documented in other articles in 5 January 1905, 19 January 1905, 7 October 1905, 10 October 1905, and 14 November 1906; and in the *Toledo News-Bee*, 2 February 1905, 5 April 1905, 5 October 1905, and 15 November 1910.

15. *Milwaukee Sentinel*, 22 January 1897; *Kansas City Daily Journal*, 8 March 1901; *Kansas City School Report*, 1903, 90. Kansas City's kindergarten teachers were active in the formation of mothers' unions starting in the 1890s. See, for example, *Kansas City School Report*, 1911, 65; as well as *Kansas City School Report*, 1913, 52, 95.

16. *Toledo Blade*, 18 November 1913. Ironville parents lobbied for electric lighting, for, as their delegation to the school board explained, "when the parents held meetings in the buildings at night . . . they had to carry oil lamps to the school." For some of the many examples, see the *Toledo News-Bee*, 9 October 1912, 7 January 1913, 18 March 1913, and 22 September 1914; and the *Toledo Blade*, 4 February 1913, 18 November 1913, and 6 October 1914.

17. *Rochester School Report*, 1904, 34.

18. *Milwaukee School Report*, 1909, 72. Although her scholarship is thoroughly uncritical of her subject, see Louise W. Sears's biography of Pearse, *Life and Times of a Midwest Educator* (Lincoln, Neb.: State Journal Printing, 1944).

19. "The Social Center Work in Wisconsin," *Playground* (September 1910): 220; Clarence A. Perry, "The School as a Factor in Neighborhood Development," *Proceedings of the National Conference on Charities and Correction* (1914): 389; Blake McKelvey, *Rochester: The Quest for Quality, 1890–1925* (Cambridge: Harvard University Press, 1956), 137; Blake McKelvey, "Historic Origins of Rochester's Social Welfare Agencies," *Rochester History* 9 (April 1947): 32–33; and "Rochester's Public Schools: A Testing Ground for Community Policies," *Rochester History* 31 (April 1969): 12–13.

20. *Rochester School Report*, 1910, 10. President George Forbes, a Good Government leader, also wrote an important essay titled, "Buttressing the Foundations of Democracy," *Survey* 27 (November 18, 1911): 1231–35.

21. Ward, *The Social Center*, 179–80; McKelvey, *The Quest for Quality*, 95: and Edward W. Stevens, "Social Centers, Politics, and Social Efficiency in the Progressive Era," *History of Education Quarterly* 12 (Spring 1972): 25–26.

22. *Labor Journal*, 22 February 1907.

23. A good overview of the administrative and curricular changes of these years is available in Herbert S. Weet, "The Development of Public Education in Rochester: 1900–1910," *Publications of the Rochester Historical Society* 17 (Rochester: Published by the Society, 1939): 183–232. For a very different perspective, consult the more critical and valuable study by Edward W. Stevens," The Political Education of Children in the Rochester Public Schools, 1899–1917: An Historical Perspec-

tive on Social Control in Public Education" (Ed.D diss., University of Rochester, 1971).

24. Joel H. Spring, *Education and the Rise of the Corporate State* (Boston: Beacon Press, 1972), 83; and Stevens, "Social Centers, Politics, and Social Efficiency," 16–33.

25. S. Baxter, "Widening the Use of the Public School House," *World's Work* 5 (March 1903): 3247; Eliot, "Full Utilization," 241; T. A. Levy, "Extended Use of the Public Schools," *American Education* 8 (December 1904): 207; and Clarence A. Perry, "Summer Use of the School House," *American City* 2 (June 1910): 265. Also see L. B. Avery, "The Wider Use of the School Plant," *School and Society* 7 (April 27, 1918): 481–85; and William A. Wirt, "Getting the Maximum Use of Our School Facilities," *American City* 18 (March 1918): 219–22.

26. J. G. Stokes, "Public Schools as Social Centers," *Annals of the American Academy* 23 (May 1904): 461; and M. E. McDowell, "Chicago's Schools Close to Discussion," *The Common Good* 5 (December 1911): 24–25; and W. H. Maxwell, "The Economic Use of School Buildings," *Journal of Proceedings and Addresses of the NEA* (1910): 326.

27. Ward, *The Social Center*, 111; Ward, "Where Suffragists and Anti's Unite," *American City* 10 (June 1914), 524. His common use of family and home metaphors is seen in "Community Cooperation in Education," *Child-Welfare Magazine* 8 (August 1914): 494–96. Also see H. L. Child, "The Rochester Social Centers," *American City* 5 (July 1911): 18–27.

28. Ward, "Community Cooperation in Education," 494. Details of Ward's life are drawn from R. S. Baker, "Do It for Rochester," *American Magazine* 70 (September 1910): 683–96; *Who Was Who in America* (Chicago: A. N. Marquis, 1950), 2:5560. Also see Ward, *The Social Center*, 141. His book is filled with slurs on the arrogance of private monopolies and the commercialization of American life.

29. *Rochester Annual Report*, 1907, 124.

30. Ward, "The Little Red Schoolhouse," 642. Ward's reports to the Rochester school board between 1907 and 1910 reflect this same sentiment. Also see Ward, *The Social Center*, chap. 8.

31. Lawrence A. Finfer, "Leisure as Social Work in the Urban Community: The Progressive Recreation Movement." (Ph.D. diss., Michigan State University, 1974), 241–42; and Edward J. Ward, "The Rochester Movement," *Independent* 67 (14 October 1909): 860.

32. Weet, "The Development," 204–5.

33. Edward J. Ward, "The Schoolhouse as the Civic and Social Center of the Community," *Journal of Proceedings and Addresses of the N.E.A.* (1912): 447. Also see *The Social Center*, chap. 2.

34. The history of the growth of the Rochester movement is detailed in several places. Besides the secondary literature previously cited, peruse Ward's many descriptions of the movement, "The Rochester Movement," 860–61; "The Rochester Social Centers and Civic Clubs Movement," *American School Board Journal* 40 (February 1910): 4–5; *Rochester Social Centers and Civic Clubs: Story of the First Two Years* (Rochester: Published by the League of Civic Clubs, 1909);

and the editorial, "Clubbed into Democracy," *The Common Good* 4 (February 1911): 3–4.

35. *Rochester Social Centers and Civic Clubs*, picture opposite page 103. Among the officers of the Men's Civic Club at the No. 14 school were "a well-to-do physician, a journeyman, a banker and a labor leader. The officers of one of the women's civic clubs are a negress, two Jewesses, two Catholics, a Unitarian, and a Presbyterian." Quoted in Ward, "The Rochester Movement," 860.

36. For a flavor of press opposition, see the following citations, usually for the editorial page: *Rochester Post Express*, 30 November 1909, 8 December 1909, 2 February 1910; the *Rochester Times*, 17 December 1908, 12 December 1909, 14 December 1909, 16 December 1909, 18 December 1909, 2 February 1910; and the *Rochester Union and Advertiser*, 1 February 1910.

37. Shedd's background and activities were described in Stevens, "Social Centers, Politics, and Social Efficiency," 28–29; and in W. Bruce Leslie, "Coming of Age in Urban America: The Socialist Alternative, 1901–1920," *Teachers' College Record* 85 (Spring 1984): 466–68. Newspaper writers and others frequently reminded Shedd of his earlier speech before the Labor Lyceum, reprinted in the *Rochester Union and Advertiser*, 26 November 1906.

38. *Rochester Times*, 14 December 1909, 16 December 1909; *Rochester Post Express*, 29 December 1909; and *Rochester Union and Advertiser*, 10 March 1909.

39. *Rochester Herald*, 30 November 1909. The Reverend A. M. O'Neill's commentary on the centers is in the *Rochester Times*, 29 November 1909. The *Rochester Post Express* support for O'Neill's stand can be found in 29 December 1909. Ward's rebuttal was reprinted in several places, including the *Rochester Union and Advertiser*, 1 February 1910.

40. *Rochester Union and Advertiser*, 3 February 1910; *Rochester Post Express*, 1 February 1910; and *Rochester Times*, 18 December 1909.

41. The Rochester newspapers were filled with editorials and comment on the activities of these organizations in February 1910. For a listing of these groups and proof of their long support for the centers, see the *Rochester Times* and the *Rochester Post Express*, 4 February 1910. Also consult *Rochester Union and Advertiser*, 25 June 1910.

42. *Rochester Democrat and Chronicle*, 9 February 1911; Blake McKelvey, *The Quest for Quality*, 106; as well as the numerous newspaper citations for early February 1910.

43. Edward J. Ward, "There are Other Rochesters," *The Common Good* 7 (April 1914): 101.

44. *Social Democratic Herald*, 7 May 1910, 23 July 1910, and 29 October 1910; and *History of the Social Democratic Victories* (Milwaukee: Social Democratic Publishing, 1911), 51–52.

45. *Toledo Evening Bee*, 28 September 1898, 25 October 1898, 11 November 1898, and 2 April 1910. The remaining documentation is in 29 September 1898, 21 January 1901, 28 February 1901, 12 January 1902; and the *Toledo News-Bee*, 16 November 1904.

46. *Toledo Evening Bee*, 7 January 1900 and 17 January 1900; *Toledo Blade*, 8 January 1900, 19 January 1900, 22 January 1900, and 29 January 1900. On 21

January 1901, the editor of the *Bee* wrote: "It is difficult to recall any venture in the history of Toledo that has met with such tremendous success as has the Complete Education League's scheme of giving free concerts every Saturday night throughout the winter."

47. *Toledo Blade*, 10 August 1902, 12 February 1900, and 5 May 1902. While the running quarrels can be sketched from the *Toledo Board of Education Minutes* (1899–1903, at the Center for Archival Research), they are more accessible in the *Toledo Evening Bee*, 23 November 1899, 7 January 1900, 17 January 1900, 23 January 1900, 28 February 1900, 29 March 1900, 7 April 1900, 13 April 1900, 17 April 1900, 13 February 1901, and 19 November 1901 ("Golden Rule Movement Is Tramped Upon.").

48. Guitteau's life is evaluated in William J. Reese, "William Backus Guitteau and Educational Reform in Toledo during the Progressive Era" (master's thesis, Bowling Green State University, 1975).

49. The ramifications of the Smith Law were widespread and the subject of considerable newspaper coverage in the *Toledo Blade*, 23 May 1911, 19 July 1911, 7 February 1913, 15 February 1913, 17 April 1913; and the *Toledo News-Bee*, 3 June 1912, 8 July 1913, 16 February 1914 through 18 February 1914, and 16 June 1914. The remaining documentation is in *Toledo Blade*, 4 April 1912, 7 May 1912, 12 October 1912, 26 November 1913; and *Toledo News-Bee*, 18 March 1913, 24 November 1913, and 26 November 1913.

50. Although Milwaukee has some excellent standard histories, like Bayrd Still's *Milwaukee: The History of a City* (Madison: State Historical Society of Wisconsin, 1948), it lacks a strong interpretive history of the schools. One useful starting point is William Lamers, *Our Roots Grow Deep* (Milwaukee: Milwaukee Public Schools, 1974). Also see William J. Reese, "'Partisans of the Proletariat': The Socialist Working Class and the Milwaukee Schools, 1890–1920," *History of Education Quarterly* 21 (Spring 1981): 3–50.

51. *Social Democratic Herald*, 17 May 1902.

52. *Milwaukee Leader*, 3 June 1914 and 15 January 1916; and *Milwaukee Free Press*, 1 April 1912. For the background of Wisconsin and Milwaukee center policy, examine "Social Center Work in Wisconsin," *Playground* 4 (September 1910): 219–20; and "Social Centers in Milwaukee," *Survey* 28 (18 May 1912): 298–99. The Social Democrats had endorsed the free and unlimited use of the neighborhood schools by the community since the turn of the century, when it became a prominent part of their municipal platform. A small sampling of their support can be gleaned from the *Social Democratic Herald*, 22 February 1902, 26 April 1902, 17 May 1902, 7 February 1903, 12 March 1904, 10 September 1904, 3 February 1906, 23 October 1909, 7 May 1910, 28 May 1910; and the *Milwaukee Leader*, 8 February 1912, 16 March 1912, 22 March 1912, 5 October 1912, 14 October 1913, and 3 November 1913 ("School Center Is Again Given Strong Impetus").

53. Though precise documentation is from the *Milwaukee School Proceedings* and the *Annual Reports*, a useful and more easily accessible sketch of the local movement is in "Social Center Work in Milwaukee," *Charities and the Commons* 21 (19 December 1909): 441–42. On the Federation of Civic Societies, see the *Proceedings*, 5 January 1909.

54. "Recreation Centers," *Playground* 6 (April 1912): 26. H. O. Berg was quoted in H. B. Dine, "The Social Center and the Immigrant," *Playground* 9 (February 1917): 459. Also see Berg, "Staying After School," *Survey* 37 (16 December 1916): 298–300, who explained how closely many activities were supervised at the local centers. Also see "Milwaukee's Recreation Movement," *Survey* 25 (18 February 1911): 832–33; Duane Mowry, "Social and Recreational Activity in Milwaukee," *American City* 6 (May 1912): 748–50; and Mowry, "Use of School Buildings for Other than School Purposes," *Education* 29 (October 1908): 92–96.

55. *Proceedings of the Milwaukee School Board*, 30 June 1909 and 30 June 1911.

56. On the Russian Self Education Club, consult the *Proceedings of the Milwaukee School Board*, 7 December 1909; on the other groups, see *Milwaukee Leader*, 25 April 1913.

57. *Milwaukee Free Press*, 7 March 1909 and 16 November 1913. For more details on community activities and neighborhood use at this particular school, see the *Milwaukee Daily News*, 16 January 1908, 11 February 1908, 22 February 1908, 27 February 1908, 13 March 1908; and *Proceedings of the Milwaukee School Board*, 2 June 1908, 30 June 1908, 1 September 1908.

58. Berg, "Staying After School," 300; and *Milwaukee Leader*, 16 April 1915.

59. Berg, "Staying After School," 298. On the popularity of Milwaukee's social centers, see Berg's "Public Schools as Municipal Neighborhood Recreation Centers," *American City* 16 (January 1917): 40, where he stated: "Our school halls, having a seating capacity of from four to eleven hundred, are taxed nearly to their fullest capacity and often people must be turned away."

60. Glueck, *The Community Use of Schools*, 18–26; and *Milwaukee School Report*, 1906, 76.

61. *The Social Center in Kansas City, Missouri* (Kansas City: Research Bureau of the Board of Public Welfare, 1913), 3–8.

62. *Kansas City School Report*, 1904, 107; and *Labor Herald*, 1 December 1911.

63. The best local publications on the social centers are the previously cited *The Social Center in Kansas City, Missouri; Fourth Annual Report of the Board of Public Welfare* (Kansas City, 1913), 41; and *Fifth Annual Report of the Board of Public Welfare* (Kansas City, 1915), 23–30.

Chapter 8

1. See the selections on Horace Mann's educational beliefs in Lawrence A. Cremin, ed., *The Republic and the School* (New York: Teachers College, Columbia University, 1957); and concerns over children's health and infant schools in Carl F. Kaestle and Maris A. Vinovskis, *Education and Social Change in Nineteenth-Century Massachusetts* (Cambridge: Cambridge University Press, 1980), chap. 3.

2. More documentation is listed later in the chapter, but examine "Facts about Vaccination," *Independent* 63 (12 September 1907): 642.

3. C. E. A. Winslow, "Poverty as a Factor in Disease," *Proceedings of the National Conference of Social Work* (1919): 154.

4. Ernest Bryant Hoag and Lewis M. Terman, *Health Work in the Schools*

(Boston: Houghton Mifflin, 1914), 4. Terman was the author of the chapter from which this quote was selected. Also see Luther H. Gulick and Leonard P. Ayers, *Medical Inspection of Schools* (New York: Charities Publication Committee, 1908), 202; and E. F. Brown, "A Firmer Physical Foundation for Education," *School and Society* 2 (9 October 1915): 505.

5. L. B. Blan, "Are We Taking Proper Care of the Health of Our Children?" *Pedagogical Seminary* 13 (1912): 220. Also see H. M. Bracken, "Health Administration of Schools," *Journal of Proceedings and Addresses of the N.E.A.* (1914): 677.

6. Quoted in John Spargo, *Underfed School Children* (Chicago: Charles H. Kerr, 1906), 5.

7. J. Kent, "Shall the State Maintain Its Children?" *Justice* 26 (1899): 4.

8. *Rochester Socialist*, 1 January 1908; and *Rochester Union and Advertiser*, 20 October 1902.

9. *Toledo Union*, 13 November 1897; *Socialist*, 12 August 1905 and 7 October 1905; and *Toledo Evening Bee*, 16 October 1909.

10. *Social Democratic Herald*, 25 September 1909; and FTC *Minutes*, 4 August 1909. Socialist support for state aid for school meals is documented in the *Social Democratic Herald*, 15 February 1902, 12 May 1906, 17 April 1909, 29 May 1909, 7 August 1909, 25 September 1909, 2 October 1909, 28 January 1911, 11 March 1911; *Milwaukee Leader*, 15 March 1913, 22 March 1913, 5 March 1915, 30 March 1915, 30 March 1917; and Meta Berger, unpublished autobiography, 54.

11. *People's Advocate*, 10 April 1902.

12. *Labor Herald*, 5 February 1904; and *Missouri Staats-Zeitung*, 21 May 1909.

13. Robert Hunter, *Poverty* (reprint, New York: Harper & Row, 1965), 191. His position was reiterated in "The Social Significance of Underfed Children," *International Quarterly* 12 (June 1906): 342; also see John Spargo, *The Bitter Cry of the Children* (reprint, New York: Quadrangle Books, 1968), 58; and Spargo, "Underfed Children in Our Public Schools," *Independent* 58 (11 May 1905): 1060–63.

14. Relevant literature includes William Leuchtenberg, "Progressivism and Imperialism," *Mississippi Valley Historical Review* 39 (December 1952): 483–504; William Appleman Williams, *The Contours of American History* (Cleveland: World, 1961); Thomas J. McCormick, *China Market* (Chicago: Quadrangle, 1967); John Morton Blum, *Woodrow Wilson and the Politics of Morality* (Boston: Little, Brown, 1956); and N. G. Levin, *Woodrow Wilson and World Politics* (New York: Oxford University Press, 1968).

15. See Gulick and Ayres, *Medical Inspection*, chaps. 1 and 12.

16. J. Taylor, "Free Schools," *Justice* 1 (1884): 2; and William T. Stead, "'Food-Aided Education': Experiments in Paris, London, and Birmingham." *Review of Reviews* 3 (July 1891): 618.

17. Hunter, *Poverty*, 216; and "The Hunger Problem in the Public Schools—What a Canvas of Six Big Cities Reveals," *Philadelphia North American*, 21 May 1905.

18. E. L. Lattimore, "School Lunches," *The Common Good* 5 (April 1912): 19; *Toledo Blade*, 6 October 1908, 4 November 1908; and *Toledo News-Bee*, 11 March 1912 and 3 November 1909.

19. *Milwaukee Free Press*, 21 October 1906 and 5 March 1911.

20. *Missouri Staats-Zeitung*, 6 April 1906: and the paper's interest in Robert Hunter's investigation on underfed children, 5 January 1906. Also see R. H. Platt, "A Consideration of State Intervention in the Field of Charity," *Proceedings of the National Conference of Charities and Correction* (1908): 21; and *New York Times*, 11 June 1909.

21. *Proceedings of the Sixth Triennial of the Council of Jewish Women* (Chicago: Toby Rubovits, 1911), 564; William J. Reese, "Between Home and School: Organized Parents, Clubwomen, and Urban Education in the Progressive Era," *School Review* 87 (November 1978): 3–28; and L. S. Bryant, *School Feeding: Its History and Practice at Home and Abroad* (Philadelphia: J. B. Lippincott, 1913), 180.

22. C. Hunt, "The Daily Meals of School Children," *U.S. Bureau of Education Bulletin*, no. 3 (Washington, D.C., 1909): 13, 21–23; L. A. Osbourne, "The School Luncheon," *Pedagogical Seminary* 19 (June 1912): 204–17; Bryant, *School Feeding*, 164; *Rochester Democrat and Chronicle*, 11 April 1895; *Women's Educational and Industrial Union Scrapbook*, 1897; *Yearbook of the Women's Educational Industrial Union, 1896–1897* (Rochester, 1897), 5, 25–26 (WEIU Papers); and K. T. Hodge, *History of Women's Educational and Industrial Union*, typescript, n.d., 10–11. (Rochester Public Library, Rochester, New York).

23. *Toledo Evening Bee*, 12 November 1905. Also see the muckraking essay in the *Toledo News-Bee*, 17 November 1904.

24. *Toledo Blade*, 15 November 1904; *Toledo News-Bee* and the *Toledo Blade*, 24 January 1908. On Steinem, see the *Bee* and the *Blade*, 8 December 1908.

25. *Toledo Evening Bee*, 12 December 1908 and 4 February 1909. On the selection of particular schools, see the *Toledo Blade*, 4 November 1908.

26. *Milwaukee Daily News*, 29 October 1904. The nutrition project's origins can be traced in the *Milwaukee Sentinel*, 1 October 1904, 1 November 1904; in the *Milwaukee Free Press*, 1 October 1904, 1 November 1904; and in the *News*, 1 November 1904, 16 February 1905, 19 February 1905, and 4 February 1906. Also see Mrs. Duane Mowry, "Penny Lunches in Milwaukee Public Schools," *American City* 4 (June 1911): 283–85.

27. This information is drawn from the *Milwaukee Daily News*, 1 December 1906, 30 March 1906, 13 April 1907, 1 February 1908, 25 February 1908, 17 April 1909; *Milwaukee Sentinel*, 15 January 1907, 31 October 1907, 30 November 1907; and *Milwaukee School Proceedings*, 4 February 1908.

28. For useful introductions to the implementation of school meals, see Bryant, *School Feeding*; Hunt, "Daily Meals"; and J. C. Gebhart, *Malnutrition and School Feeding* (Washington, D.C.: U.S. Bureau of Education, Department of Interior, 1922). The documentation on the role of women's groups and school meals is extensive. See, for example, M. E. L. Small, "Elementary School Lunches under School Department Direction, Buffalo, New York," *Journal of Home Economics* 4 (December 1912): 490–92; Small, "Educational and Social Possibilities of School Lunches," *Journal of Home Economics* 6 (December 1914): 432–39; and "School Lunches in New York City," *School and Society* 11 (3 January 1920): 20.

29. *Annual Report for 1910 of the Chief Medical Officer of the Board of Education* (London: Published by His Majesty's Stationery Office, 1911), 253; P. D. Winder, *The Public Feeding of Elementary School Children: A Review of the General Situation,*

and an Inquiry into the Birmingham Experience (London: Longmans, Green, 1913), 18, 24; and M. E. Bulkey, *The Feeding of School Children* (London: G. Bell & Sons, 1914), 59–76, 219–29.

30. *Toledo News-Bee*, 23 November 1909.

31. *Milwaukee Leader*, 5 March 1915 and 13 February 1917; and Benjamin J. Blied, *Three Archbishops of Milwaukee* (Milwaukee: 1955), 133.

32. *Social Democratic Herald*, 2 October 1909.

33. L. S. Bryant, "The School Feeding Movement," *Psychological Clinic* 6 (April 1912): 37; E. M. Sill, "Dietary Studies of Undernourished School Children in New York City," *Journal of the American Medical Association* (November 1909): 1890. Cf. "A Study of Malnutrition in the School Child," *Journal of the American Medical Association* (November 1909): 713; and C. G. Kerley, quoted in Sills, *Milwaukee*, 1891. Also see Bryant, "The School Feeding Movement," 37.

34. *Toledo Union Leader*, 24 January 1908.

35. "Medical Inspection of School Children," *Charities* 16 (17 April 1906): 3–4.

36. Leonard P. Ayres, "What American Cities Are Doing for the Health of School Children," *Annals of the American Academy* 37 (March 1911): 499; and D. V. McClure, "Medical Inspection of Schools," *American Education* 14 (February 1911): 252.

37. A. T. S., "The Public Schools as a Center of Social Service," *Education* 25 (Fall 1905): 378; "The Physician in the School," *Nation* 85 (29 August 1907): 180; and "Health in the Public Schools," *Nation* 87 (21 January 1909): 56, where the editor argues that "the good old virtues of industry and punctuality are still more effective at school than an operation for adenoids," Also consult J. D. Stewart, "Medical Inspections of School Children," *Proceedings of the National Conference on Charities and Correction* 37 (1910): 197. For other expressions of this view, consult G. W. Wharton, "Health of School Children," *Outlook* 84 (November 17, 1906): 662–66; L. D. Wald, "Medical Inspection of Public Schools," *Annals of the American Academy* 25 (March 1905): 290–98; and "The Physical Examination of School Children," *American Education* 14 (April 1911): 346.

38. J. D. Cronin, "The Doctor in the Public Schools," *Review of Reviews* 35 (April 1907): 439; L. H. Wild, "The Relation of Health to Efficiency," *Education* 33 (December 1912): 212; Brown, "A Firmer Physical Foundation," 505; and Walter S. Cornell, *Health and Medical Inspection of School Children* (Philadelphia: F. A. Davis, 1912).

39. Cronin, "The Doctor," 440. For an understanding of the eugenics movement, examine Mark Haller's *Eugenics* (New Brunswick: Rutgers University Press, 1963); and Clarence Karier, "Testing for Order and Control in the Corporate Liberal State," in Clarence Karier, Paul Violas, and Joel Spring, *Roots of Crisis* (Chicago: Rand McNally College Publishing, 1973), 108–37. Also see Russell Marks, *The Idea of I.Q.* (Washington, D.C.: University Press of America, 1981).

40. "The Physician in the School," 180. Verbal attacks on parents were commonplace, as evidenced in S. Burrage, "Medical Inspection of School Children," *Journal of Proceedings and Addresses of the N.E.A.* 37 (1898): 540; Walter S. Cornell, "Physical Care of Children," *Annals of the American Academy* 37 (March 1911):

487–93; "Health Improvement a Duty of the School," *American Education* 21 (June 1918): 480, 490.

41. W. B. Powell, "Medical Inspection of Schools," *Journal of Proceedings and Addresses of the N.E.A.* (1898): 458–59; J. B. Cronin, "School Children and their Medical Supervision," *Charities* 16 (7 April 1906): 61; "The Physician in the School," 80; and J. R. Schmidt, "Filling Teeth to Cure Dullness," *Technical World* 19 (July 1913): 738–39.

42. *Rochester Union and Advertiser*, 15 March 1901, 16 March 1901, 26 March 1901, 11 April 1901, 31 January 1905; *Proceedings of the Rochester School Board*, 11 April 1901; and these essays by George Goler: "Medical School Inspection—a Way to Child Welfare," *Proceedings of the National Conference of Charities and Correction* 38 (1911): 98–103; "Medical Inspection in Rochester," *American City* 9 (October 1913): 317–20; "The School as a Health Center," *The Common Good* 5 (July 1912): 21–23; "Medical School Inspection," 99; and M. C. Goodwin, "The School Nurse," *The Common Good* 4 (February 1911): 15–16.

43. *Toledo Evening Bee*, 19 November 1901, 20 November 1901, 26 February 1908; *Toledo Blade*, 19 November 1901, 6 December 1907, 7 December 1909, and 17 May 1910. On Milwaukee, see the numerous annual reports by medical inspectors in the *Milwaukee School Reports*, as well as *Medical Inspection in the Schools of Milwaukee* (Milwaukee: Milwaukee City Club Committee on Public Health, 1919), 1–16 (Rare Pamphlet Collection, State Historical Society of Wisconsin). On Kansas City, see the *Kansas City School Report*, 1910, 33–34; *Kansas City and Its Schools* (Kansas City: Prepared for the Members of the Department of Superintendence of the N.E.A., 1917), 10–11, 59; and M. A. Brown, "Health Program in the Kansas City Schools, 1919–1921," *Elementary School Journal* 22 (October 1921), 132–39.

44. Lattimore, "School Lunches," 19; and *Toledo School Report*, 1911, 55.

45. *Milwaukee School Report*, 1913, 167–72; and "The Dental Clinic," in *Milwaukee School Report*, 1911, 82; *Toledo School Report*, 1911, 55; and Lattimore, "School Lunches," 19.

46. J. Sobel, "Prejudices and Superstitions Met within the Medical Inspection of School Children," in *Fourth International Congress on School Hygiene* (Buffalo: Courier Company of Buffalo, 1914), 4:78; and Terman, *Health Work*, 12.

47. Cornell, *Health and Medical Inspection*, 73, 75.

48. *Toledo News-Bee*, 18 January 1907; *Rochester Socialist*, 17 January 1908; and George Goler, "The School as a Health Center," 23–24.

49. Cornell, *Health Work in the Schools*, 73–74.

50. M. Cominsky, "Report of the Fourth Ward School Nurse," *The Common Good* 6 (October 1913): 7.

51. J. W. Hodge, "Vaccination an Empirical Art," *Arena* 38 (December 1907): 664; and "Anti-Vaccinationists," *Outlook* 96 (October 22, 1910): 365.

52. *Kansas City Mail*, 6 January 1893; and W. B. Hidden, "Dangers of Vaccination," *North American Review* 159 (July 1894): 125.

53. *Rochester Democrat and Chronicle*, 9 September 1894. The details of the case are conveniently found in an article in the *Rochester Union and Advertiser*, 4 December 1912.

54. *Toledo Evening Bee,* 21 January 1903. The details on boycotts and trouble in the Lagrange area in particular are sketched in the *Bee,* 15 January 1902, 16 January 1902, 30 September 1902, 1 October 1902, 23 January 1903; and *Toledo Blade,* 20 January 1903, 26 January 1903, and 5 February 1903.

55. *Toledo Evening Bee,* 21 January 1903; *Toledo Blade,* 5 January 1914 and 27 January 1914. The boycott can be traced in the *Blade,* 16 December 1913, 5 January 1914, 6 January 1914, 16 January 1914, 17 January 1914, 19 January 1914, and 26 January 1914; and *Toledo News-Bee,* 2 January 1914, 3 January 1914, 5 January 1914, 17 January 1914, and 19 January 1914.

56. Karier, "Testing."

57. Leonard Ayres's findings in *Open-Air Schools* (New York: Doubleday, Page, 1910), were compatible with local appraisals in many cities.

58. C. Creighton, "Vaccination: A Scientific Study," *Arena* 2 (September 1890): 422; and John C. Burnham, "Medical Specialists and Movements toward Social Control in the Progressive Era," in Jerry Israel, ed., *Building the Organizational Society* (New York: Free Press, 1972), 23.

59. *Toledo News-Bee,* 14 March 1917; City Club of Milwaukee, *Medical Inspection,* 11; and Brown, "Health Program," 137.

Chapter 9

1. See especially the pertinent essays in Clarence J. Karier, Paul C. Violas, and Joel H. Spring, eds., *Roots of Crisis* (Chicago: Rand McNally College Publishing, 1973); and Joel H. Spring, "Psychologists and the War: The Meaning of Intelligence in the Alpha and Beta Tests," *History of Education Quarterly* 12 (Spring 1972): 3–15.

2. *Toledo Union,* 12 June 1897; and *Toledo Union Leader,* 24 May 1912 and 12 November 1915.

3. FTC *Minutes,* 16 June 1915. Antiwar and pacifist sentiment across the country was well documented in the *Milwaukee Leader* throughout the war years.

4. FTC *Minutes,* 4 June 1916.

5. L. P. Todd, *Wartime Relations of the Federal Government and the Public Schools, 1917–1918* (New York: Teachers College, Columbia University, 1945), 85. Also see the *Toledo Union Leader,* 24 May 1912.

6. Women's organizations did not condone war and often attacked its glorification by some citizens. Yet they often cited the past role of women in caring for the diseased and the downcast members of society. They always emphasized that men rather than women caused wars. On the domestic environment during the war, see Blake McKelvey, *Rochester: The Quest for Quality, 1890–1925* (Cambridge: Harvard University Press, 1965), chap. 10; and John M. Killits, *Toledo and Lucas County, Ohio, 1623–1923* (Chicago: S. J. Clarke, 1923), 1:201–09; H. C. Peterson and G. C. Fite, *Opponents of War, 1917–1918* (Seattle: University of Washington Press, 1957); Robert K. Murray, *Red Scare: A Study of National Hysteria, 1919–1920* (New York: McGraw Hill, 1955); David P. Thelen, *Robert M. La Follette and the Insurgent Spirit* (Boston: Little, Brown, 1976); Paul L. Murphy, *World War I and the Origin of Civil Liberties in the United States* (New York: Norton, 1979); and David

Kennedy, *Over Here: The First World War and American Society* (New York: Oxford University Press, 1980).

7. *Toledo Blade*, 22 February 1916. The plan was described in *Toledo Blade*, 8 February 1916. Labor opposition was also registered in the *Toledo Union Leader*, 18 February 1916, 3 March 1916, and 10 March 1916. Also read the *Toledo News-Bee*, 28 April 1917.

8. On Sherwood, see the *Toledo Union Leader*, 12 November 1915; *Toledo News-Bee*, 7 March 1917; and *Toledo Blade*, 7 January 1916, 10 February 1916; and 10 November 1916.

9. *Toledo Blade*, 17 March 1916; *Toledo News-Bee*, 14 February 1917; and 9 March 1917. The Nearing controversy can be traced very easily in the *Toledo Blade*, 6 April 1916, 13 October 1916, 9 April 1917; in the *Toledo Union Leader*, 9 June 1916, 16 March 1917, 23 March 1917, 13 April 1917; and in the *News-Bee*, 14 February 1917, 10 March 1917, and 12 March 1917.

10. *Toledo Blade*, 11 September 1914 and 20 March 1919; *Toledo News-Bee*, 5 July 1917, 10 October 1917, 19 October 1917, 24 October 1917, and 26 October 1917. On Guitteau and the committee, examine the *Toledo Blade* for 19 March 1917, 21 March 1917, and 5 April 1917.

11. *Toledo News-Bee*, 21 May 1917; *Toledo Blade*, 29 March 1918; and *Toledo Union Leader*, 14 September 1917.

12. *Milwaukee Sentinel*, 8 March 1918 and 27 March 1918; and Meta Berger, unpublished autobiography, 59–60.

13. The war-related tensions in Milwaukee are described and analyzed in L. L. Cary, "The Wisconsin Loyalty Legion, 1917–1918," *Wisconsin Magazine of History* 53 (Autumn 1969): 33–50; William D. Bruce, *I Was Born in America* (Milwaukee: 1937), chap. 17; and Sally Miller, *Victor Berger and the Promise of Constructive Socialism* (Westport, Conn.: Greenwood Press, 1973), chap. 9. Also see the letters from the civic secretary of the City Club to C. N. Waldron, 23 January 1917, which explains that war subjects, like religious topics, were taboo (City Club of Milwaukee Papers). Also see Oscar Ameringer, *If You Don't Weaken* (New York: Henry Holt, 1940), 305, 323–24; and see, for example, the following letters: M. K. Whitnall (S.D.P. Branch 21) to Victor Berger, August 29, 1914; Bohemian Branch "Volnost" to Victor Berger, February 1916; and Victor Berger to A. Jecmen, 16 February 1916 (Social Democratic Party Collection, Milwaukee County Historical Society, Milwaukee, Wisconsin).

14. *Milwaukee School Proceedings*, 30 June 1916. The *Milwaukee Leader* described the explosive scene on the following day. Also see the *Milwaukee Sentinel*, 1 July 1916.

15. *Milwaukee Leader*, 20 February 1917; and *Milwaukee Sentinel*, 23 March 1917. The *Milwaukee Sentinel* and many antisocialists enjoyed the war-related work and the defeats of the Social Democrats immeasurably. See the *Sentinel* on 7 February 1917, 4 April 1917, 14 February 1918, and 6 April 1918. In the last newspaper account cited, "Kiddies in the City in Loyalty Parade," the paper described the parade at the Detroit Street School in the heart of "Little Italy." Marching to the beat of fife and drum, "the children marched by fours, carrying flags, Liberty Loan posters, and other patriotic slogans." On the curtailment of

social center use and charges of sedition, consult the *Milwaukee School Proceedings,* 2 October 1917, 14 December 1917, and 2 January 1918.

16. *Milwaukee Sentinel,* 12 October 1917.

17. *Milwaukee Sentinel,* 2 July 1917.

18. These activities can be traced in the *Milwaukee School Proceedings* during the war years. Elizabeth Thomas's actions are covered in the *Milwaukee Leader,* 17 October 1917; and are more critically analyzed in the *Milwaukee Sentinel,* 18 October 1917. On Meta Berger, see her unpublished autobiography, 60.

19. *Milwaukee Leader,* 6 March 1918.

20. *Milwaukee Sentinel,* 8 November 1918; and E. Muzik, "Victor Berger: Congress and the Red Scare," *Wisconsin Magazine of History* 47 (Summer 1964): 309–39.

21. *Milwaukee School Proceedings,* 30 June 1919.

22. "1932 Municipal Platform of Socialist Party of Milwaukee," in Daniel Hoan, *City Government: The Record of the Milwaukee Experiment* (Westport, Conn: Greenwood Press, c. 1974), 336–38.

Bibliography

Because of the numerous community organizations and social reforms examined in this book, it is impossible to provide a comprehensive bibliography for national materials as well as for Kansas City, Milwaukee, Rochester, and Toledo. Instead of attempting to do so, I have provided an introduction to the historical literature and the most important sources of each city. The endnotes provided after each chapter present more complete sources.

For the local level, I examined for each of the four cities at least the major Democratic and Republican newspapers for each day between 1890 and 1920. They were supplemented by labor papers, Socialist papers, and other weekly and daily newspapers on particular subjects. Together with available manuscript collections, newspapers were the most important source in reconstructing the political and social organizations that implemented many Progressive school reforms. School reports, minutes, and proceedings are listed for each individual city.

To provide a wider understanding of national trends in social and political reform in the Progressive era, I tried to read broadly on such reforms as lunch programs, social centers, playgrounds, vacation schools, medical inspection, and other innovations. For the women's movement, I read the *Proceedings of the General Federation of Women's Clubs* (1893–1920), the *Proceedings of the National Council of Jewish Women* (1893–1920), and numerous periodicals that shed light on women and social reform.

Periodical literature for the Progressive era contains a gold mine of information on community organizations and school innovations. Space limitations prevent listing the various articles, which are contained in the endnotes of individual chapters. Consistently, the most valuable magazines and journals were the following:

American City
American Education
Annals of the American Academy
Arena
Charities and the Commons

Child-Welfare Magazine
Education
Educational Review
Elementary School Teacher
The Forum
Independent
International Socialist Review
Journal of Education
Journal of Home Economics
Ladies' Home Journal
Municipal Affairs
The Nation
National Education Association, Proceedings and Addresses
North American Review
The Outlook
Pedagogical Seminary
The Playground
Psychological Clinic
Review of Reviews
School and Home Education
School and Society
School Review
Teachers' College Record
U.S. Bureau of Education Bulletins
World's Work

Articles and Books

Ayres, Leonard P. *Open-Air Schools*. New York: Doubleday, Page, 1910.
Bell, Daniel. *Marxian Socialism in the United States*. Princeton: Princeton University Press, 1967.
Blair, Karen J. *The Clubwoman as Feminist: True Womanhood Redefined, 1868–1914*. New York: Holmes & Meyer, 1980.
Bowles, Samuel, and Herbert Gintis. *Schooling in Capitalist America*. New York: Basic Books, 1976.
Buenker, John D. *Urban Liberalism and Progressive Reform*. New York: W. W. Norton, 1978.
Buenker, John D., John C. Burnham and Robert M. Crunden. *Progressivism*. Cambridge, Mass.: Schenkman, 1977.
Buhle, Mary Jo. *Women and American Socialism, 1870–1920*. Urbana: University of Illinois Press, 1981.
Bullough, William A. *Cities and Schools in the Gilded Age*. Port Washington, N.Y.: Kennikat Press, 1974.
Butterworth, Julian. *The Parent-Teacher Association and Its Work*. New York: Macmillan, 1928.

Callahan, Raymond E. *Education and the Cult of Efficiency*. Chicago: University of Chicago Press, 1962.

Cavallo, Dominick. *Muscles and Morals: Organized Playgrounds and Moral Reform, 1880–1920*. Philadelphia: University of Pennsylvania Press, 1981.

Cohen, Ronald D., and Raymond A. Mohl. *The Paradox of Progressive Education*. Port Washington, N.Y.: Kennikat Press, 1979.

Conway, Jill. "Women Reformers in American Culture, 1870–1930." *Journal of Social History* 5 (1971–72): 164–82.

Cremin, Lawrence A. *The Transformation of the School: Progressivism in American Education*. New York: Random House, 1961.

Crunden, Robert M. *Ministers of Reform: The Progressives' Achievement in American Civilization, 1888–1920*. New York: Basic Books, 1982.

Dancis, B. "Socialism and Women in the United States, 1900–1917." *Socialist Revolution* 27 (January-December 1976): 81–144.

Davis, Allen F. *Spearheads for Reform: The Social Settlements and the Progressive Movement*. New York: Oxford University Press, 1967.

Dorr, Rheta Childe. *What Eight Million Women Want*. Boston: Small, Maynard, 1910.

Dutton, Samuel T., and David Snedden. *The Administration of Public Education in the United States*. New York: Macmillan, 1908.

Ebner, Michael H., and Eugene M. Tobin, eds. *The Age of Urban Reform*. Port Washington, N.Y.: Kennikat Press, 1977.

Edwards, Richard. *Contested Terrain: The Transformation of the Workplace in the Twentieth Century*. New York: Basic Books, 1979.

Fink, Leon. *Workingmen's Democracy: The Knights of Labor and American Politics*. Urbana: University of Illinois Press, 1983.

Frisch, Michael H., and Daniel J. Walkowitz, eds. *Working-Class America: Essays on Labor, Community, and American Society*. Urbana: University of Illinois Press, 1983.

Goodwyn, Lawrence. *Democratic Promise: The Populist Moment in America*. New York: Oxford University Press, 1976.

Gould, Lewis L., ed. *The Progressive Era*. Syracuse: Syracuse University Press, 1974.

Gulick, Luther H., and Leonard P. Ayres. *Medical Inspection of Schools*. New York: Charities Publication Committee, 1908.

Haber, Samuel. *Efficiency and Uplift*. Chicago: University of Chicago Press, 1964.

Hammack, David C. *Power and Society: Greater New York at the Turn of the Century*. New York: Russell Sage Foundation, 1982.

Hays, Samuel P. *The Response to Industrialism, 1885–1914*. Chicago: University of Chicago Press, 1957.

———. "The Politics of Reform of Municipal Government in the Progressive Era." *Pacific Northwest Quarterly* 40 (October 1964): 153–64.

———. *American Political History as Social Analysis*. Knoxville: University of Tennessee Press, 1980.

Hoag, Ernest Bryant, and Lewis M. Terman. *Health Work in the Schools*. Boston: Houghton Mifflin, 1914.

Hofstadter, Richard. *The Age of Reform: From Byran to F.D.R.* New York: Vintage Books, 1955.

Hunter, Robert. *Poverty.* New York: Harper & Row, c. 1965.

Jones, Gareth S. "Class Expression Versus Social Control? A Critique of Recent Trends in the Social History of Leisure." *History Workshop* 4 (Autumn 1977): 162–70.

Kaestle, Carl F., and Maris Vinovskis. *Education and Social Change in Nineteenth-Century Massachusetts.* Cambridge: Cambridge University Press, 1980.

Karier, Clarence J., Paul C. Violas, and Joel H. Spring. *Roots of Crisis.* Chicago: Rand McNally College Publishing, 1973.

Katz, Michael B. *The Irony of Early School Reform: Educational Innovation in Mid-Nineteenth Century Massachusetts.* Boston: Beacon Press, 1968.

Keller, Morton. *Affairs of State: Public Life in Late Nineteenth Century America.* Cambridge: Harvard University Press, Belknap Press, 1977.

Kolko, Gabriel. *The Triumph of Conservatism.* Chicago: Quadrangle Books, 1963.

Krug, Edward A. *The Shaping of the American High School, 1880–1920.* Madison: University of Wisconsin Press, 1969.

Kutler, Stanley I., and Stanley N. Katz, eds. *The Promise of American History.* Baltimore: Johns Hopkins University Press, 1982.

Lazerson, Marvin. *Origins of the Urban School: Public Education in Massachusetts, 1870–1915.* Cambridge: Harvard University Press, 1971.

Leslie, W. Bruce. "Coming of Age in Urban America: The Socialist Alternative, 1901–1920." *Teachers College Record* 85 (Spring 1984): 459–76.

Mergen, Bernard. *Play and Playthings: A Reference Guide.* Westport, Conn.: Greenwood Press, 1982.

Miliband, Ralph. *The State in Capitalist Society.* New York: Basic Books, 1969.

Nearing, Scott. *The New Education: A Review of Progressive Educational Movements.* Chicago: Row, Peterson, 1915.

O'Neill, William L. *Everyone Was Brace: A History of Feminism in America.* New York: Quadrangle Books, 1969.

Perry, Clarence A. *Wider Use of the School Plant.* New York: Charities Publication Committee, 1910.

Quint, Howard H. *The Forging of American Socialism.* Indianapolis: Bobbs-Merrill, 1953.

Rice, Bradley Robert. *Progressive Cities.* Austin: University of Texas Press, 1977.

Schlossman, Steven L. "Before Home Start: Notes Toward a History of Parent Education in America: 1897–1929." *Harvard Educational Review* 46 (August 1976): 436–67.

———. *Love and the American Delinquent: The Theory and Practice of "Progressive" Juvenile Justice, 1825–1920.* Chicago: University of Chicago Press, 1977.

Shannon, Daniel A. *The Socialist Party of America.* Chicago: Quadrangle Books, 1955.

Smith, Timothy. "Progressivism in American Education, 1880–1900." *Harvard Educational Review* 31 (Spring 1969): 168–93.

Spargo, John. *The Bitter Cry of the Children.* New York: Quadrangle Books, c. 1968.

Spring, Joel H. *Education and the Rise of the Corporate State*. Boston: Beacon Press, 1972.

Troen, Selwyn. *The Public and the Schools: Shaping the St. Louis System*. Columbia: University of Missouri Press, 1975.

Tyack, David B. *The One Best System: A History of American Urban Education*. Cambridge: Harvard University Press, 1974.

Urban, Wayne. *Why Teachers Organized*. Detroit: Wayne State University Press, 1982.

Violas, Paul C. *The Training of the Urban Working Class*. Chicago: Rand McNally College Publishing, 1978.

Weinstein, James. *The Corporate Ideal in the Liberal State*. Boston: Beacon Press, 1968.

———. *The Decline of Socialism in America*. New York: Vintage Books, 1969.

Wiebe, Robert H. *The Search for Order, 1877–1920*. New York, Hill & Wang, 1967.

———. "The Social Functions of Public Education." *American Quarterly* 21 (Summer 1969): 147–64.

Wirth, Arthur G. *Education in the Technological Society*. Scranton, Pa.: Intext Education Publishers, 1972.

KANSAS CITY

Articles and Books

Barclay, Thomas S. "The Kansas City Charter of 1875." *Missouri Historical Review* 26 (October 1931): 19–39.

Brown, A. Theodore. *Frontier Community: Kansas City to 1870*. Columbia: University of Missouri Press, 1963.

Brown, A. Theodore, and Lyle W. Dorsett. *K.C.: A History of Kansas City, Missouri*. Boulder, Col.: Pruett, 1978.

Conrad, Howard L. *Encyclopedia of the History of Missouri*. Vols. 3, 5. New York: Southern History, 1901.

Ellis, Roy. *A Civic History of Kansas City, Missouri*. Springfield, Mo.: Press of Elkins-Swyers, 1930.

Greenwood, James M. *Principles of Education Practically Applied*. New York: D. Appleton, 1887.

Griffith, William. *History of Kansas City*. Kansas City: Hudson-Kimberly, 1900.

Haskell, Henry C., Jr., and Richard B. Fowler. *City of the Future: A Narrative History of Kansas City, 1850–1950*. Kansas City: Frank Glenn, 1950.

Hollister, Wilfred R., and Norman Harry. *Five Famous Missourians*. Kansas City: Hudson-Kimberly, 1900.

Imperial Kansas City: 1900. Kansas City: Merchantile Illustrating Company, 1900.

Kansas City and Its Public Schools. Prepared for the Members of the Department of Superintendence of the National Education Association. Kansas City: 1917.

Kansas City Teachers Bulletin, 1920–1929. Kansas City: State Historical Society of
 Missouri.

McCarthy, Mary L. "Recollections of Kansas City, 1866–1916." *Missouri Historical
 Review* 45 (October 1950): 35–46.

McEwen and Dillenback. *Kansas City in 1879.* Kansas City: Press of Ramsey,
 Millett, & Hudson, 1879.

Military Training in the Kansas City High Schools. Kansas City: Birdsall & Miller,
 1881.

Missouri Educator. (State Historical Society of Missouri). 1858–60.

Missouri School Journal. (State Historical Society of Missouri). 1883–1920.

Nagel, Paul C. *Missouri.* New York: W. W. Norton, 1977.

Parrish, William E. *Missouri under Radical Rule, 1865–1870.* Columbia: University
 of Missouri Press, 1965.

Pen and Sunlight Sketches of Kansas City and Environs. Kansas City: Phoenix, 1892.

Phillips, Claude A. "A Century of Education in Missouri." *Missouri Historical
 Review* 15 (January 1921): 298–314.

Shoemaker, Floyd Calvin. *Missouri and Missourians.* Vols. 1–5. Chicago: Lewis,
 1943.

Whitney, Carrie Westlake. *Kansas City, Missouri: Its History and Its People, 1808–
 1908.* Vol. 1. Chicago: S. J. Clarke, 1908.

Wohl, R. Richard, and A. Theodore Brown. "The Usable Past: A Study of Historical
 Traditions in Kansas City." *Huntington Library Quarterly* 23 (May 1960):
 237–59.

Dissertations and Theses

Galloway, Dorothy. "James Mickleborough Greenwood: An Evaluation of His
 Service as an Educator and His Contributions to Educational Thought."
 Master's thesis, Washington University, 1931.

Glauert, Ralph Edward. "Education and Society in Ante-Bellum Missouri." Ph.D.
 diss. University of Missouri-Columbia, 1973.

Hanks, Glen Lester. "The Development of Public School Finance in the Kansas
 City School District." Ed.D. diss., University of Missouri, 1953.

McCorkle, William L. "Nelson's Star and Kansas City, 1880–1898." Ph.D. diss.,
 University of Texas at Austin, 1968.

Oster, Donald Bright. "Community Image in the History of Saint Louis and Kansas
 City." Ph.D. diss., University of Missouri, 1967.

Wagner, Patricia Youmans. "Voluntary Associations in Kansas City, Missouri,
 1870–1900." Ph.D. diss., University of Kansas City, 1962.

Manuscripts

Pertinent manuscripts are found in the Kansas City Public Library (KCPL)
and in the Western Historical Manuscripts Collection (WHMC) on the
University of Missouri-Columbia campus. The Kansas City School Re-

ports, 1869–1920, are located at the Kansas City Public Library and the State Historical Society of Missouri.

James M. Greenwood Papers (KCPL)
Missouri State Federation of Women's Clubs Papers (WHMC)
Robert T. Van Horn Papers (KCPL)

Newspapers

The following newspapers are located at the State Historical Society of Missouri (SHSM) and the State Historical Society of Wisconsin (SHSW).

Kansas City Journal of Commerce, 1864–1910 (SHSM)
Kansas City Labor, 1895 (SHSW)
Kansas City Mail, 1892–1902 (daily) (SHSM)
Kansas City Mail, 1895–1900 (weekly) (SHSM)
Kansas City Press, 1898–1912 (SHSM)
Kansas City Reform, 1900–1901, 1903–1910 (SHSM)
Kansas City Star, 1880–1907 (SHSW, SHSM)
Kansas City Times, 1872–1911 (SHSM)
The Kriterion, 1904–5, 1907 (SHSM)
Labor Herald, 1901 (SHSM)
Labor Herald, 1904–1920 (SHSM)
Midland Mechanic, 1898–1900 (SHSW)
Missouri Staats-Zeitung, 1898–1907, 1909, 1917 (SHSM)
The People's Advocate, 1902 (SHSM)
The Toiler, 1913–1915 (SHSW)

MILWAUKEE

Articles and Books

Ameringer, Oscar. *If You Don't Weaken*. New York: Henry Holt, 1940.
Borun, Thaddeus, ed. *We, the Milwaukee Poles*. Milwaukee: Nowiny, 1946.
Berger, Victor L. *Broadsides*. Milwaukee: Social-Democratic Publishing, 1913.
Blied, Rev. Benjamin J. *Three Archbishops of Milwaukee*. Milwaukee, 1955.
Bruce, William George, ed. *History of Milwaukee, City and County*. Vols. 1–3. Chicago: S. J. Clarke, 1922.
———. *A Short History of Milwaukee*. Milwaukee: Bruce, 1936.
City Club News (State Historical Society of Wisconsin). 1915–20.
Conrad, Howard Louis, ed. *History of Milwaukee*. Vols. 1–3. Chicago: American Biographical Publishing, 1986.

Conzen, Kathleen Neils. *Immigrant Milwaukee, 1836–1860*. Cambridge: Harvard University Press, 1976.

Donnelly, Patrick. "The Milwaukee Public Schools," in J. W. Stearns, ed. *The Columbian History of Education in Wisconsin*. Milwaukee: Press of the Evening Wisconsin Company, 1893.

Flower, Frank A. *History of Milwaukee, Wisconsin*. Vols. 1–2. Chicago: Western Historical Company, 1881.

Gavett, Thomas W. *Development of the Labor Movement in Milwaukee*. Madison: University of Wisconsin Press, 1965.

Gregory, John G. *History of Milwaukee, Wisconsin*. Vols. 1–2. Chicago: S. J. Clarke, 1931.

History of the Milwaukee Social-Democratic Victories. Milwaukee: Social-Democratic Publishing, 1911.

Hoan, Daniel W. *City Government: The Record of the Milwaukee Experiment*. Westport, Conn.: Greenwood Press, c. 1974.

Korman, Gerd. *Industrialization, Immigrants, and Americanizers: The View from Milwaukee, 1866–1921*. Madison: State Historical Society of Wisconsin, 1967.

Lamers, William. *Our Roots Grow Deep*. Milwaukee: Milwaukee Public Schools, 1974.

Marguilies, Herbert F. *The Decline of the Progressive Movement in Wisconsin, 1890–1920*. Madison: State Historical Society of Wisconsin, 1968.

Mears, Louise W. *Life and Times of a Midwest Educator*. Lincoln, Neb.: State Journal Printing, 1944.

Miller, Sally M. *Victor Berger and the Promise of Constructive Socialism, 1910–1920*. Westport, Conn.: Greenwood Press, 1973.

Mooney, Patricia Melvin. "Make Milwaukee Safe for Babies: The Child Welfare Commission and the Development of Urban Health Centers, 1911–1921." *Journal of the West* 17 (April 1978): 27–46.

Pienkos, D. "Politics, Religion, and Change in Polish Milwaukee, 1900–1930." *Wisconsin Magazine of History* 61 (Spring 1978): 179–209.

Pieplow, William L. *History of the South Division Civic Association*. Milwaukee: Milwaukee Times, 1947.

Schafer, Joseph. "Origin of Wisconsin's Free School System." *Wisconsin Magazine of History* 9 (1925–26): 27–46.

School Monthly (State Historical Society of Wisconsin). 1867–1970.

Stave, Bruce M., ed. *Socialism and the Cities*. Port Washington, N.Y.: Kennikat Press, 1975.

Still, Bayrd. *Milwaukee: The History of a City*. Madison: State Historical Society of Wisconsin, 1948.

Thelen, David P. *The New Citizenship: Origins of Progressivism in Wisconsin, 1885–1900*. Columbia: University of Missouri Press, 1973.

Thompson, Carl D. *Labor Measures of the Social Democrats*. Milwaukee, ca. 1911.

Wachman, Marvin. *History of the Social-Democratic Party of Milwaukee, 1897–1910*. Urbana: University of Illinois Press, 1945.

Wisconsin Comrade (State Historical Society of Wisconsin). 1914–16.

Wisconsin Journal of Education. 1857–1920.

Youmans, Theodore W. "How Wisconsin Women Won the Ballot." *Wisconsin Magazine of History* 5 (1921–22): 3–32.

Dissertations and Theses

Clark, James Ira. "The Wisconsin State Department of Public Instruction, 1903–1921." Ph.D. diss., University of Wisconsin-Madison, 1961.
Olson, Frederick I. "The Milwaukee Socialists, 1897–1941." Ph.D. diss., Harvard University, 1952.
Simon, Roger D. "The Expansion of an Industrial City: Milwaukee, 1880–1910." Ph.D. diss., University of Wisconsin-Madison, 1971.
Stachkowski, Floyd John. "The Political Career of Daniel Webster Hoan." Ph.D. diss., Northwestern University, 1966.
Van Pelt, Mark. "The Teacher and the Urban Community: Milwaukee, 1860–1900." Master's thesis, University of Wisconsin-Madison, 1978.
Waligorski, Ann Shirley. "Social Action and Women: The Experience of Lizzie Black Kander." Master's thesis, University of Wisconsin-Madison, 1969.

Manuscripts

Except for the Morris Stern Papers, which are held privately by the Stern family, the most important manuscripts on Milwaukee for the period are at the Milwaukee County Historical Society (MCHS) and the State Historical Society of Wisconsin (SHSW). The *Milwaukee School Reports*, 1848–1920, and the *Proceedings of the Milwaukee School Board*, 1880–1920, are accessible at the State Historical Society of Wisconsin and the Milwaukee Public Library.

Meta Berger Papers (SHSW)
City Club of Milwaukee Papers (SHSW)
Federated Trades Council Papers (SHSW)
Lizzie Black Kander Papers (SHSW, MCHS)
William Pieplow Papers (MCHS)
Milton Potter Papers (MCHS)
Emil Seidel Papers (SHSW)
Social Democratic Party Papers (MCHS)
Social Economics Club Papers (MCHS)
Social Science Club Papers (SHSW)
Morris Stern Papers (private)

Newspapers

All the Milwaukee newspapers for the Progressive era were consulted at the State Historical Society of Wisconsin.

Germania und Abend-Post, 1898–1910
Milwaukee Daily News, 1890–1915
Milwaukee Free Press, 1900–1915
Milwaukee Leader, 1911–1920
Milwaukee Sentinel, 1890–1920
Social Democratic Herald, 1898–1913
Voice of the People, 1910, 1918
Wisconsin Vorwarts, 1893–1920

ROCHESTER

Articles, Books, and Dissertations

The Common Good (University of Rochester Library). 1907–14.

Danforth, Mrs. Henry G. "Rochester's Gay Nineties." *Rochester Historical Society Publications* 20 (1942): 41–49.

Dow, Mrs. Harriet. "The Influence of Women in the Life of Rochester." In E. R. Foreman, ed., *Centennial History of Rochester*. Vol. 2. Rochester, N.Y.: Printed by John P. Smith, 1933.

Ellis, S. A. "A Brief History of the Public Schools of the City of Rochester." *Publications of the Rochester Historical Society* 1 (1892): 71–89.

Finfer, Lawrence A. "Leisure as Social Work in the Urban Community: The Progressive Recreation Movement, 1890–1920." Ph.D. diss., Michigan State University, 1974.

Fisler, Patricia E. "The Depression of 1893 in Rochester." *Rochester History* 15 (June 1952): 1–24.

A History of the Public Schools of Rochester, New York, 1813–1935. Rochester, N.Y.: Board of Education, n.d. (Rochester Public Library, typescript).

Hodge, Katherine Talbot. *History of the Women's Educational and Industrial Union, 1893–1943*. Rochester, N.Y.: 1943.

McGregor, A. Laura. "The Early History of the Rochester Public Schools, 1813–1850." In B. McKelvey, ed., *The History of Education in Rochester*. Rochester, N.Y.: Published by the Rochester Historical Society, 1939.

McKelvey, Blake, ed. *The History of Education in Rochester*. Rochester, N.Y.: Published by the Rochester Historical Society, 1939.

———. "Rochester Learns to Play: 1850–1900." *Rochester History* 7 (July 1946): 1–24.

———. "Woman's Rights in Rochester: A Century of Progress." *Rochester History* 10 (July 1948): 1–24.

———. *Rochester: The Flower City, 1855–1890*. Cambridge: Harvard University Press, 1949.

———. "An Historical View of Rochester's Parks and Playgrounds." *Rochester History* 11 (January 1949): 1–24.

———. "Walter Rauschenbusch's Rochester." *Rochester History* 14 (October 1952): 1–27.

———. *Rochester: The Quest for Quality, 1890–1925.* Cambridge: Harvard University Press, 1956.

———. "A History of Social Welfare in Rochester." *Rochester History* 20 (October 1958): 1–28.

———. "The Lure of the City: Rochester in the 1890s." *Rochester History* 28 (October 1966): 1–24.

———. *Rochester: The Water-Power City, 1812–1854.* Cambridge: Harvard University Press, 1945.

Stevens, Edward W. Jr. "The Political Education of Children in the Rochester Public Schools, 1899–1917: A Historical Perspective on Social Control in Public Education." Ed.D. diss., University of Rochester, 1971.

Manuscripts

The following manuscripts are located at the Rochester Public Library. Also located there are the *Rochester School Reports*, 1844–1910, and the *Proceedings of the Rochester School Board*, 1890–1920.

Women's Educational and Industrial Papers
Newspaper Scrapbook Collection, 1908–1913

Newspapers

Rochester's newspapers are available at the Rochester Public Library, but this study was based on the holdings of the State Historical Society of Wisconsin (SHSW) and the Library of Congress (LC).

Labor Journal, 1903–14 (SHSW)
Rochester Democrat and Chronicle, 1890–1915 (LC)
Rochester Socialist, 1907–8 (SHSW)
Rochester Union and Advertiser, 1890–1918 (LC)

TOLEDO

Articles and Books

Anderson, Elaine S. "Pauline Steinem, Dynamic Immigrant." In Marta Whitlock, ed., *Women in Ohio History.* Columbus: Ohio Historical Society, 1976.

Barclay, Morgan J. "Reform in Toledo: The Political Career of Samuel M. Jones." *Northwest Ohio Quarterly* 50 (Summer 1978): 79–89.

Biographical Cyclopaedia and Portrait Gallery. Vols. 1–2. Cincinnati: Western Biographical Publishing, 1984.

Boryczka, R., and L. L. Cary. *No Strength without Union: An Illustrated History of Ohio Workers, 1803–1980.* Columbus: Ohio Historical Society, 1982.

Bossing, Nelson L. *The History of Educational Legislation in Ohio from 1851 to 1925.* Columbus: F. J. Heer, 1931.

Bramble's Views: Toledo, Ohio, Diamond Anniversary, 1837–1912. Toledo: Bramble, 1912.

Burns, James J. *Educational History of Ohio.* Columbus: Historical Publishing, 1905.

Carey, Lorin Lee. *Guide to Research in the History of Toledo, Ohio.* Toledo: University of Toledo, 1977.

Carlton, Frank Tracy. "Golden-Rule Factory." *Arena* 32 (October 1904): 408–10.

Casson, Herbert N. "Draining a Political Swamp in Toledo." *Arena* 21 (June 1899): 768–71.

Commerce Club News (Toledo Public Library). 1916–1917.

Crosby, Ernest. *Golden Rule Jones.* Chicago: Public Publishing, 1906.

Downes, Randolph C. *Canal Days.* Toledo: Published by the Historical Society of Northwestern Ohio, 1949.

———. *History of Lake Shore Ohio.* Vols. 1–3. New York: Lewis Historical Publishing, 1952.

———. *Industrial Beginnings.* Toledo: Toledo Printing, 1954.

———. "The People's Schools: Popular Foundations of Toledo's Public School System." *Northwest Ohio Quarterly* 29 (Winter 1956–57): 9–26.

Folk, Richard A. "The Golden Age of Ohio Socialism." *Northwest Ohio Quarterly* 41 (Summer 1969): 91–112.

Historical Sketches of Public Schools in Cities, Villages, and Townships of the State of Ohio. Columbus: Ohio State Centennial Committee, 1876.

A History of Education in the State of Ohio. Columbus: Gazette Printing House, 1876.

Howe, Frederick C. *The Confessions of a Reformer.* Chicago: Quadrangle Books, c. 1967.

Johnson, Wendell F. *Toledo's Non-Partisan Movement.* Toledo: Press of the J. H. Crittenden Company, 1922.

Jones, Samuel M. *The New Right: A Plea for Fair Play through a More Just Social Order.* New York: Eastern Book Concern, 1899.

———. *Letters of Life and Labor.* Toledo: Franklin Printing and Engraving, 1900.

———. "American Workingmen and Religion." *Outlook* 65 (14 July 1900): 640–42.

———. "Government by the Golden Rule." *Munsey* 28 (January 1903): 506–09.

Killits, John M. *Toledo and Lucas County, Ohio, 1623–1923.* Vols. 1–3. Chicago: S. J. Clarke, 1952.

Laws, Annie, ed. *History of the Ohio Federation of Women's Clubs.* Cincinnati: Ebbert & Richardson, 1924.

Mettler, Peter J. *Chronic des Deutschen Pioner Vereins von Toledo, Ohio.* Toledo: Gilsdorf, 1918.

Nevins, Allan, ed., *The Letters and Journal of Brand Whitlock.* New York: D. Appleton-Century, 1936.

Nye, Russel B. *Midwestern Progressive Politics.* East Lansing: Michigan State University Press, 1951.

Ohio Journal of Education. 1852–55, 1910–20.

Ohio's Progressive Sons. Cincinnati: Queen City, 1905.

Perry, J. Hazard, and Mason Warner. *The Lincoln Club*. Toledo: Warner and Perry, 1899.

Portrait and Biographical Record of the City of Toledo and Lucas County and Wood County, Ohio. Chicago: Chapman, 1895.

Progressive Men of Northern Ohio. Cleveland: Plain Dealer & Publishing Co., 1906.

Scribner, Harvey. *Memoirs of Lucas County and the City of Toledo*. Vols. 1–2. Madison: Western Historical Association, 1910.

Stinchecombe, Jean L. *Reform and Reaction: City Politics in Toledo*. Belmont, Calif.: Wadsworth, 1968.

Tager, Jack. *The Intellectual as Reformer: Brand Whitlock and the Progressive Movement*. Cleveland: Press and Case Western Reserve, 1968.

——— "Progressives, Conservatives, and the Theory of the Status of Revolution." *Mid-America* 58 (July 1966): 162–75.

"The Public School System of Toledo." *Commerce Club News* 4 (1919): 1–13.

The Toledo Teacher (Toledo Public Library). 1915–19.

Toledo und Sein Deutschtum. Cleveland: German-American Biographical Company, 1899.

Tsanoff, Stoyan V. *Educational Value of the Children's Playgrounds*. Philadelphia: Published for the Author, 1897.

Waggoner, Clark, ed. *History of the City of Toledo and Lucas County, Ohio*. New York: Mansell, 1988.

Warner, Hoyt Landon. *Progressivism in Ohio, 1897–1917*. Columbus: Ohio State University Press, 1964.

Whitlock, Brand. *Forty Years of It*. New York: D. Appleton, 1914.

Winter, Nevin O. *A History of Northwest Ohio*. Vols. 1–3. Chicago: Lewis, 1917.

Dissertations and Theses

Bailey, Gary L. "The Toledo Independent Movement: A Test of the Urban Liberalism Thesis." Master's thesis, Bowling Green State University, 1977.

Bartha, Stephen J. "A History of Immigrant Groups in Toledo." Master's thesis, Ohio State University, 1945.

Brown, G. Maude. "A History of Organized Labor in Toledo." Master's thesis, University of Toledo, 1924.

Fenneberg, Davis Richings. "The Development of the American Playground As Illustrated in Toledo." Master's thesis, University of Toledo, 1927.

Folk, Richard A. "A Study of the Socialist Party of Ohio, 1900–1925." Master's thesis, University of Toledo, 1965.

Ford, Harvey S. "The Life and Times of Golden Rule Jones." Ph.D. diss., University of Michigan, 1953.

Frederick, Peter Jerome. "European Influences on the Awakening of the American Social Conscience, 1884–1904." Ph.D. diss., University of California-Berkeley, 1966.

Glockner, Marvin Jay. "Assimilation of the Immigrant in the United States As Characterized by the Poles in Toledo." Master's thesis, University of Toledo, 1966.

Hrivnyak, John M. "Birmingham: Toledo's Hungarian Community." Master's thesis, University of Toledo, 1975.

Reese, William J. "William Backus Guitteau and Educational Reform in Toledo during the Progressive Era." Master's thesis, Bowling Green State University, 1975.

Woloszyn, Andrew. "The Problem of the Poles in America As Illustrated by the Polish Community of Toledo." Master's thesis, University of Toledo, 1927.

Manuscripts

The following manuscript collections are located at the Toledo Public Library (TPL) and the Center for Archival Research (CAR) at Bowling Green State University. Both archives also contain *Toledo School Reports*, 1882–1911; these reports were not published annually, but every several years.

Samuel M. Jones Papers (TPL)
William Backus Guitteau Papers (CAR)
Schools of Toledo Collection (TPL)
Toledo Board of Education Minutes, 1849–1920 (CAR)
Women's Educational Club Papers (TPL)

Newspapers

The following newspapers are located at the University of Toledo (UT), Bowling Green State University (BGSU), the Ohio Historical Library (OHL), the State Historical Society of Wisconsin (SHSW), and the University of Washington at Seattle (UWS).

The People's Call, 1894 (SHSW)
The Socialist, 1905–6 (UWS)
Toledo Blade, 1848–1920 (BGSU, UT, OHL)
Toledo Evening Bee, 1890–1903 (UT, OHL)
Toledo News-Bee, 1904–20 (UT, OHL)
Toledo Saturday Night, 1899 (SHSW)
The Toledo Union, 1897–98 (SHSW)
Toledo Union Leader, 1907–20 (SHSW, OHL)

Index

About the Author

William J. Reese is Professor of Educational Policy Studies, History, and European Studies at the University of Wisconsin-Madison. Former editor of the *History of Education Quarterly*, he has been president of the History of Education Society and vice-president of Division F, History and Historiography, of the American Educational Research Association. He is the author of *The Origins of the American High School* and other publications in the history of education.